Passageways: An Interpretive History of Black America Volume I: 1619–1863

Passageways

An Interpretive History of Black America

Volume I: 1619-1863

Colin A. Palmer
City University of New York
Graduate School

WADSWORTH

™

THOMSON LEARNING

Preface

The proliferation of scholarship since the 1960s on various aspects of the history of black Americans provides the raison d'être for this synthesis. It is a daunting challenge because of the vast and changing literature and the inherent difficulty of interpreting a people's past. Unlike previous syntheses, the two volumes that comprise this work center blacks in their own history. The story is told from the standpoint of the volumes' subjects; blacks are not viewed through the lens of America's white majority, nor do I recount their history in terms of their roles in the making of the United States. Rather, I emphasize how a people made and remade themselves over time. Black Americans are shown as the principal architects of their struggles. The work is intended for a diverse audience of specialists, students, and the general public.

Volume I begins on the African continent, the ancestral societies of black Americans. It recounts the Africans' social, political, and cultural arrangements prior to their forced migration to America, emphasizing the centrality of their cultures in the new lives they fashioned. The ways in which these pioneering Africans and their progeny laid the foundations of black America constitute the primary focus of the volume. It is a poignant tale of a people's travail, their struggles, and ultimately their survival. The black American odyssey under slavery is not unique, however. Other black societies in the Americas experienced, in varying degrees, a similar trajectory. Consequently, Volume I, in particular, is a contribution to the larger history of the African diaspora.

Volume II addresses the struggles by black Americans to realize themselves in the aftermath of slavery, and in succeeding years. Building upon the first volume, and drawing upon the extensive secondary literature, it focuses on the enormous societal challenges they confronted after 1863, the myriad ways which they responded to them, the institutions they created, and the creative energies they unleashed. As in the first volume, the story is told from the standpoint of the subjects; black Americans are the principal actors in their struggles and attempts to achieve their possibilities.

FEATURES OF THE TWO VOLUMES

The publication of *Passageways* marks the first appearance in many years of a major new general work on the history of African Americans. The two-volume work is distinguished by the following features.

Passageways

- situates African Americans at the core of their own history
- depicts African Americans actively constructing their own paths through hostile times and environments
- reflects current scholarship and fresh interpretation on the black past
- incorporates voices of the people through speeches, prayers, poems and jokes
- combines chronological structure with thematic perspectives
- provides authoritative narrative and engaging illustrations
- includes an extensive bibliographic essay

IN APPRECIATION

This volume was conceived and begun at the National Humanities Center when I was in residence there during the academic year, 1989–1990. I thank the Center and its admirable staff for their many kindnesses. After putting the manuscript aside for a year, I continued my writing at the Center for Advanced Study in the Behavioral Sciences during the academic year 1992–1993 and was able to complete the first draft there. I am deeply grateful for the privilege of working at the Center and for the fellowship support that I received. I thank the wonderful staff for making my stay in California so memorable. I also owe a special thanks to the University of North Carolina and the Graduate School of the City University of New York for helping to support the research and writing of the two volumes that comprise this project.

During the academic year 1993–1994, my graduate students at the University of North Carolina read and commented on the manuscript. I learned a great deal from their criticisms and I deeply appreciate their efforts to sharpen my thinking on several issues. My students at the CUNY Graduate School also read the manuscript in 1994 and again in 1996. The manuscript benefited a great deal from their suggestions and for that I will always remain in their debt. Kelvin Sealey, Harris Lirtzman, and Patrick Rivers provided detailed criticisms of the manuscript thereby helping to make it a better work. I will return the favor when their own manuscripts reach a similar stage. Leslie Lindzey typed the first draft of the manuscript with skill, accuracy, and good humor. She deserves a special salute. Michael Yudell and Peter Vellon identified the illustrations and richly deserve my gratitude. James

Sweet of the City University of New York not only typed several drafts of the manuscript but served as a research assistant and friendly critic. I can never repay him for the roles he played in making this volume a reality, but I hope he knows how important he was to the project and that I will always remain very thankful.

I am grateful to the reviewers who gave their time to read and provide suggestions on an early draft of this volume:

Maceo Crenshaw Dailey, University of Texas at El Paso

Robert L. Harris, Jr., Cornell University

Judith N. Kerr, Towson State University

Gerald L. Smith, University of Kentucky

Marshall F. Stevenson, Jr., Dillard University

There are undoubtedly errors in this work, despite my best efforts. I take full responsibility for them.

Contents

Introduction

This volume addresses the principal developments in the history of the peoples of African descent in America to 1863. It begins in 1619 with the arrival of those "twenty and odd" Africans at Jamestown and concludes with the signing of the Emancipation Proclamation in 1863. I use the metaphor "passageways" to describe the ways in which blacks have had to navigate through the racially inspired minefields that circumscribed their possibilities. The enslaved and the free persons alike conceived and constructed their own passageways and struggled to preserve their humanity in a hostile environment.

The introduction of Africans into British North America as unfree workers in 1619 began a process that lasted for almost 250 years. Transported primarily from West and West Central Africa, about 500,000 Africans labored in the American colonies and in the new republic as slaves. Their ranks swelled as a consequence of natural increase and by 1860 there were about 4 million enslaved black persons and 500,000 free persons of African descent in the nation. This book is about the experiences of these people, the lives they forged, the institutions they created, and how they realized and claimed themselves over time. It explores the historical processes they struggled to shape and control.

Passageways tells the history of a *people* in formation; it is not the history of a nation-state. I place blacks at the core of their history; their experiences are placed at center stage, although external factors, actors, and influences that impacted upon them receive appropriate attention where necessary. The book does not view the history of blacks through the institutional prisms of the larger polity; nor does it situate them, willy-nilly, as a supporting cast in its construction. A people's internal history, particularly that of one defined as chattel, denied basic rights, and *excluded* from the polity is not a carbon copy of that of the nation-state and those who controlled it; its **watersheds are grounded** in the group's unique experiences. The watersheds that define a people must be rooted in their inner changes, pulls, and directions. We can no longer write and study the history of blacks—or that of any other people—through the lens of others; the chronology and grammar of their lives are not replicas of those of others.

Accordingly, I reject the existing periodization of black history–the colonial, revolutionary, and antebellum–that is patterned after that of the political history of the larger society. Focusing on the interior lives of blacks as opposed to the doings of whites, I identify three watersheds– or major points of departure–in the trajectory of black America between 1619 and 1863. I characterize the years 1619–1730 as the long first century in black American life, the time when the African-born peoples dominated the developing slave society and defined its cultural underpinnings. By the 1730s, the years that formed the first watershed, a creole or locally born population began to emerge. There would, from then on, be an annual rate of natural increase in contrast to the annual rate of natural decrease that had been the general characteristic of the earlier years. Drawing their cultural influences from the African ethnic groups of their parents and grandparents, and from the America in which they were born, these people began to lay the foundations of black society as we know it today.

The second watershed occurred around the 1820s. By 1820, at the very latest, the American-born peoples had become unquestionably dominant in black society, probably comprising four-fifths of the population or more. The texture of black life had been defined by 1820 and its distinguishing features had taken shape. Between 1820 and 1863, the inner changes in black life accelerated–the population increased by 250 percent, free blacks launched assaults on slavery, and numerous self-help and other organizations emerged. The forty years or so preceding emancipation, therefore, represented the heyday of the creoles, in contrast to the long first century, when the African-born peoples constituted the overwhelming majority.

The third watershed occurred during the Civil War, when thousands of blacks liberated themselves and abandoned the sources of their oppression. They fled to the forces that represented the Union or created sanctuaries for themselves. Many who did not flee demanded wages for their labor. While the war heightened the political consciousness of the enslaved, it was not the source of their desire for freedom. These impulses came largely from within. The war helped to undermine slavery by providing its victims with the occasion to claim themselves, and the signing of the Emancipation Proclamation by President Abraham Lincoln in 1863 was, in part, a recognition that slavery had been weakened by the removal of its human engines. For the former slaves, this was indeed a watershed in their lives; a time for new beginnings.

The volume is loosely organized around the aforementioned watersheds. Its ten chapters discuss the manner in which the enslaved peoples brought Africa with them and how their variegated cultural moorings informed life in the quarters and beyond. African-derived core beliefs and practices shaped family relationships, medical practices, religious sensibilities, and even the nature of the challenges to slavery. The African-born peoples clung to their religious beliefs, and most avoided conversion to Christianity. The creoles were more receptive to Christianity, but a high proportion remained unaffected by its theology. I argue, unlike some scholars, that the cosmological universe of the slaves included several competing religious visions or belief systems.

Most blacks were slaves before 1863, but I do not focus on the institutional arrangements of their servitude. The physical and psychological horrors that were central to the institution are not ignored, but I am more interested in the ways in which a people defined themselves in the midst of their travail, how they met their challenges, and the human price they paid. The organizing metaphor, "passageways," captures the nature of their odyssey. In as much as I bring a sympathetic understanding to the study of what the enslaved and the free people endured and created, this book is not an exercise in hagiography, nor does it romanticize slavery. The enslavement of blacks was a human tragedy of incalculable proportions, and I do not wish to temper that historical reality. In Chapter 7, I discuss the ways in which an expanding free population organized their lives and the battles they fought, but their experiences are addressed in other chapters as well.

I have, throughout the work, tried to emphasize the changes in black life over time. The cultural worlds of the African peoples of the seventeenth and eighteenth centuries differed in important ways from those of their more Westernized, Christianized, or Americanized children and grandchildren of the nineteenth century. Most students of the black past have tended to base their conclusions about the nature of slavery on evidence derived primarily from the years 1820–1863, the period that I have identified as marking the ascendancy of the creoles. While these years were of critical importance in the evolution of black America, they formed only one-fifth of the approximately 250-year history of slavery in North America. An overreliance on that period produces a picture of cultural stasis in black life. It minimizes the cultural differences between the African ethnic groups who were dominant in earlier periods and the creoles of the later years and interferes with our understanding of the ways in which the black population took shape and defined itself over the long haul.

Much of the existing work on the black presence in America has also been deeply flawed because many Western scholars are abysmally ignorant of the African peoples, their cultures, and their history. Studies of the enslaved peoples frequently ignore their African past, worldviews, and cultural understandings. Distressingly, the result has been a tendency to view these people through a Western lens and to impose Western conceptual frameworks and models on peoples whose cultural assumptions can not and should not be fitted into these ethnocentric paradigms. I have tried to avoid such pitfalls by showing–within the limitations imposed by space–how African cultures shaped the religious, familial, and other social arrangements of the enslaved, with varying degrees of intensity, over time.

This work is not designed to provide the reader with minute details about all the experiences of blacks at the expense of analysis and interpretation. Not only do the available space–and the enormous database–make this impossible, but my intention is to suggest a somewhat new and provocative reading of the black past, unencumbered by unnecessary details that do not enrich the narrative. I try to tell the story of my subjects as much as possible from their perspectives, using their voices, and in a language that seeks to capture their passion, their pain, and their joys, too.

Africa and the Peopling of Black America

The peoples of African descent in America can lay claim to a history that is as old as humankind. Excavations conducted at Olduvai Gorge in northern Tanzania and in Kenya and Ethiopia have indicated that hominids or human ancestors originated in East and Northeast Africa about two million years ago. But Africa was not only the likely ancestral homeland of human beings as we know them today. The continent saw the development of sophisticated cultures and spectacular civilizations that sustained diverse peoples and reflected their humanity, their ethos, and their creativity.

Scholars now know that hundreds of cultures emerged in Africa over time. Never static, they changed slowly over their long formative periods, both adapting to and transforming their environments. The first humans were nomadic, hunting and gathering food for their sustenance. At first, they used simple stone tools known as choppers, but they improved the technology as time went on. About a million years ago, the superior and sharper hand axe, still made of stone, made its appearance. Some of these early peoples sustained themselves by fishing and developed the appropriate nets and harpoons. The use of fire appears to have been widespread about 50,000 years ago, a development that aided the Africans in their contest with nature in a variety of ways. Among other things, their meat could be made more easily consumable and land could be cleared more quickly.

1

African societies changed more rapidly when the transition was made from gathering food to producing it. This agricultural revolution brought enormous changes and occurred at different times in different places. Egypt took the lead in food production, eventually producing a civilization of impressive proportions. It is now believed that by 5500 B.C.E. the Egyptians had begun to plant cereals, and the practice was soon adopted in Libya and in many parts of Northeastern Africa. The savanna of West Africa may have experienced a similar development by 3000 B.C.E. The domestication of food crops—wheat, barley, millet, yams, and others—was not without its difficulties, however. Once a fertile area with adequate water supply, the area now known as the Sahara dried up between 2500 B.C.E. and 2300 B.C.E. The result was the virtual disappearance of animal life and vegetation and the forced migration of the residents.

In general, African peoples became increasingly sedentary as the agricultural revolution expanded. Crops had to be tended, specialized functions developed, and communities of various sizes and degrees of complexity arose. Not all of these African peoples were alike; their diversity was, in part, a function of the impact of regional, climatic, and environmental conditions. But for those sedentary peoples who lived in substantial contact with one another for long periods of time, a fairly common gene pool was an unavoidable consequence. Accordingly, a particular population might possess a higher density of physical characteristics that distinguished it from others. In practice, however, such populations did not constitute "races," a term that has now been discredited by scientists. Rather, since there was always some degree of interaction with other groups, the observable phenotypical similarity (or skin color) of the population always masked deeper genetic variations. Thus, Africa possessed many populations that defy any easy classification based on genetic or "racial" criteria.

It may be easier to classify Africa's diverse peoples by using linguistic criteria. Languages are normally grouped into families if they possess similarities in their structure, in their words, usage, and meanings. Since languages are learned, the similarities among them are the consequence of interaction between the speakers over time. Hence, populations may be conveniently grouped in accordance with the degree to which their languages are interrelated and comprise families.

Scholars currently suggest that six principal linguistic groupings or language families are indigenous to the African peoples. The *Afro-Asiatic* family is found in North Africa, and its speakers occupy an area extending between the Mediterranean and Red seas, including the Horn as well. A number of languages comprise this family, ranging from those of ancient Egypt, northern and northeastern Africa, and the Semitic languages of southwestern Asia. Immediately to the south of the Sahara, roughly from the Niger River bend to Lake Victoria, the people speak the

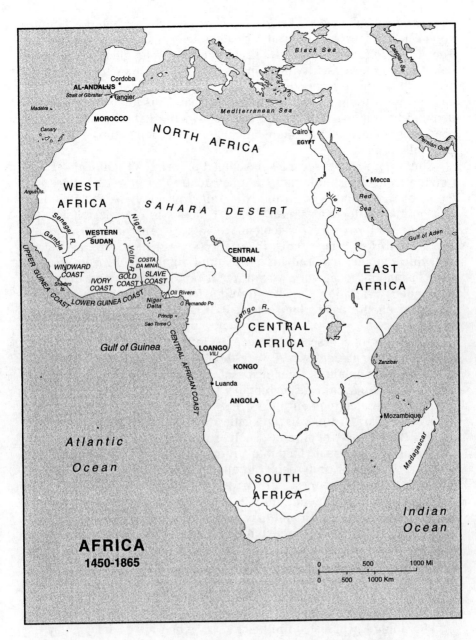

Black Sea

Caspian Sea

Cordoba

AL-ANDALUS

Strait of Gibraltar — Tangier

Madeira

MOROCCO

Mediterranean Sea

NORTH AFRICA

Cairo

EGYPT

Persian Gulf

Canary

Mecca

WEST AFRICA

SAHARA DESERT

Nile R.

Red Sea

Arguin Is.

Senegal R.

Gambia

WESTERN SUDAN

Niger R.

Volta R.

Gulf of Aden

CENTRAL SUDAN

EAST AFRICA

UPPER GUINEA COAST

WINDWARD COAST

COSTA DA MINA

SLAVE COAST

Shama Is.

IVORY COAST

GOLD COAST

LOWER GUINEA COAST

Oil Rivers

Niger Delta

Fernando Po

Congo R.

CENTRAL AFRICA

Princip

Sao Tome

Gulf of Guinea

CENTRAL AFRICAN COAST

LOANGO

VILI

KONGO

Zanzibar

Luanda

ANGOLA

Mozambique

Atlantic

Ocean

Madagascar

SOUTH AFRICA

Indian

Ocean

AFRICA

1450-1865

| 0 | 500 | 1000 Mi |
| 0 | 500 | 1000 Km |

Nilo-Saharan languages. The *Niger Congo* and the *Kordofonian* families are located in West and Central Africa and in areas south of the Equator. The *Khoisian* language family, characterized by its clicking sound, is found in southern Africa and in parts of East Africa such as Tanzania. The sixth family, the *Austronesian*, is a survivor of Southeast Asian languages and is found primarily in Madagascar. This linguistic classification may be somewhat imprecise, but it shows the diversity of the African peoples and calls into question conclusions that depict the continent as culturally homogeneous.

Similarly, African societies developed a variety of political systems ranging from the simple and the unstructured to powerful states and empires. States appeared in the Nile Valley probably as early as 3500 B.C.E. and in Ethiopia around 600 B.C.E. Ghana was organized about A.D. 400, and similar processes took place in East Africa, Central Africa, and West Africa. These states invariably viewed their king as sacred, believing that he acquired his power and right to rule from a deity. State formation, to be sure, was never a rapid process, and there was tremendous variation in the timing, form, and structure. Much depended on the particular society, its traditions, needs, and cultural imperatives.

Egypt was, of course, one of the most important and spectacular civilizations of the ancient world. With the fertile soil and water resources of the Nile floodplain at their disposal, Egyptians developed advanced irrigation and agricultural techniques by 3600 B.C.E. Efficient forms of production created food surpluses that freed some people to engage in tasks other than farming. In time, cities emerged with people specializing in a wide variety of pursuits, such as commerce and the crafts. In its early years Egypt was divided into a number of small states, however, in 3100 B.C.E., political unity began to appear when these ministates coalesced into two larger ones.

The creation of national unity in 3100 B.C.E. under the first pharaoh facilitated societal growth and expansion. Many of Egypt's accomplishments were internally inspired, but it was also exposed to the influences of black Africa and the wider Mediterranean world. During the three and a half millennia of its existence, Egyptian civilization had a major impact on the Greeks and through them on the Western world. The Egyptian peoples themselves were heterogeneous and included black Africans and lighter skinned Mediterraneans.

Pharaonic Egypt lasted until 321 B.C.E., when it was defeated by the invading armies of Alexander the Great of Macedonia. But the Pharaonic period, in spite of its considerable achievements, experienced periods of disunity and military conquest. The country was dominated by the Persians, Assyrians, and Libyans at various times. In turn, Egypt dispatched conquering expeditions to Nubia in the south, to the Sudan, and to Bedouin-controlled territories in the east.

Among ancient Egypt's cultural achievements was the development of a hieroglyphic writing system. Although literacy remained the preserve of a small elite group, the art of writing allowed for the emergence of a body of written literature—novels, poems, treatises on a range of subjects—and so on. The development of a highly complex religious system was also one of the hallmarks of Egypt's achievements. Maintained by a priestly class, religion constituted the foundation of the people's worldviews, shaped the legal and ethical systems, legitimized the power of the rulers and explained the average person's place in the universe. The great stone monuments of which the civilization is justifiably famous reflected the people's architectural and artistic genius.

Although the achievements of Egypt were the most spectacular and the best known, other societies can lay claim to significant political and economic developments. The early states of the western and central Sudan acquired great power and wealth. The earliest of these kingdoms was Ghana, located on the northern fringe of the Niger and Senegal valleys. Ghana's early history is not well known, but by the ninth century other peoples had fallen under its suzerainty and the state had become famous for its wealth. Ghana's economic power rested on the control of vast supplies of gold and the conduct of an active trans-Saharan trade in salt, copper, and other goods. The army that held the empire together numbered as many as 200,000 soldiers in 1067–68 A.D. Eventually, the empire collapsed in 1076 as a result of an invasion by a Muslim group called the Almoravids and from internal divisions as well.

Several states emerged in the wake of Ghana's demise, but none approximated the power it had enjoyed until the thirteenth century. The kingdom of Mali, Ghana's most distinguished successor, came into prominence in the second half of the thirteenth century. It soon extended control over adjacent peoples and based its power on trade and military might. Mali's capital, Niani, was located on the upper Niger. In time, Mali controlled an area far larger than the empire of Ghana, extending from the Atlantic Ocean to parts of contemporary Nigeria in the north and the Guinea forests in the southwest.

A number of contemporary North African travelers and writers reported on Mali's sophistication, prosperity, sense of internal order, and the pervasive influence of Muslim ideas and traditions. The pilgrimage that the ruler, Mansa Musa (1312–37), made to Mecca in 1324–25 provided an opportunity for the empire to display its wealth. It is said that the emperor's advance guard consisted of 500 slaves, each bearing a staff of gold that weighed 6 pounds. He was accompanied by 8,000 to 15,000 retainers and 100 hundred camels carrying 300 pounds of gold each. The Egyptian economy was adversely affected by this extravagant spending, and an inflationary spiral ensued. According to one contemporary, "So much gold was current in Cairo that it ruined the value of money."[1]

Probably because of Mansa Musa's trip to Mecca and the display of his empire's wealth, Mali became well known in Europe and in the Mediterranean. Traders and scholars were attracted to the empire, and Timbuktu became an important center of learning. To many outsiders, the western Sudan came to be known as "Rex Melli" or "Massa Mali."[2] Yet the Mali empire began to disintegrate in the fifteenth century as a result of external assaults and internal divisions. It sputtered along for many more years, however, but virtually disappeared by the early seventeenth century.

Songhai, Mali's powerful successor, rose to prominence in the late fifteenth and early sixteenth centuries. Its capital was located at Gao, and its territorial reach extended as far as areas to the southeast of the Niger bend. As in the case of Ghana and Mali, Songhai's power rested on military might and the effective control of trade and trade routes. Its greatness also derived from strong and effective leadership. Perhaps the best known of its kings was Sonni Ali (1464–92), who presided over a period of enormous imperial expansion. Wracked by internal divisions, Songhai eventually fell to an invading force from Morocco in 1591.

The states and empires of the Sudan were not atypical insofar as African political arrangements were concerned. Similar patterns existed in West, West-central, Central, Northeast Africa, and elsewhere. In recent times, historians have enlarged our understanding of the Akan, Mossi, Hausa, Yoruba, and Benin kingdoms of West Africa; the numerous Bantu kingdoms of Central Africa; the Congo; Zimbabwe; and the Muslim states and empires of North Africa, among others. We are not here concerned, however, with detailing the political history of these societies. Rather, we stress the point that the African peoples developed an impressive variety of political structures that met their needs.

The size of individual political entities varied, both in terms of the territory they claimed and the composition of the population as well. One scholar has recently speculated that the largest empires in Atlantic Africa, such as Songhai, occupied 500,000 to 1,000,000 square kilometers, or roughly equivalent to the size of France or Spain. Most states were about 50,000 square kilometers or considerably less. A number of states had a population of 20,000 to 30,000 people, but the majority were a good deal smaller.[3] Africans tended to organize their societies along lines of kin and lineage, so it is hardly surprising that states with relatively small numbers of inhabitants predominated. Regardless of their size, however, these states–and empires–possessed a military machinery for their defense, a system of revenue collection, and arrangements for the maintenance of order and the dispensation of justice. In general, their economies depended on the control of trading networks, pastoral pursuits, agriculture, and the extraction of mineral resources.

African societies, like other human societies, were never free from political tensions, warfare, and the periodic rise and fall of states and empires. Forms of slavery existed in many of these societies, and property in persons constituted one of the avenues to individual wealth as well as a form of investment. While the empires of Ghana, Mali, Songhai, and others attested to the degree of political power and sophistication that some peoples had attained, such systems were ultimately based on military might and exploitation of conquered peoples. Empires, no matter where they existed, usually acquired their power through the exercise of force, the subjugation of other peoples, and the extraction of resources from the dominated.

For this reason, we must be careful not to romanticize the existence of empires such as that of the Romans, the Aztecs, or the African peoples. While empires reflected the enormous power of a dominant entity and demonstrated the capacity to organize and administer far-flung areas, such structures also brought untold suffering to the conquered peoples. Similarly, it is worth underscoring in this context that we must avoid measuring the accomplishments of African societies with a Western yardstick. African political systems and statecraft deserve our attention because they tell us how particular peoples ordered their lives and responded to specific challenges. But we should not assess their actions in accordance with the degree to which they approximated or deviated from a familiar Western model.

Societies should be assessed, if that is called for, on their own terms, since there has not been a set of common universal priorities that transcended time and place. Thus, Westerners have had their own measures of what constitutes societal growth and development, and these may not be applicable to other societies. The peoples of the world did not all follow a common trajectory and did not ascribe the same value to all forms of human endeavor. Consequently, the history of Africa should not be told from the perspective of the West, nor should the paradigms that reflect the experiences of other societies and peoples be applied willy-nilly.

The point is worth emphasizing since Western paradigms, in particular, are permeated by racism and ethnocentric worldviews. The result has been a discourse that has distorted Africa's image. Africa and its past are usually viewed through a Western lens, and some observers present a homogeneous picture of the continent, not recognizing the profound cultural differences that existed and still exist among her peoples. The Africa that many people see, whether positively or negatively, is culturally constructed and frequently bears little or no relation to the realities of the continent, her peoples, and her history.

Negative stereotypes and distortions notwithstanding, African peoples structured their lives and fashioned their institutions in their own ways. Their complex cosmologies, kin arrangements, religious beliefs and practices, and other aspects of their lives need not detain us here since these will inform our later discussion of black life in America. We emphasize, however, that although the primary impetus for African cultural developments came from within, most societies were never immune to the influences of the outside world. In the eighth century, for example, Islam began to penetrate the northern societies and to a lesser extent the sub-Saharan region with profound religious and social consequences. East African traders visited India and China to sell their wares, and African merchants also traded with Europeans. A few Ethiopians lived in the Greek city-states from around the fifth century B.C.E. Egypt, of course, enjoyed constant contact with its neighbors in the Near East and the Mediterranean. The pace and nature of these contacts, however, changed around the start of the fifteenth century with the beginning of maritime contact with Europe. The consequences for Africa and her peoples were serious and enduring. And the human landscape of the Americas was also irrevocably altered.

Historians do not agree on the date when the first Africans arrived in what is now called the Americas. Some scholars suggest that West Africans sailed to this hemisphere to trade with the indigenous peoples centuries before Christopher Columbus made his first voyage in 1492.[4] They use a variety of linguistic, artistic, and archaeological evidence to support their arguments. Other scholars question the reliability of such evidence. We do know, however, that there was one person of African descent on board Columbus's ships in 1492. In 1494, during the second expedition, at least two black persons disembarked at Hispaniola, where the Spaniards founded their first colony. Seven years later, in 1501, the Spanish monarchs, Ferdinand and Isabella, granted permission to the settlers to import black slaves. From Hispaniola, the institution of slavery spread to the islands of Cuba, Puerto Rico, and Jamaica as well as to the mainland colonies of Mexico, Peru, and elsewhere.

We cannot claim that the Spaniards had planned to introduce African slavery when they began to colonize the Caribbean islands. Rather, the Spaniards wanted to use the indigenous peoples–misnamed the Indians– to perform the labor services that were needed. The Spaniards had not intended to work for themselves and looked with disdain on manual labor. Consequently, once they assumed effective control of Hispaniola, they began to impose labor demands upon the Indians. Before long, however, the Indian population declined drastically as a result of mistreatment and a series of epidemics of measles and typhus that struck with unrelieved ferocity. As the number of potential Indian workers began to diminish, the colonizers had to entertain the notion of an alternative source of exploited labor.

Prior to Columbus's voyages and the colonization of Hispaniola, the Spaniards, like many other peoples, were engaged in the practice of slavery. The enslaved peoples included Jews, Slavs, Muslims, black Africans, and other Spaniards. Thus, the concept of property in persons was not alien to Spanish laws and traditions. The Siete Partidas, the body of laws that formed the basis of Spanish jurisprudence, legitimized slavery although it held that the institution was unnatural and was "the most evil and the most despicable thing which can be found among men." Not surprisingly, when the need arose the Spaniards would seek to establish in the Americas an institution with which they were familiar.

The Indians and the Africans were the only two peoples, however, whom the Spaniards, and later the Portuguese and the English, enslaved in the Americas. Indian slavery was short-lived owing to the rapid decline in the number of the indigenous peoples and the difficulty of controlling them, since they fled to areas inaccessible to the Europeans. The Indians also did not readily yield to Spanish control and continued to resist efforts to deny them their liberty. By 1500, it was also clear that free workers from Spain would not be available in significant numbers to do the servile labor that the emerging colonial elite demanded.

In retrospect, it would appear that the enslavement of African peoples by the Spaniards was an inevitable consequence of the need for a dependable and exploited labor force. Such a conclusion, however, is an *ex post facto* rationalization of African slavery. Confronted by a declining indigenous population, the Spaniards had several options open to them. In the first place, the colonists could have abandoned the colonial enterprise. Alternatively, they could have overcome their disdain for manual labor and relied on their own energies to exploit the resources of the colonies. Conceivably, the Spaniards could also have introduced a system of white servile labor as the English would do a century later. There is no indication that these options was considered; the decision to import African slaves was rooted in past practice and represented a pragmatic response to the economic needs of the colonists. African slavery, therefore, was neither inevitable nor predictable in 1492, nor was it the only solution to the developing labor crisis.

The sixteenth century saw a steady expansion of the black slave population in the Caribbean and Latin America. The Portuguese became the principal suppliers of slaves, and as the colonial economies diversified the demand for labor increased. By 1570, Mexico and Peru each had 20,000 slaves and Hispaniola 5,000. Africans had clearly become a significant part of the human landscape of these societies by 1600.[5]

The English, unlike the Spaniards and the Portuguese, did not develop a sustained interest in the Americas until the seventeenth century. English privateers such as Francis Drake had made incursions into the Americas but it was not until 1607 that the first permanent settlement was established at Jamestown, Virginia. A few years later the English settled in St. Christopher (1624), Barbados (1627), Nevis (1628), and Montserrat and Antigua (1632), and they captured Jamaica from the Spaniards in 1655. By the second half of the seventeenth century, the English had become one of the major colonial powers in the hemisphere.

African slaves were first brought to what is now the United States in 1526. In that year, Vásquez de Allyón, a Spanish explorer, founded the short-lived town of San Miguel de Gualdape, a site within striking distance of Sapelo Island in contemporary Georgia. Africans were also among those who established the town of St. Augustine in Spanish Florida in 1565. Throughout the sixteenth century, their number remained small in the southeastern part of North America. But this would soon change.

As soon as the English colonists established their settlement at Jamestown, they began to experience a labor shortage. Many of the early settlers had brought with them ideas and attitudes from England that were not conducive to the sustained work necessary for the building of a colony. Some of these persons were given to sloth and idleness and included persons who "never did know what a dayes worke was."[6] Others were weakened by disease such as malaria, diptheria, and typhoid as well as by an inadequate diet. Englishmen also looked wistfully at using the labor of the Indian peoples, whom many wanted to enslave. In 1615, settler Ralph Hamor expressed optimism for the use of Indian labor "as they are easily taught and may by lenitie and faire usage . . . be brought, as being naturally though ingenious, yet idlely given, to be no lesse industrious, nay to exceede our English."[7]

The expectation that Indians were willing and available to work in sufficient numbers proved to be illusory. They died from European diseases and resisted enslavement. Indian slavery found its greatest expression in South Carolina, where a brisk slave trade in the indigenous peoples developed shortly after the colony was founded in 1670. By 1708, there were about 1,400 enslaved Indians in the colony. The Virginia colonists, and in time the others, resorted to the use of indentured labor from England to meet the labor demand. England was experiencing population pressures and there were individuals who were willing to come to America to work for a master for a given period in return for having their passage paid. This system of indentured labor was merely a modified form of the serfdom that had existed in England and continental Europe. Under the indentured labor system, unlike slavery, the person was not chattel and the master was entitled only to his labor. In addition, it was not hereditary, as African slavery would become. Although the system of indenture met some of the colonial labor needs, it was not a permanent source of labor, since the length of each person's service was limited by the terms of the contract.

As the colonial economies took shape and became more complex, the demand for labor increased. By the mid-eighteenth century, Maryland and the colonies to the south were engaged primarily in the production of export crops. The Chesapeake Bay colonies of Virginia and Maryland produced tobacco, South Carolina specialized in rice and indigo, North Carolina cultivated tobacco, and Georgia concentrated on rice. Cotton had not become a crop of any significance in these colonies by 1750. The Middle colonies of New York, New Jersey, Pennsylvania, and Delaware devoted their energies primarily to food production, meeting their own needs and those of their sister colonies in the Caribbean. In New England, Massachusetts, Rhode Island, and Connecticut also grew foodstuffs and controlled a brisk carrying trade. A few colonies developed nascent manufacturing enterprises. Pennsylvania boasted iron furnaces, North Carolina was noted for its turpentine and lumber, and New Jersey had tanneries.

These economic enterprises needed, in varying degrees, a dependable labor supply for their success. Africans would be used as slaves in all of them, and it is this crucial economic imperative that explains the origins and expansion of the slave trade and slavery. White colonists came to consider slavery a cheaper form of labor than indentured servitude, and planters frequently expressed unhappiness with the quality of their servants. Some were described as "Jaylebirds" and "desperate villans" and were seen as a threat to societal peace. In their turn, many servants expressed disappointment with the treatment they received and complained of "greate hardshipp."[8]

It must be emphasized, however, that there was nothing preordained about the enslavement of the Africans by the English despite the developing colonial economies and the increasing need for labor. No external forces compelled the English to follow the examples of the Spaniards and the Portuguese in importing Africans as slaves or in any other servile capacity. The colonists slowly but willingly and deliberately introduced slavery and came to depend on it for their economic sustenance, particularly in the South. In 1682, Dr. Samuel Wilson, a resident of South Carolina, confessed: "a rational man will certainly inquire, When I have land, what shall I doe with it? What comoditys shall I be able to produce, that will yeild me money in other countrys, that I may be inabled to buy Negro-slaves, (without which a planter can never doe any great matter)."[9] By 1757, the Reverend Peter Fontaine, an Anglican priest in Virginia, could concede, "[T]o live in Virginia without slaves is morally impossible."[10]

The availability of indentured servants declined after about 1680 largely as a consequence of improved wages and better economic opportunities in England. Colonial planters had also come to realize that it was more judicious financially to invest in black slaves than in white servants. Landon Carter, the prominent Virginia planter, gave another reason for the accelerating shift to black slave labor. "Those few servants that we have don't do as much as the poorest slaves we have."[11] By the start of the eighteenth century, African slaves outnumbered the indentured servants. In 1707, for example, Maryland had 4,657 slaves to 3,003 indentured servants in a population of 33,833. An elaborate rationale for slavery based on a virulent racist ideology would later emerge to define the institution, give it legitimacy, and sustain it.

Unlike the Europeans who came to the Americas and the indigenous peoples before them, all of the Africans were unwilling immigrants. No one among these Africans who laid the genetic foundations of black America volunteered to cross the Atlantic as a slave. Force was the defining characteristic of the slave trade. We must also underscore the point that slavery was not the normal or natural condition of Africans or of any other peoples, for that matter. Slavery was an aberration even as much as it was a feature of many ancient societies.

THE TRADE IN SLAVES

The process by which Africans came to the Americas has both institutional and human dimensions. The institutional aspects relate to the organization and structure of the slave trade, the roles of the traders, and the commercial arrangements that developed. The ethnic backgrounds, ages, gender, and individual characteristics of the enslaved constitute some of the human dimensions. We are not likely to fully understand the evolution of black society, its ethos, its tugs and pulls unless we are familiar with the persons who laid its foundations.

There were several institutional arrangements, both formal and informal, for the delivery of Africans to the mainland colonies. At first, the colonists depended upon individual traders to supply them with Africans. It appears that these persons, in the main, were transhipped from the several Caribbean islands primarily by the Dutch and the Portuguese. The colonists received only a small number of Africans in the seventeenth century. Only about 1,600 had arrived by 1650, 3,900 by 1675, and 23,000 by 1700. In contrast, between 1640 and 1700 Jamaica received 85,000 Africans and the smaller island of Barbados, 135,000.

Englishmen did not enter the slave-trading business until the second half of the seventeenth century. The privateer John Hawkins had made three slave-trading expeditions to Africa in the 1560s and sold the slaves he acquired to the Spaniards in the Caribbean. His exploits were not duplicated until 1660 when the first English joint stock company engaged in the trade–the Company of the Royal Adventurers into Africa–was chartered. The rapid failure of the company led to its reorganization and renaming in 1664 as The Royal Adventurers Trading into Africa. When this company folded in 1671, it was replaced in 1672 by the initially more successful Royal African Company.

Although the Royal African Company delivered most of its slaves directly to the Caribbean islands, an occasional cargo came to the mainland colonies. The company exercised a precarious monopoly over the trade to the English colonies until Parliament allowed the participation of private or "separate" traders in 1698. These independent entrepreneurs became the dominant traders in the eighteenth century, and London, Liverpool, and Bristol emerged as important centers for the dispatching of slave ships to the African coast. The American colonists were not principal actors in the slave trade until the eighteenth century. The first American slaver to participate in it was sent by some Boston merchants in 1644. This vessel was one of three sent to Africa to establish a trade in "negars" as well as in other goods. This ship, the *Rainbow,* was the only one to actually transport slaves, and it took a number of them to Barbados where they were sold. A few ships were dispatched to Africa by Massachusetts merchants in succeeding years, but their role in the overall trade was negligible.

The expansion of the American role in the trade in the eighteenth century coincided with the labor needs and demands of the growing plantation economies. The American merchants who controlled the trade were located largely outside of the Southern colonies that absorbed most of the Africans. Fueled by the profit motive, the human commerce attracted wealthy businessmen in Boston, Newport, Providence, New York, and Philadelphia. These merchants had agents in Virginia and South Carolina, in particular, to receive and oversee the sale of the arriving cargoes of slaves. Accordingly, Charleston and the Chesapeake Bay area with its intricate system of waterways became important entrepôts for slaves whose eventual destinations were Maryland, North Carolina, Georgia, Florida, and Louisiana.

Southern businessmen, with the exception of South Carolinians, did not play a significant role in the slave trade. If South Carolina is excluded, Southerners sent only sixteen slavers to Africa before the end of the trade in 1808. On the other hand, while only two slave ships left Charleston for the African coast before 1792, 110 were dispatched between 1792 and 1808. The heyday of the American participation in the trade was 1783–1807 as traders hurried to transport as many Africans as they could before the trade's anticipated abolition. Between 1791 and 1810, for example, American vessels delivered 180,843 slaves to the Americas, 60 percent of whom were purchased by United States citizens and the rest by the Spaniards in Cuba and on the Latin American mainland.

During the formative period of the trade, the American colonists received African slaves transshipped from the West Indies, principally from the islands of Barbados, Jamaica, and Antigua. These slaves had presumably been acclimatized or "seasoned" to the environment of the Americas and to the demands of a slave regimen. Yet the colonists were not particularly pleased with the individuals who were transshipped since they were likely to be the ones that the islanders did not want and who were generally referred to as "refuse negroes" or "rogues." Some were intractable. South Carolina was the primary recipient of these "seasoned" slaves, although a sizable number went to Virginia and later to Georgia. By the first decades of the eighteenth century, however, the colonists began to receive a high proportion of their slave cargoes directly from Africa. Between 1735 and 1769, Virginia received 83 percent of her slave imports from Africa while South Carolina got 86 percent. Maryland, to cite another example, received 92 percent of her slaves from Africa between 1720 and 1773. Georgia was an exception to this pattern, as that colony obtained most of her slaves from the Caribbean until the 1760s.

Regardless of whether these Africans arrived directly from their homelands or were transshipped from the West Indies, they had all lost their liberty in similar ways and had become items of commerce. In order to promote the slave trade, the Europeans–the Dutch, English, French, Portuguese, and others–established forts all along the African coast. The Gold Coast (contemporary Ghana) had more than fifty settlements of this type along a 300-mile coastline. The size of these forts varied, and the larger ones were called castles. Two of the best-known castles were located in Ghana. The first of these, Elmina Castle, was built by the Portuguese in 1482 but acquired by the Dutch in 1637. Cape Coast Castle was constructed by the Swedes in 1653, held by the dey (leader) of the Fetu people from 1661, then acquired by the Dutch in 1664 and the English in 1665. This castle had accommodations for about 1,500 slaves at its peak.

These forts included residences and offices for the white traders, a chapel, warehouses for the trade goods, and dungeons, sometimes underground, where the slaves were confined. Traders built these settlements with the permission of the local ruler and paid rent for the privilege. They had to be constantly defended from assaults by other Europeans and from Africans as well.

Traders on the African coast acquired their slaves in four principal ways. Most of them were captives taken in the wars that were a periodic feature of the African societies. African states went to war for a variety of reasons that included territorial, succession, and commercial disputes. Some states such as the Ashanti on the Gold Coast incorporated their neighbors into their empire and took captives in the process. In fact, it was the frequent disputes among rival African states that, in large measure, fed the slave trade. Thus, most of the victims of the trade, perhaps as much as 80 percent over time, were prisoners of war and came from a state other than that of the seller. As one eighteenth-century trader, William Bosman, observed, "Most of the slaves that are offered to us are prisoners of war, which are sold by the victors as their booty."[12]

Individuals who were likely to be sold also included persons who had lost their civil rights by virtue of crimes for which they had been convicted. Such offenses included homicide, treason, and theft. Other potential victims included persons who were abducted and sold to the traders. But such atrocities were never encouraged. Unscrupulous individuals who engaged in this practice faced severe penalties if they were caught, and these acts could lead to war between the victim's country and that of the kidnapper. "Not a few in our country fondly imagine that parents here sell their children, men their wives, and one brother the other," wrote Bosman. "But, those who think so deceive themselves."[13] A fourth category of potential slaves included those persons who lacked kinship ties to other members of their state. These persons, along with debtors and orphans, could be offered for sale, generally in times of economic distress.

Males, by far, constituted the majority of the persons offered for sale. Women were much less likely to be sold, since they were highly valued as workers in African societies. They performed most of the agricultural labor in addition to doing the domestic work. Not only did females bear the brunt of the productive labor in these societies, but they also fulfilled the normal reproductive functions as well. Young children also did not usually form a major proportion of the slaves offered for sale, except when adults were not available to meet the demand.

African traders bought their fettered slaves to the forts and castles on the coast in order to sell them to the waiting European or American purchasers. One trader noted that in Sierra Leone, "The slaves when brought here have chains put on, three or four linked together." A second trader confirmed that the slaves in the Gambia were also linked together on their long trek to the coastal markets. As he described the process, "Their way of bringing them is, tying them by the Neck with Leather-Thongs, at about a Yard distance from each other, 30 or 40 in a String, having generally a Bundle of Corn, or an Elephants Tooth [tusk] upon each of their Heads. In their Way from the Mountains, they travel thro' very great woods, where they cannot for some Days get Water, so they carry in Skin-Bags enough to support them for that Time."[14] The slave caravans from the interior often brought scores of captives, sometimes as many as 150 at a time.

A knowledge of the ethnic backgrounds of these Africans adds a necessary dimension to our understanding of the human and cultural foundations of black America. Although the mainland colonists as well as those in the Caribbean developed clear preferences for Africans from certain ethnic groups, the white traders on the coast did not control the supply and had to confine their selections to the available slaves regardless of ethnicity. South Carolina buyers, for example, were particularly eager to purchase slaves who came from the River Gambia. In 1756, Henry Laurens, one of the colony's principal slave merchants, noted, "The slaves from the River Gambia are preferr'd to all others with us save the Gold Coast."[15] His fellow colonists found the Mandinka from the Gambia region physically attractive and dependable, the Akan from the Gold Coast hostile and difficult to control, and the Ibo from the Niger Delta given to moodiness and not particularly hardy. Individuals from the Congo-Angola region were thought to have a tendency to escape and to be physically weak, although they were considered physically pleasing.

These characterizations, in retrospect, may be dismissed as stereotypes, but they indicated that the colonists distinguished between the African peoples and made their purchases accordingly. These perceptions helped determine the price of the slaves and the speed with which they were sold. In the final analysis, however, American purchasers could hardly afford to be picky given their dependence on slave labor and the frequent unavailability of the preferred slaves. Thus, although South Carolinians valued slaves from the Gambia and the Gold Coast above all others, they actually purchased more slaves from Angola than from any other part of Africa.

In general, the Africans who came to the North American mainland lived in an area bounded by Senegal in the north and extending to Angola in the south. In addition, some slaves came from Mozambique and to a lesser extent Madagascar. The catchment area, or the places from which the slaves were drawn, extended several hundred miles from the coast into the interior. Some regions, to be sure, supplied more slaves than others, and their importance to the slave traffic changed over time depending on the factors of supply and demand. A few African states also refused to participate in the human traffic.

West-central Africa, or the Congo-Angola region, supplied the majority of the slaves to the American colonies. About one-fourth of the Africans came from this region, and they belonged to such ethnic groups as the Bakongo, the Tio, and the Mbundu. Slightly fewer slaves, about 23 percent, originated in the Bight of Biafra, an area that extends from the Benin River to Cape Lopez and now comprises such nations as Nigeria, Togo, and Gabon. The ethnic groups that occupied this area included the Yoruba, the Fon, the Nupe, and the Ibo. About 16 percent of the slaves came from the Gold Coast, the third principal source of the captives. This region, which is contemporary Ghana, was home to the Akan speaking peoples and others. The Senegambia supplied 13 percent of the captives and they included such peoples as the Wolof, the Fulbe, and the Serer. Sierra Leone provided another 6 percent, the Bight of Benin 4 percent, and Mozambique and Madagascar less than 2 percent.

Once the captives arrived at the coast, they were examined by the prospective purchasers to determine the status of their health. As one trader expressed it, "The Countenace and Stature, a good Set of Teeth, Pliancy in their limbs and Joints, and being free of Venereal Taint, are the Things inspected and governs our choice in buying."[16] After the sale was completed, the enslaved person was branded with the insignia of the purchaser on the shoulder, the breast, or the buttocks.

The African trade required an assortment of goods, including several types of guns, gunpowder, woolen and textile products, East Indian

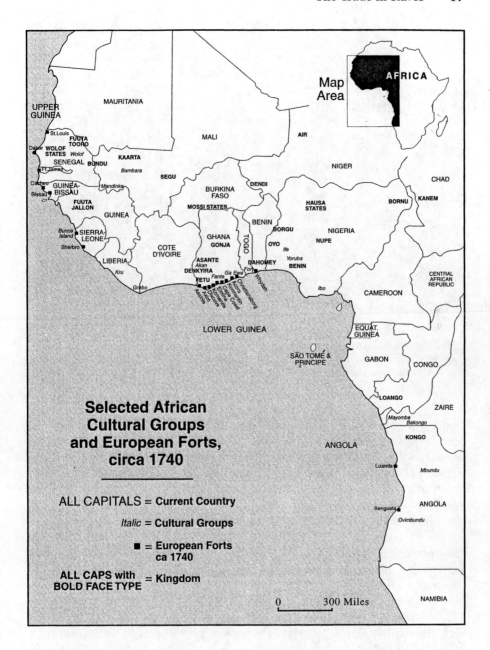

**Selected African
Cultural Groups
and European Forts,
circa 1740**

ALL CAPITALS = **Current Country**

Italic = **Cultural Groups**

■ = **European Forts
ca 1740**

**ALL CAPS with
BOLD FACE TYPE** = **Kingdom**

0   300 Miles

Slave trade was extremely competitive throughout the 1700s, as the Portuguese, Spanish, Dutch, and British rallied for dominance. Slaves were gathered in staging areas such as the Shaka market, shown here, until there were enough to fill a cargo ship.

textiles, alcohol, and such miscellaneous items as mirrors, knives, iron bars, pipes, tobacco, pots and pans, beads, and so on. All traders made sure that they had adequate quantities of these goods and that they kept abreast of local preferences and changing tastes. An ill-chosen assortment of goods for a particular area resulted in a poor market and could produce dissension between the white traders and the Africans. In 1715 the black traders at York fort at the river Sherbro vented their rage on English trader John Ball when he failed to provide the type of goods they preferred. Ball complained that the people disliked the small brass kettles that he stocked and that such items "only breed a disturbance, the natives threatening to throw them in our faces."[17]

The prices of the slaves reflected considerable variation over the life of the trade. The law of supply and demand operated just as it did for any other business. When slaves were scarce, the price rose; when they were abundant, the price declined. In fact, with the growth of the slave-based plantation economies in the Caribbean, Brazil, and the North American colonies starting in the second half of the seventeenth century, the increasing demand for African slave labor produced a steady rise in prices. The entry of a larger number of traders into the slave business, particularly after 1700, increased competition and also contributed to the inflation. Writing in 1707, one trading company bemoaned the increase in competition for the slaves, noting, "the Blacks who are a subtle people, taking advantage therof, have not only lowered the prices of our commodities, but advanced the prices of Negroes."[18]

The African traders and their white counterparts were partners in the business of slave trading on the coast. Yet it was a special kind of business because the items of commerce were human beings. No trader could deny that fact, so he had to adopt measures that implicitly recognized the humanity of the victims. Their freedom of movement had to be carefully restricted, and they had to be constantly supervised to avoid the risk of escape or rebellion. Shackled and confined in dark, damp dungeons at Cape Coast Castle, at Elmina Castle, and elsewhere, these human beings had little awareness of the fate that would befall them or of the nature of the life that awaited them. They knew, or had heard, that countless other individuals, perhaps even relatives and friends, had previously left in the white men's ships, never to be heard of again. Fearful tales of cannibalism were rumored in the interior; the trader, Captain William Snelgrave, confirmed that "these poor people are generally under terrible apprehension upon their being bought by white men, many being afraid that we design to eat them, which [I] have been told is a story much credited by the inland negroes."[19]

There was much variation in the time that these individuals waited on the coast before the departure of the ships. Much depended on the speed with which the traders acquired their cargo of slaves. This in turn depended on the supply conditions. If there were wars being fought in the interior, traders could expect a steady supply of captives. In 1712, for example, white traders at Cape Coast Castle noted with satisfaction that the neighboring states had declared war against one another. As one of them expressed it, "The battle is expected shortly, after which 'tis hoped the trade will flourish."[20] Similarly, if the nations were at peace, the ships' turnaround time could be rather lengthy. Generally, the wait was between five and ten weeks.

Many captives died on the coast as they awaited their departure. They succumbed to a variety of diseases–yellow fever, smallpox, and dysentery among others, as well as from infected wounds they had acquired during the process of their capture. The damp dungeons in which they were kept certainly contributed to the mortality rate and the joylessness of the slaves' life. For those who survived the confinement on the coast, the journey to America constituted a further assault on their personhood and posed severe challenges to their physical and mental fortitude. Each slave was limited to a tiny area in the ship's hold. Since space was at a premium, they were arranged "like books on a shelf" on various levels, each one separated from the next by a wooden platform. The space between levels was sometimes not large enough for an adult to stand. One eighteenth-century participant in the trade observed that the slaves were so wedged in that "they had not so much room as a man in his coffin either in length or breadth."[21]

The ships' crews were generally careful to ensure that the slaves were securely chained. More feared than the females, the men were chained in pairs, the right ankle of one connected to the left ankle of the other. In some cases fetters would be attached to their wrists as well. Women were subjected to the same restraints, although they were likely to be left unfettered if only a few were on board. The overall nature and duration of the physical confinement of these slaves was obviously dependent on the judgment of the crew as to whether a particular cargo of slaves would rebel if released from their fetters.

The crew did not always depend on harsh discipline and the use of shackles, handcuffs, and whips to control the slaves. The more considerate captains tried to create something approaching a pleasant atmosphere for the cargo by permitting music and drumbeating and encouraging singing and dancing. On the better managed vessels, alcohol, chiefly rum, was provided, as well as pipes and tobacco. The women received beads and other trifles with which to adorn themselves. Such concessions were evidently thought to make the slaves more contented and therefore more tractable.

The length of the slaves' journey varied over time, perhaps from twelve to sixteen weeks in the seventeenth century to between six and eight weeks in the late eighteenth and nineteenth centuries. The construction of better and faster ships explains the reduction in the crossing time. For the duration of the voyages, however, the cramped, inhospitable, and unsanitary conditions facilitated the spread of disease. The ships' holds became veritable marketplaces of contagion. Dysentery, smallpox, yellow fever, and a variety of other "fevers" attacked most cargoes with predictable ferocity. Estimates of shipboard mortality range from an average of 25 to 40 percent during the early years of the trade to between 5 and 15 percent by the nineteenth century. Since there was often a correlation between sailing time across the Atlantic and mortality rates, there was a steady reduction in deaths as ships made the journey more rapidly.

The constant presence of death and disease did not entirely crush the spirits of the captives. The slaves' moods ran the whole complex of human emotions. Moods changed as the journey lengthened and the discomfort of their surroundings exacted a physical and psychological price. Some individuals demonstrated their rejection of their condition by jumping overboard, others engaged in hunger strikes, and tempers often flared at the slightest provocation. The female slaves, according to one trader, were "the most troublesome to us, on account of the noise and clamour they made."[22]

The resort to violent rebellions was the most dramatic response of the slaves to their loss of liberty. These challenges to the power of the traders occurred with sufficient regularity to produce fear in even the most hardened trader. Revolts were more likely to occur on the African coast before the ships departed as the captives made desperate efforts to reclaim their freedom while land was still within reach. Usually, the cargoes took advantage of situations where the crew was weakened by death or disease. Similarly, slaves were able to exploit careless supervision by those in charge. We can never know the number of such incidents that occurred either on the coast or on the high seas because of an absence of systematic data.

Two contemporary participants in the trade, William Snelgrave and John Atkins, admitted that they were aware of rebellions that had taken place during the Atlantic passage. Snelgrave said he knew of several voyages during which mutinies had resulted in either the loss of the ships and crew or in the death and wounding of many slaves. And, as Atkins wrote, "There has not been wanting examples of rising and killing a ship's company distant from land, tho' not so often as on the coast."[23] Modern research, for example, has shown that between 1734 and 1807 there were eighteen revolts on slave ships that originated in Rhode Island. Some of these revolts resulted in considerable loss of lives. Thirty Africans were killed in 1762 when they revolted on the River Gaboone, and thirty-three died in a revolt at Cape Coast Castle in 1776.

Owing to the subhuman conditions in which the slaves existed aboard ship, it was difficult for them to preserve any true sense of human dignity and their own worth. These human beings—often forced to lie in their own excrement, chained together in hot and cramped quarters, and prodded by the ubiquitous whip—tried as best they could to affirm their sense of self. Trader John Atkins described how some women coped with the indignities of shipboard life. "The women retain a modesty," he wrote, "for tho' stripped of that poor clout which covers their privities they will keep squatted all day long on board to hide them."[24] It was in little ways such as this one that African slaves resisted dehumanization and retained some degree of dignity under oppression.

During the period of the slave trade a few of the Africans who had been captured and sold to traders were fortunate to be liberated and returned to Africa as free persons. One of the most celebrated cases occurred in the 1730s. Ayuba Suleiman Diallo, known in the West as Job Ben Solomon, was the son of a high priest of Bondou, a small state northwest of the Gambia River. He was kidnapped in 1730 and sold to a trader who took him to Maryland. Job and his servant Loumein Yoai, while returning home after selling two slaves, had been seized by some Mandingoes. They were shaved "to make them appear like slaves taken in war" and then sold to Captain Pike of the *Arabella*, which was anchored at Joar. Job and Pike had already met; Job had tried to sell Pike the two slaves that he had brought with him, but the captain had refused because the price was too high.[25]

Hoping to be released, Job identified himself to Pike and described the manner of his abduction. The captain agreed to allow Job and his servant to be ransomed for the price of four slaves. Job got word of his misfortune sent to his father, but Bondou was several days' journey from Joar. Consequently, by the time the ransom arrived the *Arabella* had set sail for Maryland, where Job was sold to Alexander Tolsey for £45 and put to work on his tobacco plantation. He proved incapable of doing the work and "every day showed more and more uneasiness under this exercise." Tolsey "was obliged to find easier work for him, and therefore put him to tend the cattle." Unable to reconcile himself to slavery, Job soon ran away but was arrested and jailed as a fugitive slave in Kent County, Delaware. Later, he was identified and returned to Tolsey in Maryland.[26]

Having failed to escape successfully, Job wrote to his father pleading for help in redeeming him from slavery. He had hoped that Vachell Denton, the Royal African Company's factor in Maryland, would ask Captain Pike to take the letter with him on his next voyage to Africa. Pike, however, had sailed before the letter reached him. Fortunately for Job, the letter came to the attention of James Oglethorpe, then deputy governor of the Royal African Company. Impressed by its contents, Oglethorpe decided that Job should be redeemed; to this end, he put up a bond for £45–the original purchase price. Tolsey was willing to sell Job, since he had found him "in no ways fit for his business." Job arrived in England in April 1733 and became an overnight celebrity when the details of his capture, enslavement, and redemption became known. Approximately eight months later the Court of Assistants of the Royal African Company presented Job with a certificate of manumission, making him a free man once again.[27]

During his stay in England, Job was introduced to several prominent Englishmen. According to a letter written by the officials of the Royal African Company, he was "found to be a person of Good Sence and Very Ingenious and has been taken notice of by the King and Queen as well as by sundry other persons of great wealth and worth." On July 15, 1735, Job sailed for the Gambia on board the *Dolphin,* bringing his remarkable saga to an end. In a letter of instruction to its agents in the Gambia, the company directed that Job be "given all the Assistance that lies in your Power . . . [and] possibly by that means he might be able to do the Company good Service by opening and settling a Trade and Correspondence between the nations of those parts and our highest factorys."[28] Job, like some of those who had been freed earlier, was expected to repay the company by furthering its interests in Africa.

The company provided Job with a letter of introduction to deliver to the agents at Gambia. This interesting document merits being quoted in full:

> This will be delivered to you by one Job, a free Black, and son of a
> Mahometan Priest, he was formerly taken and sold to one of the private

traders and carried to Maryland, where he was sold for a slave, but by the good offices of Mr Oglethorpe, has been redeemed in order to be sett at liberty and sent back to his own Country, he has been here in England for some time, and appears to be a very sober and Ingenious person and has met with many favours and civilitys here from many persons of great rank and worth, who have bestowed upon him several considerable presents all which he carries along with him, and as we are very desirous that he should be well and kindly used, while he stays with you, and that all due care may be taken to send him with his things safe home to his own Country, we do earnestly recommend him to your care and protection, and do strictly direct and require you to consult with him about the most proper measures for sending him safe home, and for that purpose to send him with all his things to such of our factorys up the river as lye nearest to and most convenient for him to gett to his own country under the care of some discreet person whom you shall confide in to see these our orders duly put in execution. He has likewise requested of us that if any of his religion should at any time be sold to any of our factors, that upon application for their redemption and upon paying two other good slaves for one, they may be restored to their liberty, which we have agreed to, and do therefore recommend it to you to give the necessary orders to all our factors up the river to pay due obedience to the same, and as it will be a great satisfaction to his friends and benefactors here to be informed by letters under his own hand of the treatment he meets with from you and of his save arrival in his own country, you are to desire him to write to us by all opportunity.[29]

A year after Job reached home, the company also returned a man called Eye to his African homeland. Eye, like the other returnees, was the son of a high African official at Cape Coast. Unfortunately, there is no record of the circumstances of his capture and liberation. The company evidently thought highly of the young man and was concerned about his safe return home. The Court of Assistants took pains to enjoin its officials at Cape Coast to "take care that he be safely delivered into the hands of his friends." It is unknown whether this was actually done. Two years later, in 1737, Job's servant, Loumein Yoai, was redeemed and sent back to Africa under the auspices of the company in 1738.[30]

Another African, Olaudah Equiano, was able to free himself from slavery's shackles in the eighteenth century. An Ibo who was born in what is now Nigeria, Olaudah was seized by slave traders when he was only eleven. He changed hands several times in Africa before crossing the Atlantic and ending up in Barbados. He was taken to Virginia in the 1750s and was later purchased by an Englishman who renamed him Gustavus Vassa and took him to England. Several years later, he was taken back to the Caribbean and sold. His purchaser was a Quaker merchant from Philadelphia who allowed the young man to buy and sell his own goods. Equiano saved enough money and purchased his freedom in

1766. He returned to England, received training as a barber, and became an active member of the Antislavery movement. In 1789, Equiano published his memoirs, *The Interesting Narrative of Olaudah Equiano, or Gustavus Vassa, the African.* This book described his experiences in Africa, the culture of his ancestors and his life in the Americas and in England.

Despite their travail, Job and Olaudah defeated the institution of slavery in the end. For almost all of their peers, however, their disembarkation in America meant the end of one journey and the start of another in an alien land with all of its terrible uncertainties. Most would be slaves for life, although none would have understood the meaning of that reality upon their disembarkation. Posters announcing the arrival of these human cargoes often indicated their ethnic backgrounds or the part of Africa from which they came and sometimes the asking price. Typically, such posters read "Negroes imported . . . directly from the River Gambia," or "a fine Cargoe of young healthy slaves, just imported . . . directly from the Windward and Gold Coast of Guinea."[31] Such cargoes were generally sold by auction, and if the slaves were ill, there would be attempts to dispose of them rather quickly. The following comment of a trader who sold his slaves at Annapolis, Maryland, in 1761 captures the circumstances that often surrounded the sale of the Africans and the prices at which they were offered: "We sold 14 of the Negroes yesterday very well considering the Cond'n they were in. The wenches and 1 man at [£]60 each, 1 man £68, 1 boy £60, Girls at £65, 2 sickly Girls cheap, the Maits Boy for £70, the small poor boy died coming up. . . ." The trader noted that he had wanted to sell his cargo as quickly as possible since the slaves were not in good condition "and we refused no offers . . . even upon 9 and 12 Months credt . . . it allway's helps a sale even of the best slaves to give Cred't in some Instances and we can by such people get off the worst of the Slaves and enhance the price."[32]

The role of the slave trade in the peopling of America can hardly be exaggerated. We can identify certain trends in the trade and the development of the unfree black population. The number of Africans who arrived in the immediate aftermath of the settlement at Jamestown and up to 1680 was relatively small. As a result of the decline in the supply of white servants, the period 1680–1730 witnessed an increased demand for slaves and a notable, if not dramatic, rise in the number of Africans brought by the traders. There was a fairly brisk traffic between the 1730s and 1776 as the expanding plantation economies came to depend more and more on black labor. The pace slowed during the war for the independence of the colonies, but it picked up again around 1783 and remained very active until the end of the legal trade in 1808. Traders introduced a number of contraband slaves after 1808, and this practice continued until the outbreak of the Civil War in 1861.

The sale of estates, pictures, and slaves (shown here: right, left, and center respectively) occurred almost daily during periods when cotton prices plummeted. This slave mart in New Orleans was the scene of thousands of slave sales.

Historians are not all agreed on the number of Africans who arrived. We will never know the exact figure, but reasonable estimates can be provided based on an examination of the surviving records and some intelligent guesswork. The present state of knowledge allows us to conclude, however, that earlier scholars exaggerated the extent of this forced migration to North America and elsewhere in the hemisphere. It is now known that of the estimated twelve million Africans who came to the Americas, about 95 percent, were transported to Latin America and the Caribbean. The remainder, about 498,100 persons, were brought to North America. These arrivals can be broken down in the following way, according to the periods of delivery (see Table 1.1).

The demographic data reveals that African peoples began to form a significant share of the colonial population in the eighteenth century. In 1680, they constituted only 4.6 percent of the population but by 1770 comprised 21 percent before falling to 12 percent in 1810 as the white population expanded. Specifically, blacks numbered 7,000 in 1680, 48,666 in 1710, 134,000 in the 1760s, 757,000 in 1790 and 1,377,080 in 1810. The slave trade was not the only factor that accounted for this steady growth. Unlike the other slave societies of the Americas, the North American black population was able to reproduce itself in a sustained way since

TABLE 1.1
The Demography of the Slave Trade to North America

YEARS	NUMBER IMPORTED
1626–1650	1,600
1651–1675	3,900
1676–1700	23,000
1701–1710	9,000
1711–1720	10,800
1721–1730	9,900
1731–1740	40,500
1741–1750	58,500
1751–1760	41,900
1761–1807	245,000
1808–1860	54,000
Total	498,100

SOURCE: James Rawley, *Transatlantic Slave Trade* (New York: W.W. Norton, 1981), 323–418.

about the 1730s. One authority notes that between 1700 and 1780 "the black population increased twice as rapidly as the rate of importation."[33]

There are several factors that explain this demographic growth. In the first place, American buyers of slaves seemed to have been successful in getting a higher proportion of females than was the case with their counterparts in Latin America and the Caribbean. This sexual balance was, of course, conducive to reproduction. It is also apparent that the disease environment was less harsh in North America than it was in the Caribbean and in Brazil in particular. A number of tropical diseases did not exist on the North American mainland. This resulted in a healthier slave population and a higher survival rate among the children, thereby contributing to an annual rate of natural increase. Black women in Latin America and the Caribbean also had lower fertility rates than their North American peers, a direct consequence of the sexual imbalance, poor diet, overwork, and disease.

The black population, of course, was not distributed evenly in the colonies. Much, as would be expected, depended on the demand for slave labor and the nature of the local economy. Four colonies, because of their export-oriented plantation economies, had the largest slave population, or about 85 percent of all the slaves, by 1780. The Chesapeake Bay colonies of Virginia and Maryland with their tobacco-based economy ranked first and fourth respectively. In that year, Virginia had 220,582 slaves and Maryland 80,515. South Carolina ranked second with 97,000 slaves, the vast majority of whom were employed on the rice and indigo plantations. With its 91,000 slaves in 1780, North Carolina ranked third. New York was next with 21,054 slaves, and Georgia rounded off the top six with 20,831. South Carolina alone had a black majority, but blacks constituted 40 percent of Virginia's population and approximately 33 percent in both Maryland and North Carolina. The nineteenth century would see the black population grow even more rapidly.

Africans arrived in English America a mere twelve years after the colonists established their first permanent settlement in Virginia. Many thousands more would disembark from slave ships in later years, particularly in the eighteenth century. These were not immigrants in search of a better life. They were property. But Africans were more than just property. As human beings, they brought with them their culture, ideas, and worldviews; these were the ingredients for preserving linkages with their ancestral homelands. Thus the slave trade represented more than the forced transportation of peoples; Africa came to America as well. The journey was marked by a profound anguish, pain, and suffering, and a remarkable human and cultural resilience as well. These would remain in large measure, and for a long time, the defining characteristics of black life in America.

Notes

1. E. Jefferson Murphy, *A History of African Civilization* (New York: Thomas Y. Crowell, 1972), 120.
2. Ibid.
3. John Thornton, *Africa and Africans in the Making of the Atlantic World, 1400–1680* (New York: Cambridge University Press, 1992), 104.
4. See Ivan Van Sertima, *They Came Before Columbus* (New York: Random House, 1976).
5. For the early African presence in the Americas, see Colin A. Palmer, *First Passage, Blacks in the Americas, 1502–1617* (New York, 1995).
6. Edmund Morgan, "The Labor Problem at Jamestown, 1607–18," *American Historical Review*, 76 (1971), 597.
7. Ibid., 599–600.
8. T. H. Breen, "A Changing Labor Force and Race Relations in Virginia, 1660–1710," *Journal of Social History*, 7 (1973), 5.
9. A. Leon Higginbotham Jr., *In the Matter of Color, Race and the American Legal Process: The Colonial Period* (New York: Oxford, 1978), 162–163.
10. Donald Robinson, *Slavery in the Structure of American Politics, 1765–1820* (New York: Harcourt Brace Jovanovich, 1971), 56.
11. James Rawley, *The Transatlantic Slave Trade: A History* (New York: Norton, 1981), 309.
12. William Bosman, *A New and Accurate Description of the Coast of Guinea*, reprint (New York: Barnes and Noble, 1967), 364.
13. Ibid.
14. Francis Moore, *Travels into the Inland Parts of Africa* . . . in Elizabeth Donnan, ed., *Documents Illustrative of the Slave Trade to America*, 4 vols. (Washington: Carnegie Institution, 1930–1935), ii, 345.

15. Daniel Littlefield, *Rice and Slaves: Ethnicity and the Slave Trade in Colonial South Carolina* (Baton Rouge: Louisiana State University Press, 1981), 8.
16. John Atkins, *A Voyage to Guinea, Brasil and the West Indies* (London, 1735), 179–180.
17. The Public Record Office (London), Records of the Treasury (T 70), T 70/16, p. 23.
18. Ibid., T. 70, unpaginated.
19. William Snelgrave, *A New Account of Some Parts of Guinea and the Slave Trade* (London, 1734), 163.
20. Records of the Treasury, T 70/5, p. 18, 86.
21. Great Britain, House of Commons, Select Committee on the Slave Trade (London, 1792), 35.
22. Snelgrave, *A New Account,* 105–106.
23. Atkins, *A Voyage to Guinea, Brasil and the West Indies,* 175.
24. Ibid., 180.
25. Philip D. Curtin, ed., *Africa Remembered: Narratives by West Africans from the Era of the Slave Trade* (Madison: University of Wisconsin Press, 1967), 17–59.
26. Ibid., 41.
27. Douglas Grant, *The Fortunate Slave: An Illustration of African Slavery in the Early Eighteenth Century* (London: Oxford University Press, 1968), 61–118.
28. Records of the Treasury, T 70/55, p. 221.
29. Ibid., T 70/51, p. 223.
30. Ibid., T 70/54, p. 93; Grant, *The Fortunate Slave,* 195–196.
31. Littlefield, *Rice and Slaves,* 54.
32. Darold D. Wax, "Black Immigrants: The Slave Trade in Colonial Maryland," *Maryland Historical Magazine,* 73 (1978), 42.
33. Rawley, *The Transatlantic Slave Trade,* 330.

The Foundations of Black America, 1619–1730

According to the historical record, the first Africans who came to English North America landed at Jamestown in 1619. These twenty and "odd Negroes" were delivered by a Dutch "man of warre," according to John Rolfe, an Englishman who wrote a tantalizingly brief account of their arrival. We know nothing about their ethnic backgrounds, ages, gender, or even their legal status. It is unlikely that the Dutch had acquired them in Africa, since merchants from that nation were not yet involved in the slave trade, except for one venture in 1606 and perhaps a few others thereafter. More likely, these persons had been captured by a Dutch privateer from the Spaniards in the Caribbean and then sold at Jamestown.[1]

This conclusion invites other kinds of speculation. If the Africans were sold to the English, then their status as property was established from the moment of their entry into the colony. Their purchasers could choose to hold them for life or, as was the case of the white indentured servants, for a given period of time. We cannot make any absolute claim as to which of these options was used. Since there was no law in England that recognized slavery and none existed in Virginia in 1619, it is likely that the colonists enjoyed much latitude in the status they conferred on the Africans in their midst. Conceivably, some were held for life even at this early stage; others were probably liberated after a number of years of service in accordance with the disposition of the purchaser. What appears clear, however, is that these Africans occupied a subordinate place in society from the moment of their arrival whether they were indentured servants or slaves. There is no evidence to suggest that the colonists purchased them from the Dutch in order to liberate them.

The English colonists, at least in the years after 1619, had to define the place that Africans would occupy in the society and polity that they were creating. They were no strangers to Africans, since some were present in England during the years preceding the establishment of the American colonies. Their skin color had invited speculation and pejorative comments. Writing in 1578, Captain George Best observed that an Ethiopian's "blackness proceedeth . . . of some natural infection."[2] In the parlance of the day, "Ethiopia" was a synonym for Africa.

Although the evidence is inconclusive, some of these Africans were probably treated as slaves despite the absence of such a category of persons in English law. In 1555, for example, it was reported that one John Lok brought "certaine blacke slaves" to England. These persons remained in the country only temporarily, but their designation as "slaves" indicates that the English were familiar with the institution and probably the association of slavery elsewhere in Europe with Africans. Scattered sources suggest that Africans may have worked as slaves in England by the start of the seventeenth century. Troubled by the growing number of these Africans in the country, Queen Elizabeth I ordered the expulsion of all "Negars and Blackamoors" in 1596, repeating the edict in 1601. She thought that most of the Africans were "infidels having no understanding of Christ or his Gospel." In 1601 the queen appointed a merchant to handle the expulsion and urged citizens to report those persons "which are possessed of such blackamoors that refuse to deliver them." The monarch's orders met with little success.[3] In a book that he wrote before he died in 1617 but that was not published until the 1640s, Paul Baynes, a Puritan theologian, made an unmistakable reference to black or "Blackmore" slaves in England, noting that "servants are either more slavish, or else more free and liberall: the first are such whose bodies are perpetually under the power of the Master, as [are] Blackmores with us."[4]

Black servants and entertainers served the nobility and at the royal courts in Scotland and England by the end of the sixteenth century. Whites "blacked" up in minstrelsy fashion in London to portray Africans and delight audiences.[5] It is unlikely, then, that the English colonists who came to America were unaware of the presence of blacks and the existence of slavery in their nation. Some undoubtedly shared the prevailing pejorative images of the African peoples. Nor were the colonists likely to be unfamiliar with the other forms of oppression that existed in their homeland. The English poor, in particular, were the victims of much abuse at the hands of their social and economic "betters" and the judicial system. In 1547, for example, the English adopted a law that enslaved vagrants. It allowed the master to "cause the saide Slave to worke by beating, cheyninge or otherwise in such work and Labor how vyle so ever it be." The law permitted the sale and leasing of these slaves as "any other moveable goodes or catelles."[6]

This measure was shortlived, lasting for only two years. Its importance went beyond its relatively brief duration, however. It meant that the English had developed an ethos by the mid-sixteenth century that accepted slavery as a condition suited for some people, even for aberrant Englishmen. Coming from such a hierarchically organized society and one that acknowledged servitude, the colonists were not egalitarians by any means. Not surprisingly they were receptive to the recreation of social gradations and forms of human exploitation in America.

The English were not unique in their attitudes to black Africans or in confining them to subordinate places in society. The first European colonizers in the Americas–the Spanish and the Portuguese–believed similarly and had formally enslaved black Africans from at least the mid-fifteenth century. The Iberians based their claim to superiority presumably on cultural and phenotypical, or skin color, differences. The word "race," with its modern biological connotations, was not yet a part of the intellectual and popular discourse. But although "race" was not in common usage, there was a conflation at the time between what we now call "race" with "culture." A people's culture was deemed to be a function of their essence; what they created reflected their inner capacities or what the modern reader would characterize as "genes." These were essentialist notions; the culture that the Europeans produced was thought to reflect their "whiteness" and that of the Africans was tied to their "blackness." Viewing their cultural achievements as better and more "civilized" than those of Africans–and other peoples–the Europeans concluded that this was an indication of their innate superiority. The black and "inferior Other" in their midst was accorded less human worth.

Under the circumstances, the transfer of African slavery to the Spanish colonies in the aftermath of 1492 was not a subject of any anguished discourse either in Spain or in the Americas, since the place of Africans in Spanish society had been established prior to Columbus and his voyages. On the other hand, the Spaniards had to debate the place and status of the indigenous peoples in colonial society because they had no precedent for dealing with subject peoples who were culturally and somatically different from them. The issue was not resolved until the emergence of a peculiarly colonial ethos that defined the place of the Indian peoples at the bottom rungs of the various societies.

Similarly, the proper place of those twenty or more Africans at Jamestown and the ones who came immediately after them was not easily settled in English North America. The colonists were certainly aware of the existence of African slavery in the Spanish colonies (and in Portuguese Brazil) for over a century, and on the European continent for a much longer period. But, as a people, most of them had little or no practical experience with the institution. The colonists also had to develop intellectual, moral, and cultural climates that would legitimize the denial of liberty to Africans, while claiming it for most whites. Until this ethos emerged, the place of blacks in colonial society would remain ambiguous and fluid.

A cultural personality or ethos is never a conscious creation. It emerges slowly and is ultimately the product of a dynamic interplay between material, environmental, and experiential circumstances and a vast array of societal understandings. It is never static, and its ingredients and temper may change. The culture of colonial society in formation derived its sources from the English backgrounds of the colonists, the circumstances of the American human and physical environment, and the day-to-day contests for survival. Among other ingredients, the colonists brought with them a recognition of differences between individuals and groups of persons and a tendency to make qualitative judgments on such variations, usually to the disadvantage of those who were unlike one's brethren. The America of the Indians provided a perfect locus for the application of such ethnocentrism. The cultural chasm that separated the colonists from the Indians, together with the obvious somatic differences and the conquered status of the indigenous peoples, fed the Englishmen's claim to superiority and legitimized in their own eyes their position as the new lords of the land. The Indian "Other" was accorded an inferior place in the developing polity of the colonies well before the purchase of the Africans in 1619.

The experiences of the Indians at the hands of the English served as a sort of precedent for the treatment of the Africans. As far as we can tell, all of the Africans who were imported in 1619 and in later years were purchased from European traders. The demeaning circumstances of their entry into the colonies, their alien status, culture, and skin color established their distinctiveness from the start and ultimately helped account for their debasement in a colonial society dominated by people not known for their acceptance and celebration of differences of any stripe. In time, as we shall see, the place of blacks in society crystallized as a colonial ethos emerged that simultaneously reflected and molded white attitudes toward them.

REFINING THE LEGAL STATUS OF AFRICANS

We do not know anything about the experiences of the first Africans. Arriving at the end of August, they must not have found the weather or temperature too inhospitable. Yet they must have experienced the usual difficulties of adjusting to a new environment, probably finding the language spoken to be incomprehensible, the diet strange, and the labor demands relentless and forbidding. More than likely, they had minimal contact with their shipmates, since they may have belonged to masters

Landing slaves from a Dutch man-of-war at Jamestown, Virginia.

separated by long distances. Their numbers were occasionally supplemented by new arrivals, but we can never know the degree of their
social interaction or alienation in these early years. Yet most of these
persons must have survived, at least for a while, and made the best of
their situations.

These early black workers appear in the Virginia census taken in
1624. Twenty-two Africans were listed in this early record. Unlike the
majority of the whites who were listed, no last names were cited for
any of them and almost 50 percent of their number had no name
recorded at all. The pattern was repeated in the census that was taken
the following year. The number of Africans had increased to 25, but
many were only partially identified or listed simply as "Negroes,"
"Negro woman," "Negro man." These designations took no note of their
ethnic or national origins but included them under a nomenclature
that bore no meaning other than that it described skin color, since
"Negro" meant "black." The anonymity that the Africans were granted
in the census records provides an early indication of how they were
perceived by the English. Acutely aware of the differences between
themselves and the Africans, the English by not noting the names of
the Africans had begun the process of denying them their identities
and assaulting their personhood.

In another sense, the failure to list the Africans' names established a
distinction between the whites who dominated the society and the
"Other" who occupied subordinate roles. This perception of separateness found tangible expression in 1630 when a Virginia court sentenced
a white man, Hugh Davis, "to be soundly whipped, before an assembly
of Negroes and others for abusing himself to the dishonor of God and
shame of Christians, by defiling his body in lying with a negro."[7]

The significance of this public humiliation could not have been lost
on Africans and Europeans alike. To the white Christians, this meant a
confirmation of their sense of superiority and a need to prevent contamination by the black "Other." For the Africans, the sentence and the
words that justified it rendered a pernicious assault on them as persons
and on their religious heritage. The message was clear: a white man
who had sexual relations with an African woman defiled his body in the
eyes of his peers.

The record is silent on the Africans' reactions to their peers who for-
nicated with the white "Other." The taboos against sexual contact with
outsiders, given the strength of African ethnicity, may have been rooted
just as deeply. Yet such taboos, if they existed at all in Africa, would have
merely been a recognition of ethnic particularities and would not have
been accompanied by any hierarchical judgments based on the presumed biological superiority of one group and the inferiority of the other.
As has been noted, Africans from specific regions such as West or West-
central Africa shared many cultural understandings, spoke mutually

intelligible languages, and embraced similar religious assumptions. Individuals who hailed from an ethnic group different from that to which one belonged were deemed "outsiders" but were not viewed as qualitatively inferior. It should be stressed, however, that the cultural differences between the Africans and the English were much more stark than those that divided Africans as a group. In physical appearance, language, religious beliefs and practices, family arrangements, and in numerous other ways a cultural gulf separated the European from the African.

Scattered evidence in the 1630s and 1640s provide some additional glimpses of the emerging place of Africans in early colonial polity and society. The indications are that a *de facto* slavery had become the accepted condition of blacks. White settlers continued to import Africans as workers, and most of them were probably enslaved. In 1638, four years after Maryland was settled, the legislature passed an act that stated "Be it enacted by the lord proprietor of this province of and with advice and approbation of the freemen of the same that all persons being Christians (slaves excepted) of the age of eighteen years or above brought into this province at the charge and adventure of some other person shall serve such person . . . for the full term of four years. . . ."[8] The reference in this law to "slaves" probably meant Africans. Also noteworthy is the fact that these slaves were exempted from any limitation on the period of their service. Four years later, two residents of that colony, Leonard Calvert and John Skinner, signed a contract whereby Skinner agreed to supply Calvert with seventeen slaves, comprising three women and fourteen men. There is no evidence, however, that the contract was executed. Not until 1644 is there conclusive evidence of the sale of an African slave in Maryland.[9]

Africans in the sister colony of Virginia seem to have experienced the same deterioration in their status although the word "slave" does not appear in a Virginia statute until 1662. It is apparent, however, that by 1640 some blacks were serving their masters for life. The evidence for this comes from the trial of three servants, one black and two whites, who fled to Maryland in 1640 and were apprehended. The Virginia court imposed a sentence of thirty lashes and an extension of their service by four years on the two white escapees, one of whom was a Scot and the other a Dutchman. The third escapee, "a negro named Punch," was required to "serve his said master or his assigns for the time of his natural life here or else where."[10] In addition, John Punch received thirty lashes. In a similar case, also heard in 1640, six whites and one black escaped. When apprehended, all seven were whipped, branded, and shackled for a year. The whites had their period of service extended, but not so in the case of "Emanuel the Negro." Evidently, he was already serving for life.[11]

The principal conclusion that should be drawn from these two cases is not that they were expressions of interracial cooperation because blacks and whites escaped together. Historians who do so miss the point. Among other things, the Punch case demonstrated that blacks were already being enslaved for life in Virginia (or could be). Even if we assume that John Punch was a servant, then the harshness of his punishment set an early precedent for the unequal dispensation of justice when blacks and whites confronted the law for similar crimes. This disturbing reality would not have been lost on the blacks who were familiar with the case and the differential in the punishment meted out. By 1640, Africans had lived with whites in Virginia for two decades, and none of them had occupied other than subordinate positions in society. These two cases confirmed this status differential and reflected the hardening attitudes toward the African in society.

For the next century and more, Africans and their children lived in colonies that stripped them of basic rights while simultaneously demanding their labor. Virginia and Maryland initiated this process of debasement, but no colony stood above it. By 1650, Africans were regularly purchased for life. The bills of sale noted that they would serve their purchasers "for ever." Such was the case of "one Negro girl named Jowan." In 1652, John Pott, a Virginia colonist, purchased her, and the bill of sale granted him the ten-year-old girl and "her Issue and produce duringe her (or either of them) for their Life tyme. And their Successors forever." Similarly, some individuals who made wills left their slaves to their heirs to serve them "for ever."[12]

Africans were also brought, in these early years, to New Netherland, as New York was then called by the Dutch, who occupied it until 1664. Slavery existed there as early as 1626, when the first cargo of eleven Africans arrived. Their number gradually increased as small groups of slaves were delivered in succeeding years. Some of these persons were sold to the English in Virginia and Maryland. By the time the English seized the colony from the Dutch in 1664, there were probably as many as 700 slaves there[13] Slavery as an institution was firmly established by that time and, according to one scholar, it had become "a community-wide mode of labor exploitation, regularly reinforced by importations and legitimized as a normal and desirable way of life."[14]

One of the anomalies of the 1640s and the 1650s was that the colonists in Massachusetts and Rhode Island both passed laws seemingly outlawing the institution of slavery. The Massachusetts statute of 1641 was an exercise in circumlocution in the sense that it simultaneously excluded and permitted property in persons. According to the law, "There shall never be any bond slaverie, villinage or captivitie amongst us unless it be lawfull captives taken in just warres, and such strangers as willingly selle themselves or are sold to us." In this context, "strangers" referred to Africans and Indians. The Rhode Island law of 1652 condemned slavery but allowed it for a period of ten years. It noted that "whereas, there is a common course practiced amongst English men to buy negers, to that end they may have them for service or slaves for ever; for the preventinge of such practices among us, let it be ordered that no blacke mankind or white being forced by covenant bond, or otherwise, to serve any man or his assighnes longer than ten yeares or untill they come to be twentie four yeares of age, if they bee taken in under fourteen."[15]

In fact, Africans were already present in Massachusetts in 1638, and there is evidence that slavery existed in 1639. In that year, a black woman on Noddles Island in Boston Harbor refused to have sexual relations with another African who was sent to her bed by the master. She angrily claimed that such an imposition was "beyond her slavery."[16] The Massachusetts law and that of Rhode Island did not end the institution in either of those colonies. Similarly, laws passed in New York in 1665 and Georgia in 1732 excluding slavery, became deadletters. What is more striking, however, is that slavery became entrenched in the statutes of all of the colonies by 1740. Allowing for some minor variations, these laws had four principal characteristics. They sanctioned slavery for life, made it hereditary, confined it to blacks and to a lesser extent Indians, and made the slaves chattel.

These laws, to be sure, emerged gradually as the colonists established and refined their control over the "strangers" in their midst. Englishmen developed their slave law in piecemeal fashion, as the need arose. They had no precedents, so they framed their laws in accordance with local realities and their desires. The law, as it evolved in the colonies, reflected the fears of white society and its need to legitimize the exploitation of the Africans and to debase them in the process. It became the instrument for the legitimization of the oppression of blacks by whites, and it would play that role well into the twentieth century.

Although the law increasingly circumscribed the lives of blacks, some were able to create tolerable spaces for themselves, at least for a time. In Northampton County, Virginia, almost one-third of the black population was free in 1668 and several owned land. The possession of land by free blacks brought a measure of tolerance and guarded respect from whites, much as it did in the other contemporary slaveholding societies such as Mexico, Peru, and Brazil. But none of this meant that whites anywhere in the Americas considered them equals. These free blacks earned concessions of one sort or another because they had joined a select landowning fraternity, not because "racial" or social distinctions had been blurred or held little value.

The legislators in Virginia and Maryland can claim the dubious distinction of laying the legal foundations of racial slavery. The laws they passed in the 1660s and in succeeding decades made explicit references to black slavery, thereby recognizing the state of unfreedom that had existed for many, and setting colonial society firmly on the road to making slavery the normal legal condition of the Africans and their children.

A Virginia statute of 1660 gave tacit recognition to the existence of slavery when it referred to "negroes who are incapable of makeing satisfaction by addition of time."[17] This law dealt with punishments for runaway servants, but the language clearly indicates that blacks were enslaved for life. A similar language appeared in a Maryland Act of 1663 that referred to "Negroes and Other slaves."[18] The following year, the Maryland legislature approved an act legitimizing what had been in existence for years. The law ordered that "all negroes and other Slaves to bee hereinafter imported into the Province shall serve Durante Vita [For Life] And all Children born of any Negro or other Slave shall be Slaves . . . for the terme of their lives."[19]

These acts did not alter the condition of the Africans in the colonies. For them, it meant that the law had finally caught up with social practice. The acts confirmed the white man's power over the black; they did not create it. Not surprisingly, these acts would eventually define all aspects of the Africans' life. A 1667 Virginia statute resolved the colonists' doubts as to whether conversion to Christianity conferred freedom on slaves. Traditionally, it was accepted that Christians should not hold other Christians in bondage. Consequently, conversion to Christianity was one path to liberation. Christians had also maintained that the "heathenism" of the person provided a justification for slavery. In a departure from Christian practice, the Act of 1667 provided that "baptism does not alter the condition of the person as to his bondage of freedom." Three years later, in 1670, the legislature passed an act which held that all non-Christian servants who came to Virginia by ship "shall be slaves for their lives." This clear reference to Africans established a distinction between them and Indians who came by land, as well as white servants who were Christians.[20] In 1671, Maryland adopted a statute releasing the slaveowners from their "ungrounded apprehension" that conversion to Christianity led to freedom. Evidently, this assurance was inadequate; in 1715 the legislature passed a law that more forthrightly addressed this issue. The law proclaimed that slaves who were baptized were not automatically "manumitted or sett free nor hath any right or title to freedom or manumission more than he or they had before, any Law, usage or Custome to the Contrary Notwithstanding."[21]

Unlike those in Virginia and Maryland, South Carolina's legislators were not slow in recognizing the enslavement of blacks and in asserting white authority over them. In the Fundamental Constitutions promulgated in 1669, "every freeman of Carolina" was given "absolute power and authority over his negro slaves."[22]

The slave law of the colonies elaborated on and refined the legal status of the black person as the years wore on. By 1680, the terms "negro" and "slave" had become virtually interchangeable. A Virginia law of 1680 spoke of "any negro or other slave."[23] Sixteen years later, in 1696, the South Carolinians rendered their definition of a slave. The law held that "All Negroes, Mollatoes, and Indians which at any time heretofore have been bought and Sold or now are and taken to be or hereafter Shall be Bought and Sold are hereby made and declared they and their Children Slaves to all Intents and purposes."[24] Such would become the prevailing pattern.

In addition to defining the legal status of the black person, the developing slave law after 1660 broke with the tradition of English common law and allowed children to inherit their mother's status. This was a particularly important development. It meant that children fathered by white men with black women who were slaves would be held in bondage. This was a fundamental departure from English common law, in which children took the father's status. Virginia became the first colony, in 1662, to pass such a law, and the others followed in due course. Maryland was an exception for a time but eventually fell in line with the others.

The slave law of the colonies was also noteworthy for its racist dimensions and its assertion of white supremacy. Slavery became the preserve of the black person, and a few Indians. The previously cited South Carolina law of 1696 clearly restricted slavery to "Negroes, Molattoes and Indians." A law passed in the same colony in 1712 noted that the black "Other" were "wholly unqualified to be governed by the laws, customs, and practices of this province." Such persons had "barbarous, wild, savage natures."[25] Racial and cultural origins constituted the fundamental distinction between the enslaved and the free. The slave law, as it took form, assumed a public dimension that gave all whites a superior status and power over all blacks. In theory, a black slave "belonged" to every white. Accordingly, any white person could accost a black slave and interrogate him as to his behavior and activities. Authority and power wore a white face; the law and custom enshrined the subordination and powerlessness of the black individual and upheld the social system.

The statutes, as they came to be refined, also defined the slave as chattel. The 1690 slave law of South Carolina was one of the earliest to define these persons in such a way. The Virginia slave code of 1705 was quite explicit in proclaiming that "All Negro, Mulatto and Indian slaves within this domination shall be held to be real estate and shall descend unto heirs and widows according to the custom of land inheritance."[26] One contemporary, Arthur Miller, who was acting governor of South Carolina in 1725, noted that slaves "have been and are always deemed as goods and Chattels of their Masters."[27] Consequently, slaves were always listed along with other possessions of the masters such as furniture and animals. As chattel, the slave was the master's personal possession and could be disposed of at will.

The defining of the slave as chattel was a fundamental part of the process of debasement that began with the separate treatment accorded to Africans from the 1620s. The colonists restricted their access to weapons and without exception ascribed a subordinate place to them in society. What colonial whites thought about Africans as persons, however, was most clearly revealed in their fears of sexual relations, particularly between white women and black male slaves. The language that accompanied the laws that outlawed such conduct revealed white attitudes toward blacks and explained their horror of race mixing and the depth of their developing racism.

Examples drawn from Maryland and Virginia illustrate these white attitudes and fears. A 1662 Virginia law held that "if any Christian shall committ Fornication with a negro man or woman, hee or shee so offending" would be liable to a fine that was double that which was customarily imposed for fornication.[28] In this context, the appellation "Christian" had religious, cultural, and racial connotations. The Maryland statutes used much harsher language to condemn such behavior. In 1664, the law that proclaimed the service of slaves *durante vita* denounced white women who married "Negro slaves" as acting to the "disgrace of our nation." These were "Shamefull Matches," and women guilty of such alliances "shall serve the masters of such slaves during the life of her husband."[29] The legislature returned to this issue in 1681 and lambasted such women for satisfying their "lascivious and lustfull desires . . . to the disgrace not only of the English butt also of many other Christian Nations."[30] In 1681, the colony banned marriages between blacks and whites. Ten years later, the Virginia legislature took steps to prevent "that abominable mixture and spurious issue . . . by Negroes, mulattoes and Indians intermarrying with English or other white women." According to the statute, "whatsoever English or other white men or women bond or free, shall intermarry with a Negro, Mulatto, or Indian man or woman, bond or free, he shall within three months be banished from this dominion forever." Other colonies followed suit. Massachusetts, for example, passed a law in 1705 titled "An Act for the Better Preventing of a Spurious and Mixt Issue," which banned interracial marriages and imposed stringent penalties on transgressors.[31]

White men satisfied their passions with black women even in these early years more frequently than did white women with black men, whether slaves or free. But although the conduct of these white men invited social sanctions at times, this paled in comparison to the vituperation leveled at the white women who crossed the racial divide. It was not simply that white men feared the competition of black men for their women; they wanted to preserve the "purity" of such women from "contamination" by the Africans. The Maryland law not only punished the women who demonstrated such lapses but also stated that free blacks who married them were to be enslaved.

We cannot be certain of the reaction of the blacks to these actions of the dominant society. Marriage to a white woman could hardly have been one of their central preoccupations, given the enormity of the everyday problems that bedeviled their lives. Those who demonstrated such desires and acted on them revealed the degree to which they had become a part of the American milieu and undertook a futile quest to share in the masters' world. But whether or not black men sought white women at the time, the manner in which such unions were condemned constituted a further assault on their humanity.

Clearly, then, the nature of the legal and social environment in which the Africans and their children lived must be understood before we can appreciate the texture of their lives in these formative years and their struggles to create a livable space. The white masters of the land established the legal boundaries within which the black population had to exist and tried to control its public behavior and restrict a good deal of its private activities. As the number of Africans in the colonies increased, the machinery of repression became more refined and more expansive. Although single white women never shared the same privileges as white men during the colonial period, they could testify in court, make contracts, initiate lawsuits, and own property. Married white women, on the other hand, had fewer rights and became the responsibility of their husbands. But white women, regardless of any disabilities they faced, escaped the debasement that was the lot of black men and women. In spite of their degraded legal condition, however, blacks imposed limits on the ability of the larger society to regulate and control their private lives.

DEMOGRAPHY AND CULTURE

Africans, to be sure, constituted only a small minority of colonial society up to the early years of the eighteenth century. In Virginia, for example, there were only 300 blacks to 15,000 whites in 1650. The Virginia and Maryland black populations amounted to 1,700 in 1660 and 4,600 in 1680. South Carolina, which would eventually have a black majority in the eighteenth century, had a black population of 3,000 in 1703 to a white population of 4,080. New York had 2,170 blacks and 18,067 whites in 1689. The black population in the New England colonies was proportionately smaller than elsewhere. There were fewer than 1,000 blacks in those colonies by 1700, or less than 1 percent of the overall population.

The small size of the black population and its spatial distribution in the colonies must, at first, have posed severe problems for these people. They were undoubtedly engulfed by loneliness, by feelings of profound isolation and alienation. All of these forced immigrants, including those who had been "seasoned" in the Caribbean, had to adjust to their new circumstances, establish new ties and relationships, while struggling to preserve their humanity.

The new arrivals at first confronted the daunting task of communicating with the whites and probably with other Africans who came from various ethnic groups and spoke different languages. Africans who were transshipped from the Caribbean islands may already have acquired some English, but the amount of time the captives spent on the islands varied and so did their facility in the new language. Africans were also exposed to English if they were held at forts in Africa owned by traders from England. Contemporaries reported that a pidgin (a speech deriving from several languages) developed along the African coast, and this facilitated communication. Accordingly, the captives were likely to have been exposed to a pidgin English on the coast and during their passage to the Americas.

Yet we cannot be certain of the degree to which the Africans were able to understand or to make themselves understood in the language of their owners. Most of them probably communicated through signs and gestures at the outset. In 1710, Governor Alexander Spotswood reported that slaves in Maryland spoke "A Babel of languages,"[32] a comment that suggests their difficulty in communication with one another. Olaudah Equiano, recalled that upon his arrival in Virginia in the mid-eighteenth century, "All my companions were distributed different ways and only myself was left. I was now exceedingly miserable and thought myself worse off than any of the rest of my companions for they could talk to each other, but I had no person to speak to that I could understand."

Equiano's comment revealed that he and the other Africans could communicate with their companions either because they shared a common linguistic background or had learned a pidgin during their journey. If a number of these shipmates were purchased by the same person, then they would have been able to make themselves mutually understood. In the absence of such seemingly good fortune, they would have bemoaned their fate as Equiano did. He noted that he "was constantly grieving and pining, and wishing for death rather than anything else."[33]

The learning of the masters' language hastened the Africans' creolization and adaptation to their new circumstances. The process, however, involved more than the acquisition and use of new words. The English language, in common with other languages, encoded the symbols, imagery, and values of the culture that gave it birth. Accordingly, in learning and speaking the new language, no matter how hesitantly and rudimentarily, the Africans began to operate in the cultural worlds of their masters. The grammar of their lives had begun to be altered; their ideas, hopes, dreams, and fears were being articulated in the language of their oppressors, the language of an alien land and culture. Had the Africans not placed limits on this process, their identities would have been transformed, and the slaveowners' cultural world would have invaded and controlled their very souls.

It is quite clear that the Africans, despite their difficulties, were able to retain for a time their languages, their grammatical structures, and words. Much depended on demographic conditions. Where a number of individuals with the same linguistic background resided together or in proximity to one another, then their native language could survive, but perhaps not in a pure form. Africans were sufficiently numerous in South Carolina by 1730 to maintain some degree of linguistic interaction that in time produced their distinctive tongue known as *Gullah*. Concentrated mainly on coastal South Carolina, this dialect combined several African languages with English.

In these early years and later, in their speech and in other ways, the Africans had to operate in their own worlds and in that of the whites. The retention of their languages and the creation of new dialects demonstrated their separateness from the masters and reflected the human desire and ability to preserve aspects of the past while simultaneously adjusting to new realities. Their challenge was not only to learn the language of the slave owners but also to create a form of speech that was uniquely their own. In doing this, these Africans laid the foundations of what would later be identified as black English.

The English colonists, on whose observations we are compelled to depend, frequently characterized the speech of these Africans as "bad" or "broken" English. Some whites doubted the capacity of Africans to become proficient in English. One such person was the Reverend James Falconer of Virginia, who observed in 1724 that Africans "grown up before and carried from their native country . . . are never being able either to speak or understand our language perfectly."[34] Yet, when their numbers permitted, Africans creolized the English language to suit their needs, imposed their own grammatical structure on it, added new words, and altered the pronunciation of many of the English ones. It may not be incorrect to suggest that English was Africanized in many respects. As the Reverend Hugh Jones observed in 1724, many of the Virginia-born slaves "talk good English, and affect our language, habits, and customs."[35]

The competence of slaves in the English language, understandably, varied. Numerous newspaper advertisements for runaway Africans describe them as very "fluent," "talks plain" or "talks good English." Africans who came into contact with whites more frequently than with other blacks acquired competence in English more rapidly than those whose primary associations were with speakers of African languages. Such was the case of Africans scattered throughout the New England colonies and in other settlements where the black presence was negligible.

Some Africans appear to have resisted learning the language of their owners. Reports survive of African-born persons who spoke little or no English after many years residence in the colonies. At the other extreme, there were Africans who became fluent in several European languages, including French, Spanish, Portuguese, and Dutch. These persons may have developed this facility on the African coast or in the Americas, where they were exposed to a variety of European tongues.

By about 1730 distinctive black American forms of speech had begun to crystallize. A creole or locally born population had appeared almost everywhere, and those persons' speech patterns reflected the circumstances of their American birth and their African linguistic heritages as well. While there were regional variations, this emerging language of black America was not a carbon copy of that of the whites. A 1734 advertisement that appeared in South Carolina indicated that the speech of the blacks had its own flavor. It called for the return of "Four young Negroe Men slaves and a Girl, who . . . speak very good (Black-) English."[36]

While Africans and creoles laid the foundations of black speech by 1730, there was also strong evidence that they had begun to develop a network of relationships with one another and some enjoyed settled domestic arrangements. Equally significant was the fact that by 1730 the black population in most places had begun to experience an annual rate of natural increase. This development had enormous implications for the nature and evolution of black life and culture. This native or creole population responded, in many ways, to different tugs and pulls than their parents. American born, they were socialized into the cultural, racial, and social milieu of the colonies of the Chesapeake Bay region, the Lower South, and the North. With few exceptions these black Americans had been born into slavery.

Black America, by 1730, was composed culturally of three principal groups of persons. First, there were those who had recently arrived from Africa and were not yet socialized into the ways of the colonies and whose numbers were constantly being fed by the slave trade. The second group consisted of individuals who had lived in the colonies for some time either on the mainland or in the Caribbean islands. These persons who were acculturated to the American environment, bridged two cultural worlds–that of their original homeland and the one in which they were enslaved. Their identities remained strongly that of their African ethnic group, but their experiences in the colonies had influenced them in important ways. There was, thirdly, an ever-increasing native-born population whose heritage was both American and African, but who nonetheless formed the cornerstones of a black America in formation.

Separated though they were by differences of one sort or another, the black population was also united at other levels. The overwhelming majority shared a slave status, a common phenotype, and a heritage that had many recognizably similar features–kinship arrangements, religious beliefs and practices, political systems, and so on. By 1730, new arrivals from Africa, if they were lucky, would have encountered a black population of some numerical significance in several colonies. This cushioned their entry into a new life in a strange land. Such an experience was fundamentally different from that of the early arrivals, who had to exist to a large extent solely in the white man's world.

The implications of this new demographic situation were profound. Blacks fortunate enough to be settled in sizable groups on contiguous plantations or farms could interact with one another and forge a common culture with core beliefs and assumptions. Such an environment enhanced the process of becoming black American while simultaneously fostering the retention of much of their Africanity–that combination of worldviews and culture that at once defined them and distinguished them from all other peoples. Thus, while the growing creole population was being shaped by, and was itself shaping the emerging black culture, the newly arrived Africans were adding African cultural influences while being exposed to the transforming thrusts of the American environment as well. These seemingly contradictory tendencies were perfectly normal, demonstrating as they did the pulls of the ancestral homeland and the tempering influences of their new land. Out of this bewildering and dynamic mix, an Afro-American society would emerge, complex, ever-changing and exuberant.

The roots of this society, which began to take a distinctive shape by 1730, deserve some attention. Although black society possessed a core of recognizable commonalities, there were variations as well. This was the product of demographic factors, the nature of the colonial economies and the developing slave systems. The emerging plantation society of the low country with its primary emphasis on rice cultivation constituted a region with its own rhythms of labor, demographic configurations, and cultural distinctiveness. In the Chesapeake region, the colonies of Virginia and Maryland with their tobacco-based plantation economies developed styles of black life that reflected their own peculiarities. The third region, comprising the Northern colonies, was distinguished by the absence of a plantation economy and its generally sparse black populations. Everywhere, the nature of the economy, the type of crop, and the attendant labor regime helped shape the culture of blacks and that of the whites as well.

Most blacks lived in groups of ten or fewer prior to the mid-eighteenth century. More than 50 percent of the slaves who landed in Maryland's four most populous counties on the Western Shore, for example, lived on plantations with fewer than ten of their peers between 1658 and 1760. About one-third lived on estates with fewer than five other Africans. South Carolina provides a slight variation in this picture of the distribution of blacks by household. Statistics for St. George's Parish show that there was an average of eight blacks per household in 1720 and twelve in 1726. Not all white households owned slaves, of course, but two-thirds of the slaves "resided on only 18 plantations in groups ranging in size from 25 to 94, and more than 20% were located on the largest of these."[37]

At first blush, the distribution of the black population does not appear to be generally conducive to social interaction between its members. This was probably the case in some situations. But most white households had fewer than ten residents, and this did not inhibit the growth of social cohesion among them.[38] The critical factor was less the size of the households and more the overall numerical distribution of the black population, the proximity of the households, plantations or farms, the degree of concentration of the population, and the opportunities for social interaction on a regular basis. The large plantations with a black population of 100 or more that later became features of South Carolina, Virginia, and elsewhere were small communities that facilitated the growth of social institutions. But such large communities were not a prerequisite for the development and sustenance of black society, other favorable circumstances permitting.

There is some evidence to suggest that by dint of happenstance and the economic roles they played, most blacks were concentrated in select areas of the colonies. In New England, for example, they were located principally in the Narrangansett region of Rhode Island, in the urban centers along the coast, and along the river systems that traversed the region. In New Hampshire most blacks lived in Portsmouth and in the adjacent Rockingham County. In Massachusetts, Boston had by far the largest black population, followed by Suffolk, Plymouth, and Essex counties.

A similar residential pattern may be observed in Maryland. By 1704, black slaves lived in the four counties of Calvert, Charles, Prince George's, and St Mary's, located on the colony's Western Shore. While slaves constituted only 3 percent of the population of these four counties in 1658, by 1710 the proportion had increased to 24 percent. By 1710 in Virginia, most blacks could be found in the counties of York, Stafford, Lancaster, Surry, and King William. South Carolina's blacks, by 1720, were heavily concentrated in the parishes of St. Paul's, St Andrew's, St. James Goose Creek, St. Philip's (Charlestown) and St. John's. These five parishes accounted for 76 percent or 8,983 of the colony's 11,828 slaves.

We can surmise that these Africans sought out one another and endeavored to create a network of relationships that united them in spite of distance. As early as 1687, the Virginia Council noted, disapprovingly, that masters permitted blacks to travel "on Saturdays and Sundays . . . to meet in great Numbers in makeing and holding of Funneralls for Dead Negroes."[39] A comment by the governor of Maryland in 1698 also revealed the lengths to which Africans would go to develop and preserve their social relationships. Governor Francis Nicholson complained that they traveled in groups of six and seven for distances of thirty and forty miles to visit their friends. He claimed that this was "a common practice" on weekends.[40] A few years later, there were reports of persons going back and forth to plantations on "Sabbath and holy days meeting in great numbers." This "continual concourse of Negroes" tended to get "Drunke on the Lords Day beating their Negro Drums by which they call considerable Numbers of Negroes together in some Certaine places."[41]

Such behavior, despite white disapproval, appears to have been relatively common in the colonies. Whites seldom understood the Africans' practices, defined them as antisocial, and tried, albeit unsuccessfully, to restrict these forms of human interaction. In 1712, Charleston's whites tried to prevent blacks from entering the city on holidays and Sundays. Such persons reportedly came to "drink, quarrel, fight, curse and swear, and profane the Sabbath . . . resorting in great companies together"[42] It is interesting that the whites viewed such gatherings in a purely negative fashion and in a manner that betrayed their fears of blacks assembling in large numbers. For the black persons, such social and festive occasions represented a release from their daily routine, affirmed their ties one with the other, and expressed their common humanity.

Although men and women undoubtedly enjoyed their opportunities for social interaction, it was more difficult to find spouses during these early years and live settled lives. Coming from many societies where monogamous relationships were not the norm, it must have been difficult for them to adjust to a new environment where women were not only scarce but where it was expected that one man would confine himself to one woman. Women lost much of their autonomy in monogamous relationships, in contrast to polygynous ones in which they retained control over their individual households. Some men evidently found the competition for women difficult to handle, sometimes with tragic results. Such was the case of Roger, who was enslaved at Silddow Quarter, Virginia. Sometime in December 1712 or January 1713 he "hanged himselfe in ye old 40 foot Tob house not any reason he being hindred from keeping other negroes men wifes besides his owne." Apparently, such competition was frequent and produced conflicts among the men, considering the manner in which the overseer disposed of Roger's corpse. He "had his head cutt off and stuck on a pole to be a terror to the others."[43]

The imbalance in the gender distribution also posed problems for the black population in terms of spousal selection and opportunities for reproduction. Generally speaking, the slave trade delivered two men for every one woman, more a reflection of African supply conditions than the desires of American purchasers. Consequently, most slaves ended up in households or on farms and plantations where men constituted the majority. In a sample based on four counties in Maryland's Western Shore, 80 percent of the men and 70 percent of the women lived on plantations that lacked an equal sex ratio between 1658 and 1710. The same situation obtained in South Carolina, as the data for the years 1730 and 1731 indicates. According to one scholar, "by that time the ratio of slave men to women on sizable plantations throughout the colony was 180 to 100."[44]

These data tell us little about the texture of family life, which is discussed in a later chapter. But they help explain the reasons for the inability of the black population to experience an annual rate of natural increase before the early decades of the eighteenth century. Black women, to be sure, bore children, but their fertility rates were low. Many of these women arrived in the Americas after they had passed or were advanced in their childbearing years. Others proved unable to conceive, probably because of illness or because of stress related to their new situation. African women nursed their babies for three or four years, during which time they refrained from sexual intercourse, reducing their fertility rates. The high mortality rate among babies also hindered population growth.

There was a relationship between the slave trade, fertility, and mortality rates. Slaves frequently arrived in ill health and carrying infectious diseases. As long as the trade continued, African-derived diseases, in addition to those encountered in the Americas, took their toll on the black population. This was a morbid characteristic that American slaves shared with their peers in the other societies of the Americas. Accordingly, the constant inflow of sick slaves complicated the already difficult problems that stood in their reproductive path.

Yet Africans did reproduce, and some of their children lived to adulthood. By 1720, South Carolina blacks seemed to have managed—at least for a while—an annual rate of natural increase. Between 1708 and 1721 the black population increased by over 4,000 by natural means and about 3,600 as a consequence of new arrivals from Africa. In fact, the annual rate of natural increase was a stunning 5.6 percent. This spectacular growth rate could not be sustained, however. The intensification of the slave trade after 1720 and the resulting introduction of disease had the predictable effect on fertility and mortality rates. Peter Wood also notes that the increased demands of the plantation system "may have reduced life expectancy and impaired family stability usually associated with a high birth rate."[45]

The black populations of the Chesapeake colonies of Maryland and Virginia were also able to reproduce themselves by the 1730s. One key to this development is that by 1730 a significant number of creole or native-born women had reached maturity. These women, as evidence from Maryland and Virginia underscores, had more children than their African-born counterparts. Since they may have had their first child when they were about 18 years old, they also enjoyed a longer reproductive life than their African sisters whose average age at arrival was 20 or more. Creole women also tended to marry younger, thereby increasing the possibility of their having more children.

The painfully long and formative first century of the black presence ended around 1730 with the ability of blacks to reproduce themselves in a sustained fashion in some places. An emerging creole population would, in time, become the dominant group in the black population. These creoles, the first African-Americans, bridged African and American worlds, drawing their strength and inspiration, cultural thrusts and pulls from both. Hitherto, the flavor of black life in America was primarily African in all of its richness. With the appearance of a significant number of persons born and socialized into the customs of a new land and subjected to their transforming influences, the texture of their life and their worldviews were altered. Cultural and other differences between the African-born parents and their American-born progeny appeared, predictably and inevitably. This demographic change had profound consequences for questions of black culture, consciousness, and identity. Over time, it led to a continuing and anguished search for a secure place in the land of one's birth.

These creole blacks were slaves for the most part. They, like their parents and those who would come after, were controlled by a body of laws that defined them as chattel. Their human possibilities were circumscribed by these legal boundaries, but not destroyed by them. Colonial whites defined the legal contours, and within them blacks created their own space and ordered their lives as best they could. How well these human tasks were accomplished, at least during that long first century, cannot be easily established. Three centuries later, we run the dual risk of either celebrating their accomplishments in a romantic fashion or underestimating the enormity of the problems they experienced and the complex nature of their responses.

We need to underscore the point that in the context of colonial America not even the fiction of an egalitarian society prevailed. Such a society could hardly have existed as long as only one group—whites—exercised all power. Whites made the rules and executed them, sometimes inconsistently, but they were in charge nonetheless. Whites, regardless of their social status, knew who were the lords of the land. And blacks knew that, too. White indentured servants, a declining group after 1700, knew that once their contract ended they could become upwardly mobile if fortune smiled. For the black slave there was no such predictable and believable expectation.

The years 1619–1730, then, constituted the formative period of black life in America. Slowly but surely, the larger society defined the place of its unwilling immigrants and refined its mechanisms of control in all of its heartlessness. Power always wore a white face, but its reach into the interior lives of the Africans was limited. By 1730, a creole black population had begun to claim a place in society and to lay the foundations of black America. The challenges they and their African peers confronted would test the essence of their being, but their responses give ample testimony to the fact that they would not and could not be vanquished.

Notes

1. Johannes Postma, *The Dutch in the Atlantic Slave Trade, 1600–1815* (New York: Cambridge University Press, 1990), 12.
2. Ronald Saunders, *Lost Tribes and Promised Lands: The Origins of American Racism* (New York: Harper Perennial, 1992), 223.
3. Gretchen Gerzina, *Black London: Life Before Emancipation* (New Brunswick, NJ: Rutgers University Press, 1995), 4–5.
4. Winthrop D. Jordan, *White Over Black: American Attitudes Toward the Negro, 1550–1812* (New York: W. W. Norton, 1977), 61–62.
5. Gerzina, *Black London*, 5–6.
6. Thomas D. Morris, *Southern Slavery and the Law, 1619–1860* (Chapel Hill: University of North Carolina Press, 1996), 41–42. For an important discussion of slavery in English society, see David A.E. Pelteret, *Slavery in Early Mediaeval England* (Woodbridge, Suffolk, 1995).
7. Winthrop Jordan, "Modern Tension and the Origins of American Slavery," *Journal of Southern History*, 28 (1962), 28.
8. Whittington B. Johnson, "The Origin and Nature of African Slavery in Seventeenth Century Maryland," *Maryland Historical Magazine*, 73:3 (1978), 82.
9. Ibid., 236–237.
10. Jordan, *White Over Black*, 75.
11. Ibid.
12. Ibid.
13. David Kobrin, *The Black Minority in Early New York* (Albany, NY: Office of State History, 1971), 4.
14. Joyce D. Goodfriend, "Burghers and Blacks: The Evolution of Slave Society at New Amsterdam," *New York History*, 59 (1978), 122.
15. William M. Wiecek, "The Statutory Law of Slavery and Race in the Thirteen Mainland Colonies of British America," *William and Mary Quarterly*, 3rd Series, 34 (1977), 260.
16. Carl N. Degler, "Slavery and the Genesis of American Race Prejudice," *Comparative Studies in Society and History*, 2 (1959), 62.
17. Ibid., 60–61.
18. Johnson, "The Origin and Nature," 238.
19. Ibid.; Letitia Woods Brown, *Free Negroes in the District of Columbia, 1790–1846* (New York: Oxford, 1972), 24.
20. A. Leon Higginbotham, *In the Matter of Color, Race and the American Legal Process: The Colonial Period* (New York: Oxford, 1978), 36–37.
21. Brown, *Free Negroes*, 24.
22. Degler, "Slavery and the Genesis of Race Prejudice," 62.
23. Ibid., 61.
24. M. Eugene Sirmans, "The Legal Status of the Slave in South Carolina, 1670–1740," *Journal of Southern History*, 28 (1962), 466.
25. James Oakes, *Slavery and Freedom: An Interpretation of the Old South* (New York: Knopf, 1990), 68.
26. Higginbotham, *In the Matter of Color*, 52.
27. Sirmans, "The Legal Status of the Slave," 467.
28. Jordan, *White Over Black*, 79.
29. Johnson, "The Origin and Nature of African Slavery," 239.

30. Jordan, *White Over Black*, 79.
31. Higginbotham, *In the Matter of Color*, 40–46.
32. Russel R. Menard, "The Maryland Slave Population, 1658–1730: A Demographic Profile of Blacks in Four Counties," *William and Mary Quarterly*, 3rd Series, 32 (1975), 35.
33. See the discussion of this issue in Peter Wood, *Black Majority: Negroes in Colonial South Carolina 1670 through the Stono Rebellion* (New York: Knopf, 1974), 169; Olaudah Equiano, *The Interesting Narrative of the Life of Olaudah Equiano, or Gustavus Vassa, The African* (New York: Negro Universities Press, 1969).
34. William D. Piersen, *Black Yankees: The Development of an Afro-American Subculture in Eighteenth Century New England* (Amherst: University of Massachusetts Press, 1988), 41.
35. Allan Kulikoff, "The Origins of Afro-American Society in Tidewater Maryland and Virginia, 1700–1790," *William and Mary Quarterly*, 3rd Series, 35 (1978), 226.
36. Wood, *Black Majority*, 190.
37. Ibid., 159; Menard, "The Maryland Slave Population," 204.
38. Ibid., 152–158.
39. Kulikoff, "The Origins of Afro-American Society," 239.
40. Menard, "The Maryland Slave Population," 37; Kulikoff, "The Origins of Afro-American Society," 239.
41. Menard, "The Maryland Slave Population," 37.
42. Wood, *Black Majority*, 272.
43. Kulikoff, "The Origins of Afro-American Society," 244–245.
44. Menard, "The Maryland Slave Population," 34–35; Wood, *Black Majority*, 160.
45. Wood, *Black Majority*, 153.

The Changing Structure of
Black Society, 1730–1863

T he years 1730–1863 were characterized by critical developments in the lives of black Americans. From its fledgling beginnings in 1619, black society began to take a distinctive shape around 1730, although there were regional particularities and flavors. By 1820 the inner texture of black life was well defined, constituting an important watershed. Although creole slaves outnumbered the African-born by the turn of the nineteenth century, the years 1820-63 represented their unquestioned ascendancy, saw profound structural changes in the population as a whole, the proliferation of institutions created by free blacks, the rise of black abolitionists, and the achievement of emancipation. Although black life continued to be influenced by the larger white society, the most important and enduring drives came from within.

Our primary focus in this chapter is on the internal changes in the growing slave population. (The equally expanding free population receives extended discussion in a later chapter.) We also examine the debates and political developments in white America during the period and their impact on black life. We do this at this juncture in order to demonstrate the dialectical relationship between blacks and whites in society and to provide the reader with some understanding of the national environment within which the interior changes and motions in black life–the concerns of this book–occurred.

The changes in black life during the eighteenth and nineteenth centuries took place in a larger societal environment that questioned their humanity and increasingly refined its method of control. As the institution of slavery expanded and the black population increased, whites both consciously and unconsciously created a racial order that ascribed an inferior place to blacks and legitimized their oppressive treatment. In essence, this was a systemic racism that functioned as a part of the natural order of things that few challenged or even thought about. As early as 1701, John Saffin, a Boston merchant-politician, maintained that some persons were "born to be high and honorable, some to be Low and Despicable; some to be Monarchs, Kings, Princes and Governors, Masters and Commanders, others to be Subjects, and to be Commanded . . . yea, some to be born Slaves, and so to remain during their lives."[1]

In 1858, 157 years later, this view was still being expressed, albeit in a more sophisticated fashion by James Henry Hammond, the South Carolina planter and politician. In a speech that he delivered in the United States Senate, Hammond emphasized:

> In all social systems, there must be a class to do the menial duties, to perform the drudgery of life. That is, a class requiring but a low order of intellect and but little skill. Its requisites are vigor, docility, fidelity. Such a class you must have. . . . It constitutes the very mud-sill of society. . . . Fortunately for the South she found a race adapted to that purpose to her hand. . . . We do not think that whites should be slaves either by law or necessity. Our slaves are black, of another and inferior race. The *status* in which we have placed them is an elevation. They are elevated from the condition in which God first created them, by being made our slaves.[2]

Such views were not the idle racist prattle of the ignorant or the dregs of white society. Mary Boykin Chesnut, the genteel wife of a nineteenth-century South Carolina slaveowner, confessed that she was always "studying these creatures," her contemptuous term for the black slaves who worked in her household and on the family's plantation. To her, a black person was "a creature whose mind is as dark and unenlightened as his skin." Northerners were misled into expecting an African "to work and behave as a white man." Southerners had no such expectation, Ms. Chesnut stressed, because "People can't love things dirty, ugly, and repulsive, simply because they ought to do so." In 1859, Confederate leader Jefferson Davis noted that "[T]he existence [of slavery] . . . raises white men to the same general level, . . . it dignifies and exalts every white man by the presence of a lower race."[3]

Although separated in time, the comments by Saffin on the one hand, and Hammond, Chesnut, and Davis on the other, demonstrated a profound belief in white supremacy, and by extension an embrace of an unjust and unequal social order. Saffin and Hammond saw slavery as a condition that was preordained and immutable. It was normal and natural for blacks to be confined to the bottom of the social hierarchy; the lowliest of the whites knew that they could never descend to such levels even if their condition was only marginally superior to that of the black people in their midst. Psychologically damaged in varying degrees by their racism, whites subjected blacks to assorted and heinous acts of debasement, further maiming themselves in the process.

Observing the indolence of whites in Virginia during the eighteenth century, planter William Byrd attributed it to the corruptive influence of slavery. He noted that slaves "blow up the pride & ruin the industry of our white people, who seeing a rank of poor creatures below them detest work for fear it should make them look like slaves." Businessman Elkanah Watson expressed a similar view in 1777. He thought that slavery affected "southern habits," particularly the "prevailing indolence of people." Poor white men, in his opinion, "had almost rather starve than work, because the negro works."[4]

Thomas Jefferson also made some insightful observations on the impact of slavery on the personalities of white slaveowners and their children. He noted:

> The whole commerce between master and slave is a perpetual exercise of the most boisterous passions, the most unremitting despotism on the one part, and degrading submissions on the other. Our children see this, and learn to imitate it. . . . The parent storms, the child looks on, catches the lineaments of wrath, puts on the same airs in the circle of smaller slaves, gives a loose to the worst of passions, and thus nursed, educated, and daily exercised in tyranny, cannot but be stamped by it with odious peculiarities.[5]

The human chattel were not oblivious to what slavery did to whites. Solomon Northup, a former slave, worried about the effect of the slaveowners' violence on their family members. In his autobiography, Northup recalled how his master's son abused the adult slaves, a situation that led him to wonder how the perpetrator of such violence was affected over the long haul by such tyrannical behavior. Northup noted that it was "pitiable" to see the

> "lad of ten or twelve years of age . . . chastising, for instance, the venerable Uncle Abram. He will call the old man to account, and if in his childish judgment it is necessary, sentence him to a certain number of lashes, which he proceeds to inflict with much gravity and deliberation. Mounted on his pony, he often rides into the field with his whip, playing the overseer, greatly to his father's delight. Without discrimination, at such times, he applies the rawhide, urging the slaves forward with shouts, and occasional expressions of profanity, while the old man laughs, and commends him as a thorough-going boy.[6]

Not all of slavery's victims were black.

America became two societies in the eighteenth century; this was not a twentieth-century development. Two societies—one white and free and the other black and largely unfree—could be readily observed as blacks became a significant part of the landscape and their numbers reached the half-million mark by the last third of the century. Native Americans existed on the periphery, but for the most part they were free and living in their own nations.

As their numbers increased, the white colonists extended their control over vast areas of land and managed economies that reflected regional variations. The boundaries of the colonial environment were set by the whites, who monopolized political power and legislated to protect the interests of kith and kin. White society, to be sure, possessed its internal differentiation, sharp class divisions and inequalities, as well as variations in the degree of access to the seats of power and privilege. But white society was also characterized by much fluidity. Never frozen in terms of its social boundaries, the society was elastic enough to accord rank and privilege to those who improved their economic fortunes or contracted marriage alliances that elevated their status. Yet whites as a group possessed that rambunctious confidence and overweening sense of superiority that invariably defines colonial elites *vis-à-vis* the indigenous peoples and those whom they imported to till the land, run the households, tend the animals, and care for the children.

Although there were many points of intersection, blacks stood apart from and were subordinated to whites during the colonial years and beyond. As white society began to take its distinctive form, black society also developed its peculiar features, its unique contours and internal fiber. The two societies possessed different trajectories and responded to dissimilar voices and imperatives. Blacks and whites inhabited the same space, breathed the same air, and even shared intimacies, but they lived in separate spheres that intersected but never really met. Nor did the two peoples share the same mental worlds. Slavery and race were the great unbridgeable divides; most blacks were the property of whites and could be bought and sold at will. That was the essential difference, terrifying in its implications for the owners and the owned alike.

The black person, of course, operated in the two worlds; that which was his and that which he shared with whites usually on their own terms. To function effectively in the two worlds required different skills; each one posed its peculiar challenges. The white person's world extracted its unique psychological and emotional price, because it was a world that rested on a legalized coercion, supported by the armed might of the state and strengthened by an emerging and expanding body of racist ideology. Black slaves helped to create the material conditions that sustained much of that world, although they did not belong to it and were subjected to its power and repertoire of abuse. While slaves in

North America and elsewhere existed on the fringes of the possessive society, it is not accurate, as some historians have done, to describe slavery as primarily an institution of marginality. Such a characterization is only valid if we view the enslaved exclusively through the external lens of the master class. Slaves in North America, and in many other societies, constructed their own communities, established networks of relationships, and remained centered in and central to their own lives and to those of their acquaintances and relatives.

Black society, to be sure, did not take shape immediately. This was a slow process in as much as it was a population that lacked a common provenance. The continued entry of Africans of many ethnic groups and somewhat different cultural understandings before the slave trade officially ended in 1808, militated against the rapid formation of a community or a "oneness" of goals and values. The relatively small size of the slave population and its uneven distribution in many colonies did not facilitate, although it did not prevent, interaction among its members. An African-American slave community did not begin to crystallize until after the slave trade declined, the slave population expanded significantly as a result of natural increase, and the creoles became dominant demographically. The emerging culture was neither completely African nor American but reflected the dynamic and transforming influences of various streams.

Demographically, the black population underwent profound structural changes in the years after 1730. Although the slave trade, as has been shown, continued to bring new people from Africa, its pace slackened between 1740 and 1780 but became brisk again thereafter until its legal demise in 1807. Remarkably, the black population increased at a faster rate by natural means in the second half of the eighteenth century than it did from the slave trade. In 1759 an English visitor to Virginia noted that blacks in the southern colonies "propagate and increase even faster than white men."[7] This was probably an exaggeration, but it was accurate in noticing the growing fertility of blacks.

The key to the increase of the black population through natural means can be found in the changing ratio of creoles to Africans. As one student of the demography of the black population in the Chesapeake colonies expressed it, "As the proportion of mature adults in the black population increased, the ratio of men to women declined, and this, added to an increase in the proportion of native women among blacks, led to a higher overall birth rate."[8] The rate of increase varied in each colony, of course, but generally rested somewhere between two and three percent in the second half of the eighteenth century.

The census data for the antebellum years show a steady growth of the black population as a whole. In fact, it increased by about 150 percent in the forty years spanning 1820–60. This occurred at a time when the illegal slave trade amounted to no more than a trickle; perhaps no more than 50,000 slaves entered after abolition in 1808. As Table 3.1

TABLE 3.1
The Black Population, 1820–1860

YEAR	MALES	FEMALES	TOTAL
1820	911,400	920,300	1,831,700
1830	1,158,500	1,170,200	2,328,700
1840	1,474,600	1,489,300	2,963,900
1850	1,846,000	1,865,000	3,711,000
1860	2,236,500	2,258,900	4,495,400

SOURCE: Jack Eblen, "Growth of the Black Population in Antebellum America 1820–1860. *Population Studies,* 26 (1972), 280.

shows, the ratio of male to female during those years was almost equal, a factor that was conducive to population growth. Overall, there was an average annual growth rate of about 2.4 percent; the crude birthrate of blacks was 30 percent higher than that for whites. Significantly, most blacks were children or relatively young adults. In 1820, 74.8 percent of the males and 75.42 percent of the females were under thirty. There was hardly any change in 1860. In that year, 73.52 percent of the men and 73.4 percent of the women were also aged thirty or less.

Slaves were distributed widely and unevenly throughout the states. Figures drawn from the nineteenth century underscore a wide disparity among whites regarding the number of human beings that they owned. This should not be a surprise. Despite its democratic genuflections, white society harbored a great deal of inequalities. Slaves were an expensive type of property, and only a minority of whites possessed the wherewithal to purchase them. This observation is valid for the colonial period as well as for the postcolonial years. Yet it must be stressed that the typical Southern slaveowner in 1860 was five times wealthier than the typical Northerner and 13.9 times richer than his nonslaveowning counterpart.[9]

Studies of the rural Pennsylvania counties of Chester and Lancaster provide some indication of slaveholding patterns during the colonial period. Between 1729 and 1758, for example, 30 percent of the property owners held 93 percent of the slaves in Lancaster and 83 percent in Chester. In 1860 when slavery had become a Southern and sectional institution, there were 385,000 individual slaveowners distributed among 1,516,000 families. More narrowly, 4 percent of the adult white male population owned the majority of the enslaved. Eighty-eight percent of all slaveowners owned fewer than ten persons; 50 percent of all slave owners owned an average of five persons in 1850. Thus, the slaveowning elite was confined to a small group of persons. Less than 3,000 families owned more than 100 slaves each. It should be emphasized that these statistics included all of the slaveowning states. When only the seven states of the Lower South are considered, 31 percent of white families owned black slaves in 1860. South Carolina led with 48.7 percent, followed by Mississippi with 48 percent, Florida 36 percent, and Alabama 35.1 percent. Most of these persons, to be sure, were small slaveowners.

Taken together, and viewed another way, only about 50 percent of all slaves lived in units of twenty or more in 1860. Of this number, 25 percent lived in groups of fifty or more. About 10 percent of the slaves lived in urban areas in 1860; the remainder worked on farms, industrial plants, and plantations in rural areas. Slightly more than 55 percent–2,312,000 slaves–were located in the Deep South in 1860, being primarily workers in the cotton fields. Virginia had the largest slave population in 1860, followed by Georgia, Mississippi, Alabama, and South Carolina.

The slaveowning class became more diversified in the nineteenth century, a development that has not always been recognized. About 170,000 new persons joined the ranks of the owners of other humans between 1790 and 1860. Not all of these persons could claim much wealth, challenging the notion of a homogeneous slaveowning aristocracy. By 1850, 20,000 slaveowners were artisans, 27,000 were professionals such as doctors, lawyers, and teachers, and another 21,000 were merchants, businessmen, and civil servants. The slaveholding class had also come to include a few blacks, Indians, white women, and newly arrived immigrants such as the Scots, the Germans, and the Irish. How these changes in the configuration of the slaveholding class affected slave life and the nature of slavery has not yet been carefully investigated.

THE LABOR REGIMEN

During the long first century (1619–1730), most blacks were confined principally to agricultural labor; hence they were rural dwellers. In New England, a few persons were employed in the fishing and shipbuilding industries. Of course, domestics were used everywhere, but they, too, were primarily workers in agriculturally-based households. The eighteenth century saw a diversification in the use of enslaved black workers and in their distribution; both developments were a response to the economic changes that were in motion in white society. Blacks began to be used intensively in the iron manufactories in Pennsylvania, Virginia, and Maryland and in the New England maritime industry as sailmakers, caulkers, ropemakers and so on. In the growing urban areas of New York, Boston, Philadelphia, Baltimore, Richmond, and Charleston, slaves worked as blacksmiths, carpenters, shoemakers, and at a variety of other skilled trades.

Ironically, enslaved workers played a more important role in the artisanal trades during the colonial period than in the years preceding the Civil War. Some skilled slaves were gradually replaced by white immigrants. Others were siphoned off, so to speak, to accompany their masters to the West to assist in the construction industry and in other areas where specialized talents were needed. Yet black slaves–whether as artisans, domestics, industrial workers, or manual laborers–were highly visible in the cities of the South during the nineteenth century. Free blacks and slaves constituted 58 percent of Charleston's population in 1820, 40 percent of Richmond's in the 1830s, 50 percent of Savannah's in 1830 and 25 percent of that of St Louis and Louisville in the same year. These proportions did not remain constant in the antebellum years, however. In some cities, the number increased, while there was a marked decline in others. Between 1850 and 1860, for example, the enslaved population increased by 25 percent in Richmond, 55 percent in Nashville, and 17 percent in Mobile but declined by 46 percent in Charleston.

Not all urban slaves were artisans, domestics, or manual laborers. Probably as high a proportion as 15–20 percent were industrial workers in the antebellum years. As a group, industrial slaves amounted to about 5 percent of the total slave population, or 150,000 to 200,000 persons in the 1850s. They were widely distributed throughout the slave states and played critical roles in the local economies. Various forms of labor abuse existed in these industrial plants. Long hours, absence of safety devices, exposure to life-threatening conditions, and poor ventilation made life difficult for all workers in these enterprises.

The textile mills were among the principal users of slaves in the nineteenth century. By 1860, some 5,000 unfree persons served in plants located in Georgia, the Carolinas, Virginia, Alabama, and Mississippi. The labor force was composed primarily of women and children. Most of the early mills were attached to plantations, using about ten or twenty persons. The women and children sometimes did the spinning after their other duties were concluded. One former slave from Alabama confirmed, "De Li'l niggers at night went to de big house to spin an' weave." Another recalled that "My mother was a loomer. She didn't do nothin' but weave. We all had reg'lar stints of spinnin' to do, when we come from the fiel."[10] By the 1840s large textile factories appeared employing scores of slaves.

The production of iron and the mining of coal depended on slave labor. The Chesapeake iron industry began in the early eighteenth century, and by midcentury, some ironworks were composed almost exclusively of slaves. The Virginia ironworks alone employed 7,000 slaves at various periods in the nineteenth century. Slaves were also well represented in the furnaces in Kentucky, South Carolina, Tennessee, Georgia, and Missouri. Overall, about 10,000 slaves were used in this industry at any one time in the antebellum years. The rich coal mines of western Virginia and to a lesser extent those of Tennessee, Maryland, and Kentucky also depended on unfree black labor.

The tobacco industry of Virginia and North Carolina accounted for an increasingly substantial share of slave labor in the nineteenth century. Richmond's tobacco plants employed 3,400 slaves in the 1850s, and the industry as a whole probably employed as many as 15,000 black workers in 1860. In South Carolina and Georgia, slaves worked in the rice milling industry, and in Louisiana, Texas, and Georgia they played major roles in the sugar refining industry. Others were used in the gold mines of the Piedmont, Appalachia, Georgia, and North Carolina. Lead mines in Virginia and Missouri called upon black workers, and so did the saltworks of western Virginia, Kentucky, and Arkansas. The lumber industry everywhere and those engaged in the transportation industry also relied on slave labor in significant proportions. The vast majority of the slaves, perhaps an average of 90 percent, worked on farms and plantations of various sizes throughout the period under discussion. During the long first century and later, almost 60 percent of them were located in the Chesapeake Bay area, laboring on the tobacco plantations of Virginia and Maryland. By the start of the nineteenth century, however, a dramatic shift in the distribution of the black population occurred. This redistribution of the slaves was largely a consequence of the spiralling world demand for cotton that accompanied the Industrial Revolution. Planters in the Deep South, and later Texas, responded aggressively to this demand. The climate in Alabama, Georgia, Mississippi, and Louisiana was ideally suited for cotton cultivation; all that was needed was a stable labor force to ensure maximum productivity and profitability.

King Cotton's rise to economic supremacy in the Deep South was also aided by technological improvements in the separation of the seed from the fiber. In 1793 Eli Whitney revolutionized the process by introducing a cotton gin that did the job more rapidly and efficiently. Over the next half century almost a million slaves were either sold to persons living primarily in Alabama, Louisiana, Mississippi, and Texas or were forced to move to those places with their owners. The bulk of the slaves who were involved in this interregional traffic came from the Carolinas, Virginia, and Maryland.

The majority of the enslaved were associated in some fashion with the production of cotton during the antebellum years. The 1850 census reported that 73 percent of all agricultural slaves lived on plantations where cotton was the principal crop. It should be added, however, that these persons performed other tasks as well, since the tending of the cotton fields did not require all of their attention all of the time. Large plantations were like self-sufficient villages; foodstuffs had to be produced, animals cared for, buildings constructed and repaired, clothes sewn, and so on. Fourteen percent of the slaves in the agricultural sector in 1850 worked on tobacco plantations, 6 percent cultivated sugar, 5 percent rice, and 2 percent hemp. As in the case of those on the cotton plantations, these persons were also used in other ways, as needed.

Urban slaves confronted the same set of challenges and were exposed to similar experiences as the largely rural industrial and plantation workers. There were, to be sure, some differences in the texture of daily life and work routines but not enough to impose a rigid dichotomy between rural and urban slaves. Regardless of their location and the nature of their work, the enslaved were able to negotiate a measure of control over their lives, create their own passageways in the architecture of slavery, nurture intimacies, and order their lives as best they could. Each occupation, whether rural or urban, industrial or agrarian, required its own expertise. This was the case in the making of a shoe or a house, the proper way to wield an ax and a hoe, harvest rice, or select healthy ratoons for the sugar plantation. The artisans and industrial workers acquired the specialized skills appropriate to their tasks, and so did the agricultural worker and the cook.

Generally speaking, the racial ethos of the urban areas was not qualitatively different from that of the rural environments, although it was probably more flexible or elastic in its expression. Whites still made the rules, enforced them, and established the boundaries within which the black population had to operate. American whites knew that in order for the institution to survive, they had to assert their power over their black slaves in a variety of ways. To many slaveowners and others, it was essential to make their human chattel accept white authority unquestioningly. In 1770 the wealthy Virginia planter Landon Carter observed that, "Kindness to a Negroe by way of reward for a job well done is the surest way to spoil him."[11] Writing some years later, a judge noted, "The power of the master must be absolute, to render the submission of the slave perfect."[12] But power did not always mean the use of the whip and other forms of violence. Psychological abuse went hand in hand with physical terror and debasement. The owners sought to make the slaves accept their condition as natural and their subjugation to others as normal and preordained. Slaves must know how "to keep their places, to feel the difference between master and slave."[13] In practice, this required knowing and using the proper forms of deferential address for whites, the uncomplaining acceptance of verbal and other forms of abuse, and a day-to-day obsequiousness that whites needed to assure themselves of their superiority. It also meant the demonstration of loyalty to the owner, the protection and promotion of his interests, and a seeming contentment with the condition and demands of servitude. In the words of a nineteenth-century slaveowner, slaves "must obey at all times, and under all circumstances, cheerfully and with alacrity. It greatly impairs the happiness of a negro, to be allowed to cultivate an insubordinate temper. Unconditional submission is the only footing upon which slavery should be placed."[14]

Unconditional submission was, understandably, not easily achieved. In fact, it was an ideal that most slaveowners never attained, because their often defiant chattel refused to grant it. Yet, slaveowners and the larger society could call upon its enormous machinery of control to impose an uncertain submission. Slaveowners enjoyed extensive private disciplinary powers over their human property. The ubiquitous whip represented one of the most visible symbols of white authority and power; many slaves bore the physical and psychological scars of its frequent use. Often made of ox hide, the "rawhide," as one of the whips came to be called, could sear the human flesh with each stroke, extracting screams from even the most stoic victim. A leather strap of about eighteen inches in length was also used. A "buckskin cracker" was attached to the end of the strap for the purpose of "stinging" the victim with each lash. The frequency with which the whip was employed cannot be easily determined, but it was certainly an important part of the arsenal of master control. The number of lashes varied with the offense and undoubtedly with the disposition of the owner or overseer, but particularly serious infractions would earn as many as 100 stripes.

Frederick Law Olmsted, who visited the South during the mid-nineteenth century, captured the pain, humiliation, and helplessness of slaves who were constantly at the mercy of their owners or surrogates. Olmsted's description is the most graphic of the extant accounts of white violence against black slaves. He described Sall, a girl who was required by an overseer to lie on her back and expose her genitalia. Armed with the rawhide, the overseer beat her "across her naked loins and thighs." The young victim "shrunk away from him not rising, but writhing, groveling and screaming." Overcome by the pain unleashed by each blow, she pleaded: "Oh don't sir! Oh please stop, master! please sir! please sir! oh, that's enough master! oh Lord! oh master, master, oh God, master, do stop! oh God, master, oh God, master!" When the overseer's anger had been spent and the violence ceased, Sall remained "choking, sobbing, [and her] spasmodic groans only were heard."[15] When physicians in Illinois examined the black recruits who had joined the Union army in the 1860s, they were shocked by the lacerations they observed. One lieutenant described what he saw:

> Some of them were scarred from head to foot where they had been whipped. One man's back was nearly all one scar, as if the skin had been chopped up and left to heal in ridges. Another had scars on the back of his neck, and from all the way to his heels every little ways; but

that was not such a sight as the one with the great solid mass of ridges, from his shoulders to his hips. That beat all the antislavery sermons ever yet preached.[16]

It is little wonder that during the Civil War black soldiers destroyed whipping posts with unrestrained venom. A white man who observed one such incident confided: "It seemed as though they were cutting at an animate enemy & revenging upon him accumulated wrongs of two centuries."[17]

The whip was not the only instrument of abuse. Slaves could be confined to the "stocks," a kind of barbaric instrument that prevented physical movement. Others were chained, fettered, starved, and humiliated in many ingenious ways. Occasionally, slaves' bodies were mutilated, and a few died as a result of excessive abuse. The murder of slaves constituted an offense in all of the southern states by the nineteenth century. Such laws were, however, largely unenforceable, since blacks could not testify against whites and much depended on the willingness of sympathetic whites to press charges. In a study of the extant court cases, Thomas Morris concluded, "Almost all homicides of slaves, from the colonial period to the end of slavery, ended in acquittals, or at most in verdicts of manslaughter, which meant that there had been some legal provocation from the slave."[18]

A number of states also prohibited excessive physical abuse and dismemberment of the slaves, but convictions seldom occurred. Juries were unwilling to infringe upon the masters' authority over their slaves. Nor were they disposed to convict whites for offenses committed against blacks, a practice that would survive long after slavery's demise. In reality, the courts and the criminal justice system as a whole more often than not functioned as extensions of the power of the masters. Slaves were more prone than whites to be convicted of the charges leveled against them. They were far more likely to be sentenced to death, and castration was a horrendous penalty that was reserved for black men for varying periods in North Carolina, Virginia, and Missouri. Evidence from North Carolina suggests that slaves who were executed in the eighteenth century were frequently tortured, burned, and castrated.[19]

The historical record contains innumerable examples of white mistreatment and violence and the private agony of their black victims. But it cannot capture the cumulative effect of such treatment on the slaves and on those who administered the pain or legitimized it in law, in social intercourse, and through their silence. It is certain, nonetheless, that such conduct diminished both groups; blacks bore the physical and psychological wounds, and whites as has been suggested earlier, were also maimed by the corruptive effect of the exercise of absolute power and the callous devaluing of the worth of other humans. At its most basic level, whites as a people owned blacks as a people, producing a complex set of mental conditionings, understandings, and attitudes that many have not yet been able to exorcise. Over time, a society emerged that wove racial injustice into its fabric, demonstrating marked contradictions between its professed ideals and the treatment of its peoples who were brown and black. This systemic racism trapped its perpetrators and its victims, corroded the nation's soul, and left it essentially bereft of credible claims to decency where the treatment of the peoples of African descent was concerned. Whites did not form a moral community on the twin issues of race and slavery.

In organizing their labor force, slaveowners and their overseers on large plantations adopted a number of strategies and arrangements to enhance productivity. The assignment of tasks must have presented severe psychological difficulties for the African-born persons. African societies, in the main, had gender-based labor responsibilities and duties. Since many men seldom, if ever, performed basic agricultural labor in their homeland, their assignment to such labor in America must have been the source of much role confusion and difficulty. It can be surmised that women were affected to a much lesser extent since they performed both domestic and agricultural labor in Africa and were assigned the same duties by the slaveowners. Suddenly finding themselves forced to do women's work, men reacted with sullen indignation. Perhaps this particular mode of labor organization helped explain why African men had a tendency to flee within the first few months of their enslavement.

Although the record is relatively silent on such matters for that long first century, it may be guessed that the work rhythm of the slaves, distinctive labor patterns, styles, and routines developed over time. African slaves had come from societies where work had different cultural meanings from those that existed in America. No strangers to hard work, Africans saw work as a collective endeavor in much the same way as other activities. Agricultural work had its own season, its own pace and culturally legitimized rituals and routines. The same was true of other forms of labor; each had its own rules, its own style, periods of strenuous effort and others characterized by leisure. Everything had to be undertaken and accomplished in its own time and work brought its own psychic rewards because it was done on behalf of the group to which one belonged. Independent effort had no motive force; work was just another activity situated in a culturally approved web of ritual behavior.

African attitudes to work can only be understood when placed in their proper cultural context. Those who were taken to America to work as slaves could not derive any psychic rewards from their labor because it was divorced from a cultural context that gave it meaning. This was coerced labor and it was not designed to benefit the group of which one was a part. Not surprisingly, whites viewed these workers as indolent and lazy and applied the whip to induce effort. Work had lost its deeper cultural meaning and resonance; it was something to be avoided or performed without enthusiasm.

In trying to make the most of their situation, slaves enjoyed their labor best when they worked collectively or in a gang. This practice never brought the same psychic reward as it did in Africa, but it eased the drudgery of the work and at least recaptured the spirit of communal activity. Interspersed with songs, the time passed and the routine became more bearable. Creole slaves, however, demonstrated marked differences in their attitudes toward work, reflecting their experiences as products of the American environment.

Creoles, to be sure, were never entirely free from the ethos that guided their African forbears. Work habits and the attitudes that surround them are passed on from parents to children. But they are always subject to change, particularly if work is not seen as an integral part of an intricate web of culturally sanctioned relationships. Work did not have this kind of meaning in English America, and creole slaves were exposed to a different kind of ethos with a different kind of work discipline and cultural rationale. Creole blacks enjoyed working collectively in gangs for certain kinds of labor and sang as they did so, but they were more receptive to individual or task labor in accordance with the Anglo-Saxon work ethic into which they were born.

Creole slaves, therefore, had a style of work that drew upon African rhythms as much as it was influenced by the habits of the whites and the demands of plantation agriculture, the craft workshops, and the industrial plants. Whites did not always understand the factors that influenced the performance of the slaves on the job. While some praised the extraordinary dedication of individual slaves, a far greater number evidently viewed the work habits of their labor force negatively. Whites spoke about the "laziness," "stupidity," and the overall incompetence of their slaves. One nineteenth-century white woman observed, "With negro slaves, it seemed impossible for one of them to do a thing, it mattered not how insignificant, without the assistance of one or two others. It was often said with a laugh by their owners that it took two to help one do nothing." [20] Some slaves, of course, would do things in their own time or not at all. One woman observed after the war ended, "I generally found that if I wanted a thing done I first had to tell the negroes to do it, then show them how, and finally do it myself. Their way of managing not to do it was very ingenious, for they always were perfectly good tempered and received my orders with 'Dat's so, missus; just as missus says,' and then somehow or other left the thing undone."[21] This was, of course, an exaggeration, but it did include a measure of truth. In the final analysis, however, many Southern white families had come to depend on slave labor, profiting from it in numerous ways. If slaves as a group had not been productive workers, albeit with their own styles of labor, the institution would not have expanded, and it would have been allowed to disappear. Slaveowners were nothing if not economically rational persons.

The administration of the typical plantation was the responsibility of the owner, his white overseer, and a driver, the latter being the name given to a slave who was placed in a supervisory position. The pattern varied, however. In those cases where there was an absentee owner, the overseer assumed responsibility for management decisions. A few of these overseers were black, a practice that existed without legal sanction. There was no need for an overseer on those plantations where the number of slaves was not large and the owner could handle day-to-day supervisory chores without assistance. Slave drivers, used on large plantations, supervised a number of slaves. The number of hands they supervised varied, but some were responsible for as many as fifty or sixty persons. These drivers reported to the overseer or the owner.

The slave drivers were chosen by the owner or the overseer, and they were almost always male. Obviously, slaveowners looked for certain qualities in their candidates for driver—trustworthiness, toughmindedness, leadership qualities, and the ability to gain the respect of the other slaves. As part of the managerial team, slave drivers protected and advanced the interests of the slaveowner, but they also had to be sensitive to the needs of the workers. Armed with a whip and the authority of white society behind them, slave drivers cannot be said to have been the leaders of the slaves. As far as can be presently determined, the slaves played no formal role in their selection.

In the eyes of the whites, drivers were privileged slaves. They often enjoyed such concessions as better food, clothing, and housing. The owners took pains to demonstrate to the other slaves that drivers had to be respected and obeyed, even refraining from reprimanding them publicly. As part of the management team, the drivers responded with fealty and often with affection. One driver wrote to his absent owner in 1856, "I have done all day in my power towards your benefit. . . . The hands has bin faithful to their duty."[22]

Drivers, of course, had to deal with slaves as well. They assigned tasks, encouraged, cajoled, punished, and resolved disputes. Being close to the ground, they were attuned to the slaves' moods, knew their limits, and conveyed their concerns to the white authorities. Drivers could abuse their positions as well, by inflicting severe beatings and other forms of cruelty. Theirs was a difficult task; they were slaves placed in authority over other slaves and charged with the responsibility to enhance their common oppressor's interests.

It cannot be doubted that slave drivers, if they thought about their roles at all, were racked by inner storms. Some were seduced by the confidence demonstrated in them by their owner, the acquisition of power of sorts, and their seeming elevation in the eyes of their peers. A former driver recalled:

I don't remember nothin' in particular that caused me to get dat drivin' job, 'ceptin hard work, but I knows I was proud of it 'cause I didn't have to work so hard no mo'. And den it sorta made de other niggers look up to me, an you knows us niggers, boss. Nothin' makes us happier dan to strut in front of other niggers.[23]

Such a point of view may or may not have been representative of the perceptions of drivers. There is no way to tell. Yet drivers were multidimensional persons who had to walk a tightrope between their allegiance to their owners and their identification with the black group of which they were a part. The people whom they supervised were their kin, friends, and associates, and this must have had a tempering effect on the exercise of their power. Drivers probably looked the other way if wives, children, or lovers failed to complete assigned duties. On the other hand, drivers who distanced themselves from their fellow slaves and abused their power showed the degree to which slavery could pervert the sensibilities of some of its victims.

As slavery evolved on the plantations, two principal forms of organizing labor emerged—the gang and task systems. The former drew upon the African work cultures and was ideally suited for crops where the labor force had to be supervised and regimented. This was true of tobacco, cotton, and sugarcane. Workers had to know about each stage of the process, from cultivation to harvesting, and it did not easily lend itself to tasking or individual effort. Under this system, slaves worked for a stipulated period of time each day at various tasks. This was collective effort at its best, each person having to keep pace with the next whether the job was ploughing, hoeing, or harvesting. With the rise of a creole population in the nineteenth century with different skills and work attitudes, slaveowners tended to use the task system in almost all forms of agriculture.

Under the task system, the enslaved worker was given a job to be completed for the day. The person worked independently at his or her pace. Once the assignment was accomplished, the slave was free to do whatever he or she pleased. This was the ideal situation since for the system to work efficiently, slaves had to be assigned a task that could be reasonably completed in the time allotted for it. This was not always the case, and it led to conflicts and negotiations between the slaves and their supervisors.

The task system developed during the early years of the eighteenth century and was in widespread use, particularly in South Carolina and coastal Georgia, throughout the antebellum years. Rice farmers in South Carolina adopted the system quite early, generally assigning a quarter of an acre of land as the daily task unit. The responsibilities included clearing the land, planting, and harvesting. As time went on, tasking expanded to include work in the lumber industry such as sawing, the

This picture, taken at Drayton's plantation in Hilton Head, 1862, portrays a typical slave labor force.

cultivation of sea island cotton, corn, and sugarcane. In Georgia, according to one nineteenth-century observer, tasking was used in the canefield "whenever the nature of the work admits of it; and working in gangs as is practiced in the West Indies and the upper country, is avoided. The advantages of this system are encouragement to the labourers by equalizing the work of each agreeably to strength and the avoidance of watchful superintendance and incessant driving."[24]

Slaves who had been influenced by the Anglo-Saxon work ethic preferred the task system. For them, work had no ceremonial meanings as it did for the African-born in their own societies. Work was something that had to be done, an inescapable obligation. The task system allowed the individual to control the pace of the work. Those who worked at an accelerated pace knew that once the task was completed, they could turn to their own pursuits. We can never be certain how frequently slaves completed their task before day's end. If this was a regular occurrence, slaveowners, overseers, and drivers would certainly have increased the amount of work that each task required. It is clear, nonetheless, that some slaves completed their tasks early but probably not all that frequently. Not superpersons by any means, slaves who regularly sped to the completion of their tasks would surely have paid a physical price and would not have had the energy to do much for themselves after sundown.

Tasking, if the amount of work assigned was manageable, allowed some slaves a degree of control over their work rhythms. Some devoted their time after the early completion of their task to tending their own crops on those plantations where they were allowed to plant provisions. Throughout the South, slaves grew a variety of crops—corn, rice, peas, vegetables—which they consumed or sold to their masters and other whites, sometimes in contravention of local laws. Others reared fowl, hogs, horses, and cattle.

In some cases, slaves hired themselves out to whites to earn money, a practice that seemed to have begun in the early eighteenth century. Most whites, it may be recalled, did not own slaves and could not afford them even if the desire existed. Such persons, resources permitting, were willing to hire other people's slaves to perform certain services. This was a practice that existed in both rural and urban areas, although it was more prevalent in the cities during the nineteenth century. Not all hired slaves were persons who had completed their tasks; many were individuals whose owners allowed them to be hired for substantial periods of time. A few masters had no need for the labor of their chattel but used them as income-earning human machines.

Slaves who were hired negotiated the terms of the labor arrangement or left it up to their masters. Those who were hired for long periods of time—as long as a year—frequently lived with their employer or in rented places, particularly in the cities. Owners worried about the fate of their property in such situations, recognizing that blacks confronted enormous day-to-day difficulties. A Beaufort, South Carolina, owner who allowed two of his slaves to find work in Savannah, thirty miles away, pleaded with his cousin "to be kind enough and protect them if anything may occur that will want a white person's interference. . . . In fact I wish you would take them under your charge while in Savannah."[25] That these persons did not run off raises questions about slavery's mechanisms of control. The whip was not always needed; slaveowners who had done their job well could command fealty even from a distance.

Hired slaves in the cities worked in factories and as domestics, artisans, and manual laborers. Such persons often signed a contract stipulating the wage, period of service, and the conditions of labor. Whites, to be sure, received higher wages for the same jobs, but such was the nature of everyday business in America. The slaveowners expected a certain sum of money from their chattel either weekly or monthly. The slave kept any amount beyond that. This, understandably, gave such slaves an incentive to work for long hours and at different jobs where that was possible. One traveler, writing in the mid-nineteenth century, observed, "At the Christmas holidays, some of the Southern cities and towns are alive with negroes, in their best attire seeking employment to come, changing places, and having full liberty to suit themselves as to their employers."[26]

Slaves, undoubtedly drawing upon their African commercial traditions, were quite active as vendors in urban markets, at least from the mid-eighteenth century. They plied their own wares as well as those entrusted to them by their owners. Whites frequently objected to the competition and to the assertion of black economic independence. A group of disgruntled white citizens in Charleston complained in 1740 that such practices constituted "a very great Grievance and an intolerable Hardship" on them. They disliked the fact "that Negroes are suffered to buy and sell, and be Hucksters of Corn, Pease, Fowls &c. whereby they watch Night and Day on the several Wharfes, and buy up many Articles necessary for the Support of the Inhabitants and make them pay an exhorbitant Price for the same."[27]

Women played a much more prominent role in trade than did the men, developing a reputation for sharp business practices and acumen. An eighteenth-century visitor to Charleston, which had a sizable number of black women traders, left a vivid description of a market scene. The women, the traveler wrote, were

> seated there from morn 'til night, and buy and sell on their accounts, what they please in order to pay their wages, and get as much more for themselves as they can; for their owners care little how their slaves get the money so they are paid. These women have such connection with and influence on, the country negroes who come to that market, that they generally find means to obtain whatever they choose, in preference to any white person; thus they forestall and engross many articles, which some hours afterwards you must buy back from them at 100 or 150 per cent advance. I have known those black women to be so insolent as even to wrest things out of the hands of white people, pretending they had been bought before, for their masters or mistresses, yet expose the same for sale again within an hour afterwards, for their own benefit. I have seen country negroes take great pains, after having been spoken to by those women, to reserve what they choose to sell to them only, either by keeping the articles in their canoes, or by sending them away, and pretending they were not for sale, and when they could not be easily retained by themselves, then I have seen the wenches as briskly hustle them about from one to another that in two minutes they could no longer be traced.[28]

As a consequence of the sale of their own provisions and their skills, many slaves had money in their pockets to spend on their own needs. These persons accumulated varying amounts of cash as a result of their enterprising spirit and participated in a thriving domestic economy. Some could even be called successful entrepreneurs, although there is no evidence, except in rare cases, that their capital exceeded more than a few hundred dollars. Such persons, however, constituted a very small minority in the overall slave population, and their exceptional performance in the system should not blind us to the fact that the vast majority remained propertyless and lived a materially spartan existence. Those who created economic passageways for themselves reduced their dependence on their owners and became participants in an economy built partially on their own oppression. As in other ways, their "success" carried a terrible price tag.

Slaves who reaped material rewards from the system were likely to be less inclined to challenge the status quo. Whites knew that too, and some encouraged black economic initiative. One South Carolina slaveowner said it well in 1828: "No negro with a well-stocked poultry house, a small crop advancing, a canoe partly finished or a few tubs unsold, all of which he calculates soon to enjoy will ever run away." Another owner admitted that he permitted his slaves "to own and have their property and have little crops of their own for it Encouraged them to do well and be satisfied at home."[29] Such masters were overly optimistic or practiced a form of self-deception, but having a stake in the system made it harder, though not impossible, for individuals to distance themselves from it and to seek its destruction.

Plantation slaves were not all men, although much of the existing literature creates that impression. In fact, as has been shown, slave women slightly outnumbered men in the antebellum years. This was not always the case, since the slave trade introduced mostly men, and not until the rise of the creole population did the sexual imbalance diminish. Except in managerial positions, slaveowners used women in much the same way as they did men, although women tended to dominate as domestics and men in the artisanal trades. Women must have been particularly valuable as fieldworkers in that long first century, given their experience with agrarian labor in many African societies.

Women, to be sure, played important roles in the lives of the white folks as well as in those of their own families and community. For whites, particularly in the households, they served as nursemaids, seamstresses, washerwomen, chambermaids, cooks, confidantes, and in numerous other ways. Over time, an unfriendly white society stereotyped these women as libidinous, promiscuous temptresses and jezebels. But the origins of the stereotype, its persistence, and the complex psychic needs it met for its perpetrators should not be confused with the internal history of enslaved women and will not receive much attention here. The study of white images and stereotypes of black women or of blacks in general, however important, is not synonomous with the history of a gender or a people

The slave woman–the Mammy–who was the tough-minded but sensitive manager of the kitchen and in most respects the white household has survived in popular lore as the epitome of the black woman in service to whites. Mammy nursed the children with love, disciplined them, gave advice, and comforted them in difficult times. She oversaw the preparation of the food, protected the interests of the household, and made them her own. A figure of much authority, Mammy commanded respect from blacks and whites alike.

But Mammy and all the other women in the Big House and in the fields had families of their own and lives that existed independently of those of the Massa and the Missus. By the nineteenth century, black women had their first child at an average age of nineteen, two years earlier than white women. The responsibility of caring for their children was primarily theirs, in addition to their usual work requirements. Domestics also had to attend to the white children, a responsibility that many white slaveowning women avoided.

Slave women bore all of the burdens of slavery along with their men but there were additional ones that came as a consequence of their gender. They gave birth to the children, and assumed much of the routine work in their households. But childbirth and childrearing were not cheerless endeavors. For the African-born woman, pregnancy and childbirth were the occasions for celebration; both occurrences were invested with great meaning, since fertility was the gift of the gods and meant the creation of life and the survival of a people. Creole women were less deeply affected by the ceremonial significance of these events but derived their quiet pleasures from them nonetheless.

The demographic parity between men and women that was achieved by the nineteenth century must have had a major effect on the texture of slavery and slave life in general. But this process remains largely unstudied. Certainly, this provided greater opportunities for spousal selection and ensured a steady increase in the population. The increased presence of women may have affected the pace and development of black social institutions, affected work assignments, altered the ways in which certain jobs were done and transformed daily routines in countless ways. Women must have brought their own distinctive styles to their work, just as men did. Over the long haul, the interaction of men and women in the context of numerical equality must have changed the lives of both and the institution of slavery in significant ways.

As important as women were to the owners, their mark on their own families and society remained impressive, varied and significant. Whether as wives, mothers, cooks, or midwives, women performed a variety of duties in their private spheres. Most survived well enough, demonstrating resilience and holding family units together as husbands and lovers were sold away or ran off to claim their freedom. The image of the strong black woman owes its origins to these early travails, but it is an image that does not capture her constant pain, muted cries, and human vulnerabilities. The Mammy in the Big House discharged her responsibilities in the best way she knew how, but she was no stranger to hurt and abuse. The proverbial strength of these women was not a function of any genetic transmission. Often working together in the fields or in the households, women created networks of relationships among themselves, shared intimacies, and cemented affective bonds born of their gender and condition. Women, it appears, handled better or differently from the men the storms that constantly buffeted them. The burdens they bore as slaves and as women were formidable, but they found ways to cope even as they wrestled with and met the often-conflicting demands of their owners and those of kith and kin.

Although the structure of black life changed fundamentally between 1730 and 1863, with the impetus coming essentially from within, developments in the larger white society were not without substantial effects. Yet it must be emphasized again that the history of black America cannot be defined primarily by these external historical markers, as important as they were. The war for independence, for example, had enormous consequences for black America, but it was a white man's war and it cannot be accorded a central place in the periodization of black life. The war broke the colonial tie with England and in time it ushered in deeper changes in American society as a whole. But it did not alter fundamentally the structure of black life, its woof and warp; those were the creations of blacks themselves.

DEVELOPMENTS IN THE LARGER SOCIETY AND THEIR IMPACT

As the colonial society that the whites presided over matured in the eighteenth century, tensions arose with England. By 1760 the colonists had begun to challenge imperial policies. They opposed the Sugar Act of 1764, which interfered with commerce between New Englanders and the Caribbean islands. Later, they chafed under the Navigation Acts, which placed severe restrictions on colonial trade, requiring, for example, that tobacco, sugar, rice, and other products be sold only to the mother country or to their sister colonies.

Possessed of a growing sense of nationalism, some colonists questioned the right of the British Parliament to pass legislation that they were bound to accept. Accustomed to electing representatives to their own Assemblies, whites bemoaned the absence of their own people in the halls of Parliament. They likened themselves to slaves, a role they would never accept at the hands of the British. "*Those who are taxed* without their own consent expressed by themselves or their representatives, are *slaves*." wrote John Dickinson, a Pennsylvania pamphleteer. "We *are taxed* without our consent. . . . We are therefore–SLAVES."[30]

Colonists railed against any perceived limitations on their much cherished "liberty," while being simultaneously blind to the entreaties of the human property in their midst. "How is it that we hear the loudest yelps for liberty among the drivers of negroes?" inquired Samuel Johnson.[31] The tensions and conflicts between the colonists and London that characterized the 1760s and the 1770s were a manifestation of the fact that the American elites and probably others as well saw themselves as different from their English kin, the products of a different environment and experiences, peoples with a different agenda, needs and priorities. Colonial peoples then, and since, have asserted differences from the Imperial power and claimed their freedom by resorting to violence. British intransigence and colonial belligerence ultimately led to the outbreak of fighting in 1776. The first shots were fired in Boston. Six years earlier, on March 5, 1770, a skirmish between the British soldiers and an enraged crowd, known historically as the Boston Massacre, had led to the death of a black man. Crispus Attucks would be celebrated later as the first person to give his life in the cause of freedom for the new nation. It was the cruelest of ironies, because Attucks and his people could not lay claim to the liberty for which his life was ostensibly sacrificed.

As the war developed, it produced a passionate discourse on liberty, the natural rights of "man," and the need to create a society based on egalitarian principles. Thomas Jefferson, the Virginia legislator, intellectual, and slaveowner, penned the words that would immortalize the principles upon which the War of Independence was fought. The Declaration of Independence affirmed that "All men are created equal," and asserted their untrammelled right to the pursuit of life, liberty, and happiness. But this was more a distant ideal than an accurate expression of the reality of the time. Among the signatories to the document were such prominent slaveowners as Thomas Jefferson, George Washington, Edmund Randolph, and George Mason.

Few who subscribed to such principles in 1776 were fully aware of their revolutionary implications and how their implementation would transform the society. More than two hundred years later, the nation that arose out of the war still struggles with the full meaning and implication of the ideology that gave it birth. Yet, in a fundamental sense, the ideals that justified the war were incompatible with the existence of slavery; they could not coexist forever regardless of the compromises that were hammered out to delay the triumph of principle over interested prejudice.

The victory of the colonists was enshrined in the federal Constitution of 1787. The document established the bases of the relationship between the states and the central government and underscored the ideological principles upon which the new republic rested. The word "slavery" never appeared in it, although euphemistic references to the enslaved were made. Thus, slaves were referred to as "such persons," "other persons," and as a person "held to Service and Labour."[32] Perhaps the absence of the words "slave" or "slavery" in the document betrayed a queasy conscience or a moral ambivalence on the part of some to the institution. James Madison, one of the document's framers, believed that it was "wrong to admit in the Constitution the idea that there could be property in men."[33] The fact, of course, was that there were almost 500,000 slaves in the new nation at the time, sophistry notwithstanding.

Critics of the Constitution later claimed it to be a pro-slavery document because it sanctioned slavery whether or not the word was used. Scholars are divided on this issue, but it is clear that the document confirmed the ownership of property in persons. Article 1, section 2 of the Constitution, for example, allowed three-fifths of the slave population of each state to be counted, along with the free persons, in order to determine congressional representation. Known as the "three-fifths clause," this ingenious device allowed Southern whites to increase their representation in Congress. The same three-fifths concept applied in the allocation of tax responsibility to the states. In addition, the Constitution permitted the capture and return of runaway slaves and prevented states from freeing such persons who sought sanctuary in them. It also extended the life of the slave trade for two decades, forbidding Congress to take up the issue of its abolition before 1807.

Slaveowners at the time understood that the Constitution included no provisions for the emancipation of the slaves, despite its libertarian orientation. General Charles Cotesworth Pinckney assured South Carolina lawmakers, "We have a security that the general government can never emancipate them, for no such authority is granted; and it is admitted, on all hands, that the general government has no powers but what are expressly granted by the Constitution, and that all rights not expressed were reserved by the several states."[34] Others concurred, some seeking to distance themselves from the document's legitimizing of slavery. To one New Yorker, the Constitution was "drenching the bowels of Africa in gore, for the sake of enslaving its free-born innocent inhabitants." Three contemporary critics of the Constitution in Massachusetts spoke prophetically: "This lust for slavery, [was] portentous of much evil in America, for the cry of innocent blood, . . . hath undoubtedly reached to the Heavens, to which that cry is always directed, and will draw down upon them vengeance adequate to the enormity of the crime."[35] The framers of the Constitution had worked out a compromise between white Southerners and white Northerners on the divisive issue of slavery. Southerners had their property in persons tacitly recognized and protected; Northerners took comfort in the fact that the Constitution did not include firm guarantees against emancipation in the future. Blacks were the victims of all this maneuvering and circumlocution; it was not the last time that whites would resolve their differences at blacks' expense.

ACHIEVING THE FIRST EMANCIPATION

The War of Independence set in motion events that led to the emancipation of slaves in the North. This development was not necessarily a consequence of the benevolence of the slaveowners but a pragmatic response to the need for manpower to fight the war and the ideological forces unleashed by the conflict. The British were the first to entice the slaves to participate in the war with a promise of freedom. In 1775, the royalist governor of Virginia, Lord Dunmore, offered freedom to all the slaves who deserted to the British ranks. Many slaves who heard of this extraordinary offer found it difficult to resist. Alarmed, slaveowners responded by threatening severe punishment, including death, to those who accepted Lord Dunmore's invitation. The promise of freedom to those who joined the British forces was repeated in 1779 by General Henry Clinton, the commander in chief. Thousands joined the British, and many achieved their freedom at the end of the war as a consequence. But others were not so fortunate and were sold as slaves to Caribbean purchasers. Several of the freedpersons migrated to Nova Scotia, Canada, and eventually to Sierra Leone, while others took up residence in various parts of the United States.

The colonists who fought for independence also enlisted blacks in their ranks by 1777 with promise of freedom, but not without some apprehension. Slaves with guns and military experience posed a threat to the survival of slavery. Slaveowners also disliked releasing their slaves for military service because this represented a loss of their labor. But these objections dissipated as the war dragged on, and some colonists began to openly recruit blacks into the army. The practice was more prevalent in the North and to a lesser extent in the Upper South. In Virginia, Delaware, and North Carolina, slaveowners were allowed to send slaves to war in their place and that of their sons. Maryland permitted slaves to enlist and drafted free blacks. Virginia also encouraged the enlistment of free blacks. Whites in the Lower South–Georgia and South Carolina–with their large black populations resisted all attempts to employ slaves in military service. In so doing, they followed in the fearful tradition of a group of North Carolina settlers who noted in 1715, "there must be great caution used [in the military employment of Negroes] lest our slaves when armed might become our masters."[36]

At war's end, however, many slaves who had participated in it had their freedom confirmed. A few were liberated as a result of the special acts of the legislatures, but many more were freed by their masters. Some masters sought to deny their slaves the freedom they had promised them for their war service, but the extent of such duplicity is uncertain. It is believed, however, that several thousand blacks received their freedom as a result of military service, swelling the ranks of the free population.

The war of independence and the ideology of freedom that nourished it had a major impact on the course of slavery in the North. At the outbreak of the war, few whites could have foreseen that the arguments used against British rule could also be applied to the denial of liberty to the black person. Yet, this was precisely what happened, and a number of voices were raised to oppose the ownership of fellow human beings and to contrast the high ideals of the Declaration of Independence with its emphasis on equality, liberty, and justice and the simultaneous existence of slavery. Thus the ideology of the war helped to create a climate conducive to a discussion of the place of slavery in society.

One can overstate the pervasiveness of such a climate, however. With the exception of many Quakers, some Evangelicals, and others who endorsed the revolutionary ideology, most whites took no public position on the issue. Of course, there were those who had an economic stake in the preservation and expansion of slavery. Others had come to accept slavery as the natural, unchanging condition of the black person. Much of the challenge to the institution appeared in the North, where the institution was less economically entrenched, although there were a few pockets of opposition in the South as well.

The Northern states, however, were the only ones to adopt legislation emancipating their slaves, immediately or gradually. The primary impetus behind such momentous acts is not easily unravelled. It is certain that the libertarian ideology of the independence war played a role in shaping opinion on the issue but it cannot fully explain Northern behavior. Most whites clung to a belief in their own superiority although this did not prevent some of those persons from opposing slavery or property in persons. This belief, combined with the fear of losing the funds invested in their slaves and concern about the aftermath of freedom ensured that the struggle for emancipation would be prolonged almost everywhere.

In the end, Northern whites responded to conscience, pragmatism, and their own self-interest on the matter of emancipation. They had to be convinced that slavery had a corruptive influence on their society, that it was sinful, and that emancipation was the just thing to do. One Philadelphia Quaker, Anthony Benezet, urged the liberation of the slaves because it was "a Debt due to them, . . . or their Ancestors." Slaveowners, he pleaded could "avert the Judgments of GOD" by so doing.[37]

Such appeals, no matter how persuasive, however, had to be linked to more political arguments. Thomas Paine, one of the ideologues of the War of Independence, held that slavery was "contrary to the light of nature, to every principle of Justice and Humanity, and even good policy."[38] An anonymous commentator enquired how his countrymen could "reconcile *the exercise* of SLAVERY with our *professions of freedom.*" He goaded them with the admonition that "Were the colonies as earnest for the preservation of liberty, upon its *true* and *genuine* principles, as they are opposed to the supremacy of an English Parliament, they would enter into a virtuous and *perpetual* resolve, neither to import, nor to purchase any slaves introduced amongst them."[39] Undoubtedly, some persons were convinced that slavery was morally wrong and contradicted the egalitarian and libertarian ideals upon which the new nation was based. Yet for all of these high-sounding principles, slavery would not have ended when it did in the North if it were of crucial economic importance. It was not a necessary evil.

The slave population in the North was quite small. In 1776, Pennsylvania had 3,761 slaves or less than 1 percent of the population. In the case of Massachusetts, there were 4,377 blacks in 1784 and 353,133 whites. New Hampshire had only 46 slaves in 1786, and Rhode Island had a black white ratio of 1 to 22 in 1783. The number of slaves in New York in 1786 stood at 18,889 or about 15 percent of the population. Also in that year, New Jersey's black population numbered 10,501 or 8 percent of the residents. Overall, black slaves formed a small proportion of the population everywhere outside of the Upper and Lower South.

Seen in a demographic context, slaves could be freed in these states without undue economic distress, and those who had become increasingly embarrassed by the practice of slavery could claim the moral rewards that resulted therefrom. Even so, most states did not adopt measures for immediate emancipation, preferring to do so reluctantly and gradually.

The passage of the emancipation acts in the North was, in part, the result of pressure exerted by the slave population. In some instances, slaves sought to test the legitimacy of their enslavement in the courts. In other cases, they petitioned the legislatures for their freedom. One of the earliest examples of a Massachusetts court battle occurred in 1765 when "Jenny Slew of Ipswich in the County of Essex," brought a suit against John Whipple for having taken her "with force of arms" and enslaved her. She lost the case in the Court of Common Pleas, but the decision was later reversed in a higher court.[40] In 1781 Elizabeth Freeman, an enslaved woman, sued for her freedom, citing the Bill of Rights enshrined in the 1780 Massachusetts Constitution. She maintained that her enslavement violated the Constitution's principles that all human beings were born free and equal. The county court of Great Barrington ruled in Freeman's favor in 1781 and awarded her damages against her former master. This landmark suit represented the first time that a slave had challenged slavery on the grounds that its existence violated a state's constitution.

The most celebrated and controversial case was heard between 1781 and 1783. Quock Walker was a Massachusetts slave who fled his master's farm and sought refuge on a nearby one. Nathaniel Jennison, Walker's master, found him at John Caldwell's farm, whipped him, and took him home. Walker sued Jennison for battery and assault and asked for £300 in damages. The point at issue was whether Walker was legally a slave, since his previous owner had promised to free him at age twenty-five. In an interesting twist to the case, Jennison had married the widow of Walker's former master, and Walker claimed that she was aware of the promise of manumission. The court found in Walker's favor, holding that "said Quo[c]k is a Freeman and not the proper Negro slave of the Deft."[41]

The trial on the battery and assault charge occurred in 1783. It was heard by the Supreme Judicial Court, with Chief Justice Cushing presiding. The attorney general argued that Walker was a free man at the time of the beating in view of the previous master's promise of manumission. The defense claimed that he was a slave and that Jennision had acted within his rights when he punished him. In his charge to the jury, the chief justice invoked the principles of the Massachusetts Constitution of 1780 to show that slavery violated the "natural rights of mankind." He maintained that the court was "fully of the opinion that perpetual servitude can no longer be tolerated in our government." The jury was convinced and upheld Walker's suit. The decision did not immediately lead to a wholesale liberation of the slaves, but it was clear that its days were numbered in Massachusetts and that the suits of such slaves like Freeman and Walker had speeded up the process.[42]

Equally impressive were the petitions that the slaves submitted to the Massachusetts legislature. In January 1773 a number of slaves in Boston submitted "a humble petition" to the Governor, Council, and House of Representatives asking that "their unhappy state and condition [be taken] under your wise and just consideration." The petition is noteworthy for its absence of stridency and it shows the role that Christianity played in sanctioning slavery. The slaves were prepared to continue in their condition, however, "so long as God, in his sovereign providence, shall *suffer* us to be holden in bondage." Other petitions followed, but with a more accusatory tone. In 1777, a petition described slavery as "an unnatural practice . . . a scandal to professors of ye Religion of Jesus, and a disgrace to all good Governments, more especially to such who are struggling against Oppression and in favor of ye natural and unalienable Rights of human nature."[43]

Pennsylvania became, in 1780, the first state to adopt a gradual emancipation law, setting a precedent for others. Adults continued to serve, but all children born after February 1780 would be freed at age twenty-eight. In New Hampshire, slavery had all but disappeared; the constitution of 1783 included a provision that said that "all men are born equal and independent." It is not clear whether this was an antislavery measure, but the institution steadily went into extinction. There were 674 slaves in New Hampshire in 1773 and 8 in 1800. Suffice it to say, there were no statutes that specifically liberated blacks in that state.

The Connecticut legislature, like its counterpart in Pennsylvania, adopted a gradual emancipation law in 1784. The state had a sizable slave population when compared with its neighbors, about 6,000 in 1782. The proslavery forces defeated emancipation bills in 1777, 1779, and again in 1780. A watered-down version of the bill was passed in 1784, with its proponents arguing that "sound Policy" required the emancipation of the slaves.[44] Children born after March 1, 1784, would be freed, but only after they reached age twenty-five. Similarly, a Rhode Island law of 1784 required that boys born after March 1 of that year be apprenticed to their masters for twenty-one years, and girls for eighteen years.

The New England states were unable to liberate their slaves forthrightly and unequivocally even as they laid public claim to the libertarian ideology of the War of Independence. Black slaves were property, and few owners welcomed the opportunity to put their ideology above their material interests. Their behavior was not at all unusual. New York and New Jersey, with their somewhat larger slave populations, demonstrated a great deal of intransigence in the struggle for emancipation.

The issue of emancipation was first considered by the New York Assembly in 1785. Not until 1799, however, were the legislators able to pass an emancipation bill. The law permitted the freedom of all children born after July 4, 1799. As in the case of the other states that passed similar measures, the New York law required the men to be completely free only after they had reached twenty-eight years of age and the women twenty-five. New Jersey did not pass an act of gradual emancipation until 1804. Men were to be freed at age twenty-five and women at twenty-one. As late as 1860, eighteen blacks remained in servitude in New Jersey.[45]

The striking fact about the emancipation process in the North is that it took such a long time. The statutes freed no one immediately. Adults remained legally slaves until they were manumitted or death intervened. Children born after the passage of the emancipation acts could look forward to their freedom only after two decades of service or longer (see Table 3.2). Northern whites legislated against slavery not primarily from a principled ideological stance but from a pragmatic assessment of their own needs. Voices were raised in opposition to slavery and high-minded principles invoked, but these debates merely created the climate within which Northerners could examine whether public policy and societal needs were best served by the presence of slaves.

The answer was not immediately clear to many people. Some saw slaves as posing a threat to public order. Others disliked the presence of blacks in their midst and wanted to keep their number low or exclude them entirely. Only when it became evident that northern society would not have to depend on slaves to meet its essential needs was abolition generally embraced. Slavery was not the economic or racial necessity it would later become in the South. Not surprisingly, the various emanci-

TABLE 3.2
Age of Emancipation for the "Free-Born"

STATE	DATE OF ENACTMENT	AGE OF EMANCIPATION	
		MALE	FEMALE
Pennsylvania	1780	28	28
Rhode Island	1784	21	18
Connecticut	1784	25	25
New York	1799	28	25
New Jersey	1804	25	21

SOURCE: R. W. Fogel and S. L. Engerman, "Philanthrophy at Bargain Prices: Notes on the Economics of Gradual Emancipation," *Journal of Legal Studies*, 3, (1974), 381.

pation measures contained loopholes that worked against the interest of the black population. Slaves could still be sold to individuals in those states where the institution was not in danger. Masters could still abuse their slaves and abandon the aged and the infirm. The laws permitted slaveowners to continue using their property to their advantage and to lay claim to their slaves' children, at least for two decades or more.

In addition to the slaves who became free as a result of the legislative and judicial process, there were some who were manumitted by their masters. In the aftermath of the war, a number of states passed laws liberalizing the process of manumission. In 1782, Virginia allowed slaveowners to free slaves under the age of forty-five by will or deed. This was followed by other Southern states with the lone exception of North Carolina, where slaves could be freed only under unusual circumstances and then only with the authorization of the county court. Most slaveowners had no desire to liberate their slaves. Although there are no comprehensive figures available on the number of persons who were manumitted after 1782, it is clear from scattered statistics and qualitative evidence that the number may have been a few thousand at best or a few hundred at worst.[46] Slaveowners in the Upper South were more likely than their peers in South Carolina and Georgia to engage in private acts of manumission.

The emancipation of the slaves in the North did not slow or prevent the expansion of the institution to other places. In the aftermath of the war, slavery spread to Kentucky, Mississippi, and Alabama. In 1803 President Jefferson acquired Louisiana, a vast formerly French area where slavery had long existed. He agreed that the French and Spanish slaveowners who occupied the territory could keep their slaves. In time, Louisiana joined the ranks of the slave states.

For blacks, the exclusion of slavery from the territory north of the Ohio River was one of the major developments of the period. The huge area included the contemporary states of Indiana, Illinois, Ohio, Michigan, and Wisconsin. Known as the Northwest Ordinance, the law was passed by Congress in 1787. There were a number of slaves in the Northwest at the time, but their status was not affected by the legislation; it also left slavery south of the Ohio untouched. But the law did place limits on the expansion of slavery north of the Ohio River.

It is not clear why the measure that included this prohibition of slavery was approved. There was hardly any debate on the matter, a surprising development since in 1784 a Jeffersonian proposal to exclude slavery from all of the nation's territories after 1800 was rejected. As passed, Article VI of the Ordinance declared that

> There shall be neither slavery nor involuntary servitude in the said territory, otherwise than in the punishment of crimes, whereof the party shall have been duly convicted: provided always, that any person escaping into the same, from whom labour or service is lawfully claimed in any one of the original states, such fugitive may be lawfully reclaimed and conveyed to the person claiming his or her labour or service as aforesaid.[47]

Accordingly, the ordinance permitted the return of runaways, although it rejected slavery in the territory. Southerners may have been inclined to support the measure because of its endorsement of the return of those who fled. The ordinance's silence on whether slavery could exist in the Southwest must also have helped to garner Southern support for it.

The ordinance was not greeted enthusiastically by those who owned slaves in what would later become the states of Indiana and Illinois. Arguing that the measure violated their right to property, they petitioned to be allowed to keep their chattel. Congress lent a deaf ear to these petitions but winked at the continuation of slavery in the territory. In fact, slaves were brought into the territory after 1787, and the institution continued to exist, albeit weakly, until the 1830s in Indiana and more vigorously until 1848 in Illinois.

The abolition of the slave trade can also be attributed, in part, to the ideology of the war. Opposition to the trade had preceded the outbreak of hostilities with England. The Quakers were among the first to express their abhorrence of it. In 1688 the Pennsylvania Quakers denounced the trade because it was morally wrong, but the impact was negligible. Groups of Quakers continued their protest with some regularity thereafter, but many of their colleagues, like a growing number of other colonists, were deeply involved in the trade and slavery and turned a deaf ear. The Yearly Meeting–the governing body of the Quakers–hedged on the issue from time to time; the anti-slavery theology of the group and their belief in the spiritual equality of all humans notwithstanding. In 1715, for example, the Yearly Meeting in Pennsylvania refused to endorse a proposal to exclude members who traded in black slaves. The majority decided "in Condescention to such Friends as are streightnd in their minds against the holding them, it is desir'd that friends generally do as much as may be avoid buying such Negroes as shall hereafter be brought in, rather than offend any friends who are against it. Yet this is only caution and not Censure."[48]

The voices opposed to the trade remained in the wilderness as slavery took a deeper hold in the colonial economies and the psyche of the colonists. A shift in attitude would not come on this issue until three important developments had occurred. The first was the recognition on the part of some of the immorality of the trade and its inherent violation of human rights. The second major development was the outbreak of the great slave rebellion in St. Domingue in 1791 and the fear it produced in whites, particularly the fear of slaves introduced via the slave trade from Africa or the West Indies. The third, and perhaps the most significant development, was the growth in the creole slave population and the recognition by the slaveowners that they did not have to depend completely on the international trade to obtain their slaves. Not only were their own slaves reproducing at a steady rate, but there was a brisk domestic slave trade as well.

Philadelphia Quaker and schoolteacher Anthony Benezet was the white person who provided the most effective and persistent intellectual leadership for the movement to abolish the slave trade after 1750. He denounced the trade as un-Christian, unjust, cruel, and oppressive. An indefatigable pamphleteer, Benezet asked his fellow Quakers, "Can we be innocent and yet [be] silent spectators of this mighty infringement of every humane and sacred right?"[49] Benezet and other humanitarians linked the struggle against the slave trade to the eventual abolition of slavery, seeing the two evils as being intertwined. Support grew, especially in the North, for both causes, and in 1774 the First Continental Congress, which met in Philadelphia, endorsed an end to the slave trade. Northern legislators followed suit, and by 1787 all the New England and Eastern states had outlawed the importation of slaves. Virginia had long been associated with antislave-trade activity, and in 1778 the Old Dominion prohibited that form of commerce.

Never dependent on slaves for their economic sustenance, the Northern states could end the slave trade without undue disruption of their economies. Most of the statutes had loopholes, however, effectively nullifying the dubious intent of the measures. Virginia legislators, on their part, recognized that their society was well supplied with domestic slaves, so an end to the trade would not constitute a serious disadvantage to them. Other Virginians feared rebellions and sought to limit the entry of additional slaves. During their disputes with the British, Virginians even blamed the mother country for imposing the slave trade on the region, conveniently ignoring their own complicity in it.

South Carolina and Georgia waged a relentless opposition to any interference with the slave trade, since their own economies depended for their survival on black labor. General Charles Cotesworth Pinckney of South Carolina even maintained that "the importation of slaves would be for the interest of the whole Union. The more slaves, the more produce to employ the carrying trade; the more consumption also, and the more of this, the more of revenue for the common treasury." His colleague Rawlins Lowndes agreed with the need for the trade, arguing that it "could be justified on the principles of religion, humanity, and justice; for certainly to translate a set of human beings from a bad country to a better, was fulfilling every part of these principles. . . . Without negroes this state would degenerate into one of the most contemptible in the union. . . . Negroes are our only wealth, our only natural resource."[50]

Sentiments such as these help explain why the Constitutional Convention decreed a moratorium on any federal tampering with the trade for twenty years. Voices were raised in pious denunciation of the human traffic but there were equally passionate defenses of it on the grounds of economic necessity and even Christian charity. Yet by 1798, all of the states had passed legislation ending the trade although most lacked the slightest intention to enforce the law. In fact, the heyday of the slave trade to America fell in the two decades preceding Federal abolition in 1807. The traffic after 1790 was particularly brisk, this despite the proscription of the trade by the states. Those who anticipated an end to the nation's involvement in the commerce after the twenty-year moratorium elapsed, hastened to purchase the chattel they needed. Not surprisingly, legislators from Southern states bristled at any discussion of antislave trade petitions in Congress in the 1790s, and Northerners thought twice before they picked a fight on the issue. Accordingly, the new nation revealed much moral bankruptcy on one of its most important early challenges; the slave trade, slavery, and racism compromised its innocence and made it difficult for it to claim that it kept an abiding faith with its ideals.

In 1803, South Carolina abandoned the fiction of having ended the trade and reopened it. An uproar followed in Congress, but that was as far as the response went. The righteous indignation of the antislave-trade legislators lacked any effective force. In December 1806 President Jefferson reminded members of Congress that it was their constitutional responsibility to address the issue of the trade the following year. Although still a slaveowner, Jefferson expressed the view that Congress should "interpose" its "authority, constitutionally, to withdraw the citizens of the United States from all further participation in those violations of human rights which have so long continued on the unoffending inhabitants of Africa, and which the morality, the reputation, and the best interests of our country have long been eager to proscribe."[51]

That Congress acted in 1807 to end American participation in the international slave trade remains somewhat a surprise. The passage of the law reflected a fortuitous convergence of many motivations and interests. Some legislators voted affirmatively because of their principled opposition to the trade. Many who had watched the St. Domingue slave revolution destroy property and persons wanted to keep potentially troublesome Africans out of the country. Others, particularly Southerners, knew that slavery had become self-sustaining because of the growing creole population, so the trade was not as crucial as it had been fifty years earlier. The nation, some surmised, lacked the desire and the will to enforce abolition. Even so, an overwhelming majority of Southerners opposed the bill. For them, it was not merely a question of the economic role that slaves played in their region. Georgia Congressman Peter Early could not support the bill since his fellow Southerners "do not believe it immoral to hold human flesh in bondage." Early was certain that a "large majority" of people in the Southern states did not find slavery to be morally wrong.[52] Until they came to such a conclusion, the slave trade and slavery would continue, unless more powerful forces intervened.

The federal prohibition of the trade took effect in 1808. Predictably, the law did not end the international slave trade to America, as traders and slaveowners alike evaded its enforcement. Nor were the federal authorities particularly vigilant in policing the nation's ports of entry and apprehending the offenders. President James Madison complained in 1810 that "American citizens are instrumental in carrying on a traffic in enslaved Africans, equally in violation of the laws of humanity and in defiance of those of their own country."[53] American authorities, however, steadfastly refused to cooperate with the British, who had taken the lead in suppressing the international trade. England had abolished the slave trade in 1807 and in later years tried to get other European nations to do likewise. The British also undertook an aggressive campaign to board slavers on the high seas, seize their cargoes, and return the victims to Africa.

In order to facilitate the execution of their mission, the British stationed a fleet of ships—a squadron—off the African coast. England also signed a number of treaties with other nations giving her sailors the right to board ships flying those nations' flags and search for slaves. Alone among the major slave-trading nations, the United States refused to sign the "right of search" treaty. In 1820, however, the Americans dispatched a small naval force to the African coast to aid in the fight against the illegal slave trade. Although it was strengthened in 1842, the naval force discharged its duties in a halfhearted fashion and hardly made an impact on efforts to seize ships that flew the American flag. In fact, citizens of other nations flew the American flag to avoid being pursued and boarded by the British squadron. The British could not normally board such ships because of the absence of a right of search treaty with the United States.

The start of the Civil War resulted in a change in American policy. Confronted by turmoil at home and the need to use the ships on the African coast against the Confederate states, the squadron was recalled. In 1862, the federal government finally signed a right of search treaty with the British; a function of the struggle with the South. The two nations established a judicial machinery–mixed courts–for trying offenders. The treaty came too late; the market for slaves had already dried up in the South as a bitter war was in progress and slavery faced an uncertain future.

In the final analysis, the international trade continued as long as a demand for slave labor existed in the South. Some South Carolina slave-owners and sympathetic legislators even proposed legalizing the trade, once again, in the 1850s. Support for the proposal came from voices in Alabama, Georgia, and Louisiana. The South Carolina legislature rejected the measure on several occasions between 1856 and 1859, but not before producing a national outcry among the opponents of slavery.

The slave trade had two dimensions, the one international and the other domestic. Creole blacks also faced the prospect of being sold, not once but several times. This internal trade must be distinguished from the movement of those persons with their masters such as that which occurred from the border states and the Upper South to the Lower South and Texas after 1790. The domestic trade, properly speaking, refers to those persons sold by their owners to others, in state or out of state. This was a very active commerce, particularly in the nineteenth century, as demand for enslaved workers increased in the cotton-producing states. Somewhere between 750,000 and 1,000,000 persons exchanged owners as a result of sale between 1790 and 1860, the majority of them originating in the Upper South. Almost equally balanced between males and females, they consisted principally of individuals between the ages of twelve and twenty-five.

SLAVERY EXPANDS

As the nation struggled to define itself in the half century after its independence, it swayed back and forth under the weight of slavery. But it was a problem that was of its own making; the constitutional compromises of 1787 on the issue of slavery deferred the day of reckoning. In 1819 when Missouri applied for admission to the Union as a slave state, the fragile national unity on the slavery question was challenged. Northerners wanted to contain the institution and Southerners thought otherwise. Southerners fought to ensure that Missouri would be admitted as a slave state, because that would preserve the political balance in the

Senate between free and slave states. In the end, both sides compromised. The agreement, know as the Missouri Compromise, was worked out in 1820. It allowed for the admission of Missouri as a slave state and Maine as a free state. The compromise prohibited slavery in the vast area west and north of Missouri that had been acquired from the French in the Louisiana Purchase. The prolonged debate before the compromise was achieved laid bare the fault lines in the nation's soul that slavery had created and merely postponed the inevitable crisis.

The issue of slavery and its expansion was not solved in 1820 and remained at the centre of the conflicts between white Americans for the next four decades. As the *Charleston Mercury* concluded in 1858: "On the subject of slavery, the North and South . . . are rival, hostile Peoples."[54] Some whites, particularly in the North, shared a revulsion of property in persons. Others, such as the Southerners who had emigrated to the Northwest, brought a virulent racism with them and sought to avoid any contact with blacks, either as free persons or as slaves. These immigrants also proclaimed the virtues of individual effort and free labor. In another sense, the free states looked askance at slavery's expansion because it meant increased political power for the slavocracy, since each slave counted as three-fifths of a person in the allocation of congressional representation.

The controversy over slavery's expansion took on a new immediacy during the 1830s and the 1840s with the acquisition of much of Mexico's territory. Texas, which was a part of Mexico, had become the home of many Americans who moved there and purchased land cheaply. These settlers were angered in 1830 when Mexico abolished slavery in Texas and banned the entry of additional Americans. The conflict eventually produced a war between the Americans in Texas and the Mexican government. Led by the bellicose Sam Houston, the settlers defeated the Mexican army in 1836 and formed the Republic of Texas.

The prevailing assumption was that the new republic would have a short life and that it would be annexed by the United States. In that eventuality, Southern whites insisted that slavery be allowed to exist there, and Northerners objected. The controversy dragged on seemingly interminably, a visible symbol of a deeper sectional struggle. In the end, Congress voted its approval of annexation in 1844 and Texas joined the ranks of the slavocracy a year later.

The incorporation of Texas into the American fold seemed to whet the appetite for additional Mexican territory. In the process, the United States would fulfill its self-proclaimed Manifest Destiny to extend its power and control over the hemisphere. Propelled by such imperatives and facilitated by the weakness of the Mexican government, it is little wonder that an excuse was found to go to war with the southern neighbor. When the Mexicans attacked an American army that had invaded their territory in 1845, the ensuing war and peace treaty led to Mexico's loss of what are now New Mexico, Arizona, Utah, and California and an extension of the boundary claimed by Texas.

Slaveowners looked wistfully at these new areas as potential slave states. Despite his pro-slavery stance, President James Polk who presided over the war believed, however, that there was "no probability that any territory will ever be acquired from Mexico in which slavery would ever exist."[55] Opponents of expansion were not so sure. Congressman David Wilmot of Pennsylvania wanted Congress to ban slavery from Mexico's former territory and introduced a measure to that effect in August 1846. The Wilmot Proviso, as the measure came to be called, would prohibit slavery and "involuntary servitude" from "any part of said territory." Wilmot was not moved by any profound affection for the black slave. He wanted to "preserve for free white labor a fair country . . . where the sons of toil, of my own race and own color, can live without the disgrace which association with negro slavery brings upon free labor."[56] Thus he embraced the "cause and rights of the free white man." In order to protect whites, "the African and his descendants" should be excluded from the new territories. Wilmot's racist rantings rested in part on a belief that he shared with others that slave labor debased free labor. The free labor of whites had been diminished by "the servile labor of the black," as he put it.[57]

The Wilmot Proviso was condemned by Southerners, and it died in the Senate after a lengthy and acrimonious series of debates. Southern leaders, energized by this latest assault on their institution and on their honor, began to question the constitutional basis of such restrictions on slavery as the Northwest Ordinance and the Missouri Compromise. Some warned of secession if their views went unheeded. Senator John Calhoun was convinced that fellow Southerners faced serious threats to their "property, prosperity, equality, liberty, and safety."[58]

Seemingly, nothing could mollify white Southern fears about the safety of slavery and the security of their way of life and society. Alternating between bombastic threats of secession and a quiet willingness to compromise, Southern slaveowners and politicians were consistent only in their belief in white supremacy and the rightness of slavery. They denounced the tyranny of the federal government in its attempts to control the expansion of slavery, but they simultaneously urged it to be vigorous in promoting the recapture of runaway slaves. Members of the slavocracy railed against a perceived abrogation of their rights as citizens, but they justified the enslavement of the millions of blacks in their midst.

Northerners who opposed slavery or sought to contain it struggled to reconcile their principles with the practical need to keep the Southerners in the Union. Few desired disunion, and most were willing to allow slavery to continue to exist where it was already entrenched. Horace Greeley, a New York editor, noted in 1854 that he had "never been able to discover any strong, pervading, overruling Anti Slavery sentiment in the Free States." He thought "that if every voter in the Free States were to have half a dozen negro slaves left him by some Georgia uncle or cousin's will, that a decided majority would hold on to their chattels and make as much as possible out of them."[59]

Perhaps such sentiments helped to temper the assaults by Northerners on their Southern brethren. They also fed a disposition to compromise. Greeley, for one, believed that "a large majority" of Northern voters "are impelled by interest rather than principle."[60] Under the circumstances, it is entirely understandable why the legislators in 1850 hammered out a compromise on the slavery question. The Compromise of 1850 was an attempt to reconcile the irreconcilable and to paper over the deep chasms that had come to separate the sections. The South won the right to have its escaped slaves returned, while Northerners settled for the abolition of the slave trade in the District of Columbia but not the emancipation of the slaves there. Similarly, in accordance with the wishes of the South, Utah and New Mexico were organized as territories without any mention of slavery. Northerners were satisfied with the admission of California as a free state.

The compromise was remarkable for the absence of any identifiable principles; it was pragmatically judicious but morally bankrupt. No one acknowledged the fact that the details of the agreement affected the lives of the real people who were slaves. The white arbiters of black fate settled their disputes among themselves with little regard for the lives of those who would be apprehended as runaways in Pennsylvania or Ohio or potentially confined to servitude in Utah or New Mexico. Their concern was not with the slaves as people; they were more preoccupied with the crippling burden that the institution imposed upon the political life of the nation. Seen from the standpoint of the more than three million slaves in 1850, the compromise was made at their expense. The overriding issue that it addressed–the place of slaves and slavery in the Union–did not go away precisely because the settlement lacked moral legitimacy. Jubilant crowds of whites greeted the apparent resolution of the conflict with shouts of "The Union is saved." But slavery remained untouched and the whirlwind was yet to be reaped.

Despite the deep national divisions over slavery, the slave population continued to expand after 1820 and slavery became more deeply woven into the societal fabric of the South. Louisiana, Missouri, Arkansas, Mississippi, Alabama, Florida, and Texas were all embraced as slave states after 1800. Slaveowners continued to reap healthy returns on their investment in human property as good or better than what they would have made in a range of other enterprises. Slavery remained economically viable throughout the antebellum years and there were no signs of its impending death by the time the Civil War occurred. Its existence remained at the center of most quarrels between the North and the South; Southern spokespersons defending it as a good and Northern opponents attacking it as a national cancer.

These quarrels between whites did not, and do not, of course, constitute the core of black history. The issues concerning slavery that divided white men showed where power really resided; the compromises that temporarily abated these disputes were made without reference to blacks, whether slaves or free. The legislation to end the slave trade, the passage of gradual emancipation laws, the Missouri Compromise, the Wilmot Proviso, and others were battles fought by whites, but the results had some impact on the evolution of black life in the nation, even if blacks were excluded from the political process. These debates and conflicts tell us much more about whites, their internal struggles, and their history than they do about the ebb and flow of black life.

Yet blacks were also at the center of much of national life, affecting its course in important ways and quietly shaping their own terrain and influencing white society. America's story in these and later years could hardly be told in racially particularistic terms, or wholly from the perspective of the white and the free. The peoples of African descent transformed the American experience during the period, even as they were transformed by it. The real stuff of an internal black history during the period, however, must be found in the enormous structural changes that the population experienced. Creoles emerged as the dominant group, and black society developed its own contours and inner form. Called upon to perform all manner of duties for whites, blacks established their own institutions and struggled to define themselves as a people. The burden of slavery blighted their possibilities, but the peoples of African descent created passageways that enabled them to ease their pain. It is to the texture of their lives and the nature of their struggles and passageways that we now turn.

Notes

1. James Oakes, *The Ruling Race: A History of American Slaveholders* (New York: Knopf, 1982), 3.
2. Eric McKitrick, ed., *Slavery Defended: The Views of the Old South* (Englewood Cliffs, NJ: Prentice-Hall, 1963), 122–123.
3. George Fredrickson, "Masters and Mudsills: The Role of Race in the Planter Ideology of South Carolina," *South Atlantic Urban Studies*, 2 (1978), 46; David R. Goldfield, *Black, White, and Southern: Race Relations and Southern Culture 1940 to the Present* (Baton Rouge: Louisiana State University Press, 1990), 14.
4. Mechal Sobel, *The World They Made Together: Black and White Values in Eighteenth Century Virginia* (Princeton: Princeton University Press, 1987), 62.
5. Oakes, *Slavery and Freedom*, 18.
6. Solomon Northup, *Twelve Years a Slave*, reprint (Baton Rouge: Louisiana State University Press, 1968), 201.

7. Allan Kulikoff, "A 'Prolifick' People: Black Population Growth in the Chesapeake Colonies, 1700–1790," *Southern Studies,* 16 (1977), 391.
8. Ibid., 403.
9. Peter Kolchin, *Unfree Labor, American Slavery and Russian Serfdom* (Cambridge, MA: Harvard University Press, 1987), 166.
10. Randall M. Miller, "The Fabric of Control: Slavery in Antebellum Southern Textile Mills," *Business History Review,* 55 (1981), 473.
11. Kolchin, *Unfree Labor,* 18.
12. Kenneth Stampp, *The Peculiar Institution: Slavery in the Antebellum South* (New York: Knopf, 1956), 141.
13. Ibid., 145.
14. Ibid., 144–145.
15. William W. Freehling, *The Road to Disunion: Secessionists at Bay, 1776–1854* (New York: Oxford, 1990), 62.
16. Joseph T. Glatthaar, *Forged in Battle: The Civil War Alliance of Black Soldiers and White Officers* (New York: The Free Press, 1990), 77.
17. Ibid., 201.
18. Morris, *Southern Slavery and the Law,* 181.
19. Marvin L. Michael Kay and Lorin Lee Cary, *Slavery in North Carolina, 1748–1775* (Chapel Hill: University of North Carolina Press, 1995), 70–95.
20. Eugene Genovese, *Roll Jordan Roll: The World the Slaves Made* (New York: Pantheon Books, 1974), 299.
21. Ibid., 301.
22. Ibid., 375.
23. Genovese, *Roll Jordan Roll,* 370; Kolchin, *Unfree Labor,* 348.
24. Philip Morgan, "Work and Culture: The Task System and the World of Lowcountry Blacks, 1700–1800," *William and Mary Quarterly,* 3rd Series, 35 (1982), 583.
25. Claudia Goldin, *Urban Slavery in the American South, 1820–1860: A Quantitative History* (Chicago: University of Chicago Press, 1976), 39.
26. Richard Wade, *Slavery in the Cities: The South, 1820–1860* (New York: Oxford, 1964), 48.
27. Loren Schweninger, *Black Property Owners in the South 1790–1915* (Urbana: University of Illinois Press, 1990), 14.
28. Peter Wood, "'Taking Care of Business' in Revolutionary South Carolina: Republicanism and the Slave Society," in Jeffrey Crow and Larry Tise, eds., *The Southern Experience in the American Revolution* (Chapel Hill: University of North Carolina Press, 1978), 275.
29. Philip Morgan, "Work and Culture," 597.
30. Donald Robinson, *Slavery in the Structure of American Politics,* 63.
31. Ira Berlin, "The Revolution in Black Life," in Alfred Young, ed., *The American Revolution: Explorations in American Radicalism* (DeKalb: Northern Illinois University Press, 1976), 356.
32. Paul Finkelman, "Slavery and the Constitutional Convention: Making a Covenant with Death," in Richard Beeman et al., eds., *Beyond Confederation: Origins of the Constitution and American National Identity* (Chapel Hill: University of North Carolina Press, 1987), 190.
33. Robinson, *Slavery in the Structure of American Politics,* 245.
34. Finkelman, "Slavery and the Constitutional Convention," 193.
35. Ibid., 225.
36. Benjamin Quarles, *The Negro in the American Revolution* (New York: W. W. Norton, 1973), 13–14.
37. Arthur Zilversmit, *The First Emancipation: The Abolition of Slavery in the North* (Chicago: University of Chicago Press, 1967), 87.
38. Ibid., 96.
39. Ibid., 97.

40. Higginbotham, *In the Matter of Color,* 84.
41. Ibid., 92.
42. Ibid., 94–97.
43. Ibid., 86–87.
44. Zilversmit, *The First Emancipation,* 123.
45. Edgar J. McManus, *A History of Negro Slavery in New York* (Syracuse: Syracuse University Press, 1966), 181.
46. Morris, *Southern Slavery and the Law,* 390–398.
47. Paul Finkelman, "Slavery and the Northwest Ordinance: A Study in Ambiguity," *Journal of the Early Republic,* 6 (1986), 349.
48. Jean R. Soderlund, *Quakers and Slavery: A Divided Spirit* (Princeton: Princeton University Press, 1985), 21.
49. Zilversmit, *The First Emancipation,* 88.
50. Robinson, *Slavery in the Structure of American Politics,* 297–298.
51. Ibid., 324.
52. Ibid., 330–331.
53. Ibid., 338.
54. James McPherson, *Battle Cry of Freedom: The Civil War Era* (New York: Oxford, 1988), 41.
55. Ibid., 51.
56. Ibid., 55.
57. Eric Foner, *Politics and Ideology in the Age of the Civil War* (New York: Oxford, 1980), 84.
58. McPherson, *Battle Cry,* 65.
59. Larry Gara, "Slavery and the Slave Power: A Crucial Distinction," *Civil War History,* 15 (1969), 9.
60. Ibid., 10.

The Development of Family Life

The black population depended upon a network of kin relationships under slavery to provide its members with emotional support and psychic sustenance. Coming from societies where ethnicity and kinship ties constituted the foundation upon which all other relationships rested, Africans endeavored to reconstruct this world in America. The obstacles that stood in their path were forbidding and their efforts, no matter how relentless and sustained, were not always successful. Nevertheless, an intricate web of kin relationships and a precarious family life evolved over time, reflecting the needs of the black population and drawing its inspiration from African traditions and the realities of life in the quarters and in America as a whole.

Any analysis of the kin arrangements and the family life of the African-born slaves and to some extent those of the creoles must be approached with caution. We must be careful not to impose a Western conceptualization of the family upon them and seek to identify only examples of Christian marriages, monogamy, and the standard nuclear family. Organized into lineages and kinship units, Africans enjoyed kin and familial traditions that were quite different from those of the Christian English, and it is unfortunate that historians and others have applied Western models of kinship arrangements such as the nuclear family, simple family, extended family, and so on to peoples who did not organize themselves in such a way. The result is that we have used a measure of the Africans' kin arrangements that lacks cultural validity. It is only when the black population becomes creolized, and to some extent Christianized, that we can begin to apply Western concepts. Even

93

so, these arrangements must not be seen as simple extensions of, or carbon copies of, those of the whites. To do so would be to seriously misunderstand the evolution of black life and the ideas that informed and legitimized social relationships. Even slaveowners, who should have known better, tended to use their own yardsticks to measure the kin arrangements of their slaves. Cheryl Ann Cody, who has studied the naming patterns of the slaves, recently concluded that the majority of the slaves "conceived of their families in a broad sense, including extended kin," while their owners "saw the nuclear family as the primary unit."[1] Along these lines, a former Louisiana slave recalled, "in our family am pappy, mammy, and three brudders and one sister, Julia, and six cousins."[2] In some African societies households included a man, his wives, their children and their spouses, grandchildren, and other assorted kin.

Under the circumstances, it may be misleading to use the term "family" to describe all of the variegated kin relationships and household compositions that the Africans created in the early years, particularly during the long first century. The same could be said, with some qualifications, about some members of the creole population in later years. "Family" is probably inappropriate because it immediately conjures the more narrowly constructed Western images of a man, a woman, and their children, living together in a union sanctioned by the church or the state. The relationships that the enslaved created, often without Christian sanction, and certainly without state approval, ran the gamut of what would be characterized in contemporary Western terms as "monogamy," "polygyny," "serial marriages," "consensual unions," and perhaps other combinations as well. We should avoid homogenizing such diverse kin relationships under the general rubric of "family" with the attendant connotation. Consequently, we use the term cautiously throughout this chapter and only when it is fairly clear that the arrangement that we are discussing is similar, at least in form, to the Western and Christian ideal.

In many important respects, African–born slaves understood the meaning of a union between a man and a woman quite differently from their more Westernized and creole counterparts. For the African, the primary relationship in a marriage was that which was established between the two lineages from which the partners hailed. The relationship between the husband and the wife was secondary to that which was forged between the lineages precisely because of the transcendental importance of kinship obligations and the precedence of the needs of the community over those of individuals.

Generally speaking, the fundamental purpose of marriage was to produce children, increasing the size of the group and enlarging the network of kin relationships. Parenthood was ascribed a special meaning and value because it meant the fulfillment of the highest obligations to the community. Under the circumstances, fertility was highly prized and infertility could constitute appropriate grounds for the annulment of the marriage. Since the procreative aspect of the relationship was so important, it becomes readily understandable why women of childbearing age were at a premium and tended to be offered for sale as slaves less frequently than the men. Childless and unmarried women failed to fulfill their culturally assigned roles and probably became pariahs. Polygyny was one appropriate response in those societies and at those times when there was a numerical superiority of women.

Since the bond that united the man and the woman was secondary to that which cemented the two lineages, it meant that the parents of the couple and the elders of the community played the principal roles in spousal choices. They initiated the discussions concerning the union, decided on its timing, the gifts that accompanied it, and the ceremonies that gave it legitimacy. Some of these societies had patrilineal descent systems, while others were matrilineal.

Under patrilineal systems, the children of the marriage belonged to the father's kin; in matrilineal systems, they belonged to the mother's kin. The problem of descent was, and still is, of paramount importance in such societies because it determines the distribution of property. The wife's kin inherit the estate under matriliny and the father's kin are the recipients under patriliny. Societies that practice matriliny or patriliny are characterized as unilineal in contrast to those that are bilateral, with descent flowing from both men and women.

It is important to keep the nature of the Africans' traditional kin arrangements in mind as we examine the evolution of family life under slavery. Their violent removal from their ethnic group destroyed the web of kin relationships that secured their place in society. The resulting kinlessness must have exacerbated their emotional pain and despair in ways in which we can never begin to understand. To be without kin was to be the perpetual outsider, to be socially dead. Parents and community elders were not present with the African captive in America to determine spousal choices in those situations where marriageable partners were available. We may also guess that when marriages occurred they were not usually accompanied by the customary ceremonies given the absence of kin and the appropriate ceremonial leaders and authorities.

The systems of patriliny and matriliny also broke down as a consequence of the slave trade and slavery. During the long first century, Africans were never present in significant numbers to recreate these crucial aspects of their lives. In addition, individuals who were socialized into one system or the other probably found themselves together in the same household or on the same farm, further complicating the problem of cultural reconstruction. In any event, most slaves possessed little if any property to bequeath to their kin. Then, too, slave marriages lacked legal standing in America, so the partners were afforded none of the legal protection, such as inheritance rights, that the law gave to white couples. Louisiana legislators found it necessary to remind residents of the state in 1824, "Slaves cannot marry without the consent of their masters, and their marriages do not produce any of the civil effects which result from such contract."[3]

Although African-born slaves could not recreate–except with considerable difficulty–their traditional domestic and kin arrangements, it is certain that the memory of these and other aspects of their heritage survived and were transmitted, albeit in modified forms, to their descendants. In fact, the moorings and sensibilities of traditional Africa were reflected in such ways as the high premium placed on fertility, the manner in which a birth was celebrated, the naming patterns, the respect accorded elders, the nature of burial rites, and the sanctity of kin ties. These and other African-inspired practices and sensibilities continued to inform life in the quarters throughout the period of slavery and beyond.

RECONSTRUCTING AND CONSTRUCTING KIN

The evidence is clear that blacks developed a network of relationships as soon as chance, the demographic situation, and the sex ratio facilitated it. The emergence of these ties of kin and nonkin should not be seen primarily as acts of resistance to the efforts of the slaveowners and the larger society to diminish them as persons. Rather, they represented the perfectly normal expressions of their humanity and their conscious desire to recreate kinship systems and social relationships to help give meaning to their lives. The systems they created tell us much about their efforts to define themselves and to order their intimate lives according to their own rules.

The nature of the slaves' network of relationships changed over time. Understandably, their beliefs, behavior, and social organizations were largely a function of their place of birth and the culture into which they had been socialized. While African-born persons engaged in polygynous unions where they could, nineteenth-century Christianized creoles were more likely to accept monogamous relationships, at least in principle. By the mid-nineteenth century, it appears that the ideal was approximating that of the Christian/Western practice of one man to one woman.

Although it is certain that black women and men established amorous liaisons whenever they could, there is little information on the factors that determined spousal selection. Quite likely, as was the case in colonial Mexico and Peru, Africans tended to choose their partners from among individuals of the same ethnic group. Creoles were also more likely to choose other creoles as their spouses in those societies, and free persons tended to marry other free persons. Evidence from Christ Church and St. Peter's Church in Philadelphia indicate that between 1727 and 1780, in 25 percent of the marriages contracted by blacks, both partners were free. In 14 percent of the cases, the marriages were between a slave and a free person, and those between slaves constituted 29 percent of the sample.[4]

These choices were perfectly understandable. It made practical sense for individuals of the same legal status to contract marriage alliances. Marriages in which one spouse was free and the other was a slave must have presented great difficulties for both persons. Conceivably, the couple could not live under the same roof and visitation rights could be denied the free person by the master of the slave spouse. Although we do not know the ethnic backgrounds of the couples in the Philadelphia sample, ethnicity must have informed their choices as well. By the nineteenth century, however, when the creole population became dominant, the role of ethnicity in marriage choices would have declined in importance. Black American society was well on the way to becoming solidified by then; the primary lines of demarcation were no longer between the African-born and the creoles, but increasingly between the free and the enslaved.

The choice of a spouse represented an important watershed in the lives of the enslaved couple as much as it did for free persons. Most slaves appear to have selected their spouses freely and without the coercive interference of their masters. There were instances, to be sure, where slaveowners sought to impose partners on their human property. One former slave who had lived in Texas recalled that in those days "Massa pick out a portly man and a portly gal and just put 'em together; what he want am the stock."[5] A distinction should be made between formal marriages, of course, and forced sexual relationships.

One woman, Rose Williams, graphically related her anguished and futile struggle to resist the advances of the man her master selected for her. It is a story that tells much about what it meant to be chattel and female.

> Dere am one thing Massa Hawkins does to me what I can't shunt from my mind. I knows he don't do it for meanness, but I allus holds it 'gainst him. What he done am force me to live with dat nigger, Rufus, 'gainst my wants.
>
> After I been at he place 'bout a year, de massa come to me and say, "You gwine live with Rufus in dat cabin over yonder. Go fix it for livin'." I's 'bout sixteen year old and has no larnin', and I's jus' igno'mus chile. I's thought dat him mean for me to tend de cabin for Rufus and some other niggers. Well, dat am start de pestigation for me.
>
> I's took charge of de cabin after work am done and fixes supper. Now, I don't like dat Rufus, 'cause he a bully. He am big and 'cause he

so, he think everybody do what him say. We'uns has supper, den I goes here and dere talkin', till I's ready for sleep and den I gits in de bunk. After I's in, dat nigger come and crawl in de bunk with me 'fore I knows it. I says, "What you means, you fool nigger?" He say for me to hush de mouth. "Dis my bunk, too," he say.

"You's teched in de head. Git out," I's told him, and I puts de feet 'gainst him and give him a shove and out he go on de floor 'fore he knew what I's doin'. Dat nigger jump up and he mad. He look like de wild bear. He starts for de bunk and I jumps quick for de poker. It am 'bout three feet long and when he comes at me I lets him have it over de head. Did dat nigger stop in he tracks? I's say he did. He looks at me steady for a minute and you's could tell he thinkin' hard. Den he go and set on de bench and say, "Jus' wait. You thinks it am smart, but you's am foolish in de head. Dey's gwine larn you somethin'."

"Hush you big mouth and stay 'way from dis nigger, dat all I wants," I say, and jus' sets and hold dat poker in de hand. He jus' sets, lookin' like de bull. Dere we'uns sets and sets for 'bout an hour and den he go out and I bars de door.

De nex' day I goes to de missy and tells her what Rufus wants and missy say dat am de massa's wishes. She say, "Yous am de portly gal and Rufus am de portly man. De massa wants yu-uns fer to bring forth portly chillen."

I's thinkin' 'bout what de missy say, but say to myself, "I's not gwine live with dat Rufus." Dat night when he come in de cabin, I grabs de poker and sits on de bench and says, "Git 'way from me, nigger, 'fore I busts yous brains out and stomp on dem." He say nothin' and git out.

De nex' day de massa call me and tell me, "Woman, I's pay big money for you and I's done dat for de cause I wants yous to raise me chillens. I's put yous to live with Rufus for dat purpose. Now, if you doesn't want whippin' at de stake, yous do what I wants."

I thinks 'about massa buyin' me offen de block and savin' me from bein' sep'rated from my folks and 'bout bein' whipped at de stake. Dere it am. What am I's to do? So I 'cides to do as de massa wish and so I yields.[6]

The degree to which such forced intrusions into the private lives of the slaves occurred will remain contentious. It was in the slaveowners' material interest to encourage and promote childbearing among female slaves since the children assumed their mother's status. But the men and women who were slaves must have been able to exercise a far greater degree of control over their intimate lives and choices than they have so far been credited. Neither slave men nor women had become sexual robots to be controlled and manipulated by those who owned them. Nor can it be concluded that the men and the women had become so dehumanized that they lacked the capacity to form and nourish basic human bonds and affectional ties.

There is, on the other hand, an abundance of evidence indicating that male slaveowners, their sons, and overseers abused slave women sexually. Not only did women perform the labor that was required of them, but their bodies also were used to satisfy the sexual passions of those who owned or supervised them. Consequently, women experienced the burdens and horrors of being human property, at least in this context, quite differently and perversely from men. Harriet Jacobs, who wrote *Incidents in the Life of a Slave Girl*, recalled that slavery was "far more terrible for women. Superadded to the burden common to all, *they* have wrongs and sufferings, and mortifications peculiarly their own."[7] In contrast to the abuse of these women by men, there is little documentation on same-sex relationships between the owners and the owned or between white slave mistresses and slave men, but both existed.[8] Whatever its nature, owners' exercise of sexual power over their slaves, particularly the women, affirmed the domination of white over black and underscored the tyrannical nature of the institution of slavery.

We can never know the full psychological impact of sexual assaults on those who endured them, or on their kin. But we can be certain that they elicited a range of emotions, including resentment, fear, resistance, bitterness, contempt, and even resigned and sullen accommodation. In a celebrated case that occurred in Missouri in the 1850s, Celia killed her master because of his repeated sexual demands. She was tried, convicted, and executed for homicide. The decision meant that in the eyes of the law and the larger society, slave women did not control their bodies or their sexuality. Not all sexual contacts between white men and black women were coerced. A number were consensual and lasted for varying periods of time. Some white men, more the exception than the rule, acknowledged their affairs, even formally accepting the progeny of such unions. Historians still debate whether a healthy emotional relationship could exist when one of the lovers was legally owned by the other.

Although it should be readily conceded that some slaveowners tried to select lovers or spouses for their slaves, the question of whether slaves were systematically bred for the domestic market is more troublesome. It has been suggested that slaveowners, in some cases, established breeding farms where young men and women were coerced or somehow induced to produce children who would be sold. The paucity of explicit references in the historical record to this activity has led some scholars to doubt whether it was widely practiced, if at all. Others suggest that "slave breeding" was not something of which masters were proud and, consequently, records would not have been kept.

It is generally recognized, however, that some border states and others in the Upper South—Delaware, Maryland, Kentucky, Tennessee, Virginia, and North Carolina—were major exporters of slaves to Arkansas, Texas, Louisiana, Mississippi, and Florida in the antebellum years. Between 1850 and 1860, for example, about 250,000 slaves were uprooted and delivered to the buying states. Males comprised a higher proportion of the sales than females, and individuals between the ages of 15 and 39 were at a premium.[9] In addition, slaves were more likely to be sold as individuals, thereby breaking up families and creating untold emotional misery. Scholars who support the "slave breeding" thesis point out that the "breeder states" held disproportionately large numbers of women in the childbearing age group. These women, it has been said, also had a suspiciously high fertility rate compared to their counterparts in other states.

Still, conclusions about the practice and incidence of "slave breeding" are based largely on circumstantial evidence. Slaveowners, of course, offered inducements of one sort or another to their slaves to bear children and rewarded particularly fecund women. Women who bore several children received special privileges. One nineteenth-century rice planter reported that "women with six children alive at any one time are allowed all Saturday to themselves."[10] Some slaveowners rewarded women with gifts when they gave birth. A few women, on the other hand, were so damaged by the institution that they derived a perverted satisfaction from producing children that became the masters' property. "Tho' we no able to work, we make little niggers for massa," explained one woman on a Georgia rice plantation in the nineteenth century.[11]

Did slave men and women respond affirmatively to the coercion or blandishments of their owners or was the decision to bear children essentially their own? Several facts indicate that most slaves procreated because it responded to their own human needs and cultural pulls. The notion that they were coerced to produce children on breeding farms suggests a degree of debasement of the black population that contradicts almost everything we currently know about slave life. It ignores the widely accepted conclusion that the enslaved exercised much control over their private lives and placed limits on the extent to which slaveowners could regulate their intimate behavior. Interference by slaveowners does not explain the slaves' decisions to reproduce and the high fertility rates that have been noticed, especially for the nineteenth century.

Most, if not the majority of slave women, as we shall later underscore, lived in long-term unions with one man during the nineteenth century. This hardly presents a picture of indiscriminate sexual activity. The high fertility rates of slave women reflected the premium placed on reproduction in the African societies from which they descended and suggests that these sensibilities continued to prevail in the quarters. Consequently, we should situate our explanation for the high fertility rates of the slaves more in their cultural and human tugs and less in the power of unscrupulous slaveowners over their intimate lives. Some states exported slaves because of their declining economic need for human chattel and their inability to absorb the increasing number that lived to adulthood in the nineteenth century. Accordingly, we must distinguish between the economic imperatives that explain the sale of the slaves and the private reasons why these human beings bore their children.

We do not know a great deal about the courting and marriage practices of black lovers, particularly for the formative years. Yet, evidence from the largely nineteenth-century creole population indicates that courting rituals were suffused with much playfulness, braggadocio on the part of the men, love poems, stories and songs. Usually the initiator, the man signalled his interest by impressing the woman with his wit, his elegant turn of language, and his charm. The intent was to arouse the woman's interest and to proclaim one's admiration through figurative and playfully boastful speech. If the woman went along in her responses, then the possibility of a romance existed. The following nineteenth-century conversation between two prospective lovers captures the spirit of the initial stages of courtship.

He: My dear kin' miss, has you any objections to me drawing my cher to yer side, and revolvin de wheel of my conversation around the axle of your understanding?

She: I has no objection to a gentleman addressin' me in a proper manner, kin' sir.

He: My dear miss, de worl' is a howlin' wilderness full of devourn' animals, and you has got to walk through hit. Has you made up your min' to walk through hit by yerself, or wid som bol' wahyer?[12]

Courting normally took place whenever and wherever individuals gathered on social occasions such as parties, dances, and cookouts. Sometimes it occurred at night. A former slave remembered that the men "would come to the girl they liked, and talk to them at night after the work was done." Obviously, there were practical difficulties that stood in the way of the lovers, particularly if they were owned by different masters. They could not visit each other as they would have wished, owing to work routines and the lack of freedom of movement. As one former slave expressed it, "Niggers didn't have time to do much courting in them days. White folks would let them have suppers 'round Christmas time, then after that it was all over and no more gatherings till the next summer; then they would set out under the shade trees on Sunday evening, and all like that."[13]

Once the couple made the decision to marry, parental approval was sought, where feasible. This was a feature of the creole population, particularly in the nineteenth century, since the African-born would not have had their parents with them. As noted earlier, African traditions left spousal selection up to the parents and the elders of the community. But a variation of this practice seemed to continue in the quarters with the couple making their choice but still seeking a ratification of it by their parents. One Virginia tobacco planter observed the custom of obtaining parental approval in 1812, adding, "young people might connect themselves in marriage to their own liking, with consent of their parents who were the best judges."[14]

The couple also had to obtain their master's approval. In some cases, particularly on large plantations, the couple shared one master. In other instances, probably the vast majority, the slaves belonged to different masters and lived apart. In the previously cited sample from Philadelphia, fewer than one-fourth of the slave couples had the same master.[15] Sensitive owners were more likely to grant permission to marry if, in their judgment, it led to a more contented labor force and added to their economic advantage through the bearing of children. As early as the 1750s one perspicacious slaveowner maintained, "It is necessary that the Negroes have wives, and you ought to know that nothing attaches them so much to a plantation as children."[16] Thomas Jefferson, who owned slaves on his Virginia plantations, recognized the economic benefits of family life and reproduction among the slave population. He characterized "a woman who brings a child every two years as more profitable than the best man on the farm [for] what she produces is an addition to capital, while his labor disappears in mere consumption."[17]

The marriage customs and practices of the slave couples were creative and varied. Again, most of the descriptive evidence comes from the nineteenth century and reflects the influences of the creole environment and Christian practices. Weddings were generally festive occasions and took place most frequently on weekends or on holidays such as Christmas. These could be grand affairs and involved much planning. Friends were invited from neighboring plantations, farms, and households, and whites frequently attended, particularly if the happy couple were domestic slaves. On occasion, the marriage rites were performed by the slaveowners. At other times a white clergyman or a black preacher officiated. The location of the ceremony varied; it could occur in a church or in the open as circumstances dictated. One couple or several couples could be married simultaneously.

The Christian ceremonies followed the customary pattern of the exchange of vows. The celebrant normally avoided the use of the words "Till death do you part," however, because of the precariousness of slave marriages, subject as they were to being broken up by masters at will. Black preachers often added their own realistic twist to the ceremony, recognizing the arbitrariness of white control but expressing simultaneously a moral judgment on those who disrupted the private lives of the slaves. As one Alabama black preacher intoned, "Now before God and the witness, I pronounce you man and woman. And whomsoever God hap solated to be jined together, let no man part a thunder. Cursed is he that part man and wife–Amen."[18]

Slaves who avoided Christian marriage ceremonies resorted to other practices to legitimize their unions. A report from early eighteenth-century North Carolina indicates that blacks in Edenton retained some of their West African practices. The description of one such ceremony may have missed the deeper cultural meanings of the act, but it does provide a glimpse of a surviving practice,

> Their Marriages are generally performed amongst themselves, there being very little ceremony used upon that Head; for the Man makes the Woman a Present, such as a Brass Ring or some other Toy, which she accepts of, becomes his wife.[19]

One of the most popular practices, at least in the nineteenth century, was that of "jumping the broom." In this ceremony, the origin of which is uncertain, the couple joined hands and jumped over a broomstick. There was no set pattern to this ceremony. One former slave recollected that the couple jumped "backwards and forwards over a broom." Another maintained, "after supper dey puts the broom on the floor and de couple takes de hands and steps over the boom, den dey am out to bed." A third informant, a former Tennessee slave, related, "Day go in the parlor and each carry de broom. Dey lays the broom on the floor and de woman puts her broom front the man and he puts the broom front the woman. Dey face one 'nother and step 'cross the brooms at the same time to each other and takes hold of their hands and that marries them."[20]

Slaves may even have exchanged their own marriage vows privately. When the Sea Island blacks observed during the war, "We married ourselves," they may have been referring to their privately expressed vows or to the custom of solemnizing a union by sharing a blanket. The practice of sharing a blanket as a marriage ritual seems to have been fairly widespread throughout the South. As a former Georgia slave reported, "We comes together in the same cabin, and she brings her blanket and lay it down beside mine; and we gets married that a-way."[21]

Regardless of the nature of the marriage ceremony, it had a profound meaning for the couple and for those who witnessed it. Although they lacked legal standing, these marriages affirmed the humanity of the enslaved, established an enduring network of relationships with the kinfolk of the two individuals, and ultimately helped people to have some normalcy in their lives. There were limits to this, of course. A marriage ceremony did not a marriage make. Major difficulties remained for the couple, only one of which was the constant threat of separation. The Gullah preacher who performed slave marriages and pronounced the couple united "Till death or buckra (whites) part you," recognized, as did all his listeners, that once the festivities ended, an uneasy and uncertain future awaited.[22]

The family life of the enslaved cannot be characterized in simple and absolute terms. Never static, the texture of these relationships changed over time as the number of the enslaved in some areas increased, as the net of kin relationships expanded, and as the proportion of creoles to Africans increased. By 1820, the slave population had become highly concentrated in the South and numbered about 1,800,000. This provided a critical mass that enhanced the development and sustenance of a network of kin and nonkin relationships. With the declining presence of the African-born, the emerging creole majority drew much of its inner compass and ways of doing things from the fact of its birth and socialization in the slave quarters of America.

The black families of the seventeenth and eighteenth centuries remain largely unstudied, in part because of an absence of appropriate historical sources. Census and probate court records provide useful statistical information, but they do not illuminate the nature of family and kin arrangements. Yet family practices in the early years must have been shaped by the life the Africans knew before their forced transportation to America. Polygynous family arrangements existed, but it is not clear to what extent. Francis Le Jau, an eighteenth–century Anglican missionary, admonished his black flock, noting, "The Christian Religion does not allow plurality of Wives," an indication that such practices had been brought to America.[23] Scattered evidence suggests that during the eighteenth century in New York and New England, some couples changed partners with some degree of ease. In 1775, one observer in Rye, New York, noted that the slaves "will not or cannot live up to the Christian covenant in one notorious instant at least, viz., matrimony, for they marry after their heathen way and divorce and take others as often as they please." Similar complaints came from Boston.[24]

The black slaves who married could not normally expect to share the same conjugal household unless they belonged to the same owner. Given the sexual imbalance that often existed even on large plantations in the nineteenth century and the fact that most slaves lived in households or on farms in groups of ten or less, both men and women experienced difficulties in finding partners. Many found spouses "'broad," or away from their own farm or plantation. If they were lucky they lived within easy reach, but in many cases they were separated by long distances. Slave owners discouraged these 'broad unions. Thomas Jefferson thought such persons acted "independently." "There is nothing I desire so much," he added, "as that all the young people on the estate should intermarry with one another and stay at home." Jefferson and other slaveowners knew from experience that provisions had to be made for "time off" for conjugal visits by slaves involved in 'broad unions, particularly on weekends. Then too, there was an economic argument against these marriages. Only the owner of the wife could lay claim to the children of such unions, since they took the mother's status.

Jefferson probably had this in mind when he noted that slaves who married "at home" are worth a great deal more in that case than when they have husbands and wives abroad."[25]

There is not much doubt that such long–distance relationships posed emotional and other difficulties for the couple. While each person retained some degree of personal autonomy, husbands revealed the depth of their emotional attachments by making frequent visits to their wives' abode. There are some historians who conclude that the slaves actually preferred such residential arrangements, since the couples would not have to witness the humiliations inflicted upon their partners by their respective owners or those in their employ. Henry Bibb, who escaped in the nineteenth century, had an anguished recollection of being "compelled to stand and see my wife shamefully scourged and abused by her master, and the manner in which this was done, was so violently and inhumanly committed upon the person of the female."[26] A number of slaves recounted similar scenes and a few, under the circumstances, expressed a preference for 'broad spouses. A nineteenth-century Georgia slave mistress was also certain that the slaves "all preferred having husbands off the plantation [and] thought it was exceedingly hard if they could not marry away from home."[27]

Such observations were probably exaggerated. 'Broad marriages exacerbated the burdens of slavery because the distance denied the couple the mutual and constant emotional support that they were likely to have enjoyed had they shared the same conjugal unit. The situation was made much worse when children were involved. The lot of the slaves–adults and children–was unenviable enough without the added complication of parents and children living away from one another. Commuter marriages afforded the couple the opportunity to visit another household, farm, or plantation and to be free–albeit temporarily–from the supervision of one's master or overseer. Yet such psychic benefits must have been tempered by the transitory nature of the contact with spouses and children, the burden of having to travel particularly after a day's labor, and the painful recognition that such familial travails came as a consequence of being some one else's property.

There is an increasing body of statistical evidence that illuminates the household structure and reproductive patterns of the slave population. Much of this evidence deals with the nineteenth century, although there are a few studies for the eighteenth century as well. These data allow us to reconstruct residential patterns, size and composition of household units, fertility rates, and so on. But they tell us little about the day-to-day relationships within families, the stuff of human interaction at that intimate level and the texture of domestic life. We must also remind ourselves that the farms and plantations constituted artificial communities of slaves in the sense that their residence in them was involuntary. The fact and circumstances of racial slavery limited the options of its victims and forced them to make creative adaptations to their condition in familial arrangements as well as in other aspects of their interior lives.

Unlike free persons, slaves lacked the mobility to establish and nurture ties with individuals separated by long distances. There were exceptions, of course, but as a rule individuals had to confine their social relations to people on their own farms and plantations or those nearby. Slaves on plantations with fifty or more of their peers were more likely to be able to find marriage partners from among themselves than were the residents of smaller units. The chances were best on those plantations with several hundred slaves, a demographic reality that also served to enlarge the networks of blood ties and kin relationships. On the Ball plantation in South Carolina, 26 percent of the slaves were related by blood during the late eighteenth and nineteenth centuries.

But such large concentrations of slaves were nonexistent during the long first century. The situation began to change in the eighteenth century, particularly after about 1740. By the mid-nineteenth century, 25 percent of the slave population lived in units of fifty or more. But this must be balanced against the fact that in 1850, fully 43 percent of the enslaved also resided in groups of fifteen or less. The structure of the kin and family arrangements of this atomized majority remains largely unstudied, and it may well be that the pattern of their intimate relationships varied significantly from that of the residents of the large plantations. Consequently, statistics relating to marriage and family arrangements that are drawn from the large plantations may have dubious applicability to the majority of the enslaved.

These comments are worth underscoring in light of the recent tendency among historians to homogenize the family relationships among the slave population and to paint a static and idyllic portrait of their life. Generalizations about the experiences of slaves cannot be based solely on the antebellum years any more than they can be on the conditions that existed on life on the largest plantations. With these caveats in mind, we turn to some of the more recent findings on the structure of the family at specific times and places.

A close study of the approximately 400 slaves owned by Charles Carroll of Maryland in 1773 gives us some clues as to the structure of family life on a large plantation during the eighteenth century. Some of the slaves were African-born and others were creoles. It is not clear what proportion of the population each group constituted. Nor is there any information on whether the family arrangements of the African-born were different from the creoles or whether the two groups intermarried. Without this information, we are not likely to fully understand the nature of the domestic and intimate lives of the slaves. We should not ignore the Africans' primary socialization and experiences, since these undoubtedly shaped their response to the realities of slavery in America.

In any event, almost 60 percent of the slaves who were on the Carroll plantation in 1773 lived in the standard nuclear family, with the presence of parents and children. Another 31.6 percent of the households consisted of a mother and her children, and 5.1 percent were formed by a father and his children.[28] Further evidence of the structure of the slave family comes from three additional large plantations in Prince Georges and Anne Arundel counties in Maryland between 1759 and 1775. In this sample of 576 slaves, 47 percent lived in households comprising the two parents and their children, 14 percent consisted of mothers and their children, 2 percent included a father and his children, and 9 percent had the husband, wife, children, and other kin living in them.[29]

Not surprisingly, the evidence for the existence of settled unions is far richer for the nineteenth-century creole population. One of the best studies of household structure was done on slightly over 10,000 slaves who resided in 155 communities in rural Louisiana between 1810 and 1864. The researcher found that on farms with fewer than 100 slaves, there was a higher percentage of unmarried persons living alone than in units with higher concentrations of persons. On farms with fewer than 20 slaves, 20 percent remained unmarried, 24 percent on those farms with 20 to 49 slaves, and 20 percent on those with 50–99 slaves. Single persons living alone comprised 18 percent of the slaves on plantations with a population of 100-199, 11 percent on those with 200–299 persons and 5 percent on those who had 300-399 slaves. Taken together, 18 percent of the slaves lived alone, 49 percent resided in households comprising parents and their children, 8 percent consisted of married couples living alone, 14.5 percent lived in female-headed households, and 2 percent in those led by men.[30]

The Louisiana sample, with its mix of farms and plantations of different sizes and extending over five decades (1810–64), shows that an overwhelming majority of the enslaved resided with their kinfolk. About 80 percent of them lived with kin either in the nuclear family, in the extended family, or in households where the residents shared blood ties of one sort or another. This pattern reflected the continuing salience of traditional African kinship arrangements as well as the need to cement and cherish familial bonds as a means of psychic sustenance in an oppressive environment.

We must be careful, however, about the overall applicability of these conclusions to the entire slave population. The sample included a smaller number of slaves (296) on farms with fewer than 20 persons than for any of the other categories. For farms with 20–49 slaves, the sample was 1,618 persons, and for those with 50–99, the corresponding figure was 3,800 slaves. In the 100–199 category, 2,819 persons were sampled; 1,113 in the 200–299 category; and 683 on farms with 300–399 slaves. Since the census of 1850 reported that 86 percent of the slaveowners had fewer than 20 slaves each, it is clear that the number of such slaves in the sample is inadequate for the making of generalizations about the structure of the family for a significant proportion of the slaves in Louisiana or elsewhere in the nation.

It is apparent, however, that the structure of the creole family became increasingly similar to that of the whites. The standard nuclear family was becoming the dominant form of marital arrangement in the nineteenth century. As in other ways, creoles were not immune to the larger cultural influences of the land in which they were born, and it is certain that slaveowners would not have encouraged polygynous relationships even if some slaves so desired. The role of Christianity and its opposition to polygyny cannot be discounted as a factor that gave legitimacy to a nuclear family organization.

Structural similarities between the black family and that of the whites, however, obscure fundamental differences in the interior rhythm of the slaves' lives, rules of marital behavior, kinship networks, sexual mores, and so on. We do not even understand the attitudes that surrounded premarital sexual behavior. Unlike those of the Christians, many of the societies from which Africans came in the seventeenth and eighteenth centuries appear to have lacked taboos on sexual relations before the formal celebration of matrimony. In any event, the first African arrivals seemed to have engaged in sexual activity before marriage, at least often enough to invite negative comment from white observers. Whites, to be sure, were no more likely to abide by the Christian strictures against premarital sex. If we are to believe the recent literature on African sexuality, blacks enjoyed greater sexual freedom than did whites and were not overcome by guilt as a result of their indulgence. We cannot be certain, however, about the accuracy and general applicability of this observation for the early period or even the later years for that matter. Robert Smalls, who later became a congressman from South Carolina, observed in 1863 that "the majority" of black women had sexual intercourse before marriage, "but they do not consider this intercourse an evil thing."[31] Smalls did not volunteer any information about the habits of the men, and the evidence upon which he based such a sweeping assertion is not entirely clear.

In the end, however, the point is not whether blacks practiced sexual restraint or not before marriage. If their values and mores sanctioned such conduct, and were strong enough to act as countervailing forces against the Christian teachings, then such behavior was quite normal. It was not an aberration and only became so in the eyes of Christian whites who kept watchful eyes on black sexuality in the quarters.

The slaves' values, at least in the nineteenth century, dictated that premarital pregnancies should lead to marriage. This did not always occur, however, as some persons cavalierly avoided their responsibilities in this regard and others feared an unhappy marriage. Furthermore, sanctions against those who contravened these codes could have been enforced only where slaves had the demographic strength and social organizations to do so. Similarly, extramarital relationships, at least for Christianized slaves, were discouraged. The situation would not arise for those who did not embrace Christianity or monogamous relationships. The point is worth underscoring, because not all slaves were Christians and hence did not adhere to norms that characterized the behavior of believers.

It is, of course, against this religious background that one should view efforts of some slaves to punish those who engaged in extramarital conduct. Prior to the Civil War the Beaufort Baptist Church in South Carolina imposed a variety of penalties on its members who committed adultery and fornication. Adulterers were suspended from the church for three months upon conviction for a first offense. For a second offense, they were punished with a six-month suspension.[32] Whether similar sanctions existed elsewhere is uncertain, but the Beaufort strictures could have held meaning only for church members and fellow Christians.

Sexual fidelity or infidelity aside, the life of the average couple was harsh and difficult, regardless of where they lived and the time period. It could not have been otherwise, lacking as they did control over their lives, marriages free from separation, and the constant humiliations that came with being chattel. Some of these daily indignities must have affected relationships between men and women, parents and children. Not "super persons" by any means, or possessed of "Teflon–coated" personalities; slaves saw much, endured much, and were affected by much. The indictment by a black woman that "white folks got a heap to answer for the way they've done to colored folks" captures both pain and anguish, but it does not reveal the invisible scars that slaves possessed.[33] If white society did not wholly determine the texture of social relations in the quarters, it had the capacity to set some of the boundaries and influence a great many choices.

How men and women organized their lives in the quarters, if they shared one, remains imperfectly understood. Perhaps there was no common pattern given the variety of ethnic backgrounds from which the Africans came and the diverse experiences of the creole population. It is certain that in the formative period African men and women stuck to carefully defined gender roles reflecting their traditions and belief systems. When working for their families, women did most of the productive labor and domestic work, while the men performed tasks requiring specialized skills such as carpentry, fishing, the trapping of animals, and shoemaking. These strict gender-based roles were modified in time as a consequence of the creolization process. Men and women worked together in the fields, performing the same tasks, and generally had the same work routine. In terms of social relations in the

Slave quarter at Sotterly plantation, St. Mary's County, Maryland.

quarters, however, women still bore the primary responsibility for child-rearing and the domestic chores. Gender–defined roles were more elastic in the nineteenth century than they had ever been, but they never disappeared.

Partners in suffering and much else, slave men and women tried to cope with their condition, loved and quarreled, and reared their children as best they could. John Collins, a former slave in South Carolina, remembered, "Daddy used to play with mammy just lak she was a child. He'd ketch her under the armpits and jump her up mighty high to the rafters in de little house us lived in."[34] Couples not only shared intimacies in their cramped quarters, but they fought in them too. Wife beating existed, and its occurrence should not be a surprise. Slavery exacerbated the tensions of everyday life, and men, without understanding the roots of their violence, could unleash it on their women.

FAMILIAL PRESSURES

Slave marriages, like those of other folk in other times and places, had different degrees of longevity. One observer, writing from Boston in 1733, disliked the tendency of slaves "to take husbands and wives at their pleasure, and then leave them again as they please, and then take others again as fast and as suddenly as they will and then leave them again."[35] This comment may have reflected a misunderstanding of African polygyny and the ease of "divorce" if the woman proved to be infertile. The presence of such a minuscule black population in eighteenth-century Massachusetts could hardly have favored the taking of partners at one's "pleasure." In any event, slavery and the slave trade certainly disrupted African traditional practices, so the comment probably contained a kernel of truth.

Many marriages in the antebellum years, however, were of a relatively long duration. In 1866, 24 percent of the former slave couples in Nelson County, Virginia, had been married 10 to 19 years, 16 percent between 20 and 29 years, and 8 percent between 30 and 39 years. Forty-five percent, comprising the majority, had been married for less than 10 years. A sample from North Carolina for the same year consisting of 9,452 marriages showed that almost 25 percent had lasted between 10 and 19 years, 20 percent for about 20 years, and almost 10 percent for more than 30 years.[36] Similar patterns probably existed in other states.

Some cautionary notes are in order. The existence of long–lasting marriages should not lead to the conclusion that slave marriages were "secure." As long as such marriages could be broken up at will by the masters, slave marriages must be considered to have been insecure, subject as they were to outside forces that exercised arbitrary power over them. Secondly, in the aforementioned samples of the longevity of marriages, the majority of the couples had lived together for less than ten years. While this is not in itself unusual and should be expected in a growing population and one with a life expectancy of forty years or less, the raw statistics often do not reveal whether these were first, second, or third marriages, and if so, the reasons for the termination of the previous ones. While death and divorce undoubtedly accounted for the end of some earlier marriages, forced separations by the masters explain a significant percentage as well.

While such forced separations occurred throughout the entire period of slavery, their incidence increased after 1790 with the intensification of the cotton plantation-based economy in the Lower South. We will never know the exact numbers, but as we indicated in Chapter 3, between 750,000 and 1 million black men and women and their children were relocated from the border states and the Upper South to the Lower South and Texas between 1790 and 1860. Entire families were sometimes uprooted, but in many instances, marriages and families were disrupted. Such atrocities not only reaffirmed where power resided but also revealed yet again the travails that characterized the experiences of human chattel.

This massive uprooting of slaves and their families is often emphasized, in part because of its horrible dimensions. But the breakup of marriages and the disruption of families occurred in less spectacular ways most of the time. Slaveowners everywhere sold the spouses of their slaves in times of economic distress, offered them in settlement of debts, gave them as gifts, and bequeathed them to their heirs. In some cases, sale could be used as a means of punishment for slaves who could not be easily controlled. Not all slaveowners, to be sure, acted so callously. Sensitive to the bonds that united couples and their families, and to moral considerations as well, they tried to keep families intact even under difficult economic circumstances.

Yet slaves were disposable and movable property, and the moralizing of their owners did not, ultimately, prevent their sale if there was no economic alternative. Thomas Chaplin, a South Carolina planter, revealed his inner turmoil in 1845 when he had to sell some of his slaves in order to meet his debts. He agonized over the decision to sell "ten prime negroes." "Nothing," Chaplin wrote, "can be more mortifying and grieving to a man, than to select out some of his negroes to be sold–You know not to whom, or how they will be treated by their new owners, and negroes that you find no fault with–to separate families, mothers & daughters–brothers & sisters–All to pay for your own extravagance." Chaplin was relieved when the sale ended, since it was the "most unpleasant thing I have ever had to do. . . . The Negroes at home are quite disconsolate, but this will soon blow over." And, the slaveowner added, "They may see their children again in time."[37] Thomas Chaplin's anguish cannot, obviously, be equated with the suffering of the victims of his "extravagance" and power. Nor should we ignore the fact that to be placed on the auction block was one of the most terrifying and deeply humiliating experiences that an enslaved person endured. Nothing revealed more starkly the awesome power of whites over blacks, of master over slave, and nothing captured more painfully and graphically the debasement of America's human chattel. Contemporary descriptions of auctions are rare, but the following one captures the demeaning procedure. It occurred in Richmond, Virginia, in 1853. The male slave was

> ordered to take off his clothes, which he did without a word or look of remonstrance. About a dozen gentlemen crowded to the spot while the poor fellow was stripping himself, and as soon as he stood on the floor, bare from top to toe, a most rigorous scrutiny of his person was instituted. The clear black skin, back and front, was viewed all over for sores from disease; and there was no part of his body left unexamined. The man was told to open and shut his hands, asked if he could pick cotton, and every tooth in his head was scrupulously looked at.[38]

The overall incidence of forced marital separation is, however, uncertain. But Herbert Gutman's analysis of this issue based on the recollections of 9,000 former slaves in Mississippi is instructive. This sam-

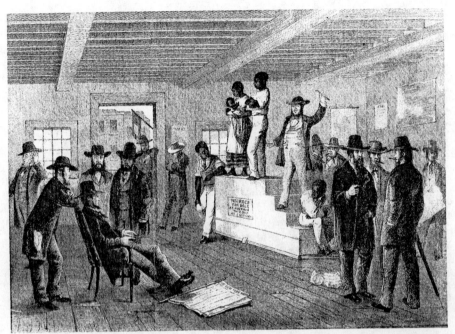

Slave auctions were not only humiliating to the slave, but there was also the probability that family members would be separated and sold to different owners.

ple, derived from evidence collected in 1864-65, shows that one-sixth of these persons, aged twenty or older, had a marriage forcibly terminated.[39] The percentage was higher for persons aged thirty and older. According to Gutman, "nearly one in four men and one in five women had suffered such a separation." Significantly, 35 percent of the couples (in which one or both parties were at least forty years old) reported the termination of an earlier marriage by force. Overall, it has been estimated that 29 percent of all slave marriages were broken up between 1820 and 1860.[40]

The separation of spouses was bad enough, but children were sold as well. Probably as many as 2,000,000 families experienced some form of disruption through sale between 1820 and 1860.[41] An advertisement in a New Orleans newspaper tells the grim story. "NEGROES FOR SALE– A negro woman 24 years of age, and two children, one eight and the other three years. Said negroes will be sold separately or together as desired."[42] Observing an auction in Wilmington in 1778, Elkanah Watson reported that the victims were

driven in from the country, like swine for market. A poor wench clung to a little daughter, and implored, with the most agonizing supplication, that they must not be separated. But alas, either the master or circumstances were inexorable–they were sold to different purchasers. The husband and the residue of the family were knocked off to the highest bidder."[43]

Harriet Jacobs captured the anguish of the slave mothers as they awaited the inevitable pain of separation from their children. "To the slave mother," Jacobs recalled,

> New Year's day comes laden with peculiar sorrows. She sits on her cold cabin floor, watching the children who may all be torn from her the next morning; and often does she wish that she and they might die before the day dawns. She may be an ignorant creature, degraded by the system that has brutalized her from childhood; but she has a mother's instincts, and is capable of feeling a mother's agonies.
>
> On one of these sale days, I saw a mother lead seven children to the auction-block. She knew that *some* of them would be taken from her; but they took *all*. The children were sold to a slave-trader, and their mother was bought by a man in her own town. Before night her children were all far away. . . . I met that mother in the street, and her wild, haggard face lives to-day in my mind. She wrung her hands in anguish, and exclaimed, "Gone! All gone! Why *don't* God kill me?"[44]

Slaves who were fortunate enough to be able to keep their families intact, nevertheless lived with the fear of the ultimate tragedy. Consider the painful memories of a liberated man:

> "After my master died, my mistress sold a number of her slaves from their families and friends–but not me. She sold several children from their parents–but my children were with me still. She sold two husbands from their wives–but I was still with mine. She sold one wife from her husband-but mine had not been sold from me. The master of my wife, Mr. Smith, had separated members of families by sale–but not of mine. . . . We knew and, what is more, we felt that we were slaves."[45]

Although the break up of families was a regular occurrence, no amount of psychic preparation was enough to mute the pain when the dreaded event occurred. Parents and children pleaded to remain together but their entreaties went unanswered. Such was the unenviable lot of the enslaved and the societally powerless. Once the separation was effected, those who were left behind had to adjust and prepare for the next time. Those taken away were almost never heard from again, but they too, had to be sustained by their memories and their inner resolve.

But human beings have remarkable adaptive capacities. Slaves drew upon their elaborate kin and nonkin networks to cushion the psychic blows that forced separations inflicted upon them. Children whose parents were removed from them or from whom they were removed could normally expect to find other adults willing to be surrogates. And an adult who was sold away might be welcomed by their new brethren and gradually eased into the community. The new ties that were forged as a result of the forced separations aided the healing process but the scars and the painful memories would remain.

Regardless of the threat of separation, slaves continued to have children and to hope for the best. Predictably, the number of children born to the women varied. African women during the formative years had fewer children than their nineteenth–century creole counterparts. As women married younger, nursed their children for shorter periods of time, and enjoyed better health, their fertility rates increased. Recently available evidence suggests that the typical black woman gave birth to seven children in the nineteenth century. A high proportion of these children did not live to become adults. Overall, three out of every ten infants died during the first year and almost 50 percent died before reaching their tenth birthday. They succumbed to the usual childhood diseases—diphtheria, dysentery, diarrhea, whooping cough, pneumonia, and so on. A considerable number of infant deaths were reported as being the consequence of smothering (overlaying) by the mothers. In 1850 four-fifths of the deaths attributed to smothering were slave children, a figure that was twenty–eight times higher than that for whites. According to Michael Johnson, "Between 1790 and 1860 smothering was responsible for the deaths of over 60,000 slave infants."[46]

The mothers of the infants were sometimes blamed for these deaths. Some were accused of carelessness and others of deliberately committing infanticide. In time, historians and others attributed such conduct to the attempts by slave mothers to prevent their children from becoming slaves and their masters' property. While one may grant some of this argument, modern science has produced a convincing explanation for the majority of these infant deaths. These babies were actually the victims of sudden infant death syndrome (SIDS). It is now known that such deaths are, in part, nutritionally related and may be a consequence of certain mineral deficiencies.

The mortality rate of children was evidently much higher in the unhealthy rice swamps of the lower South. Some plantations experienced much difficulty in maintaining an annual rate of natural increase even in the nineteenth century. At the Gowrie rice plantation in Georgia, 90 percent of those who were born between 1833 and 1861 died before their sixteenth birthday. In his outstanding analysis of these grim statistics, William Dusinberre notes that the mortality rate does "not fully measure the sorrows of the slave women, for it takes no account of stillbirths. . . . The number of stillbirths was almost certainly at least 5 percent as large as the total number of live births. Nor does the child mortality rate of 90 percent take into account miscarriages." Dusinberre paints a picture of unrelieved horror for the enslaved who labored in these arenas of death. Slave families at Gowrie, Dusinberre concludes, were "devastated" by child mortality "so that the most common nuclear grouping was a husband and wife with *no* surviving children. So many adults died young, and so many couples split up voluntarily, that over half the women who reached the age of twenty-eight married at least twice, and not uncommonly three, four, or even five times."[47]

While medical science has seemingly solved the riddle of some of the deaths in infancy, the problem of the extent of infanticide cannot be so easily resolved. There is very little data to support expansive claims by some historians that women slaves frequently murdered their children as an act of resistance. While there were isolated acts of infant killings, some were conceivably the actions of deranged minds, a phenomenon that is not confined to the enslaved. Others were designed to protect the children from a life of enslavement. One such reported incident concerned a South Carolina woman who poisoned one of her children after the others had been sold.[48] There were undoubtedly similar cases, but infanticide cannot be said to have been a characteristic of the slave population.

The same observation can be made about the incidence of abortions by slave women. Admittedly, this was a practice that would have been shrouded in such secrecy that documentary and other forms of evidence would not be readily accessible. Slave women, to be sure, were aware of the ways in which a pregnancy could be terminated. One Tennessee physician, John Morgan, reported in 1860 that "the remedies mostly used by the negroes to procure abortion" consisted of "the infusion or decoction of tansy, rue, roots and seed of the cotton plant, penny royal, cedar gum, and camphor, either in a gum or spirits."[49] Whether these and other "remedies" were efficacious is, of course, another matter. So too, is the question of the degree to which pregnant women resorted to such practices and the circumstances under which they did so. Slave-owners were only too quick to accuse the women of abortions when reliable evidence to support their claims seldom existed. It seems reasonable to suggest that many of these women experienced what modern physicians describe as "spontaneous abortions," a condition resulting from overwork, poor nutrition, deformities of the fetus, and so on.

It is unlikely that abortions received much, if any, approval in the quarters. The practice of terminating pregnancies and infanticide did not find any legitimization in the African societies from which the slaves descended, and there were strong taboos against such practices. Pregnancy and childbirth were events greeted by life-affirming rituals. Such cultural precepts continued to inform the behavior of American slaves. Given the strength of the kinship structure in the quarters, it may be further doubted that attempts to terminate pregnancies would have found general acceptance. Christianized slaves would surely have opposed the practice or experienced profound guilt if they transgressed in this manner. Thus, while some women ended their pregnancies for their own private reasons, the incidence of such behavior may have been quite low over time.

NAMING A CHILD

The successful delivery of a child brought its own joy to the parents. Children had a special place in African sensibilities, the households, and the larger community, despite the uncertainties surrounding their life chances and fate. Naming ceremonies were important, particularly in the early years, when African parents predominated. The name and the ceremony that accompanied it established the identity of the child, defined the newborn's place in the family and the community, and simultaneously renewed and cemented treasured kin relationships. African-born parents must have tried to name their children after kin left behind and in other traditional ways, but it was not always that easily accomplished.

The names of adult slaves in the early records suggest that the majority had been renamed by their owners. Names such as "Mary," "Antoney," "Isabell," and "William" that appear in the 1625 Virginia census are certainly not African in origin. By renaming these persons, slaveowners not only affirmed their power over their human property but also sought to create a new identity for them. African names, however, had deep cultural significance and meanings and could not be discarded at will. Olaudah Equiano, who was African–born, emphasized, "our children were named from some event, some circumstance, or fancied foreboding at the time of their birth. I was named Olaudah, which, in our language, signifies vicissitude or fortune also, one favored, and having a loud voice and well spoken. I remember we never polluted the name of the object of our adoration; on the contrary, it was always mentioned with the greatest reverence."[50] A name represented the essence and the uniqueness of a person. It was much more than one's individual identity; it bound an individual to the ancestors and established certain obligations and responsibilities for the bearer. The slaveowner's imposition of a new name violated more than just the African's personhood; it broke the symbolic links to the past and threatened to disrupt his entire world.

Slaveowners may not have understood the cultural meanings of African names but some of them surely recognized that it was important to rename their human property, thereby breaking their symbolic links to the past and emphasizing the owners' authority and power. The new name was devoid of any deeper meaning for the slave; it was not culturally sanctioned and it was not even ceremonially conferred. Nevertheless, he was forced to respond to it even if it lacked the emotional resonance of his given name. Some individuals, of course, used the new name with whites, but their friends in the quarters and outside knew them by their African name and respected its meaning. Masters knew about the survival of these African names even if they did not understand the reasons for their persistence. Newspaper advertisements for escaped persons clearly show the duality in nomenclature. One owner, for example, advertised for the return of "TWO NEW NEGRO YOUNG FELLOWS; one of them calls himself GOLAGA, the name given him here ABEL; the other a black fellow . . . calls himself ABBROM, the name given him here BENNET."[51] The following are some other examples from the advertisements that underscore the Africans' struggle to retain their original names and hence their separate identities.

John, Aug. 27, 1757 ("he will more readily answer to the name of FOOTBEA, which he went by in his own country")
Tyra, Aug. 10, 1765 ("The wench's country name Camba")
Somerset, Sept. 20, 1773 ("his country name Massery")
Limus, Sept. 20, 1773 ("his country name Serrah")[52]

African names persisted throughout the colonial period, undoubtedly nourished by the slave trade, and continued into the nineteenth century. In fact, during the colonial period "as many as 15 to 20 percent of the slaves in the two Carolinas had African names."[53] This group obviously consisted of the African–born who retained their names with or without their owner's approval and those who named their children in accordance with the old ways. Unfortunately, the symbolic meanings of such names as Quamino, Ankque, Warrah, Annika, and Monimea cannot now be determined.

Many of the surviving names were African "day" names, reflecting the custom of naming the child for the day on which he or she was born. Since Africans spoke different languages, there would have been variations in these names, a fact that is not often acknowledged. One eighteenth-century attempt in Jamaica to produce the English equivalent of one version of these names follows.[54]

Male	Female	Day
Cudjo	Juba	Monday
Cubbenah	Beneba	Tuesday
Quaco	Cuba or Cubena	Wednesday
Quao	Abba	Thursday
Cuffee or Cuff	Phibba	Friday
Quamin	Mimba	Saturday
Quashee or Quash	Quasheba	Sunday

In time, some slaves used the English equivalent of these names. Thus, it was not unusual for someone to be called "Monday" or "Friday." One variation on this pattern was to be named after the month in which one was born. It is not entirely clear what deeper meanings were held by these names, but their persistence suggests their cultural importance, continued vitality, and efficacy.

While slaveowners invariably sought to rename the Africans they purchased, they did not always interfere in the naming of the children born in the quarters. Such interference was more prevalent where the slave population was small but became less so on large plantations. There were exceptions, of course, and even on large plantations masters sometimes chose the name of the child of a favorite slave. For the most part, however, parents named their own children, although there was probably some deference to the wishes of the owners when appropriate.

The changes in the choice of names tell us a great deal about black society in formation. While there was more of a tendency to choose African names in the colonial period, this had changed somewhat by the nineteenth century, when the creole population had become dominant. Along the way, slaves gave their children (or had given to them) a wide range of names that reflected their uneasy groping for place within their communities and the larger world. There was, consequently, much experimentation with naming; Anglicized names had not yet acquired special familial significance and had not yet assumed generational meanings by association with grandparents and other kin. Thus, the pool of names appeared to be larger in the late eighteenth century than in the nineteenth century, at least on those plantations that have been subjected to systematic analysis.

As soon as slaves began to develop networks of kin relationships, they began to name their children after revered grandparents, fathers, aunts, uncles, brothers and sisters, and so on. Not only did this reflect the importance of kin but it also reduced the pool of names and made the naming process more systematic and imbued with greater meanings. In a sense, second- and third-generation slaves replicated the African practice of attaching deep significance to names. The actual names changed as the process of creolization continued, but the deep cultural significance attached to names persisted. Among the creoles, names came to symbolize blood relationships and celebrated those linkages much as they did in the African societies.

When seen in this light, the actual names that the slaves chose reveal much about the process of their acculturation. The adoption of classical names–such as Pompey and Caesar–that were probably imposed by the masters, reflected a stage in the evolutionary process. Similarly, the tendency to embrace biblical names–Mary, Joseph, Abraham, Samson, Hannah, and so on indicated the slaves' exposure to Christianity and their embrace of that religion's heroes and heroines. In time, many of these names began to be culturally refashioned, assuming special meanings for the black population and serving to unite kinfolk, both the living and the dead.

Children probably did not always appreciate the significance of their names. But that would surely come with time as they became socialized into the network of relationships that provided the foundation of the community. In spite of the idyllic picture that some scholars have painted for the early childhood of slaves, the reality was probably quite different. As previously mentioned, a high proportion of them could expect to die before the tenth birthday. Fathers could be sold away and mothers too, but to a lesser extent. Labor demands, however trifling, could be imposed on them by their masters at an early age, cutting short the abandon associated with these early, formative years.

Children, at least in the years immediately preceding emancipation, grew up in an expanding slave community with its own ethos and social and cultural mechanisms. They played with their kin and black friends and with young white boys and girls, blurring with the innocence of childhood the racial and status differences. Lunsford Lane, a former slave who lived in North Carolina, recalled that he played "with the other boys and girls, colored and white, in the yard." Lane "knew no difference between myself and the white children, nor did they seem to know any in turn." But this would change as he got older. He noted that when he began to work at ten or eleven, he "discovered the difference between myself and my master's white children. They began to order me about, and were told to do so by my master and mistress. I found, too, that they had learned to read while I was not permitted to have a book in my hand."[55]

Like Lunsford Lane, Frederick Douglass had a pleasant recollection of his very early childhood. "The first seven or eight years of the slave-boy's life," Douglass wrote, "are about as full of sweet content as those of the most favored and petted *white* children of the slaveholder . . . freed from all restraint, the slave–boy can be, in his life and conduct, a genuine boy, doing whatever his boyish nature suggests." Others remembered a much harsher life in the early years. Thomas Jones, for example, said that he was "made to feel, in my boyhood's first experience, that I was inferior and degraded."[56] Jones's comment, of course, referred to the impact of slavery on one's sense of self, while Douglass addressed the playful childhood pursuits and seemed to ignore the larger question of how a young person was affected and his self-understanding shaped by being human chattel.

The very troubling issue of the impact of slavery on the young must be addressed, but it does not yield any neat or easy answers. Since the majority of the slaves by the mid-nineteenth century had been born into slavery, it is important to understand their childhood experiences and their socialization in order to fully appreciate their adult personalities.

The normal playfulness that characterized their young lives and the idyllic depiction of the early years by some former slaves and contemporary observers do not tell the complete story. In ways that were subtle and not so subtle, children were being socialized into a life of servitude.

From an early age, sensitive children could hardly have been unaware of the fact that they and their parents belonged to "massa." They may not have grasped the full implications of that reality, but they observed their parents' humiliation at the hands of white society and the frequent powerlessness of those who lived in the quarters. The former slave, William Wells Brown, vividly recalled his mother's lament as she was whipped by the overseer. The young child heard "every crack of the whip and every groan of and cry of my poor mother." Unable to help his mother, but overcome by her screams, he found a temporary surcease in his bed, where he "wept aloud."[57]

No one can claim that children who witnessed such scenes remained unaffected by them. We remain uncertain, however, how they were processed and the nature of their long-term psychological consequences. James W. C. Pennington, a former slave, described the lacerations on his father's back as "the most savage cruelty." "How would you expect a son to feel at such a sight?" he enquired.[58] The children also observed that even their white counterparts could assert power over adult black men and women. A former slave recounted one such episode in terms that capture the painful realities of being human property and the constant assaults on the personhood of the enslaved. He reported that on one occasion a young white girl went into the kitchen "and for some trifle about the dinner, she struck my mother, who pushed her away, and she fell to the floor." The girl reported the incident to her father, who responded by whipping his mother and then "called his daughter and told her to take her satisfaction of her, and she did beat her until she was satisfied."[59]

Parents tried to shield their children as much as they could from witnessing such humiliation and abuse. But it is doubtful whether they achieved much success in this regard. No one could always predict when whites would inflict physical pain on their chattel or hurl verbal abuse at them. Impressionable children saw where real power resided, and no amount of parental protection and support could obscure that fact. Nevertheless, parents probably never ceased trying to protect their offspring from the bullets of the master class and white society. They did this by promoting in their children a sense of self-worth and sometimes by a resort to violence. Fannie Moore brimmed with pride as she recalled how her mother "stand up for her children. . . . De old overseer he hate my mammy, cause she fought him for beatin' her chillen. Why she get more whippin' for dat dan anythin' else."[60]

Children, in some cases, accompanied their mothers to their place of work whether that was in the kitchen, the fields, or elsewhere. In some cases, particularly on the larger plantations, they were placed in the care of an elderly woman or nurse once their mothers resumed their regular duties after giving birth. The ages of these children varied, but the oldest could be as old as ten or twelve. The quality of the supervision depended on the nurse's age, her disposition, and the number of children entrusted to her care. A Scandinavian woman who visited the South in the 1850s reported that she had seen "Sometimes as many as sixty or more [small children] together, and their guardians were a couple of old Negro witches who with a rod of reeds kept rule over these poor little black lambs, who with an unmistakable expression of fear and horror shrank back whenever the threatening witches came forth, flourishing their rods."[61]

Infants were also placed in the care of their slightly older siblings. Frances Kemble reported that on the Butler Island Plantation in Georgia:

> The poor little Negro sucklings were cared for (I leave to your own judgment how efficiently or how tenderly) by these half-savage slips of slavery–carried by them to the fields where their mothers were under the lash, to receive their needful nourishment, and then carried back again to the "settlement," . . . where they wallowed unheeded in utter filth and neglect until the time again returned for their being carried to their mother's breast.[62]

Childhood was a relatively short period of time in the lives of slave children. Both sexes assumed regular household and plantation chores by the time they were ten or twelve. Ties of friendship with white children gradually snapped as the worlds of work, emerging adolescence, and the racial divide sent them in different directions, with different possibilities. Parents could no longer shield their children from the realities of slavery, the only life that most of them would know. Harriet Jacobs was acutely aware of the differences between the life chances of a young child who was a slave and her free white counterpart. She recalled:

> I once saw two beautiful children playing together. One was a fair white child; the other was her slave, and also her sister. When I saw them embracing each other, and heard their joyous laughter, I turned sadly away from the lovely sight. I foresaw the inevitable blight that would fall upon the little slave girl's heart. I knew how soon her laughter would be changed to sighs. The fair child grew up to be a still fairer woman. . . . How had those years dealt with her slave sister, the little playmate of her childhood? She, also, was very beautiful; but the flowers and sunshine of love were not for her. She drank the cup of sin, and shame, and misery, whereof her persecuted race are compelled to drink.[63]

In spite of the inevitable problems that the slaves faced in maintaining their kin and family relationships, many were not overwhelmed by the task. It is worth stressing, however, that the emergence of enduring kin relationships was a double-edged sword. On the one hand, the enslaved derived enormous social and psychic rewards from being anchored in communities united by blood. On the other, these developments helped ensure the continuing strength of the institution of slavery and, ironically, the perpetuation of the oppression of the black population. Slaves who enjoyed their kin and family relationships did not usually want to risk such comforts by challenging the institution. Consequently, they tended to be more quiescent and responsive to the demands of their owners. Then, too, the children of these unions, if fortune did not intervene, added to the size of the exploited labor force. Thus, in a pernicious way, strong kin and family arrangements served the interests of the masters as much as they met the needs of the slaves. The kin and family arrangements of the slaves emerged slowly over the long haul. The process began during that long first century but accelerated as the population increased and became more concentrated in the eighteenth century. By 1750 the structure of their kin and family life had begun to take a distinctive shape with its own configurations, naming patterns, and gender roles. Kin and family arrangements were constantly evolving and adjusting to the realities of slavery and Christian norms. These arrangements were always subjected to enormous external pressures. But in the end, they proved to be remarkably resilient. The expanding networks of relationships that the enslaved created met their needs as best they could.

Notes

1. Cheryl Ann Cody, "Naming, Kinship, and Estate Dispersal: Notes on Slave Family Life on a South Carolina Plantation, 1786 to 1833," *William and Mary Quarterly*, 3rd Series, 39 (1982), 193.
2. Ann Patton Malone, *Sweet Chariot: Slave Family and Household Structure in Nineteenth-Century Louisiana* (Chapel Hill: University of North Carolina Press, 1992), 241.
3. Oakes, *Slavery and Freedom*, xvii.
4. Jean R. Soderlund, "Black Women in Colonial Pennsylvania," *Pennsylvania Magazine of History and Biography*, 107 (1983), 54.
5. Genovese, *Roll Jordan Roll*, 464.
6. Herbert Gutman, *The Black Family in Slavery and Freedom 1750-1925* (New York: Vintage, 1976), 84–85.
7. Harriet Jacobs, *Incidents in the Life of a Slave Girl: An Authentic Historical Narrative Describing the Horrors of Slavery as Experienced by Black Women*, ed. L. Maria Child (New York: Harcourt Brace Jovanovich, 1973), 77.
8. Morris, *Southern Slavery and the Law*, 303–321.
9. Richard Sutch, "The Breeding of Slaves for Sale and the Westward Expansion of Slavery, 1850-1860," in Stanley Engerman and Eugene Genovese, eds., *Race and Slavery in*

the Western Hemisphere: Quantitative Studies (Princeton: Princeton University Press, 1975), 177–178.

10. Gutman, *The Black Family,* 77.
11. Jacqueline Jones, "'My Mother was much of a Woman': Black Women, Work, and the Family Under Slavery," *Feminist Studies,* 8 (1982), 238.
12. John Blassingame, *The Slave Community: Plantation Life in the Antebellum South,* revised edition (New York: Oxford, 1979), 158.
13. Genovese, *Roll Jordan Roll,* 469.
14. Gutman, *The Black Family,* 159.
15. Soderlund, "Black Women in Colonial Pennsylvania," 54.
16. Genovese, *Roll Jordan Roll,* 452.
17. Ira Berlin, "Time, Space, and the Evolution of Afro-American Society on British Mainland North America," *American Historical Review,* 85 (1980), 74.
18. Genovese, *Roll Jordan Roll,* 481.
19. Gutman, *The Black Family,* 348.
20. Ibid., 276–277.
21. Ibid., 275.
22. Genovese, *Roll Jordan Roll,* 481.
23. Gutman, *The Black Family,* 331.
24. Piersen, *Black Yankees,* 89–90.
25. Mary Beth Norton et al., "The Afro-American Family in the Age of Revolution," in Ira Berlin and Ronald Hoffman, eds., *Slavery and Freedom in the Age of the American Revolution* (Charlottesville: University of Virginia Press, 1983), 176–178.
26. Gilbert Osofsky, *Puttin' On Ole Massa: The Slave Narratives of Henry Bibb, William Wells Brown, and Solomon Northup* (New York, 1969), 80–81.
27. Genovese, *Roll Jordan Roll,* 474.
28. Norton et al., "The Afro-American Family," 178.
29. Allan Kulikoff, "The Beginnings of the Afro-American Family in Maryland," in Aubrey Land, Lois G. Carr, and Edward C. Papenfuse, eds., *Law, Society, and Politics in Early Maryland* (Baltimore: Johns Hopkins University Press, 1977), 179.
30. Malone, *Sweet Chariot,* 14–15.
31. Gutman, *The Black Family,* 63.
32. Ibid., 70.
33. Genovese, *Roll Jordan Roll,* 458.
34. Ibid., 463.
35. Piersen, *Black Yankees,* 89–90.
36. Gutman, *The Black Family,* 12–16.
37. Freehling, *The Road to Disunion,* 71.
38. Oakes, *Slavery and Freedom,* 71.
39. Gutman, *The Black Family, 146.*
40. Ibid., 21; Paul David et al., *Reckoning with Slavery: A Critical Study of the Quantitative History of American Negro Slavery* (New York, 1976), 94–113.
41. David, *Reckoning with Slavery,* 94–113.
42. McPherson, *The Battle Cry,* 38.
43. Kay and Cary, *Slavery in North Carolina,* 154.
44. Jacobs, *Incidents in the Life of a Slave Girl,* 14.
45. Oakes, *Slavery and Freedom,* 23.
46. See Eblen, *Growth of the Black Population,* 288; Kenneth F. Kiple and Virginia H. Kiple, "Slave Child Mortality: Some Nutritional Answers to a Perennial Puzzle," *Journal of Social History,* 10 (1977), 299; Michael Johnson, "Smothered Slave Infants: Were Slave Mothers at Fault?" *Journal of Southern History,* 47 (1981), 495.
47. William Dusinberre, *Them Dark Days: Slavery in the American Rice Swamps* (New York: Oxford, 1996), 51, 84–85.
48. Genovese, *Roll Jordan Roll,* 497.

49. Gutman, *The Black Family*, 81.
50. Olaudah Equiano, *The Life of Olaudah Equiano, or Gustava Vassa the African*, 2 vols., reprint (London: Dawson, 1969), i, 31.
51. John C. Inscoe, "Carolina Slave Names: An Index to Acculturation," *Journal of Southern History*, 49 (1983), 533.
52. Hennig Cohen, "Slave Names in Colonial South Carolina," *American Speech*, 28 (1952), 103–104.
53. Inscoe, "Carolina Slave Names," 532.
54. Cohen, "Slave Names in Colonial South Carolina," 104.
55. Charles H. Nichols, ed., *Black Men in Chains: Narratives by Escaped Slaves* (New York, 1972), 97–98.
56. Frederick Douglass, *My Bondage and My Freedom* (New York, 1855), 40–41; Thomas Jones, *The Experiences of Thomas Jones, Who Was a Slave for Forty-Three Years* (Boston, 1850), 5.
57. Osofsky, *Puttin' On Ole Massa*, 180.
58. James W.C. Pennington, *The Fugitive Blacksmith; or Events in the History of James W.C. Pennington* (Westport, CT: Negro Universities Press, 1971), 211.
59. John Blassingame, *Slave Testimony: Two Centuries of Letters, Speeches, and Autobiographies* (Baton Rouge: Louisiana State University Press, 1977), 132–133.
60. Genovese, *Roll Jordan Roll*, 499.
61. Wille Lee Rose, *Slavery and Freedom*, ed., William Freehling (New York: Oxford, 1982), 44–45.
62. Frances Kemble, *Journal*, 359–360.
63. Jacobs, *Incidents in the Life of a Slave Girl*, 28–29.

Religious Life Under Slavery

Slave societies of the Americas have been noted for the vitality and exuberance of their religious practices. While this has evoked much comment and even admiration, the roles that the multiplicity of religious beliefs and practices played in the quarters have never been satisfactorily explained, at least from the standpoint of the practitioners. In many instances, contemporary scholars, often Christians themselves, have viewed the religious behavior of African slaves through Christian lenses, an approach that distorts more than it reveals. The challenge is to determine the actual religious beliefs of American slaves over time and to understand how they shaped behavior, morals, values, and worldviews.

This is no easy task under the best of circumstances. But it becomes more complex when one tries to understand the belief systems of other peoples in the past, particularly those who left few written records about such matters. From a theoretical and methodological standpoint, it is also necessary to understand these beliefs on their own terms and avoid seeing Christianity as the norm or the standard against which they should be measured. We must appreciate the fact that the Africans, as we shall see, came from societies with deeply held religious beliefs and traditions. The Christians did not normally respect these religious beliefs and some of them thought that it was their duty, and their right as Christians, to try to convert the Africans to their religious practices and precepts. Such a position, of course, was rooted in the ethnocentric notions of Western cultural and religious superiority.

The contemporary historian and reader must avoid such pitfalls. We must abandon any Western and Christian biases in reconstructing the religious history of the peoples of African descent. In other words, we should not start with the assumption that what Christianity had to offer was superior to what the African religions represented. Not only does such a position interfere with our understanding of the African peoples and their religions, but it often leads us to criticize some slaveowners and representatives of Christian denominations for neglecting the souls of the Africans. Historians have frequently done this because of their assumptions, usually not recognized, that Christianity was a "good thing" for the African peoples. That may be a justifiable theological position to hold, but it has no place in a historical discussion of the beliefs of the slaves, to say nothing of the perverse judgment on African cosmologies that it conveys. The reader should also not confuse the important and varied role of Christianity in contemporary black America with that which it played at an earlier time and should also not minimize the meanings and implications of religious conversion for the African-born.

The peoples who came to North America from West and West Central Africa brought with them a coherent set of religious ideas and practices. Their societies had developed elaborate and complex cosmologies long before the start of the slave trade. Although many of the ethnographic sources upon which we rely for information on African traditional religions lack historical depth and depict them in a static, timeless fashion, certain generalizations can be cautiously advanced. First, African religious ideas cannot be meaningfully isolated from those that inform economic, political, and social life. Thus, they are part of a tightly woven fabric of interrelated ideas that explain the origins of the universe and the nature of human beings and connects them to the worlds of the living and the dead. Their cosmologies explain evil and misfortune, establish codes of behavior, and elucidate the relationship of human beings to the Supreme Being. All of these societies have highly systematized rituals and archetypal symbols or sacred images of gods, ancestors, or things. In addition, there is a hierarchy of religious specialists, such as priests, prophets, and diviners.

In spite of considerable variations in the nature of these beliefs and in their expression, there was a common set of principles, broad cores of understandings that appear to have transcended ethnic boundaries. Most, if not all, of these societies accepted the concept of a Supreme Being, believed in lesser gods, ancestor worship, the efficacy of spirits, and so on. Similarly, their cosmologies tended to make no distinctions between the religious and the secular aspects of life. Religious beliefs both shaped and were reflected in their art, their music, their dance, their worldviews, and assumptions. One's identity and personhood and one's sense of who one was in a society came from, and was inextricably bound up with, one's religious beliefs and heritage.

Seen in this light, to divest the Africans of their religious beliefs was, in effect, to destroy their core, their personhood. The African-born persons who embraced Christianity underwent a cultural and psychic transfiguration with all of its awful and awesome consequences. It meant a remaking of themselves, a state that few achieved. It may be argued, of course, that the transformational leap for Christianized Africans was not as wide as this argument implies, since there were similarities between Christian beliefs and those of the Africans.

Such a claim may not be without merit, but it is risky nonetheless. African religious behavior was shaped, conditioned, circumscribed, as well as legitimized by a whole series of rituals that had profound meanings in their particular context. The ceremonies imposed meanings on the activity, artifact, or practice. Thus, the ceremonial context was all-important; nothing had any meaning unless it was conferred by the appropriate rituals and by those empowered to do so. Beneath the apparent similarities with Christianity, more complex principles and meanings often functioned. Thus, African beliefs and practices cannot be abstracted from their cultural setting, and perceived similarities with Christian practice may obscure more than they reveal. No scholar would seriously maintain that European Christians confused the deeper meanings and symbolism of their cross with that used by the Bakongo, but somehow the reverse is repeated by several authorities, betraying perhaps Western condescension to the Africans' beliefs.

The forced African immigrants, then, brought highly complex belief systems that had served them well. Scattered across the colonies in that long first century, it must have been difficult for them to find meaningful religious expressions and interaction. Many rituals had to be performed collectively, and a priest or some other religious authority had to be present to do the honors. Other activities took place only in sacred places with objects that possessed special meaning and efficacy. In some cases, only the priests knew the religious secrets and determined the moment for their revelation and expression. None of this could be recreated easily. For a people whose lives were built around ceremony and ritual and who drew strength from their religious practices conducted in a particular setting, they must have experienced a spiritual death. Not until their numbers increased were they able to reconstruct the broad contours of their beliefs, and even this would have been exceedingly difficult to accomplish.

The records are silent on the private pain of these Africans, uprooted and bereft of the psychic balm that a community-centered religion helped to produce. Being separated from kinfolk as well added to the sense of profound loss. In such a state, some Africans were likely to blame their misfortune on themselves, on some transgression that brought forth such punishment. Some would have questioned the power of their own deity, who had failed to protect them from such adversity.

In their despair, as Monica Schuler has shown for African immigrants in Jamaica, some probably came to accept the white man's sorcery and magic, that is, his religious power, as superior to their own.[1]

It is this acceptance of the superior power of the white man's sorcery that helps to explain the receptivity to Christianity on the part of some Africans. On another level, it may also be surmised that Christianity would appeal to those who, having lost everything, sought to reorganize their lives in a new land. Christianity gave structure to their emotional and spiritual thrashings even as it exacted its own price.

CHRISTIANIZING THE AFRICANS

The English paid no systematic attention to the religious care of their slaves in the early years. This stemmed, in part, from the conviction that Christians should not enslave fellow Christians. Accordingly, to baptize the African slave would be to contribute directly to his manumission. In spite of this belief, some Africans were baptized, presumably after an appropriate period of instruction. It is clear that a few slaves achieved their freedom as a result of their conversion, although their liberation was not always granted without a fight. Two court cases illustrate this latter observation.

The first case was heard in Northumberland County, Virginia, in 1655. Elizabeth Key petitioned for her freedom on the grounds that she was a Christian; that her father was a free person, thereby making her free at that time; and that she had been sold to her present master to serve only for a period of nine years and that time had elapsed. It is instructive, in this context, that the litigant argued that her Christianization should have guaranteed her freedom. We may presume that she based this submission on perceived behavior. The court upheld her suit, but the verdict was appealed. Not until several months later was Key able to claim her freedom.[2]

The second suit was brought in 1667 in Lower Norfolk County by a slave known only as Fernando. Fernando maintained that he "was a Christian and had been several years in Ingland" and that he should not serve for a period of time longer than that of a white servant. Unlike that brought by Key, Fernando's suit failed since his supporting documents, according to the record of the proceedings, were written "in Portugell or some other language which the Court could not understand."[3]

Probably fearing a proliferation of such cases, the Virginia Assembly soon resolved the question of whether baptism brought freedom. As we noted in Chapter 4, the House of Burgesses passed a law in 1667 stating that baptism did not confer freedom. Freed from the uncertainty that manumission followed conversion, the legislators hoped that masters "may more carefully endeavour the propagation of christianity by permitting children, though slaves, or those of greater growth if capable to be admitted to that sacrament."[4] By 1706, five other colonies–Maryland, the Carolinas, New York, and New Jersey had endorsed this principle.

It should be emphasized that Christian instruction was intended to accomplish more than just the substitution of one set of religious beliefs for another. Christianity had a political function as well. In time, it came to be perceived as a central agency in the cultural remaking of the Africans, imparting to them the values and worldviews of the Europeans. Normally, the view was expressed that the adoption of Christian principles would improve the moral character of the Africans. In practice, this ethnocentric and Eurocentric view meant that the Africans and their progeny had to divest themselves of what Sterling Stuckey has called their Africanity and embrace a set of new beliefs and ways of doing things. Accordingly, it is a mistake to focus solely on the purely religious dimensions of Christianity and to ignore the other fundamental changes in the lives of the Africans it was intended to bring in its wake. The British colonial secretary, Lord Bathurst, said it well in 1823 when he saw the adoption of Christianity by slaves in the Caribbean as an "indispensable necessity . . . the foundation of every beneficial change in [their] character and future condition."[5]

The religious life of the slave constituted one of, if not the principal, terrain upon which the battle for the control of the African's personhood was fought. Africans who embraced Christianity had to reject much of their past assumptions and beliefs, a not-too-easy process given the integrated nature of the religious and the secular. Not surprisingly, Christianity's impact on the African-born person in America, in contradistinction to its effect on the creoles, was relatively minor. Most African-born persons would not pay the price that Christian conversion demanded. Fundamentally, conversion to Christianity meant the embrace of a new cosmological world.

During the long first century, English colonial policy, however, gave some encouragement to the Christianization of the Africans. In 1660, for example, the Crown asked the Council for Foreign Plantations

> to consider how such of the Natives or such as are purchased by you from other parts to be servants or slaves may be best invited to the Christian Faith, and be made capable of being baptized thereunto, it being to the honor of our Crowne and of the Protestant Religion that all persons in any of our Dominions should be taught the knowledge of God, and be made acquainted with the misteries of Salvation.[6]

Colonial governors were urged sporadically to promote the Christianization of the black population. The Church of England also favored the conversion of the Africans. In 1680 the Reverend Morgan Godwyn published a book in which he suggested that attention be paid to "those

Myriads of hungry and distressed Souls abroad . . . our Peoples Slaves and Vassals, but from whom also the Bread of Life is most sacrilegiously detained."[7] The Bishop of London, who exercised jurisdiction over the colonies, recommended conversion from time to time. Similarly, the missionary arm of the church, the Society for the Propagation of the Gospel in Foreign Parts, took an interest in the spiritual welfare of the slaves from the time of its foundation in 1701. A few years later, a group known as The Associates of Dr. Bray was created. Named after Dr. Thomas Bray, a famous Anglican priest, the groups sought to instruct "in the Christian Religion the Young Children of Negro Slaves [and] such of their Parents as shew themselves inclinable [and] desirous to be so instructed."[8] None of these organizations had much success.

In fact, the Church of England and the other denominations could hardly have approached their mission to the slaves with much moral fervor. As slaveowners and as Englishmen, religious leaders shared the same negative assumptions about the Africans, recognized their "otherness," and acted from a sense of cultural and racial superiority. None of the denominations, with the possible exception of the Quakers, found slavery to be incompatible with Christianity. The Bishop of London observed as late as 1727 that conversion to Christianity did not result in "the least Alteration in Civil Property; that the Freedom which Christianity gives, is a Freedom from the Bondage of Sin and Satan, and from the Dominion of those Lusts and Passions and inordinate Desires; but as to their outward condition they remained as before even after baptism."[9] The church acknowledged the receipt of slaves as gifts, and priests owned Africans as well.

The record of the other denominations and sects was similar. Congregational clergymen were slaveowners, and so were the Puritans. Both groups lacked a general representative body, so slaveowning was a matter left to the determination of each congregation. Presbyterians, Baptists, and Methodists arrived after 1740 and attracted substantial support from whites. More elitist in their orientation, the Presbyterians counted many slaveowners in their ranks. The Baptists and the Methodists attracted the less wealthy whites and had a tendency to make statements critical of slavery. Not until 1780 did the Methodists condemn the institution, but they compromised their position later. The Pastoral Address of 1836 declared that the church lacked the "right, wish or intention to interfere in the civil and political relation as it exists between master and slave in the slaveholding states of this union."[10]

The Society of Friends, as the Quakers were called, consistently supported the conversion of the Africans. The Yearly Meetings frequently urged masters to foster the spiritual care of the Africans and to provide them with opportunities for worship. The position of the Friends on the question of property in men is less clear-cut. Individual members were troubled by this practice, but it was not until the 1770s that members were expressly prohibited from owning slaves. Yet the Friends had the most consistent record of all the religious groups in discouraging their members from slaveholding, even if it took them a century to outlaw it.

The task of converting the slaves was difficult at best in the face of much African disinterest and the opposition of many masters. Bishop George Berkeley reported in 1731 that the planters had an "irrational contempt of the blacks, as creatures of another species, who had no right to be admitted to the sacraments." Writing in 1758, one Anglican missionary complained that "Americans look upon their slaves, to have no Souls at all, and a favourite Dog or Horse meet with more humane treatments than they."[11] Slaveowners everywhere had to be convinced that it was in their interest and that of the larger society to Christianize the Africans. Masters were reluctant to release their slaves from work to receive religious instruction and to attend worship services. As one contemporary writer in the *Athenian Oracle* noted, "Talk to a *Planter* of the *Soul* of a *Negro,* and he'll be apt to tell you (or at least his Actions speak it loudly) that the Body of one of them may be worth twenty Pounds; but the Souls of an hundred of them would not yield him one Farthing."[12]

Some colonists also feared that conversion might lead slaves, now equal in the eyes of God, to expect some social interaction with whites. Others even refused to receive the Eucharist at the same table. The Reverend Francis Le Jau, who served as an Anglican priest in South Carolina during the early eighteenth century, noted that one of his parishioners "resolved not to come to the Holy Table while slaves were "Rec[eive]d there." Some planters expressed a different kind of opposition to religious instruction for their slaves. They believed that Christianity made slaves less dependable as workers. Francis Le Jau reported that some of these persons maintained that "Baptism makes the slaves proud and undutiful."[13] Others held that "a slave is ten times worse when Xn, Yn in his State of Paganism."[14] Le Jau, for one, was careful to ensure that baptized slaves knew exactly what their conversion entailed. Each one had to swear to the following:

> You declare in the presence of God and before this congregation that you do not ask for the holy baptism out of design to free yourself from the duty and obedience you owe to your master while you live, but meekly for the good of our soul. . . ."[15]

The Reverend Cotton Mathers, the eighteenth-century New England divine, also recognized Christianity's ability to sustain and sanction slavery even in the eyes of the enslaved. This is clearly revealed in the rules of the Negro Society of Boston that were developed with his assistance. They show in an unmistakable fashion how Christianity was used to serve the interest of the master class from an early date.

IV. Wee will, as often as may bee, obtain some wise and good Man, of the *English* in the Neighborhood; and especially the *Officers* of the Church to look in upon us, and by their Presence and Council, do what they think fitting for us.

V. If any of our Number fall into the sin of *Drunkenness,* or *Swearing,* or *Cursing,* or *Lying,* or *Stealing,* or notorious *Disobedience* or *Unfaithfulness* to their Masters, wee will *admonish* him of his Miscarriage . . .

VII. Wee will, as wee have Opportunity, sett ourselves, to do all the good wee can to the other *Negro-Servants* in the Town; and if any of them should *run away* from their Masters, wee will afford them *no shelter;* but wee will do what in us lies, that they may bee discovered and punished. . . .

VIII. None of our Association, shall be *absent,* from our Meeting, without giving a *Reason* of the Absences; and it bee found that any have pretended unto their *Owners,* that they came unto Meeting, when they were otherwise and elsewhere emplo'd, wee will faithfully *inform* their owners. . . .[16]

Another example, drawn from Georgia, reveals the role that Christianity was expected to play in the lives of the slaves. William Knox, a prominent eighteenth-century Georgian slaveowner, recommended that blacks be told

There is one God in heaven who never dies and who sees and knows everything. . . . That he punishes all roguery, mischief, and lying, either before death or after it. That he punishes them for it before they die,. by putting it into their masters hearts to correct them, and after death by giving them to the Devil to burn in his own place. That he will put it into their masters hearts to be kind to those who do their work without knavery or murmuring. To take care of them in old age and sickness, and not to plague them with too much work, or to chastise them if they are not able to do it. That in the other world, after they die, he will give all good Negroes, rest from all labour, and plenty of all good things.[17]

William Knox was in good company. The Reverend Joseph Ottolenghe, an Anglican missionary who was sent to minister to the slaves in Georgia in the mid-eighteenth century, maintained that a slaveowner "would be a greater gainer if his servant should be converted to christianity, [since] he would have, instead of an immoral dishonest domestic, a faithful servant."[18] Years later, Clarissa Leavitt, a Louisiana slaveowner, reported the consequences of Christian instruction. She thought that the slaves in a particular congregation were "very much interested in the subject of religion at this time. I rejoice at it for it makes them happier here, and a promise of this bliss hereafter. And it makes them much better servants and more easily managed."[19]

Many slaveowners, as well as other colonists, were only nominally Christian, and attendance at church on Sundays was not one of their frequent activities. Not surprisingly, they saw little merit in their human property being allowed time off to go to a place of worship. Such concessions, they argued, also had an economic cost because of the labor lost while the slaves were being instructed. This attitude would change, however, when some masters realized that the Christian message, if carefully packaged, could serve as an effective means for the social control of the black population.

Chronically understaffed and overworked, even well-intentioned clergymen lacked the time and energy to minister to the slaves, planter opposition not withstanding. Farms, plantations, and households were often separated by long distances. One missionary in Hempstead, New York, noted that distance prevented more than just a handful of slaves to be gathered at one time for religious instruction. Similar complaints came from other parts of that colony such as Westchester and Albany counties.[20] One North Carolina clergyman spoke for many others when he complained in 1761 that it was "impossible for the Ministers in such extensive Parishes to perform their more immediate Duties in them, and find time sufficient for those poor Creatures Instructions, and very few if any of their masters will take the least Pains about it."[21]

As valid as these explanations were for the relative lack of success in converting the slaves, the principal cause was the resistance of the Africans to the new religion. Hugh Bryan, an early eighteenth-century slaveowner in South Carolina, reported sadly, "My servants were called to prayers, but none came."[22] Thus the reluctance of some whites in these formative years to encourage Christianization coincided with the opposition of many slaves to such efforts. Missionaries frequently referred to the Africans as "infidels" and "heathens," blissfully refusing to grant any efficacy to African beliefs and practices. One Anglican minister, the Reverend Powell, observed in 1722 that in his North Carolina parish few Africans "knew any Thing of God or Religion." Another rector, reporting from Craven County, North Carolina, claimed that "most of the Negroes may too justly be reckoned Heathens." The rector of Christ Church parish in South Carolina also noted in that year that the 700 slaves there were "in Infidelity."[23] Five years later, the Bishop of London thought that the greatest impediment to the Christianization of West African slaves was that they were "accustomed to the Pagan Rites and Idolatries of their own Country [and] prejudiced against all other Religions, particularly the Christian."[24] All too often the clergymen equated the absence of Christian beliefs among the Africans with the absence of religious beliefs. This was, of course, a serious error.

This confusion certainly complicated the task that the clergymen and missionaries set for themselves. Their condescension and failure to understand and respect the Africans' beliefs made them underestimate their tenacity and explain the inability to devise effective strategies to achieve their objectives. Long before the Protestants arrived in North America, the Catholic friars in Latin America had used creative methods in their proselytizing of the indigenous peoples. Among other things, they endeavored to understand the cosmology of the Indians and built upon what they determined to be similarities in the beliefs and symbolisms of Christianity and the local religions.

By 1750, the missionaries could show little results for their efforts. Most surveys showed that only a small minority of the slaves could be characterized as Christian. Not immune to the racist assumptions that affected the laity, white clergymen blamed their failure on the intellectual incapacity of blacks. In 1748, the Reverend Phillip Reading maintained that they "seem to be of a species quite different from the whites, have no abstracted ideas, cannot comprehend the meaning of faith in Christ, the nature of the fall of man, the necessity of a redeemer, with other essentials of the Christian scheme." Jonathan Boucher, another Anglican priest, was convinced of "the incorrigible Stupidity of the Majority of these wretched Creatures."[25]

Recognizing the failure of Christian proselytizing among the slaves, the Reverend Alexander Hewath reported during the War for Independence that with "a few only excepted," the slaves in South Carolina "are to this date as great strangers to Christianity, and as much under the influence of Pagan darkness, idolatry and superstition, as they were at their first arrival from Africa."[26] Similarly, a recent study of slavery in New England concluded that "after more than a century of slavery and proselytizing, the vast majority of New Englands' blacks were still outside the white churches, unconvinced and unconverted, as the eighteenth century ended."[27] In New York, the situation was much the same. John McManus notes, "Only fifty three slaves were baptized in Huntington over a period of fifty-six years, a conversion rate of less than one slave per year." He reports that in the township of Rye, "only one slave in every hundred was a Christian after ten years of proslytization."[28]. And, finally, only 7 percent of Virginia's slaves belonged to the Methodist and Baptist churches in 1790, the denominations that most actively sought their membership.[29]

The black population of the New England colonies and New York was, relatively speaking, quite small. Consequently, one would have expected that the Christianization process would have proceeded more rapidly in contrast to other colonies where there were larger concentrations of Africans and hence greater opportunities to preserve and practice their own religions. But demography was evidently not the crucial factor in determining the extent of conversion. The African-born proved to be remarkably impervious to the new religion. The old ways continued to serve them well. Swedish traveler Peter Kalm betrayed his ethnocentric bias, but he was nevertheless correct when he observed in 1748 that the blacks in the colonies "live on in their pagan darkness."[30]

Even those Africans who had been baptized cannot be said to have experienced many changes in their belief systems and interior lives. The Reverend Lang, who was the rector at St. Peters in New Kent, Virginia, in the mid-eighteenth century, said as much when he charged:

> Some people are fond of bringing their Negroe Servants to Baptism, how soon they are capable to rehearse the Creed, Lord's Prayer & Commandments and yet these live together afterwards in common without marriage or any other Christian decency's as the pagan Negroes do who never were entered into the Church membership. Those who stand Godfathers and Godmothers for children at their Baptism are extremely ignorant and never mind the solemn engagements nor can they endure to be instructed or catechiz'd so as to improve in knowledge and understanding.[31]

The opposition of the whites or their condescendingly benign tolerance not withstanding, African religious beliefs and practices endured, probably with modifications, although this dynamic process is difficult to trace. On one level, the existence of these beliefs demonstrated a profound resistance to the attempts of the Christians to change their religious assumptions, the ways in which they viewed the world around them and defined themselves. But to see this exclusively in terms of resistance is to ignore the enormity of the challenge the Christians confronted. John S. Mbiti has observed that traditional African religions "permeate all the departments of life, there is no formal distinction between the sacred and the secular, between the religious and the nonreligious, between the spiritual and the material areas of life." Conversion to Christianity would mean a fundamental change in the African's interior being, his "thought patterns, fears, social relationships, attitudes and philosophical disposition."[32] The African would undergo a metamorphosis and emerge as a new person with an altered sense of identity, bereft of a healthy belief in his past and immersed in the ways of his societal oppressors, probably more as a caricature than as a real person.

Under the circumstances, it is no wonder that some of these early Africans laughed at their peers who were seen with the Bible. According to some eighteenth-century North Carolina masters, when slaves converted, "all other slaves do laugh at them."[33] That conversion severely shook the personhood of the Africans is revealed in some of the comments they made about the slave trade, their heritage, and themselves. Chloe Spear, an African-born person who labored in New England was certain that "[Whites] meant [the slave trade] for evil, but God meant it for good. To his name be the glory."[34] To Chloe, the slave trade had brought her from Africa, but the Christian experience was a worthy compensation, ordained by God.

Ginney, an African-born person who served in Connecticut, showed how the assimilation of Christian beliefs explained her status. While she awaited death, Ginney who was the slave of the Reverend William Worthington, asked to see the Reverend Dr. Goodrich and revealed to him her hopes for the afterlife.

> "Yes, Maasa Goodrich," said Ginney, "When I die I shall go right to heaven, and knock at de door, and inquire for Massa Worthington. . . . Maasa Worthinton will come right to me; and I will say, 'Ginney's come. I want you to tell God that Ginney was always a good servant. She never lie, never steal, never use bad language.' And he will come back to the door and say, 'Ginney, you may come in.' And I will go right in, and sit in the kitchen."[35]

The poet Phillis Wheatley (circa 1753–84), who was brought to New England from Senegal in 1761 as a seven-year-old, expressed much gratitude for her forced transportation and her eventual conversion to Christianity.

> 'TWAS mercy brought me from my *Pagan* land,
> Taught my benighted soul to understand
> That there's a God, that there's a *Saviour* too:
> Once I redemption neither sought nor knew.

The imagery, "black as Cain," that she employs in the same poem, associates that color with one of the renegades of Christian lore and equates Christianity with refinement and the possibility of joining the "angelic train."

> Some view our sable race with scornful eye,
> "Their colour is a diabolic die,"
> Remember, *Christians, Negroes,* black as *Cain,*
> May be refin'd, and join th' angelic train.

In a similar vein, the creole slave and poet Jupiter Hammon (1720?–1806?) showed the ability of Christianity as packaged for slaves to sanction the system in their eyes. Hammon wanted his fellow slaves to accept their condition as ordained by the Christian God since

> . . . who of us dare dispute with God! He has commanded us to obey, and we ought to do it cheerfully, and freely. This should be done by us, not only because God commands, but because our own peace and comfort depend upon it. As we depend upon our masters for what we eat and drink and wear, and for all our comfortable things in this world, we

cannot be happay unless we please them. This we cannot do without obeying them freely. . . .[36]

In a poem that he dedicated to Phillis Wheatley in 1778, Hammon extolled the virtues of Christianity and his view that it liberated Africans from a "dark abode."

I
O come you pious youth! Adore
The wisdom of thy God,
In bringing thee from distant shore
To learn His holy word.

II
Thou mightst been left behind,
Amidst a dark abode;
God's tender mercy still combin'd,
Thou hast the holy word.

IV
God's tender mercy brought thee here;
Tost o'er the raging main;
In Christian faith thou hast a share,
Worth all the gold of Spain.

The authorities, in time, came to appreciate the potentially transforming power of Christianity for the Africans. They failed, however, to appreciate the limits that Africans as people could place on their efforts. The retention by the Africans of much of their basic beliefs demonstrated not only their deeply held nature but also the impossibility of the transfiguration that the Christians sought.

While many, if not most of the African-born remained beyond the reach of Christian proselytizers, the same cannot always be said so confidently about the creoles. Uniquely the products of the American environment, creoles were exposed to Christian influences from birth. Those who had parents who were already Christianized grew up in an atmosphere encouraging of such a religious orientation. Others could hardly have escaped, in varying degrees, some exposure to Christian beliefs and practices. The creoles who were born of African parents in the eighteenth century would have been familiar with African religious practices at firsthand, given the continuation of the slave trade. Nineteenth-century creoles, for the most part, would have had a somewhat different experience. By 1820, at the latest, an Afro-American Christianity with its distinctive flavor had taken shape, even if many slaves still distanced themselves from it.

The mid-eighteenth century represents the time when Christianity began to make appreciable inroads in the black population. This was the consequence of internal as well as external developments. A creole population of some significance had emerged by then, and its members formed the group that was most responsive to Christian appeals. By midcentury, the enslaved population had also begun to increase at a faster rate naturally than it did from the slave trade, a fact that had a direct bearing on the success of the missionary efforts. These persons lacked the socialization into the complex African religions and world-views of their parents, so baptism did not mean a fundamental break with the past, the embrace of a new spiritual order, and the inner tur-moil that conversion undoubtedly produced. These creoles shared in the cultural heritages of their parents but they were also nurtured in an environment much different from that of their ancestors. Africa and the ethnic groups from which their parents hailed would continue to have profound symbolic and emotional meanings for them, but none could claim familiarity with its terrain, none could speak authoritatively about the old ways. As new peoples, in a sense, creoles could not have been shielded from or immune to the effects of the religious forces operating in the land of their birth.

The creoles' familiarity with the English language from birth (or variations of it) facilitated their understanding of Christian dogma, and ultimately their conversion. Missionaries had claimed consistently that the Africans' lack of proficiency in English was a major impediment to their Christianization. In 1754, for example, the Anglican missionary Joseph Ottolenghe complained that Georgia's African-born slaves "are so ignorant of ye English Language, & none can be found to talk in their own, yt it is a great while before you can get them to understand what ye Meaning of Words is, & yt that without such a knowledge Instructions would prove Vain, & the Ends proposed abortive, for how can a Propo-sition be believed, without first being understood? And how can it be understood if the Person to whom it is offer'd has no Idea even of the Sound of those Words which expresses the Proposition?"[37] Such nega-tive assessments declined as the ratio of creoles to Africans increased and seemed to have disappeared altogether in the nineteenth century.

The series of religious revivals known as the Great Awakening and which began in the late 1730s played a significant role in the process of making Christians of some of the slaves. From New England to the Lower South, the renegade Anglican priest George Whitefield and oth-ers electrified thousands of whites and blacks, bringing them a message of redemption and hope. Theirs was a message presented with vigor and emotion, rich in metaphors and in a vernacular easily understood by the literate and the unlettered alike. At revivals held in churches and outdoors, large numbers of blacks, probably mostly creoles, were pro-foundly touched by Whitefield's fiery oratory, his denunciation of evil, and his promise that all could achieve eternal salvation.

Whitefield promoted a form of peoples' Christianity that encouraged congregational participation and an open and free expression of emotions when possessed by the Spirit. The slaves were attracted to this style of worship; it gave them a sense of communal release and opportunities to proclaim an ecstatic joy in their beliefs. One observer reported from Virginia that the slaves who attended these services "are more noisy in time of preaching than the whites, and are more subject to bodily exercise, and if they meet with any encouragement in these things, they grow extravagant."[38]

To the slaves who heard the message, the promise of an afterlife free from pain, toil, and servitude must have been particularly appealing. Whitefield, for one, explained that their earthly travail was a necessary prerequisite for their redemption. "Shew them, O Shew them," he pleaded, "the necessity of being deeply wounded before they can be capable of healing by Jesus Christ."[39] For a people reeling from daily wounds and whose possibilities were circumscribed by their condition, the expectation of a healing and a deliverance through Christ must have taken on a compelling immediacy.

The combined impact of the demographic changes and the appeal of Evangelical Christianity produced a surge of black Christians. Statistics from Virginia for the second half of the eighteenth century show an increasing number of black members in the Baptist and Methodist churches in particular. Membership figures are, of course, misleading because not all who accepted the Word became formal members of a church. The stringent rules of membership excluded some persons. One Presbyterian Church in Hanover County, Virginia, baptized the enslaved only "after they had been Catechumens for some time, and given credible evidence, not only of their acquaintance with the important doctrines of the Christian Religion, but also a deep sense of these things upon their spirits, and a life of the strictest Morality and Piety."[40] Others must have wanted to avoid the ugly sneers of white Christians. The Reverend Isaac Browne, a Methodist minister in New York, would hardly have welcomed these converts into his church. He noted that blacks "who were lately called Heathens, seem many of them now to be a miraculous compound of Paganism and Methodism."[41]

The fact is, however, that blacks did enroll in white churches, usually constituting a minority of the membership. Some historians have seen this development as a form of egalitarianism that, unfortunately, was shortlived. This is a misreading of the situation as it existed. Masters and servants the world over have always worshipped together, but this practice has never served to blur and confuse legal and social distinctions. Each group knew its place and undoubtedly honored the rules of appropriate social conduct. When George Whitefield preached at a church in Hanover County, Virginia, in 1762, he was "obliged to make the negroes go out to make room for the white people."[42] Slaves occupied separate pews and were sometimes hidden from general view. White Christians in these churches recognized blacks as possessing souls, accorded them membership, and held them to the same standards of morality, but there could be no doubt as to who enjoyed a superior status. A former slave who labored in Louisiana reported, "I seed my mammy whipped for shoutin' at white folks' meetin'. Old massa stripped her to the waist and whipped her with a bullwhip."[43] In some Virginia churches a slave could be expelled for disobeying his master.

The institutional arrangements that the slaves made for their Christian worship tell us a great deal about the development of black America and the emergence of a distinctive black consciousness. Separate or independent congregations gave expression to and shaped this nascent identity. It should not surprise anyone that black America's first institutions were of a religious nature, given the profound spiritual traditions of the people, the transcendental importance of the supernatural and the psychic and other needs that religion met.

As far as is known, the first independent black congregation was established at Silver Bluff in Aiken County, South Carolina, between 1773 and 1775. This Baptist congregation started out rather small, having no more than eight members at the outset although it soon increased to thirty. Most, if not all, of the original members were the slaves of George Galphin, a businessman who allowed them to worship at his mill. The first regular pastor was David George, a creole slave. This congregation spawned others. George Liele, a slave who later received his freedom, founded a church at Yama Craw, adjacent to Savannah, Georgia, in 1777. Liele remained at this church until 1782, when he undertook missionary work in Jamaica. He established a church in Kingston that boasted a membership of 350 in 1791, most of them slaves.

The decades of the 1780s and the 1790s saw the establishment of additional congregations. By 1801 there were a total of ten such congregations in Kentucky, South Carolina, Georgia, and Virginia. The Savannah Georgia First Colored, a reincarnation of the congregation at Yama Craw, was the largest of them all. By 1800, it had a membership of 700 persons under the pastorage of Andrew Bryan, who had been converted by George Liele.[44] A creole, Bryan was born in Goose Creek, South Carolina, in 1737. He purchased his freedom around 1787 or 1788, just about the time of his ordination. A religious leader of some influence, Bryan was an unfortunate child of his times. He acquired eight slaves, joining the ranks of those free blacks before him—and later—who like the whites, debased their fellow men by owning them.

Many other black preachers appear in the records as the eighteenth century waned and black Christianity took firmer roots. The children of the Great Awakening, several preachers received licenses from the Baptists and to a lesser extent from the Methodists. Most were probably creoles and few had much formal education. An Anglican priest spoke contemptuously of the Evangelicals in 1776 when he observed that the "most illiterate among them are their Teachers, even Negroes speak in their meetings."[45] Some of these preachers spoke before integrated audiences and on occasion even pastored white congregations. The primary importance of these developments, however, does not reside in the interracial nature of some of their ministrations. They were the persons who began to lay the institutional foundations of the black church and that was no mean achievement. Other blacks, particularly free persons would build on these foundations in the nineteenth century (see Chapter 7).

The creation of an institutional framework was not indispensable for the practice of religious beliefs in the nineteenth century, or for any other time. Most converts were evidently not formal members of a church. Several tendencies may be observed. Some slaves worshipped in independent black congregations where those existed. By 1865 there were 563 black congregations of various sizes in the South.[46] Not all of the members were slaves, of course. The Methodists led the way with 329 congregations, and the Baptists were next with 130. Other denominations included the African Methodist Episcopal Zion with 3 congregations and the African Methodist Episcopal with 89 churches. Overall, it is estimated that between one-sixth to one-quarter of the slaves had some association with these churches in 1865.[47]

Some slaves attended the white churches with their masters. Their proportion is unknown, but the practice was widespread throughout the South. Much depended on the degree of the master's own religious beliefs and his concern for the spiritual life of his human chattel. If he were a regular churchgoer or held strong beliefs, he would encourage the slaves to attend worship services and may even have insisted on it. Much also rested on the willingness of the white congregation to accept black worshippers, even if they were not likely to be seated in the sanctuary. In some cases, probably a majority, separate services would be held for the black congregants in order to mollify white sensibilities. A number of masters, in the absence of a preacher, conducted religious services for their slaves.

Perhaps the majority of the Christian converts worshipped at their own Praise meetings and lacked any institutional affiliations. In some cases, the two were not mutually exclusive. Clara Brim, a former Louisiana slave recalled:

> When Sunday came old Massa ask who want to go to Church. Dem what wants could ride hoss-back or walk. Us go to the white folks church. Dey sot in front and us sot in back. Us had prayer meetin' too, regular each week. One old culled man a sort of preacher. He de leader in 'ligion.[48]

Whether these prayer meetings were held in the open air, or in log cabins or other convenient places, the faithful could listen to their own preachers and pursue their own styles of worship.

OTHER RELIGIOUS OPTIONS

Studies of the religious life of the slaves often convey the impression that the vast majority were Christianized. This conclusion cannot be sustained for the period before 1800, and it may even be doubted for the largely creole population of the nineteenth century. Undoubtedly, the conversion rates increased in the decades immediately preceding Emancipation, but no credible measure of its extent exists. It would have been perfectly normal for some of the enslaved to avoid any association with Christians or to pay only perfunctory attention to the attempts to convert them.

There is an increasing amount of evidence indicating that a considerable number of Muslim slaves were included in the slave cargoes. Islam had penetrated West Africa from around the eighth century, gaining many converts over time. In fact, almost 50 percent of the African-born slaves hailed from such areas as the Senegambia, the Gold Coast, and the Bight of Benin, all of which had significant Muslim populations. It is safe to assume, therefore, that practitioners of Islam were enslaved and sold to the traders, although this assertion cannot be supported statistically.

Many slaves in the quarters retained names such as Mustapha and Mahomet, which were unquestionably Muslim in origin. Scattered evidence suggests that the faithful struggled to sustain their religion in a society that was not supportive of it. Some offered their customary daily prayers to Allah and celebrated the holy days. A few may even have possessed copies of the Qur'an. A former slave recalled that a Muslim named Israel:

> . . .pray a lot wid a book he hab wut he hide, an he take a lill mat an he say he prayuhs on it. He pray wen duh sun go up and wen duh sun go down. . . . He alluz tie he head up in a wite clawt an seem he keep a lot uh clawt on hand.[49]

Muslim slaves were probably most numerous during the era of the slave trade as new recruits were being brought constantly from their African homelands. Some of these people passed on their religion to their American-born children, but the numerical strength of Islam diminished as Christianity gained an increasing number of converts among the creoles during the nineteenth century.

The presence of Muslim slaves means that we must be careful not to exaggerate the extent of Christian beliefs and practices among the slaves. Slaves had many sacred worlds, and Christianity was only one of them and hardly the dominant one before the nineteenth century. Observing the behavior of creole slaves in Maryland's Eastern Shore in the 1740s, the Reverend Thomas Bacon reported that they were "living in as profound Ignorance of what Christianity really is (except as to a few outward Ordinances) as if they had remained in the midst of those barbarous Heathen Countries from whence their parents had been first imported."[50] Almost a century later, the Reverend Charles C. Jones, a Presbyterian clergyman, noted that slaves refrained from embracing Christianity. Writing in 1834, Jones concluded, "It is true that they have access to the house of God on the Sabbath; but it is also true that even when the privilege is in their reach a minority (and frequently a very small one) embraces it."[51]

Albert Raboteau seems to be on secure ground when he recently concluded, "The majority of slaves . . . remained only minimally touched by Christianity by the second decade of the nineteenth century."[52] It appears that Christianity achieved its most enduring successes after emancipation, but this hypothesis deserves further examination. Similarly, since only a minority of the slaves were exposed to Christianity before the nineteenth century, we should not focus our attention exclusively on the ethnocentric question of the degree of Christianization among the slaves as if that were the norm for them. We should also examine the religious beliefs and practices of the majority who embraced other options.

The nature of the beliefs of those who embraced Christianity is also a matter of considerable interest and controversy. Several historians have reconstructed versions of the slaves' religious life based primarily on evidence drawn from the antebellum years. This, of course, is questionable, particularly when the findings are presented as if those years were representative of the two and a half centuries of black servitude. Other scholars see the Christianity of the slaves as constituting a culture of resistance to their oppression, giving them autonomy and space to survive as persons. While this position is credible, it does ignore the variegated roles that Christianity played in the quarters. Such a position also exaggerates the degree to which Christian beliefs—no matter how reinterpreted and Africanized—were able to shield the slaves from those real but invisible wounds that slavery could inflict on its victims. In her memoirs, Harriet Jacobs, a former slave, cautioned against ascribing too much weight to the singing of the Christianized slaves who "struck up a hymn" and "sung as though they were as free as the birds that warbled round us." She noted:

> Precious are such moments to the poor slaves. If you were to hear them
> at such times, you might think they were happy. But can that hour of

singing and shouting sustain them through the dreary week, toiling without wages, under constant dread of the lash?[53]

One can recognize the strength, vitality, and exuberance of the Christian beliefs and practices of the enslaved without ascribing to them a role that they did not and could not have effectively played. No one would seriously argue in our own times that black Christianity is an effective countervailing force against racism and its effects.

We must be careful also not to equate religious beliefs with Christian beliefs, or religion with Christianity. This is a mistake that is often made by Westerners. Nor should we be preoccupied with determining whether some of the Africans' beliefs should be characterized as "magic" or "religions" in the sense in which social scientists use those terms today. It seems unnecessary to underscore the point that much of this scholarship is culture bound, and a contemporary Western or Christian definition of what is a magical belief may be inapplicable to other peoples at other times, to say nothing of the ethnocentricity that is implied. Jeffrey Russell's view that "no religions lack magical elements" seems entirely plausible. It is also not without some interest in this context that Western scholars and those who have been influenced by them use the phrase "black magic" to describe that which is used for malevolent or socially destructive purposes and "white magic" for "productive, protective, and curative" objectives.[54]

Traditional African religious beliefs and practices had an extraordinary tenacity and elasticity everywhere in the Americas. Studies of the belief systems of African slaves in colonial Mexico, Brazil, Haiti, Suriname, and other societies show that the central tenets of African cosmologies were retained, although not always in a pure form. Africans continued to believe in the spiritual efficacy of their charms and amulets, the existence of a Supreme Deity as well as lesser gods, the power of spirits, their abilities to control their environments, the celebration of the ancestors, and so on.

As far as North American slaves were concerned, African cosmologies and traditions also remained living and essential parts of their consciousness. There were several dimensions to their constantly developing religious realities. In the first place, what could be characterized as an African religious sensibility prevailed, that is to say, a style of worship that was exuberant, joyfully unrestrained, celebratory, filled with energy, drumming, song, and dance. The mood, the tempo, the essence of these observances, then and now, defies any easy description and can hardly be recaptured on paper. Simon Brown, a creole slave who was born in 1843 and who labored in Virginia, gave a tantalizing hint of the atmosphere that engulfed the worshippers. "But, oh, my, When my people got together to Wishop [worship] God, the spirit would move in the meeting."[55] Another practitioner, this time a preacher, recalled

The way in which we worshipped is almost indescribable. The singing was accompanied by a certain ecstasy of motion, clapping of hands, tossing of heads, which would continue without cessation about half an hour; one would lead off in a kind of recitative style, others joining in the chorus. The old house partook of the ecstasy; it rang with their jubilant shouts, and shook in all its joints.[56]

Frederika Bremmer, who attended black worship services in the 1850s, also found the proceedings "indescribable," noting the "stamping, jumping and clapping of hands."[57] A visitor to a Georgia plantation reported that the slaves sang

with all their souls and with all their bodies in unison; for their bodies rocked, their heads nodded, their feet stamped, their knees shook, their elbows and their hands beat time to the tune and the words which they sang with evident delight."[58]

And finally, a South Carolina rice planter confirmed:

Their whole religious worship is proverbially emotional, frequently running into boisterous shoutings, with noisy demonstrations of hands and feet, and extravagant, wild hysterical gyrations of the body, which are contagious and exhaustive, sometimes ending in a swoon or semi-cataleptic condition.[59]

This particular worship style appears to have been common throughout the Americas. It did not originate from the Africans' exposure to Christianity. Nor was it, in its fundamentals, a creation of the slave quarters. Such styles of worship and praise were deeply associated with African religious ceremonies and found continued expression and vitality in the Americas. They were grafted onto Christian practices, infused with new life, probably with their meanings modified over time. Christianity sustained these patterns of behavior and provided a hospitable vehicle for their expression. Albert Raboteau notes, "The crucial factor linking the two traditions was a conviction that authentic worship required an observable experience of the divine presence." This was precisely the view of the former slave who maintained, "It ain't enough to talk about God, you've got to feel him moving on the altar of your heart."[60] Similarly, the Louisiana slave who insisted, "The angels shout in heaven. The Lawd said you gotta shout if you want to be saved" reflected his African-inspired religious sensibilities.[61] As a Catholic, he had embraced the Christian God, but the ways of his ancestors were never destroyed; they were incorporated into his Christian theology and practice to give them vitality and added meaning. Thus the practices that characterized the religiocultural lives of the Africans were passed on to their progeny, who in turn transmitted them to their children, creatively adapting and transforming them along the way.

Not only did the peoples of African descent retain certain distinctive styles of religious expression, many traditional beliefs continued to have some salience. There was probably more continuity than discontinuity in their theological assumptions and religious wellsprings. The claim is not being made, of course, that these beliefs were transmitted unchanged over time in a deliberate fashion. Rather, there were some core understandings that survived the passage of time and remained influential in the slave quarters. The forms they took and the manner of their observance may have been modified, but many of the underlying assumptions had a remarkable tenacity. A few beliefs may have disappeared, however, or become less deeply held as the creole population increased.

Many Africans, at least through the eighteenth century, believed that when they died their spirits would return home to be with the ancestors. Jin Cole, who was brought from Africa in 1715, for example, spent her life believing that "at death, or before" she would "be transported back to Guinea; and all her long life she was gathering, as treasures to take back to her motherland, all kinds of odds and ends, colored rags, bits of finery, peculiar shaped stones, shells, buttons, beads, anything she could string."[62] Such beliefs declined in intensity, since few could claim an African homeland in the antebellum years.

Other beliefs remained strong in North America and elsewhere. Thus, many African slaves in the Americas, regardless of the century, continued to believe in the efficacy of their charms and amulets. These objects, deemed to be sacred by the possessor, presumably had the power to thwart malevolent actions by one's enemies, to bring good fortune, or to offer protection from a master's punishment or abuse. These charms could be anything–nails, bags, feathers, special sticks, statues, bones, and so on. But once they were embraced as being the vehicles through which divine power could be manifested, they took on an authority that few doubted or questioned.

One of the persons who knew the potency of these charms and had the power to neutralize harm or to inflict it was the practitioner of conjure. This mysterious but highly feared and respected person derived his power from God or from the devil, depending on one's point of view. The conjurer was often employed to avenge a wrong, divine the future, harm a foe, cure an illness, cast a spell, or help win the affections of a man or woman. His bag often contained the frightening tools of his trade–grave dirt, reptiles, scorpions, and bones. One peered in the bag at one's peril. One slave, Hagar Brown, expressed his fear at so doing: "I know I ain't goin' be the one peep in there. Cause I ain't make my peace yet. Know it will make you fall dead. . . ."[63]

Of course, not all slaves believed in conjure, but the unbelievers could resort to him in times of distress. Even a skeptic like Frederick Douglass availed himself of the service of a conjurer when he wanted to avoid being beaten by his master. Some slaves also believed in the power of hags, or malevolent creatures who could fly to their victims and "ride" them during the nights, sometimes sucking their blood in vampirelike fashion. Witches abounded, and they were feared by blacks and whites alike. Four blacks, along with several whites, were defendants in the Salem witch-hunt trials of 1692. We cannot, however, establish the intensity of the belief in witches or hags or conjurers by the time slavery ended. There were many believers, but a healthy skepticism also existed.[64]

The aforementioned beliefs and practices are not necessarily peculiar to the peoples of African descent in general or to slaves in particular. Many Europeans and others also believed in witches, diviners, and evil spirits. Yet what is important in this context is that these beliefs existed with others that could be considered Christian in their genesis and content. These were parallel beliefs, seemingly contradictory at times, but to the believer and the practitioner they formed a coherent system.

In essence, the African-born slaves who became Christians incorporated Christian theology into their existing belief system, reinterpreting it and transforming it in the process. This new complex of beliefs–this emerging Afro-Christianity–met their spiritual needs under some circumstances, but it did not replace core African beliefs nor did it suffice all the time. In fact, the Africans continued to express a profound faith in the efficacy of their charms, rituals, and religious principles even as they consulted a Christian clergyman to seek his comforting ministrations at various times, including while they were on their deathbeds.

This should not astonish anyone; human beings have the capacity to integrate ideas, particularly religious ones, that appear to the outsider to be in conflict with one another. The often repeated proposition that Africans did not understand much of what the Christians taught them may only be partially correct. Two belief systems, in time, coexisted. There was, on the one hand, that dynamic, evolving blend of some African and Christian beliefs that can be called Afro-Christianity. On the other hand, there were some African core beliefs that never blended at all, remaining beyond the reach of Christian influence. That which was given primacy at a particular time depended upon the needs of the moment and on what was considered to be most efficacious under the circumstances. Accordingly, our efforts to understand the texture of religious life in the quarters should not be centered simply on whether African slaves were Christianized, the nature of their Christian or traditional beliefs, and the degree of syncretism that occurred. Rather, we should recognize a dynamic, complex set of beliefs–at once coherent, at once contradictory–that defy any dogmatic characterization.

The Afro-Christianity of the early converts, creole and African, drew as heavily upon African cosmologies as much as it did upon Christian theology. But the Christian elements seemed to have acquired greater salience as the creole population increased, although this observation must remain tentative. Sterling Stuckey's insightful observation in this context deserves to be noticed. He suggests,

> "in most "Christian" ceremonies on plantations Christianity provided a protective exterior beneath which more complex, less familiar (to outsiders) religious principles and practices were operative. The very features of Christianity peculiar to slaves were often outlawed manifestations of deeper African concerns, products of a religious outlook toward which the master class might otherwise be hostile. By operating under cover of Christianity, vital aspects of Africanity, which some considered eccentric in movement, sound and symbolism, could more easily be practiced openly.[65]

The religious life in the quarters must have been richly varied, since it drew upon many theological streams. Even the Christian message was not uniformly packaged given the varieties of denominations–Anglican, Methodist, Baptist, the African Methodist Episcopal Zion, the AME, and the Catholics in southern Louisiana and Maryland. Here and there adherents of Islam could also be found. The Christian message as proclaimed by the white preachers with its emphasis on obedience to the master's will, fidelity, honesty, and acceptance of one's condition as divinely ordained had a different kind of resonance from that generally articulated by the black preacher. Not only was much of the white Christian message designed to promote the legitimacy of the system, but it also sought to foster the psychological enslavement of the black brethren as well. Consider the following, reported as a "catechistic exchange" between a Methodist clergyman and a slave in Alabama.

Q.   What did God make you for?
A.   To make a crop.[66]

The Episcopal bishop of Virginia, William Meade, enjoined slaves to obey their masters since they were the Christian God's representatives on Earth: "What faults you are guilty of towards your masters and mistresses are faults done against God Himself. . . . I tell you that your masters and mistresses are God's overseers, and that, if you are faulty towards them, God Himself will punish you severely for it in the next world."[67] Slaves, at least some of them, were not likely to accept such injunctions uncritically. Accordingly, they sang:

Ole Satan's church is here below;
Up to God's free church I hope to go.[68]

Slave preachers, on the other hand, did not usually preach a gospel of meek submission to white authority. Most of these proselytizers were

Baptists or Methodists, and some were licensed by those denominations. Others simply preached the Word without any official denominational sanction. In any event, they facilitated the spread of Christian doctrines filtered through the lens of a black person and a slave. Invariably, these proselytizers interpreted and packaged Christian dogma to meet the needs of a servile black population in a world dominated by whites. Enjoying a far greater appeal among the slaves than the white preachers, theirs was a message laced with strong emotional appeal, delivered in the language of the congregation, rich in metaphors that had meaning for the listener and preached with verve.

Black preachers were highly respected in the quarters. Some were literate, but the vast majority were not. On occasion some pretended that they could read, perhaps to lend greater authority to the proceedings at hand. As one former slave reported,

> De preacher I laked de bes' was name' Mathew Ewing. He was a comely nigger, black as night, an' he sho' could read out of his han'. He neber learned no real readin' an' writin' but he sho' knowed his Bible an' would hol' his han' out an' mak lak he was readin' an' preach de purtiest preachin' you ever heared.[69]

In general, slave preachers tried to imbue their listeners with a sense of self-worth and, if they could get away with it, others preached a gospel of equality. Since preachers operated with the sufferance of the masters and of white society, they had to be careful about the nature of their public utterances. Anything that could be construed as inflammatory and subversive of white society's control had to be avoided.

Generalizations about the nature of the Christian message delivered by the black preachers can be dangerous, however. We can find evidence to suggest, not surprisingly, that some black preachers, as did their white counterparts, enjoined the believers to accept their fate as one ordained by the Christian God. Recent discussions of the religious experiences of the slaves do not appear to grant a range of black responses to the Christian message. These carelessly made generalizations depict an incredibly uniform religious and political response to the religion of the white folks. One can only speculate on the Christian message of a free black preacher, for example, who not only looked with disfavor on the abolitionists but would not proselytize in Africa, he said, because of the absence of whites there. A former slave, Charley Williams, recalled, "We had meetings sometimes, but the nigger preacher just talk about being a good nigger, and doin' to please the master."[70] Since the Christian message as delivered by whites to blacks was partially designed to foster their spiritual and physical enslavement, it would have been surprising if it had found no disciples among the black preachers. There is evidence to suggest, on the other hand, that

black preachers were so carefully watched that they were forced to proclaim a gospel that was reassuring to whites even as it made a travesty
of Christian teachings. According to a former slave, "If a collud man
take de notion to preach, he couldn't preach 'bout the gospel. Dey didn't
low him to do that. All he could preach 'bout was obey de massa, obey
de overseer, obey dis, obey dat."[71]

There is no doubt, however, that many of the slaves who embraced
Christianity redefined aspects of its theology, if not its symbolism, to
meet their own needs. As one preacher recalled:

> When I starts preaching I couldn't read or write and had to preach
> what the master told me, and he say tell them niggers iffen they obeys
> the master they goes to Heaven; but I knowed there's something better
> for them, but daren't tell them, 'cept on the sly. That I done lot's. I tells
> 'em iffen they keeps praying the Lord will set 'em free.[72]

Despite such examples, it can hardly be disputed that Christianity
was the religion of the oppressor, and Jesus the "savior" was represented as having a phenotype different from that of the black slave. The
psychological impact on a black slave socialized into accepting a "savior" whose physical features resembled those of the master can only be
conjectured. To accept Christianity, even if the slaves were able to divest
it of the more pernicious aspects of its theology as packaged for them,
was still to share somewhat in the spiritual and religious worlds of the
master.

It is not only that the message of Christianity was often packaged in
a perverse way, but the "conversion" to it by some African slaves must
have posed considerable internal difficulties. The anguish felt by slaves
who were baptized and renamed by priests in Brazil, their identities and
past obliterated by the celebrant "who flourished a broom dipped in
holy water over their heads, until they are well sprinkled, and, at the
same time, bawls out to them, what their name is to be" can only be
imagined.[73] Nor can one ignore the effects of involuntary or forced con-
versions. We can find only glimpses of this in the record. Take, for
example, the following account of the case of the individuals who went
to Rio de Janeiro from the region along the Zaire River.

As part of the baptismal ceremony, the new converts had to answer
a series of questions designed to test their superficial knowledge of
Catholicism. One of these questions, "Do you want to eat the salt of
God?" would, according to Mary Karasch, have created severe problems
for individuals from this area. To the Kongo people, the consumption of
salt meant that one would "become like a European." This meant the
loss of certain powers such as the ability to fly back to Africa or to
"interpret all things." Since those who did not eat salt enjoyed powers
similar to those of the spirits, it is not difficult to understand why this

was a fearsome ritual for these people and one that exacted a psycho-logical price. It is no wonder that slaves were reported to be depressed at the prospect of being baptized. João Rugendas, who visited Rio in the nineteenth century, observed that some baptized slaves considered the unbaptized to be "savages."[74] This was one indication that they had absorbed the prejudices of the master class and the degree to which they had come to view their heritage in negative terms.

At one level, the missionaries and other Christian proselytizers were pleased with the enthusiasm that some slaves displayed in their embrace and practice of Christianity. This sharing in the cosmology of the master brought them closer to their oppressors while distancing them from the religious heritages of their ancestors.

But Christianity was a mixed blessing for its black followers. Its appeal was unquestionably strong, since it helped provide, for a people with strong religious traditions, a moral code, an explanation of the world around them, and the comforting promise of an afterlife. Chris-tianity helped provide psychic sustenance for the enslaved. In some cases it also legitimized resistance to slavery. Drawing upon their Chris-tian beliefs, slaves on one of the islands off the South Carolina coast sang the following "Hymn of Freedom" in the early years of the nine-teenth century:

> Look to Heaven with manly trust
> And swear by Him that's always just
> That no white foe with impious hand
> (Repeat)
> Shall slave your wives and daughters more
> or rob them of their virtue dear.
> Be armed with valor firm and true,
> Their hopes are fixed on Heaven and you
> That truth and justice will prevail
> And every scheme of bondage fail.[75]

Christianized slaves and free persons also used their religious beliefs to justify their violence against the institution of slavery. Churches and other religious meeting places provided the perfect locales for the recruitment of participants in conspiracies and rebel-lions. There is much evidence to suggest that Christianized slaves com-pared their condition to that of the children of Israel who were held in bondage in Egypt. Denmark Vesey, the freedman who conceived a major conspiracy in Charleston in 1822, read to the slaves "from the Bible how the *children of Israel were delivered out of Egypt from bondage.*"[76] He assured his fellow conspirators that the Almighty would find their efforts "pleasing." Nine years later, Nat Turner was certain that he was doing his God's will when he led his famous revolt in Southampton, Virginia. To his followers, he was "Prophet Nat." Even as they awaited their deaths, Turner's troops "declared that they were going happy fore that God had a hand in what they had been doing."[77]

The legitimization of the desire for liberation through the application of Christian symbolisms testifies to the influence of the master's religion on the enslaved and the free alike. But there is considerable danger in extrapolating too much about the role of Christianity in resistance from these rather isolated acts of physical rebellion. There can be no doubt that some of those involved in the leadership of these challenges were Christianized, but the documentation is often silent on the religious beliefs of the rank and file. It should be emphasized, however, that Christian religious gatherings provided opportunities to recruit potential participants in rebellions, so to that extent it can be assumed that these persons were Christians although the actual content of their religious beliefs cannot be ascertained.

The religious practices in the Praise House, churches, or quarters must also have provided solace for the slaves, as they are wont to do for believers everywhere. But whether this psychic balm could produce more than temporary relief from the spiritual ravages of servitude is open to question. Christian beliefs–the promise of an afterlife, the gospel of forgiveness–undoubtedly tempered the harshness of their reality and contributed to their acceptance of the status quo. As an expression of her Christian faith, for example, one enslaved woman offered the following prayer in 1816:

> O Lord, bless my master. When he calls upon thee to damn his soul, do not hear him, do not hear him, but hear me–save him–make him know he is wicked, and he will pray to thee.
>
> I am afraid, O Lord, I have wished him bad wishes in my heart–keep me from wishing him bad–though he whips me and beats me sore, tell me of my sins, and make me pray more to thee–make me more glad for what thou hast done for me, a poor [N]egro.[78]

An examination of the religious lives of the Gullah shows considerable vitality and a profound accommodation to servitude and a seeming contentment on the part of some with their situation. One new convert, or seeker, in response to the question "You think you are converted?" replied "Yes, . . . I' so lovin! I loves ebery body–all de trees, an' de chicken, an' de peoples; I loves ebery ting an' ebery body."[79] This joy in Christ, whether short-lived or permanent, was precisely the kind of feeling that could militate against any sustained challenges to their earthly realities. Obviously, the Christianized slave drew much more from his religion than a justification for resistance. The search for a tradition of slave protest legitimized by Christianity, therefore, must not lead us to ignore what may well have been that religion's more enduring impact, namely fostering an acceptance by many of the status quo. As one former slave recalled in the 1930s,

> God gave it [Christianity] to Adam and took it away from Adam and gave it to Noah and . . . Noah had three sons, and when Noah got drunk on wine, one of his sons laughed at him, and the other two took a sheet and walked backwards and threw it over Noah. Noah told the one who laughed, "your children will be hewers of wood and drawers of water for the other's two children, and they will be known by their hair and their skin being dark," so . . . there we are, and that is the way God meant us to be. We have always had to follow the white folks and do what we saw them do, and that's all there is to it. You just can't get away from what the Lord said.[80]

The practice and the survival of religious beliefs that were not Christian represented a far greater threat to slavery and the hegemonic influence of the master class. The tenacity of Islam, voodoo, conjuration, and belief in spirits, hags, and witches, among other African-based cosmologies, suggest their salience in the lives of these people. These practices constituted living parts of the realities of the enslaved and created an alternative vision of their place in the world.

Nevertheless, the Christian beliefs of the slaves sustained them psychologically, gave them strength, explained the world around them, justified their resistance on occasion, and paradoxically served as a means of social control. Christianity's tantalizing promise of an afterlife of freedom must have had a profound appeal. A special hope and expectancy led slaves to sing

> We'll soon be free
> We'll soon be free
> When the Lord will call us home

Yet, in spite of Christianity's important role in helping the believers to exercise some spiritual autonomy, it must be said that blacks in the Americas were placed in environments where the religious symbols of Christianity were cast in the phenotypical mold of their oppressors. Although Christianity linked blacks to whites in a religious sense, it was at bottom the religion of the masters. Thus, the Virgin Mary, the Savior, the angels, and most of the saints were depicted phenotypically in the image of the master class. In societies where power wore a white face, the symbols of economic and political power converged with those that reflected religious authority. While it is possible to argue, as we have done, that the believers "Africanized" Christianity to meet their needs, many slaves, particularly the creoles, must have fought major psychological battles against a body of religious dogma that often sought to sanction their oppression and whose symbols supported that stance.

The most pernicious aspect of slavery, it could be argued, was not the physical and legal chains that linked the slave to the master but rather the psychological battles it forced the enslaved to wage to define themselves as whole persons and to reject white definitions of them. The Christian message, as packaged by whites for slaves, tended to make this struggle more difficult. No one can claim that this battle was completely won. The shackles that did the most damage were frequently the ones that could not be seen.

Notes

1. Monica Schuler, "*Alas, Alas, Kongo*": A Social History of Indentured African Immigration into Jamaica, 1841–1865 (Baltimore: Johns Hopkins University Press, 1991), 33–36.
2. Warren M. Billings, "The Cases of Fernando and Elizabeth Key: A Note on the Status of Blacks in Seventeenth-Century Virginia," *William and Mary Quarterly*, 3rd Series, 30 (1970), 468–469.
3. Ibid., 468.
4. Marcus W. Jernegan, "Slavery and Conversion in the American Colonies," *American Historical Review*, 21 (1916), 506.
5. Lord Bathurst's observations are reprinted in Frank J. Klingberg, *The Antislavery Movement in England: A Study in English Humanitarianism* (New Haven: Yale University Press, 1926), 338–350.
6. Jernegan, "Slavery and Conversion," 508.
7. Ibid., 509.
8. John B. Boles, ed., *Masters and Slaves in the House of the Lord: Race and Religion in the American South, 1740–1870* (Lexington: University of Kentucky Press, 1988), 4.
9. Jernegan, "Slavery and Conversion," 511.
10. Lewis M. Purifoy, "The Southern Methodist Church and the Proslavery Argument," *Journal of Southern History*, 32 (1966), 325.
11. Kay and Cary, *Slavery in North Carolina*, 191.
12. Jernegan, "Slavery and Conversion," 516.
13. Wood, *Black Majority*, 135.
14. Betty Wood, *Slavery in Colonial Georgia, 1730–1775* (Athens: University of Georgia Press, 1984), 162.
15. Margaret Washington Creel, *"A Peculiar People": Slave Religion and Community Culture among the Gullahs* (New York: New York University Press, 1988), 101.
16. Piersen, *Black Yankees*, 56.
17. Betty Wood, *Slavery in Colonial Georgia*, 162.
18. Julia Floyd Smith, *Slavery and Rice Culture in Low Country Georgia, 1750–1860* (Knoxville: University of Tennessee Press, 1985), 142.
19. Malone, *Sweet Chariot*, 245.
20. McManus, *A History of Negro Slavery in New York*, 75.
21. Jernegan, "Slavery and Conversion," 520.
22. Creel, *A Peculiar People*, 103.
23. Jernegan, "Slavery and Conversion," 521–523.
24. Betty Wood, "'Never on Sunday?': Slavery and the Sabbath in Lowcountry Georgia, 1750-1830," in Mary Turner, ed., *From Chattel Slaves to Wage Slaves: The Dynamics of Labour Bargaining in the Americas* (London: James Currey Ltd., 1995), 85.

25. Kay and Cary, *Slavery in North Carolina*, 191.
26. Lawrence Levine, *Black Culture and Black Consciousness: Afro-American Folk Thought From Slavery to Freedom* (New York: Oxford, 1977), 61.
27. Piersen, *Black Yankees*, 49.
28. McManus, *History of Negro Slavery in New York*, 76.
29. Allan Kulikoff, *Tobacco and Slaves: The Development of Southern Cultures in the Chesapeake, 1680–1800* (Chapel Hill: University of North Carolina Press, 1986), 358.
30. Jernegan, "Slavery and Conversion," 526.
31. Mechal Sobel, *Trabelin' On: The Slave Journey to an Afro-Baptist Faith* (Westport, CT: Greenwood Press, 1979), 60–61.
32. John S. Mbiti, *African Religions and Philosophy* (New York: Praeger, 1969), 146.
33. Albert Raboteau, *Slave Religion: The "Invisible Institution in the Antebellum South* (New York: Oxford, 1978), 121.
34. Piersen, *Black Yankees*, 52.
35. Ibid., 76.
36. Stanley Austin Ransom Jr., America's First Negro Poet: The Complete Works of Jupiter Hammon of Long Island (Kennikat Press, Port Washington, NY, 1970), 108.
37. Betty Wood, *Slavery in Colonial Georgia*, 160.
38. Piersen, *Black Yankees*, 69.
39. Sobel, *The World They Made Together*, 182–183.
40. Ibid., 183.
41. Piersen, *Black Yankees*, 70.
42. Sobel, *The World They Made Together*, 186.
43. Malone, *Sweet Chariot*, 247.
44. Sobel, *Trabelin' On*, 189.
45. Albert Raboteau, "The Slave Church in the Era of the American Revolution," in Berlin and Hoffman, *Slavery and Freedom*, 203.
46. Sobel, *Trabelin' On*, 221–222.
47. Ibid., 221.
48. George Rawick, *From Sundown to Sunup: The Making of the Black Community* (Westport, CT: Greenwood Publishing Co., 1972), 34.
49. Michael A. Gomez, "Muslims in Early America," *Journal of Southern History*, LX:4 (1994), 697.
50. Kulikoff, "The Origins of Afro-American Society," 256.
51. Sterling Stuckey, *Slave Culture*, 37.
52. Raboteau, *The Invisible Institution*, 149.
53. Jacobs, *Incidents in the Life of a Slave Girl*, 72–73.
54. Jeffrey Burton Russell, *Witchcraft in the Middle Ages* (Ithaca: Cornell University Press, 1972), 10–17; M.G. Marwick, "Witchcraft and Sorcery," in M. Fortes and G. Dieterlen, eds., *African Systems of Thought* (London: Oxford University Press, 1966), 21.
55. Stuckey, *Slave Culture*, 33.
56. Blassingame, *The Slave Community*, 134.
57. Stuckey, *Slave Culture*, 60.
58. Levine, *Black Culture and Black Consciousness*, 42.
59. Charles Joyner, *Down By the Riverside: A South Carolina Slave Community* (Urbana: University of Illinois Press, 1984), 160.
60. Albert Raboteau, *A Fire in the Bones: Reflections on African-American Religious History* (Boston: Beacon Press, 1995), 190.
61. Malone, *Sweet Chariot*, 247.
62. Piersen, *Black Yankees*, 76.
63. Joyner, *Down By the Riverside*, 147.
64. Ibid., 149.
65. Stuckey, *Slave Culture*, 35.
66. Levine, *Black Culture and Black Consciousness*, 45.

67. Ibid., 46.
68. Jacobs, *Incidents in the Life of a Slave Girl,* 77.
69. George Rawick, ed., *The American Slave: A Composite Autobiography,* 19 vols. (Westport, CT: Greenwood, 1972), 9:171–172.
70. Genovese, *Roll Jordan Roll,* 260, 263.
71. Rawick, *The American Slave,* vol. 5, pt. 3, 3169.
72. Quoted in William Banks, *Black Intellectuals: Race and Responsibility in American Life* (New York: W. W. Norton, 1996), 6.
73. Mary Karasch, *Slave Life in Rio de Janeiro, 1808–1850* (Princeton: Princeton University Press, 1987), 257.
74. Ibid.
75. John Hammond More, "A Hymn of Freedom–South Carolina, 1813," *Journal of Negro History,* L:1 (1965), 52–53.
76. Vincent Harding, "Religion and Resistance Among Antebellum Negroes, 1800–1860," in August Meier and Elliott Rudwick, eds., *The Making of Black America,* vol. 2 (New York: Atheneum, 1973), 185.
77. Ibid., 188.
78. James Melvin Washington, *Conversations With God* (New York: Harper Collins, 1994), 19.
79. Creel, *A Peculiar People,* 287.
80. Rawick, *The American Slave,* vol. 6, 335–336.

Social and Cultural Life
in the Quarters

As human beings, black slaves could not avoid creating a variety of social and cultural forms and institutions that met their needs and affirmed their humanity. There was nothing deliberate or conscious about this; cultures never emerge that way. Nor was the slaves' culture in its genesis and evolution primarily a reaction to white society. Blacks created a culture not because they were slaves, but because that was a function of being human even if they lived in a hostile environment. They drew upon their African heritage, their daily experiences in the quarters and beyond, their interaction among themselves and with the physical landscape to create a culture that bore their own imprint, one that reflected their values and worldviews and provided psychic sustenance. Never a carbon copy of white culture, the culture they created must be assessed on its own terms and must be seen as the normal expression of a people struggling to define themselves as autonomous beings and not simply as persons lacking inner pulls and always operating on the masters' terrain.

A distinctive black culture did not emerge immediately, but its foundations were laid during that long first century. African influences prevailing in those early years were reflected in religious beliefs and practices, naming patterns, language, the socialization of children, and in other ways. Much of this began to change as the creole population began to increase, and out of their interaction with the African-born would emerge the kind of cultural compromises and common ground that would become distinctive by the nineteenth century.

The social context within which the cultural moorings would be nurtured is difficult to reconstruct. We can speculate that in the early years the slaves derived their ideas about social formation from the worlds they had known. Conceivably, the persons who exercised authority and commanded most respect were individuals who would have been revered in African societies as well. These included religious leaders, elders, and senior members of the lineage. These criteria may have become less salient with the passage of time as new determinants of social status evolved. It is unlikely that those of African provenance would have lost their respect in the quarters, however. In fact, as the African-born component became less strong, their standing may even have improved among the population as a whole. In 1851, for example, four African-born slaves who were then laboring in Georgia "were treated with marked respect by all other Negroes for miles and miles around."[1]

Status in slave society depended on many factors. The dichotomy that is usually drawn between house slaves and field slaves is somewhat false, since this occupational division was not all that clear-cut for a significant number of slaves. This was particularly the case on small farms. Yet there is some evidence that during the nineteenth century the majority of slaves in the Cotton Belt did not experience much occupational mobility. Most performed the same jobs for the duration of their working life, and children were likely to inherit their parents' jobs. As Michael Johnson explains, "Whether a slave would become a field hand, a house servant, or a skilled tradesman was more or less predictable at birth."[2] In practice, however, there was some flexibility in the system, since job assignments could change depending on the wishes of the master or overseer and the circumstances of the moment. Frances Kemble, who resided on a Georgia plantation in the 1830s, reported on the occupational demotion of a cook who stole a ham. The slave's owner

> was in a state of towering anger and indignation, and, besides a flogging, sentenced the unhappy cook to degradation from his high and dignified position . . . to the hard toil, coarse scanty fare, and despised position of a common field hand.[3]

As in most human societies, there was internal social differentiation among the slaves, although the criteria that determined it were neither universal nor fixed. Slave society was nothing if not dynamic. Any analysis of the social structure of the slave population must recognize the fact that the criteria by which status was ascribed had their origins primarily within black society and were not imposed from without. Viewing slaves from the outside, slaveowners ascribed a higher status to those like the house servants, coachmen, and valets who served them directly and met their needs. Slaves, at the other extreme, valued those of their number who possessed certain skills and talents that could be used for the benefit of their community. There were instances, however, when an exceptionally gifted person such as a sugar boiler or a skilled carpenter enjoyed a high status in both worlds even though his talents were used to enhance the interests of the master class. Thus, service to the master and service to the enslaved were not mutually exclusive.

Two broad but overlapping social classes of slaves may be distinguished: the elites and the nonelites. It is tempting to impose the usual social ordering of upper, middle, and lower class upon the slave population, but this is probably too neat a classification, and the evidence to support it is at best imprecise and elusive. Furthermore, the numerous networks that linked slaves together served to mediate social divisions that resulted from occupational assignments and skills. Domestic servants, for example, often found their spouses from among the ranks of the field hands. Elaborate kin networks united slaves on many plantations, a fact that tended to temper incipient class distinctions.

This does not mean that social divisions were nonexistent. The slave narratives reveal that nineteenth-century slaves were conscious of status differences and acted upon them. These differences could be particularly sharp between the house slaves and the field hands. House slaves, at least some of them, assumed the superior airs of the whites, a perverse indication of their internalization of white society's attitudes to blacks. One former slave, Ellen Betts, recalled, "All the niggers have to stoop to Aunt Rachel [the cook in the Big House] jes' lak dey curtsy to Missy."[4] A second person, Lucy Thurston, reported that sometimes the house servants "get mighty upidy 'cause they served the Marster an' his family. . . ." And Lucy McCullough remembered, "De house servants hold that dey is uh step better den de field niggers. House servants wuz niggah quality folks."[5] Henry Bibb, who escaped from slavery and wrote his autobiography, was certain that "the distinction among slaves is as marked as the classes of society are in any aristocratic community; some refusing to associate with others whom they deem beneath them in point of character, color, conditions, or the superior importance of the respective masters."[6]

Domestic slaves, according to Frederick Douglass, formed "a sort of black aristocracy."[7] Those who were racially mixed also had difficulty identifying with the black side of their heritage, an indication of the unhealthy impact of slavery and racism on their sense of self. One servant whose father and grandfather were Caucasian explained that "like my . . . Mother I thought myself of a superior caste and would have felt it a degradation to put myself on a level with those of a few shades darker than myself."[8]

Whatever the basis of their presumed superiority, these slaves worked intimately with their owners and shared bonds of affection. A woman who owned slaves in Virginia recalled that they were the "repositories of our family secrets. They were our confidants in all our trials. They joyed with us and sorrowed with us; they wept when we wept, and they laughed when we laughed. Often our best friends, they were rarely our worst enemies."[9] Owners mourned the death of their domestics and celebrated the birth of their children. Some worried about the inevitable separation of their families and the pain that it produced. A young woman, overcome by the sale of some domestic servants, confessed, ". . . it is really distressing to be compelled to sell good, faithful servants that have raised you and that you love like your own blood and the worst of all to hear of those best of servants that were treated with so much respect and were such great favorites being so unkindly treated. . . . . These are trials I've had to bear."[10]

Such attitudes showed that sensitive whites recognized the essential humanity of their chattel, even as they embraced the notion that they belonged to an inferior species. At one level, they came to know some of their enslaved workers as persons and mutual bonds of affection did develop between them. But the status and racial differentials were never blurred, as each group knew its place. Slaveowners who tempered their claim to absolute control of their chattel with acts of compassion and a concern for their physical and emotional well-being acted from a sense of enlightened self-interest as well as from their own human pulls and sensibilities. The two sentiments—self-interest and humanity—were intertwined, although the former could take precedence depending on the circumstance.

Some nineteenth-century slaveowners protested that their slaves formed a part of their extended family. These metaphorical formulations assuaged the consciences of those who embraced them and gave expression to their paternalistic impulses. Many masters believed that their benign paternalistic reach penetrated the quarters, shaped the consciousness of their chattel, and influenced their behavior. But this was largely a delusion. Skilled in the art of dissemblance as a means of survival, some slaves feigned much affection and fealty to the master and the families that owned them. Former slaveowner John S. Wise, who wrote his memoirs at the end of the Civil War, tried to understand why such seemingly loyal slaves had abandoned their master:

Were not the negroes perfectly content and happy? Had I not often talked to them on the subject? Had not every one of them told me repeatedly that they loved "old Marster" better than anybody in the world, and would not have freedom if he offered it to them? Of course they did—many and many a time.[11]

Most slaves who had lived long enough knew that they were not really a part of the master's family. They recognized that the patriarch could sell them at will and that he presided over their abuse and debasement. Slaves, particularly the creoles, could hardly have escaped internalizing–in varying degrees–some of white society's attitudes toward them. But as a group, their mental world remained distinct from that of their oppressors, and they never reached the point where their contests with the masters for their own space had been muted and the patriarchical power of the slaveholders reigned triumphant. As it turned out, the masters knew the slaves a good deal less than the slaves knew them. One white Virginian who viewed, uncomprehendingly, the exodus of seemingly loyal slaves during the Civil War, revealed the limits of the masters' paternalism and their misreading of their slaves' attitudes and behavior. "Those we loved best, and who loved us best–as we thought–were the first to leave us," he reported.[12]

Still, we must recognize that some degree of intimacy with the masters existed in particular situations. Such bonds often distanced domestics from the other slaves in the quarters and linked them with whites in a manner that shows the corruptive power of slavery and the hegemonic influence of the masters. The noted South Carolina slave trader, Henry Laurens, described a welcome he received from his domestics on his return home in the following manner.

> I found nobody there but three of our old domestics–Stepney, Exeter, and big Hagar. These drew tears from me by their humble and affectionate salutes. My knees were clasped, my hands kissed, my very feet embraced and nothing less than a very–I can't say fair, but full-buss of my lips would satisfy the old man weeping and sobbing in my face . . . they . . . held my hands, hung upon me; I could scarce get from them. 'Ah," said the old man, 'I never thought to see you again; now I am happy; ah, I never thought to see you again.'[13]

House servants, it would appear, were more likely to internalize the values of the white master class to a much greater extent than their peers in the field. Some even succeeded in identifying their masters' interests with their own and looked contemptuously at those who wanted to liberate themselves. One traveler in the South recalled that a domestic slave upbraided a coachman who had run away as "a disgrace to we black gentlemen–I neber 'sociate with you 'gain." Another escapee who was caught and returned by a fellow slave listened to his captor report, "Master, I done bring John home. . . . I wish master sell him where 'ol nigger nebber see him more, if he run away 'gain: he disgrace he family."[14]

Although some domestic slaves identified with the masters and had an ambivalent relationship with the field hands, it is important to remember that they shared the same legal status and were as vulnerable to abuse by their owners as any other category of chattel. Thus, reported cleavages among the slaves may obscure the deeper bonds that held them together as a people. It is certain also that house slaves did not all share the same attitudes, anymore than field hands spoke with one voice.

There can be no doubt, however, that domestic slaves with specialized skills–along with skilled craftsmen, literate slaves, and those who possessed medical knowledge or were spiritual leaders–occupied elite status in slave society. Those who had accumulated modest sums of money as a result of their agricultural and commercial enterprises also occupied the upper ranks of the social hierarchy. Charles Ball, a man who escaped during the nineteenth century, emphasized the class differences among the enslaved. "It may well be supposed, that in our society, although we are all slaves, and all nominally in a condition of the most perfect equality, yet there was in fact a very great difference in the manner of living."[15] As a rule, preachers, conjurers, midwives, doctors, cooks and workers in the Big House, butlers, coachmen, craftsmen, and entertainers were included in the elite group. The nonelite group, which may have lent itself to further internal differentiation, included the field hands (except those with important specialized skills) and the unskilled in general. Obviously, what defined elite status varied in accordance with the plantation, farm, or household, so status was not necessarily transferable.

CREATING A CULTURE

Despite social distinctions, the slaves as human beings developed strategies for coping with their life situations. One would expect such a normal evolution over two hundred years so the existence of a slave culture should not be an occasion for amazement. On the contrary, the absence of such an identifiable culture would be more noteworthy. Slavery, it has been suggested, represented a prolonged period of historical crisis for its victims. One cannot take serious issue with this conclusion, but it raises some questions. How long does a crisis last? At what point does the "abnormal" even in its perversity assume some degree of predictability and constancy? No people could have survived for 250 years in a state of sustained crisis, their energies sapped, their lifeblood drained. They had to create some inner sanctuary, find some corner, seize some terrain upon which to construct human relationships even as the system within which they operated represented a travesty of all that was normal and just.

The slaves' culture, then, reflected their own experiences, values, and ethos. Its flowering prevented slaves from existing wholly in the world of the masters. Yet, although the culture of the slaves represented a viable alternative to that of the masters, it did not replace it, since they had to function in the world beyond the quarters as well and largely in accordance with its rules. The slaves' culture affirmed their humanity and anchored them in their own ground, but it did not make the burden of being human property any less real; it could not stanch the flow of abuse nor could it stay the atrocities that were visited upon them. The culture of the slaves did not negate the institutional structure of slavery and the forces that sustained it. On the other hand, their culture afforded them crucial psychological space and cushioned the impact of slavery's blows, but it did not weaken the intensity and the force of their delivery. The slaves' culture blunted some of slavery's weapons and prevented the destruction of their being.

At the core of slave life was a set of beliefs that determined and explained the nature of the individuals' daily existence and their reactions to natural and supernatural phenomena. Some of these beliefs would probably be called secular today, others were more decidedly religious, and many cannot be so easily classified. We have already discussed the belief of some slaves in the efficacy of magic, hags, conjurers, and witches, and these could be considered essentially religious in their orientation. As late as 1842, the Reverend Charles C. Jones complained that the slaves "believe in second-sight, in apparitions, charms, witchcraft, and in a kind of irresistible Satanic influence. The superstitions brought from Africa have not been wholly laid aside."[16]

The African "superstitions"–or, more accurately, beliefs–continued to inform behavior among the peoples of African descent under slavery and later. Other beliefs were borrowed from the Europeans and undoubtedly from the Indians as well. In fact, many whites also believed in forms of magic, witchcraft, spirits, ghosts, divination, and so on. Thus it may be a futile effort to try to determine with any specificity the provenance of some of the beliefs in the quarters. Yet, striking similarities across the black world regarding the belief in dreams, signs, ghosts, and the efficacy of certain burial customs suggest a common African origin.

African slaves, everywhere, engaged in very elaborate burial practices. They were designed to give the deceased an appropriate send-off. Among the African-born, the belief existed that the spirit would return to Africa to be with the ancestors, but this became less widely embraced as the creole population became dominant. Funerals were occasions on which kin and friends gathered to pay respect to the dead and to renew acquaintances. Peter Randolph, a former slave, recalled that in Virginia "when one of their number dies they go to the overseer, and obtain leave to sit up all night with their dead, and sing and pray. This is a very solemn season. First, one sings and another prays, and this they continue every night until the dead body is buried."[17] Another former slave who labored in Georgia reported that on his plantation "if a slave died . . . nobody went to the fields till after the burying."[18]

Once a death had occurred, relatives and friends conducted a vigil around the body. The deceased was never left alone, not only because of the respect accorded to the person but also as a consequence of the profound meaning of dying in African traditions. A former slave, probably a creole, recalled, "Wen one uh doze Africans die, it was bery sad. Wen a man's countryman die, he sit right wid um all night. . . . Attuh dey pray, deh come in and put deah hand on duh frien an say goodbye."[19] (see p. 167.) Death was the continuation of life, albeit in another form, and the spirit now joined the ranks of the revered ancestors. This belief may have weakened as the population became more creolized, but it does not appear to have disappeared.

The corpse was usually carefully bathed, dressed, and prepared for burial. Undoubtedly, distinctive African practices were associated with the procedure, but the evidence for this is not particularly strong. It is known that the body was usually shrouded in white cloth, but the precise meaning of this is unclear. Funerals were marked by processions, singing, ceremonial dancing, and a variety of rituals. One eighteenth-century clergyman in New York complained, "Heathenish rites are performed at the grave of their countrymen."[20] Funerals were not necessarily somber occasions, although the undercurrent of pain and loss was never absent. Perhaps, the feeling that the spirit still remained a part of day-to-day life must have tempered the anguish of the passing. There was much food and drink available to celebrate the passage to the world of the ancestors, to enliven the spirits of those present, and to act as a balm at a time that was not without its stress.

Funerals often took place at night because that afforded the largest possible attendance. Their day's toil over, slaves had the time to participate in the lengthy ceremonies. Whites attended as well, particularly if the deceased were a trusted domestic. The last rites could be conducted by any slave selected for that purpose or by a slave preacher or clergyman. In keeping with African traditions, particularly those of West-central Africa, the body was placed in the coffin with the head facing the west. Then, as one informant described the scene at one funeral,

> . . . the men an' boys begin to fill up the grave. When it was full they roun' it up real purty-like, an' put a wood shingle at the head an' another at the foot of the grave. The women-folk lay some flowers an' 'ribbon-grass' on the top an' put different color' bottles, broken glass an' sea-shells all 'roun' the grave.[21]

There was much singing at the grave as those in attendance wished goodbye to the earthly form of the deceased, assuring him or her that their spirits would one day be reunited.

As the above quotation shows, a variety of articles could be placed on top of the graves. These included personal possessions, pieces of

pottery, jewelry, cooking utensils, and mirrors. This custom, undoubtedly African in origin, has been observed among several West African
and West-central African peoples. The articles were placed for the use of
the deceased in the spirit world and reflected what were presumed to be
his or her most enduring needs. As one former slave expressed it,
"Them dishes and bottles what put on the grave is for the spirit and ain't
for nobody to touch them that's for the spirit to feel at home."[22] One
recent authority has indicated that the custom had an even deeper significance. Robert Fariss Thompson suggests,

> The fusion of slaves from the Gold Coast, the Congo-Angola area, and
> the other parts of the Guinea Coast in Southern slavery could mean the
> reinforcement of the African notion that the funeral is the climax of life
> and that the dead should be honored by having their possessions placed
> upon the top of their graves.[23]

After the interment of the body, the singing continued at the grave or
at an appropriate venue elsewhere. A memorial ceremony or service
could be held later, probably on the ninth day after death. This brought
to an end the formal ceremonial proceedings associated with the death.
For those still adhering to African cosmologies, the spirit of the deceased
now joined the ranks of the ancestors, symbolizing the continuity
between life and death.

Funerals also provided the occasion for cooking and feasting. A former slave, Jane Lewis, recalled:

> . . . dey would cook a regluh meal and dey would kill a chicken in
> front of duh doe, wring he neck an cook um fuh duh feas. Den wen we
> all finish, we tak wut victuals lef and put it in a dish by duh chimley an
> das fuh duh sperrit tuh hab a las good meal.[24]

There is much documentation for the continuation of a variety of
other supernatural beliefs. In accordance with their African traditions,
the residents of the quarters believed that the spirits of the dead retained
an interest in the welfare of the living and were still available to provide
help, guidance, and protection. The spirits of those persons who lived
admirable lives and who "died good" were benevolent and not to be
feared. On the other hand, those individuals whose lives were marked
by wrongdoing and evil and who did not "die good" had malevolent
spirits who excited much fear. Mean-spirited masters fell into this category as well.

There were certain practices that could neutralize the potential
malevolence of the ghost of a wicked person. The individual could be
buried facedown, or certain objects such as nails, or coins, and brooms
could be placed in the coffin. This meant, in the language of West Indian
slaves, that the person's spirit was "planted" and it would remain forever

underground, unable to visit its evil upon the living. Belief in the power of ghosts and their ubiquity was also common in the black world in the Americas. Very deeply held, it reflected the continuing efficacy of beliefs that linked the world of the spirits to the world of the living. As such, they remained a vital part of the consciousness of African peoples that not even Christianity could destroy.

In an age when diseases struck with predictable regularity and many victims died early, it is understandable that slaves, and others as well, embraced an elaborate body of beliefs regarding the causes of illnesses and the appropriate remedies for them. Some of these beliefs were carried from Africa while others had their origins in America. Human beings the world over have always responded creatively to assaults on their bodies and have developed rational explanations for their occurrence. Some Africans, for example, believed that sickness was caused by the malevolence of an enemy and by powerful forces outside of one's body. Some persons possessed the sorcery or the power to do harm to others by investing certain objects with the qualities to create mischief. For the objects to be effective, the victim had to ingest them or come into contact with them in some particular way. They could be buried at one's doorstep, thrown in one's residence, or rubbed on one's clothes. Virginia Hayes Shepherd, a former slave, recalled that when her stepfather became ill, "He believed he had a bunch something like boils. White doctor bathed it. After a few days it burst and live things came out of the boil and crawled on the floor. He thought he was conjured. He said an enemy of his put something on the horse's back and he rode it and got it on his buttocks and broke him out."[25]

The target of such malevolence could adopt appropriate countermeasures, usually by wearing certain objects or performing time-tested rituals. The gum resin asafetida was a most effective antidote. If worn around the neck, it could protect one from harm and thwart the evil intentions of others. This belief in the capacity of others to cause one to become ill is still prevalent in many black societies in the Americas. Essentially, it is a religious belief, since it ascribes power to certain supernatural forces, acting through particular objects, to do good or evil.

Most historians who have discussed matters relating to the health of the slaves have characterized this kind of spiritual response to disease as "folk" medicine. It should be more properly seen and understood within the context of their cosmology, where disease often had a spiritual basis and therefore required a spiritual response. As a former slave expressed it: "Every time somebody gets sick, it ain't natchel sickness."[26] Under the circumstances, the measures taken to counteract such malevolence cannot be fitted into the Western and secular model of what constitutes "medicine." More properly, they represented the long reach of religious beliefs and the notion that sickness and disease were the result of religious infractions or the malevolence of another person. Accordingly, the efforts to restore a sick person to health formed a normal and integral part of religious practice. Religious rituals constituted the means to good health.

The belief that illness could be the product of sorcery, or malevolence, existed alongside the recognition that there were other causes as well. Slaves knew what happened to them if they were bitten by a poisonous snake, if they ingested poison, or if a wound were left untreated. Under these circumstances, they had a range of remedies that had seemingly worked over time. The average person knew what herbs to take or teas to drink to cure some physical distress. In more difficult cases, the "root" doctor or slave doctor might be consulted.

The slave doctor commanded much respect, since he could diagnose the problem and often had prescriptions that were effective. Slaves preferred their own doctors to the white ones, probably with good reason. White doctors had a tendency to bleed their patients, a practice that must have impeded their recovery. Dr. Hardison, who attended to the sick slaves on the Pettigrew plantation in North Carolina, reported an instance of a slave who resisted his treatment in 1845. Hardison complained:

> I cannot persuade Jack to Submit to the operation of having his tooth extracted nor do threats avail anything–It was with great difficulty I succeeded in fixing the instrument on the tooth and as soon as I did so he gave my hand and instrument a violent knock and broke the tooth even with the gum. . . .[27]

Slave doctors must not be confused with conjurers, who relied upon supernatural powers to treat disease, as opposed to the prescription of what would be referred to today as drugs. The nature of the treatment was dependent upon the diagnosis; if evil forces were involved, then the conjurer would be the person to effect the cure. If that were not the case, then the root doctor provided the treatment. Of course, the same person could wear the two hats; the approaches were not mutually exclusive. Many whites consulted slave doctors, evidently leaving as satisfied patients. Conjurers were another matter, of course, and white physicians seemed to have tried to reduce their influence over those who believed in them. One white physician reported in the 1850s how he humiliated a few conjurers in Louisiana after an outbreak of cholera on a sugar plantation had killed forty persons.

> I took about three hundred negroes, sick and well, a mile or two back into a dry, open place in the swamp, where there was no house to be seen, or any preparation begun for building any. . . . They encamped in the open air and built fires, although the weather was warm, and some booths were directed to be made over the sick to protect them from the sun and the rain. The ashy-coloured, dry skin conjurers, or prophets, who had alarmed their fellow-servants with the prophecies that the cholera was to kill them all, and who had gained, by various tricks and

artifices, much influence over their superstitious minds, were by my orders, at twilight, called up, stripped, and greased with fat bacon, in the presence of the whole camp—a camp without tents or covering of any kind, except some bushes and boards over the sick from the carts that conveyed them to the camp. After being greased, the grease was well slapped in with broad leather straps, marking time with the tam tam, a wild African dance that was going on in the centre of the camp among all those who had the physical strength to participate in it. This procedure drove the cholera out of the heads of all who had been conjured into the belief that they were to die with the disease; because it broke the charm of the conjurers by converting them, under the greasing and slapping process, into subjects for ridicule and laughter, instead of fear and veneration. The next morning . . . all who had been able to join in the dance the over night, were ordered into the cane-field to work. There were no more cases of cholera, or deaths from that disease after the removal, except one man who had strayed away from the camp, and except also among some half dozen who had been left to take care of the houses, about half of them died.[28]

Black midwives were also highly respected by blacks and whites alike. Most black babies, and many white ones, were delivered with a midwife in attendance. In addition, slave women tended to the sick. One white woman recalled that on her plantation in Virginia: "One of the house-servants, Amy Green—'Aunt Amy' we children called her—was a skilled nurse. My father kept a store of medicines, his scales, etc. So with Aunt Amy's poultices of horseradish and plattain-leaves and her various cuppings and plasters the ailments of the hundred negroes were well taken in hand."[29] These "doctor women" seemed to have assumed the major responsibility for the health care of the slaves on the larger plantations, a fact that has not always been appreciated. A former slave in Georgia remembered that "one had to be mighty sick to have the services of a doctor." Furthermore, "old women were . . . responsible for the care of the sick."[30]

Many slaveowners assumed the primary responsibility for the medical care of their human property. They studied the medical manuals, practiced medicine by trial and error, and became accomplished quacks. One such person was the nineteenth-century North Carolina planter Thomas Pettigrew. He demonstrated a keen interest in the health of his slaves and treated them on the family plantations in Tyrrell and Washington counties. Pettigrew prescribed all kinds of remedies, ordered drugs, and freely dispensed advice on the medical care of slaves. White physicians, understandably, disliked such competition from slaveowners. In the 1850s Dr. D. Warren Brickell of the New Orleans School of Medicine criticized "the almost universal practice, on the part of owners and overseers, of tampering with their sick negroes."[31] Others denounced the widespread use of "negresses" as midwives. One Louisiana doctor complained that "such uneducated persons should be generally successful is owing to the fact that in a great majority of cases no scientific skill is required, and thus a lucky negress becomes the rival of the most learned obstetrician."[32]

White physicians shared the racist assumptions of others in society. Some physicians maintained that blacks had different constitutions from whites. Hence, they had to receive medical care appropriate to that difference. Dr. Samuel A. Cartwright was one of the most aggressive purveyors of the view that there were fundamental physiological differences between blacks and whites. Writing in 1851, he argued that the head of the black person

> . . . is hung on the atlas differently from the white man; the face is thrown more upwards and the neck is shorter and less oblique; the spine more inwards, and the pelvis more obliquely outwards; the thigh bones larger and flattened from before backwards; the bones more bent; the legs curved outwards or bowed; the feet flat; the gastrocnemii muscles smaller; the heel so long, as to make the ankle appear as if planted in the middle of the foot; the gait, hopperhipped, or what the French call l'allure dehanchee, not unlike a person carrying a burden. The projecting mouth, the retreating forehead, the broad, flat nose, thick lips and wooly hair, are peculiarities that strike every beholder.[33]

Cartwright was a staunch defender of the slave system, and his views were more extreme than many of his peers. Their racist views not only fed claims to white superiority but also propagated the notion that slavery was the natural condition of the black person. Free blacks deteriorated as persons, they suggested, because they lacked white supervision. It is now known that the 1840 federal census was deliberately falsified to show that free blacks in the North suffered a higher rate of insanity than did slaves in the South. The intention was to blunt any assault on slavery. John C. Calhoun, the white supremacist who held the post of secretary of state in 1844, observed that the flawed 1840 census revealed that "in all instances in which the states have changed the former relation between the two races the condition of the African, instead of being improved has become worse."[34]

Medical science joined hands with the proslavery politicians to provide an elaborate defense of slavery. But even while physicians asserted the doctrine of white biological superiority and maintained that there were physiological differences between the two races, they were quick to use black bodies for all kinds of scientific experiments. Medical students in such states as Virginia, South Carolina, Alabama, Kentucky, and Georgia learned their craft by observing the course of various diseases particularly on black patients. Medical school faculties advertised for slaves who would become the victims of surgical experimentations. In 1834, one observer noted that in Baltimore, "The bodies of coloured people exclusively are taken for dissection, because the whites do not like it, and the coloured people cannot resist."[35] Dr. T. Stillman, who practiced in Charleston, advertised in 1838 offering to pay "the highest cash price" for fifty slaves "affected with scrofula or king's evil, confirmed hypochondriasm, apoplexy, diseases of the liver, kidneys, spleen, stomach and intestines, bladder and its appendages, diarrhea, dysentery, etc."[36] Undoubtedly, these persons were needed as experimental subjects.

There is abundant evidence suggesting the abuse of blacks by white physicians in the nineteenth century. The procedure for Caesarean operations was perfected on black women. So, too was the painful surgical treatment for vesico-vaginal fistula, defined as "a break in the wall separating the bladder from the vagina."[37] The art of performing ovariectomies (removal of an ovary) owed much to the experiments conducted on black women in Kentucky. Surgery performed on an anesthetized person was also first tried on a black man in 1842. No wonder blacks feared admission to hospitals and the butchery that went on in them. A poem written, presumably by a white person, after slavery was abolished captures these real fears in four of its stanzas:

The Dissecting Hall
Yuh see dat house? Dat great brick house?
Way yonder down de street?
Dey used to take dead folks een dar
Wrapped een a long white sheet.

An' sometimes we'en a nigger'd stop,
A– wondering who was dead,
Dem stujent men would take a club
An' bat 'im on de head.

An' drag that poor dead nigger chile
Right een that 'sectin hall
To vestigate 'is liver–lights–
His gizzard an' 'is gall.

Tek off dat nigger's han's an' feet
His eyes, his head, an' all,
An' w'en dem stujent finish
Dey was nothin' left at all.[38]

Some of the diseases that afflicted the slaves were closely related to dietary deficiencies. Throughout the nineteenth-century South, the slaves' diet consisted primarily of fat pork, vegetables, cornmeal, molasses, rice, meat, and fish. Its nutritional adequacy has been a matter of some controversy. But the issue is a difficult one to resolve because of the wide variation over time in the nature and volume of the slave's diet. The situation becomes even more complicated because human beings have different nutritional requirements at the various stages of their life cycle. Children and pregnant women, for example, have special nutritional needs.

One way to determine the nutritional adequacy of the slave's diet is to examine the kinds of diseases from which they suffered and to determine the degree to which they were nutritionally related. In the case of slave children, data for the years 1849-50 show that they died in large numbers from tetany, rickets, and sudden infant death syndrome. Modern science has suggested that these maladies tend to affect those who are deficient in vitamin D, magnesium, and calcium. Slave children, and adults as well, also engaged in "dirt eating," sometimes with lethal results. This potentially deadly compulsion is the symptom of a disease known as pica, and its cause has been traced in part to deficiencies in potassium, iron, calcium, and magnesium. Southern physicians also described a disease "to which Negro children are liable between the second and the fifth year. . . . It is literally a 'wasting away'–a tabes . . . styled provincially [as] 'the drooping disease of negro children.'"[39] We now know that such symptoms are associated with protein caloric malnutrition.

Adults had their share of nutrition related disorders as well. Pellagra, or "black tongue," a disease that leads to death, was a consequence of a poor diet and vitamin and mineral deficiencies.[40] Adults, as has been mentioned, also suffered from pica. Studies also show that diet-related deficiencies resulted in poor bone formation, eye diseases, skin lesions, anemia, and dental caries. About all that can be safely said about the diet of the adults is that they received adequate amounts of carbohydrates and the attendant calories, but their rations were deficient in foods rich in iron, niacin, thiamine, and many of the amino acids that we now know to be essential to good health.

Slaves, of course, made the best of the foods available to them, whether these came from the masters or from their own resources. They supplemented their weekly rations, if circumstances permitted, with vegetables from their own gardens, fish that they caught, meat from such hunted animals as the opossum, rabbit, and squirrel, as well as provisions pilfered from the plantation. There must have been tremendous variations, however, in the degree to which such additions to the diet were possible. Urban slaves would have had fewer opportunities to supply their own needs, and for the others much would depend on the size of their farm or plantation, the resourcefulness of the individual, and the availability of game.

Whatever the source or nature of their diet, slave women, in particular, developed reputations for culinary triumphs. Their liberal and creative use of seasonings enhanced the appeal of each meal, regardless of its actual composition. Special meals were prepared on Sundays, holidays, cornshuckings, and most festive occasions. A former slave remembered the mood of the cornshuckings: "Oh my Lord, dey would have de big eats on dem days. Would have a big pot out to the barn where dey was shuckin' corn and would boil it full as it could hold wid such as peas, en rice, en collards."[41]

Christmas was an occasion for elaborate meals and consumption of alcohol. Masters provided their human property with drink on that day and looked on approvingly as the slaves drank to their health. But it was the food that made the occasion special. As one former slave reminisced:

> Christmas Day! What a time us Niggers did have dat day! Marse Landnorth and Marse Alec give us evvything you could name to eat: cake of all kinds, fresh meat, light bread, turkeys, chickens, ducks, geese and all kinds of wild game. Dere was allus plenty of pecans, apples, and dried peaches too at Christmas. And the pewter pitcher full of whisky was passed 'round.[42]

Such festivities, of course, gave slaves a chance to enter the white man's world, since Christmas celebrations were not a part of African ancestral traditions. They had a chance to participate in moments of real pleasure even as they were pulled into a world that exacted a price for such seemingly healthy and innocent indulgences.

The festive gatherings of the slaves were invariably accompanied by music and dancing. The African societies from which the slaves came were characterized by the central role that music and ritual dance played in their entertainment and religious observances. The slave trader John Atkins wrote of the people of Sierra Leone in 1721:

> Dancing is the Diversion of their Evenings: Men and Women make a Ring in an open part of the Town, and one at a time shews his skill in antick Motions and Gesticulations, yet with a great deal of Agility, the Company making the Musick by clapping their hands together during the time, helped by the louder noise of two or three drums made of a hollowed piece of Tree, and covered with Kid-Skin. Sometimes they are all round in a Circle laughing, and with uncouth Notes, blame or praise somebody in the Company.[43]

American-born slaves, many scholars have observed, continued the circle ritual. Sterling Stuckey, the most insightful student of this ceremony, notes, "The use of the circle for religious purposes in slavery was so consistent and profound that one could argue that it was what gave form and meaning to black religion and art."[44] The counterclockwise movement of the circle dance seemed to have existed in many of the societies from which the enslaved came, but perhaps with different symbolisms and meanings. In any event, it became ubiquitous in the quarters and, according to Stuckey, it formed the basis of slave culture and society. As he puts it, "The ring in which Africans danced and sang is the key to understanding the means by which they achieved oneness in America."[45]

The record is largely silent on the nature of the slave's music and dancing in that long first century. Their number was small, and they were scattered throughout the colonies. Yet slaves must have gathered together where it was feasible to play their own music, sing, and dance. Certainly, there are reports from the Caribbean islands in the seventeenth century of their cultural life and its ingredients of music, dance, and song. One observer in Barbados described the behavior of the slaves in 1687 as follows:

> Every Sunday (which is the only day of Rest, and Should be set apart for the Service of God) they employ either in . . . making Ropes . . . or else spend the Day in Recreation, as Dancing or Wrestling . . . in their Dancing they use Antick Actions, their hands having more of motion than their feet, and head than either; nor do the men and women dance together, but apart; the Musick to which they dance being a sort of Kettle-Drums, one bigger than another, which makes a strange and various noise.[46]

Eighteenth-century sources provide a glimpse of the music and dance of the slaves. The descriptions are often couched in pejorative language, reflecting the fears and biases of the reporter. In 1709, an Anglican missionary in South Carolina, Frances Le Jau, condemned the "feasts, dances, and merry Meetings" of the slaves on Sundays. Thirty years later George Whitefield denounced the whites of Maryland, Virginia, and North and South Carolina for allowing slaves "to prophane the Lord's Day, by their Dancing, Piping and such like." The slaves who took part in the revolt at Stono, South Carolina, in 1739 were described as "dancing, Singing and beating Drums."[47]

Over the long haul, slaves played numerous kinds of musical instruments. The banjo, known variously as the bandore, banjar, and banza was brought from Africa and appears in the writings of eighteenth-century observers. Banjos were often made from a gourd or wood and animal hide. A former slave recalled, "When we made a banjo we would first of all catch what we called a ground hog, known in the north as a woodchuck. After tanning his hide, it would be stretched over a piece of timber fashioned like a cheese box." In time, as one person wrote in 1856, the banjo became "the real musical instrument of the Southern negroes."[48]

Slaves also played "quills" or panpipes. This instrument was made from reeds. In the words of a former slave: "We plays de quill, made from willow stalk when de sap am up. You takes de stick, and pounds de bark loose and slips it off, den split the wood in one end and down one side, puts holes in de bark and put it back on the stick. De quill plays like the flute."[49] Other slaves played the French horn, tambourine, percussion instruments, and the flute. Drums were also a feature of slave life, sometimes surreptitiously, because of legal prohibitions against their use. Fearful slaveowners believed that slaves could communicate by drumming and would use it as a means of planning uprisings. After the abortive Stono Rebellion of 1739, for example, the South Carolina legislature banned "wooden swords, and other mischievous and dangerous weapons, or using or keeping of drums, horns, or other loud instruments, which may call together, or give sign or notice to one another of their wicked designs or purposes."[50] Drumming survived, however, and there are reports of the practice in the nineteenth century. In 1808, a visitor to New Orleans offered this description of a group of slaves' behavior on a Sunday morning. He saw "twenty different dancing groups of the wretched Africans. . . . They have their own national music, consisting of the most part of a long kind of narrow drum of various sizes, from two to eight feet in length, three or four of which make a band."[51]

The fiddle was one of the most popular instruments used by musically gifted slaves. The earliest reference to such individuals appears in an advertisement for the recovery of a runaway slave in 1734: "Runaway the 26th of June, last, from Samuel Leonard of Perth Amboy, in New Jersey . . . Wan. He is half Indian and half negro. He had on when he went away a blue coat. He plays the fiddle and speaks good English." Fiddlers entertained both black and white audiences. One traveler to Baltimore in 1785 reported how a black fiddler entertained white revelers: "We sent for a violin in the evening and had a most agreeable dance. . . . After the poor Negro's fingers were tired of fiddling, I took the violin and played them the 'Pleasures of Youth' and the 'Savage Dance.'"[52]

Fiddlers and banjoists often earned money for their performances, particularly when they played for whites. This gave them a measure of economic independence although customarily they had to share their earnings with their masters. One such person was the famous Solomon Northup. A free man, Northup was kidnapped in New York in 1841 and sold into slavery. A violinist of much distinction, he earned substantial sums of money entertaining whites for ten years in Louisiana. He was reputed to be one of the wealthiest slaves. Many slaves who did not play the violin or the banjo became accomplished flutists or players of the French horn.

Along with their music, slaves enjoyed the occasions on which they could sing. Whether at work, on festive occasions, in the quarters or at funerals, these persons entertained or consoled themselves with their singing. The fondness for this means of expression often puzzled whites and has been the subject of much confusion. Frederick Douglass, the escaped slave who wrote his first autobiography in 1845, was surprised "to find persons who could speak of the singing among slaves as evidence of their contentment and happiness."[53] Douglass drew upon his own experience to confess, "I have often sung, to drown my sorrow, but seldom to express my happiness. Crying for joy, and singing for joy, were alike uncommon to me while in the jaws of slavery."[54] Dr. Benjamin Rush, a white Philadelphian who disliked slavery, expressed the view, "Instead of considering the songs and dances . . . as marks of their happiness, I have long considered them as physical symptoms of Melancholy Madness, and therfore as certain proofs of their misery."[55]

Such assertions undoubtedly contained a degree of truth. No one can ignore the therapeutic value of the singing and the songs. Yet it is also true that the slaves, as persons, sang because singing had a very deep cultural significance, and a profound spiritual resonance. It was not something that could be programmed; they sang in moments of sadness and pain, and in moments of pleasure and joy. The choice of songs reflected the occasion and the mood, and only those who knew them well could tell the difference. Frances Kemble knew of slaveowners who understood the meanings of the songs and tried to interfere with the singing:

> I have heard that many of the masters and overseers on these planta-tions prohibit melancholy tunes or words, and encourage nothing but cheerful music and senseless words, deprecating the effect of sadder strains upon the slaves, whose peculiar musical sensibility might be expected to make them especially excitable by any songs of a plaintive character, and having any reference to their particular hardships."[56]

The slaves' singing was not solely an expression of contentment or pain or even of melancholy madness; it could be all of these depending on the circumstances. The slaves' mood was not always shaped by the masters. They had a life of their own with all of its private ecstasy and pain, its simple pleasures and times of disappointment and loss. Their singing reflected some of these personal moments when their own needs were paramount and they could be themselves.

For purposes of analysis, the slave songs may be divided into two categories—the secular and the religious. The work songs are among the best known of those that can be called secular. Slaves sang while they cut roads, rowed boats, or worked the tobacco, rice, corn, and sweet potato fields. This was probably not an everyday occurrence, but it was done frequently enough. Describing this practice at St. Helena island, one observer wrote in 1862: "Sixty-eight hands in the potato field plant-ing sweet potatoes, swinging their hoes in unison, timed by a jolly song, words undistinguishable. They work with a good will and plant about thirteen acres during the day."[57]

These songs were often improvised so the words changed often with each rendition. As one traveler noted, "The blacks themselves leave out old stanzas, and introduce new ones at pleasure. Travelling through the South, you may, in passing from Virginia to Louisiana, hear the same tune a hundred times, but seldom the same words accompanying it. This necessarily results from the fact that the songs are unwritten, and also from the habit of extemporizing."[58]

Some of the songs were overtly political in tone, reflecting the slaves' perception of the injustice of their condition:

Missus in the big house,
Mammy in the yard
Missus holdin' her white hands,
Mammy workin' hard.
Old Marse ridin' all time,
Niggers workin' round
Marse sleepin' day time,
Niggers diggin' in the ground.

Or they could celebrate their skill and physical prowess:

When I was young and in my prime (hah!) (hah!)
Stuck my axe deep every time, (hah!) (hah!).

Others could be playful. Consider the following, which was sung in Savannah by slaves as they rowed a boat.

We are going down to Georgia, boys Aye, Aye.
To see the pretty girls, boys; Yoe, Yoe.
We'll give 'em a pint of brandy, boys Aye, Aye.
And a hearty kiss, besides, boys. Yoe, Yoe.

The song "Sold off to Georgy" captures the pain of their condition and the psychic cost of being human property:

Farewell, fellow servants! Oho! Oho!
I'm gwine way to Leabe you; Oho! Oho!
I'm gwine to leabe de ole county Oho! Oho!
I'm sold off to Georgy! Oho! Oho!

Farewell, ole plantation, Oho! Oho!
Farewell, de ole quarter Oho! Oho!

Un daddy, un mammy, Oho! Oho!
Un marster, un missus! Oho! Oho!

My dear wife un one chile, Oho! Oho!
My poor heart is breaking; Oho! Oho!
No more shall I see you, Oho! Oho!
Oh! no more foreber! Oho! Oho!

The religious songs, commonly called spirituals, appeared in the early nineteenth century. These sacred songs were created by an increasingly Christianized slave population. Drawing upon their experiences as Christians, it is entirely understandable that the slaves would develop their own forms of religious expression, whether in song or in other ways. The songs grew from their own souls, their pain, frustrations, and hopes for redemption, much as the hymns of other folk in society reflected their peculiar experiences.[59]

Spirituals had a tremendous appeal for the slaves, and they could be sung on any occasion, not necessarily on religious ones. As the Reverend C. F. Sturgis observed in Alabama in 1851:

> The negro is a great singer, and he sings religious songs in preference to any other; indeed, unless now and then a comic song, often, as I suspect, falsely attributed to them, they sing but few others. They sing at their work, at their homes, on the highway, and in the streets; and, in the large majority of the cases, their songs have a decidedly religious character. How common to see an old woman at her work, "lining out" a hymn to herself and then singing it in a spirit of rapt abstraction from earth and all earthly things.[60]

Spirituals expressed in song a need for freedom, a desire for personal autonomy as in:

When I get to heaven, gwine be at ease
Me and My God gonna do as we please.

Gonna chatter with the Father, argue with the Son,
Tell um' bout the world I just come from.

Or:

Is'e been on the road into heaven, my Lord!
I can't stay behind
O, room in dar, room in dar,
Room in dar, in de heaven, my Lord!
I can't stay behind!

Spirituals also reflected the pain of their earthly condition:

Nobody knows de trubble I sees,
Nobody knows de trubble I sees,
Nobody knows de trubble I sees,
Nobody knows but Jesus.

The lyrics of some spirituals also provided encouragement in the face of adversity:

Breddren, don' get weary, breddren' don' get weary,
Breddren don' get weary. Fo' the work is mos' done.
Keep yo' lamp trim' an' a burnin',
Keep yo' lamp trim' an' a burnin',
Keep yo' lamp trim' an' a burnin',
For the work is mos' done.

The spirituals and the secular songs were the creative expressions of a people trying to make the best of their situation, creating space for themselves and tending to their own needs. Slavery had not left them bereft of pleasures or means of psychological sustenance. Their songs helped meet their inner needs, but they could not lighten the physical burdens of their condition; they provided temporary surcease.

Similarly, the slaves' tales were important as a means of entertainment in the quarters. In a real sense, tales were a form of oral literature, filled with humor, drama, mystery, moral lessons, and strategies for survival. Animals figure prominently in these tales, particularly the crafty Brer Rabbit and the scheming Brer Fox. Brer Anansi, the West African spider and accomplished trickster, appeared in many stories, particularly those told by the slaves in the Caribbean islands. Undoubtedly, the enslaved enjoyed the Brer Rabbit and other stories, humanized these animals in their telling and must have derived vicarious delight from seeing the weak overwhelm the strong, often making fools of them in the process. Slaves also appeared as tricksters in these stories, often using guile to escape from difficult situations.

One such story involved a male slave who stole a chicken from the master and proceeded to cook it. Unfortunately, the master turns up unexpectedly and asks the slave what is being cooked. Thinking rather quickly, the slave announces that it is an opossum, whereupon the master indicates his desire to partake of it as well. Now in a frenzy, the slave devises a plan to thwart the master's desire and to save himself from punishment for the theft of the chicken. He now tells the master, "Dis possum am done to a tu'n. Mus' be all dat good spittin' we done. . . . Us nigguhs allus spits in possum gravy. Makes the meat mo' tenduh. Aunt Janie done spit in it; Uncle Amos done spit in it; de chilluns done spit in it; an' I spit in it myse'f fo' er five times. You wants nice big piece, Massa?" The master, predictably, declines the offer and the slave triumphs.[61]

In a second story, the slave Pompey exposes his master's pretensions:

"Pompey, how do I look?" the master asked.
"O, massa, mighty. You looks mighty."
"What do you mean 'Mighty,' Pompey?"
"Why, massa, you looks noble."
"What do you mean by noble?"
"Why, suh, you looks just like a lion."
"Why, Pompey, where have you seen a lion?"
"I saw one down in yonder field the other day, massa."
"Pompey, you foolish fellow, that was a jackass."
"Was it, massa? Well, suh, you looks just like him."[62]

Not only were such tales entertaining, but they also socialized the listeners into important survival strategies. Yet, these were tales and nothing more, and slaves did not confuse them with the realities of their daily lives, anymore than contemporary children or adults in the Caribbean confuse their own situations with the cunning exploits of Brer Anansi. Contemporary historians analyze these tales for symbolic meanings, irony, ambiguity, and so on. While this approach undoubtedly has intellectual merit, we must be careful lest we apply these artificial and theoretical constructs willy-nilly to slave life and to social reality. These modern and ingenious analyses of the slaves' stories make for good reading as exercises in literary criticism, but regrettably they often blur the real distinctions between fact and fiction, reality and unreality. Slaves enjoyed their stories, simultaneously drawing lessons from some of them, but none of these tales, no matter how powerful in the telling and their symbolic meanings, could lighten the burden of their daily oppression. Moreover, the tales did not always reflect the realities of the slaves' everyday experiences.

In addition to storytelling, the enslaved engaged in other forms of entertainment. Slaves in New England and New York, starting from around the mid-eighteenth century, held annual elections for "kings" and "governors" and other notables. At the appointed time each year, they would gather to celebrate the occasion with music, dance, food, games, and parades. Slaves

. . . decked themselves out in striking or fantastic costumes, and on horseback or on foot accompanied their "governor" through the streets. The parade included an accompaniment of hideous music, and was followed by a dinner and dance in some commodious hall hired for the purpose. Sometimes, however, the dinner and dance were not preceded by the parade.[63]

The elected officials exercised some power in their communities. In Hartford, Connecticut, for example, the "governor" reportedly "settled all grave disputes in the last resort, questioned conduct and imposed penalties and punishments sometimes for vice and misconduct."[64]

Slaves, particularly those living on the Eastern Shores and in North Carolina celebrated a festival at Christmas known as John Canoe, or John Kuner. On Christmas morning, the revelers donned colorful costumes and masks, played music, danced through the streets soliciting gifts in return for their performance. Evidently African in origin, this custom was also observed in the slave societies of the Caribbean, particularly in Jamaica. A description of its practice in North Carolina merits being quoted in full.

> Every child rises early on Christmas morning to see the Johnkannaus. Without them, Christmas would be shorn of its greatest attraction . . . companies of slaves [come] from the plantations. . . . Two athletic men, in calico wrappers, have a net thrown over them. . . . Cows' tails are fastened to their backs, and their heads are decorated with horns. A box, covered with sheepskin, is called the gumbo box. A dozen beat on this,. while others strike triangles and jawbones, to which bands of dancers keep time. For a month previous they are composing songs, which are sung on this occasion. These companies, of a hundred each, turn out early in the morning, and are allowed to go round till twelve o'clock begging for contributions. . . . It is seldom that any white man or child refuses to give them a trifle. If he does, they regale his ears with the following song:

> "Poor massa, so dey say
> Down in de heel, so dey say;
> Got no money, so dey say;
> Not one shillin', so dey say;
> God A'mighty, bress you, so dey say."[65]

While John Kunering recalled an African past in music, costume, and dance, the arts and crafts of the slaves also reflected the continuing vitality of the aesthetic of their ancestral lands. Their basketry, particularly the coiled baskets of South Carolina and the Sea Islands, preserved African styles. Talented slaves carved richly detailed walking sticks, human figures, animals, a variety of weapons, musical instruments, and household wares. One man recalled that "the African men used to all the time make little clay images. Sometimes they like men sometimes they like animals. . . . Sometimes they try to make the image out of wood."[66] Slave women also developed quilting into a fine art form. The design of the quilt tops reflected African influences, but according to one

Face vessel with handle, stoneware, kaolin, c. 1860. Height 4″. South Carolina, Bath, Thomas Davies Pottery.

Jar, stoneware, ash glaze. Inscription reads: "Lm Aug 24 1857/Dave." On opposite side: "Pretty little girl on the virge/volca[n]ic mountain how they burge." Dave the Potter, South Carolina. Miles Mill, 1780–1863.

scholar, the "techniques of quilt construction were largely derived from Euro-American sources."[67] His comments about quilting have a broad applicability to other aspects of the slaves' cultural life:

> Some of the geometric combinations of odd scraps of cloth that decorate American quilts have African analogs. It is possible that some of the quilts made by slaves simultaneously served the requirements of their masters and preserved a cultural memory. The Afro-American quilt provides us with an example of how European artifacts may be modified by African canons of design and thus stand as statements of cultural survival rather than tenacity.[68]

Slaves, as has always been the case with human beings regardless of their condition, had no choice but to create the cultural bases of their sustenance. Drawing upon their African heritages and the experiences in America, they fashioned a culture that was their own. It grounded them in their own space, but it never made their oppression lighter or any less real. The slaves' cultural practices responded to and shaped their inner needs. But it left their condition of servitude untouched, the legal barriers in place, and the daily abuse unabated.

Notes

1. Inscoe, "Carolina Slave Names," 554.
2. Michael P. Johnson, "Work, Culture and the Slave Community: Slave Occupations in the Cotton Belt in 1860," *Labor History*, 27 (1986), 343.
3. Frances Kemble, *Journal*, 189.
4. Johnson, "Work, Culture, and the Slave Community," 546.
5. Ibid., 345-346.
6. Henry Bibb, *Narrative of the Life and Adventures of Henry Bibb, An American Slave* (New York: Negro Universities Press, 1968), 33.
7. Frederick Douglass, *My Bondage and My Freedom* (New York: Arno Press, 1968), 9.
8. C. W. Harper, "Black Aristocrats: Domestic Servants on the Antebellum Plantation," *Phylon*, 46 (1985), 134.
9. Leon Litwack, *Been in the Storm So Long: The Aftermath of Slavery* (New York: Random House, 1979), 17.
10. Harper, "Black Aristocrats," 129.
11. Genovese, *Roll Jordan Roll*, 111-112.
12. David Herbert Donald, "A Generation of Defeat," in Walter J. Fraser Jr., and Winfred B. Moore Jr., *From the Old South to the New: Essays on the Transitional South* (Westport, CT: Greenwood Press, 1981), 11.
13. David Duncan Wallace, *The Life of Henry Laurens* (New York: G. P. Putnam's Sons, 1915), 436.
14. C.W. Harper, "House Servants and Field Hands: Fragmentation in the Antebellum Slave Community," *North Carolina Historical Review*, 55 (1978), 54.
15. Charles Ball, *Fifty Years in Chains* (New York: Dover Publications, 1970), 275.
16. Levine, *Black Culture and Black Consciousness*, 61.
17. Dena Epstein, *Sinful Tunes and Spirituals: Black Folk Music to the Civil War* (Urbana: University of Illinois Press, 1977), 235.
18. David R. Roediger, "And Die in Dixie: Funerals, Death, and Heaven in the Slave Community 1700-1865," *The Massachusetts Review* (Spring 1981), 166.
19. Ibid., 170.
20. Piersen, *Black Yankees*, 77.
21. Sterling Stuckey, *Slave Culture*, 40-41.
22. Ibid., 41.
23. Robert Faris Thompson, "African Influences on the Art of the United States," in Armstead Robinson et al., eds., *Black Studies in the University* (New Haven: Yale University Press, 1969), 150.
24. Josephine A. Becker-Butts, "'She Make Funny Flat Cake She Call Saraka': Gullah Women and Food Practices Under Slavery," in Larry E. Hudson Jr., ed., *Working Toward Freedom: Slave Society and Domestic Economy in the American South* (Rochester: University of Rochester Press, 1994), 219.
25. Todd Savitt, "Black Health on the Plantation: Masters, Slaves, and Physicians," in Ronald L. Numbers and Todd L. Savitt, eds., *Science and Medicine in the Old South* (Baton Rouge: Louisiana State University Press, 1989), 354.
26. Rawick, *The American Slave*, vol. 13, pt. 4, 276.
27. Bennett H. Wall, "Medical Care of Ebenezer Pettigrew's Slaves," *Mississippi Valley Historical Review*, 37 (1950), 465.
28. John S. Haller Jr., "The Negro and the Southern Physician: A Study of Medical and Racial Attitudes, 1800-1860," *Medical History*, 16 (1972), 242.
29. Savitt, "Black Health on the Plantation," 354.
30. Deborah Gray White, *Ar'n't I a Woman?: Female Slaves in the Plantation South* (New York: W. W. Norton, 1985), 125.

31. Walter Fisher, "Physicians and Slavery in the Antebellum Southern Medical Journal," *Journal of the History of Medicine and Allied Sciences,* 23 (1968), 42.
32. Ibid., 43.
33. Haller, "The Negro and the Southern Physician," 247-248.
34. Leon Litwack, *North of Slavery: The Negro in the Free States, 1790-1860* (Chicago: University of Chicago Press, 1961), 43.
35. Todd Savitt, "The Use of Blacks for Medical Experimentation and Demonstration in the Old South," *Journal of Southern History,* 48:3 (1982), 337.
36. Ibid., 343.
37. Ibid., 344.
38. Ibid., 341.
39. Kenneth F. Kiple and Virginia H. Kiple, "Slave Child Mortality: Some Nutritional Answers to a Perennial Puzzle," *Journal of Social History,* 10 (1977), 297.
40. See Kenneth F. Kiple and Virginia H. Kiple, "Black Tongue and Black Men: Pellagra and Slavery in the Antebellum South," *Journal of Southern History,* 43 (1977), 411-428.
41. Charles Joyner, "Soul Food and the Sambo Stereotype: Foodlore from the Slave Narrative Collection," *Keystone Folklore Quarterly,* 16 (1971), 176.
42. Ibid., 176-177.
43. John Atkins, *A Voyage to Guinea, Brasil, and the West Indies . . .* (London, 1735), 53.
44. Stuckey, *Slave Culture,* 11.
45. Ibid., 12.
46. Epstein, *Sinful Tunes and Spirituals,* 29.
47. Ibid., 38-39.
48. Ibid., 146.
49. Norman Yetman, *Life Under the "Peculiar Institution": Selections from the Slave Narrative Collection* (New York: Holt, Rhinehart and Winston, 1970), 170.
50. Epstein, *Sinful Tumes and Spirituals,* 59.
51. Ibid., 52.
52. Ibid., 113-115.
53. Frederick Douglass, *Narrative of the Life of Frederick Douglass, an American Slave, Written by Himself* (Cambridge: Harvard University Press, 1960), 38.
54. Ibid., 38.
55. Epstein, *Sinful Tunes and Spirituals,* 42.
56. Frances Anne Kemble, *Journal of a Residence on a Georgian Plantation in 1838-1839* (New York: Knopf, 1961), 129.
57. Epstein, *Sinful Tunes and Spirituals,* 163.
58. Dena Epstein, *Slave Music in the United States Before 1860: A Survey of Sources,* Part 1, Music Library Association (Spring 1963), 70.
59. See Epstein, *Sinful Tunes and Spirituals,* for the lyrics quoted here; Blassingame, *The Slave Community.*
60. Epstein, *Sinful Tunes and Spirituals,* 224.
61. Levine, *Black Culture and Black Consciousness,* 128.
62. Mel Watkins, *On the Real Side: Laughing, Lying, and Signifying-The Underground Tradition of African American Humor* (New York: Simon and Schuster, 1994), 67.
63. Hubert H. S. Aimes, "African Institutions in America," *Journal of American Folk-Lore,* 18 (1905), 15.
64. Joseph P. Reidy, "'Negro Election Day' and Black Community Life in New England, 1750-1860," *Marxist Perspectives,* 1:3 (1978), 106.
65. Jacobs, *Incidents in the Life of a Slave Girl,* 121-122.
66. John Vlach, *The Afro-American Tradition in Decorative Arts* (Athens: University of Georgia Press, 1990), 27.
67. Ibid., 44.
68. Ibid.

Toward Freedom

For almost the duration of slavery in colonial and independent America, there were two legal categories of black persons: the enslaved and the free. Free blacks appear in the Virginia records as early as 1650, and by 1860 their number had increased to about 500,000 in the nation as a whole. Always occupying an insecure place in the larger society, free blacks were denied many of the basic rights of full citizenship. Yet they played a fundamental role in laying the institutional foundations of black America, in the struggle for equal rights, and in the assault on slavery in the nineteenth century.

Scattered evidence indicates that a few blacks enjoyed a free status during the long first century of their presence. Some of these individuals were probably indentured servants who had completed their service; a few may have purchased their freedom, and others were probably manumitted by their masters for various reasons. Their number hardly exceeded a handful, but whites acted quite early to confine them to a subordinate place in society. As early as the 1660s, the Virginia House of Burgesses declared that they "ought not in all respects . . . be admitted to a full fruition of the exemptions and impunities of the English."[1]

By the eighteenth century, a sizable proportion of the growing free black population consisted of mulattoes. They were frequently the progeny of white male servants and black women or white female servants and black men. These kinds of alliances offended the sensibilities of other whites, even as they became increasingly commonplace. Colonial laws usually punished white women who had sexual relations with black

185

men, and there were laws that required that any children produced by such unions were to be enslaved for the first thirty-one years of their lives. We can never be certain about the number of free persons who claimed such ancestry, but qualitative evidence suggests that the children of black and white couples dominated the early free population.

Not all mulatto children were descended from white servants. In fact, the number of indentured whites drastically declined by the eighteenth century. Many, if not most, mixed children were probably the offspring of the slaveowners. A federal census taken in 1850 found that with the exception of the North, mulattoes comprised a significant share of the free population everywhere. The breakdown was as follows:

North	28.9%
Upper South	38.5%
Lower South	68.6%

South Carolina and Louisiana, in particular, had free populations that were overwhelmingly of a mixed racial ancestry. In 1860, for example, only 5 percent of South Carolina's slaves were mulattoes but they comprised about three-quarters of the free population of 9,914 persons. Not all of these persons were the product of white-black unions; a high proportion were the sons and daughters of mulatto parents.

As a group, the free population numbered 59,000 in 1790, 108,000 in 1800, 186,000 in 1810, 234,000 in 1820, 434,000 in 1850, and 488,000 in 1860. The War of Independence and its aftermath, as we have seen, led to a dramatic growth in the free population as these figures demonstrate. The ranks of the free also increased as some slaves who were in a position to do so purchased their freedom or had it done for them by relatives or other benefactors. The masters, obviously, had to approve these transactions. Not only did some slaves buy themselves, but they also purchased their spouses and children as well. One can hardly ignore the pain involved in such business arrangements, of persons saving their paltry sums to buy a freedom that others in society claimed as their birthright. A former slave recognized the stark irony inherent in such realities when she described her grandfather's purchase of her mother: "Now mind you, for his own child, they charged him $350, just think of that."[2] Such awful dilemmas notwithstanding, thousands of persons made enormous sacrifices to be able to purchase themselves and their loved ones, even if freedom did not confer on them all of the rights that whites enjoyed. A Virginia slave, Godfrey Brown, took twenty-three years to accumulate the $2,375 required to purchase his freedom and that of his wife and nine children. We can never know how long it took most slaves to raise the requisite funds, but the record shows that a high percentage became free as a result of self-purchase. Fully 42 percent of the free persons in Cincinnati in 1839, for example, had bought their own freedom.[3]

The ranks of the free population also swelled as a consequence of flight. Slaves in the Upper South were more likely to find this an attractive means of claiming their freedom during the nineteenth century because of their proximity to the states that had passed emancipation acts. Philadelphia, New York, Boston, and elsewhere witnessed the arrival of many fugitives. The North Star had a profound emotional resonance. In this context, it may be added that thousands of refugees came to Louisiana, Georgia, South Carolina, and Virginia during and after the great slave rebellion that began in St. Domingue (Haiti) in 1791. Between 1791 and 1804 when Haiti became a free republic, the slaves fought a series of wars against their masters. Fearing for their lives, several thousand persons fled to the United States. Although most of the refugees were white, a significant proportion were free persons of African descent, generally mulattoes. Anxious Southerners, fearing the virus of rebellion, hastily passed laws banning the entry of these people, but such hysteria frequently failed to achieve its objective.

The free population also increased by natural means. In time, most became the residents of urban areas, where it was easier to establish networks of relationships, find employment, create institutions of their own, and avoid some of the virulent racism that existed in the society as a whole. There were no sanctuaries, of course, but life was somewhat easier where there was a critical mass of other free blacks, where solace could be found in numbers, and support mechanisms nurtured. By 1860, 61 percent of the free blacks in the North were urban dwellers, compared to 35 percent in the South.

LEGAL STATUS

In many respects, however, the term "free black" or "free negro" was a misnomer. Believing that slavery was the natural condition for blacks in the United States, some whites found the presence of the freed persons an anomaly. The Southern ideologue George Fitzhugh enquired:

> What Shall be Done with the Free Negroes? A free Negro! Why, the very term seems an absurdity. It is our daily boast, and experience verifies it, that the Anglo-Saxons of America are the only people in the world fitted for freedom. The negro's [condition] is not human freedom, but the wild and vicious license of the fox, the wolf or the hawk.[4]

No matter where they lived, free blacks lacked the basic rights that freedom conferred upon whites, particularly men. Free blacks, it can be argued, existed at the sufferance of whites. Measured against white men and women, they did not possess "rights" but a small pile of concessions, but even those were never secure, never inviolate. Referring to the status of free blacks in Georgia and by extension free blacks in the South as a whole, Justice Joseph Lumpkin of the Georgia Supreme Court noted just before the outbreak of the Civil War:

> The status of the African in Georgia, whether bond or free, is such that he has no civil, social or political rights or capacity, whatever, except such as are bestowed upon him by statute, . . . the act of manumission confers no other right but . . . freedom from the domination of the master, and the limited liberty of locomotion.[5]

Free blacks occupied a legal middle ground, an intermediate stage between slavery and freedom. Not legally owned, they were perceived, nonetheless, by those who made the rules as inferior and destined to occupy only a subordinate place in society. As Philip Barbour, who was later to become a U.S. Supreme Court justice, observed in 1820, free blacks "are just enough elevated to have some sense of liberty, and yet not the capacity to estimate or enjoy all its rights . . . and being between two societies, above one and below the other, they are in a most dissatisfied state."[6]

Racist ideology legitimized the denial of rights to free blacks and their separate treatment. Although the number of free blacks was relatively small during the colonial period, whites developed a body of legislation that confined them to their own sphere, excluding them from the benefits of freedom and making them pariahs. In 1723 the governor of Virginia was convinced that by the imposition of a "perpetual Brand upon Free-Negroes [and] Mulattos by excluding them from the great Priviledge of a Freeman," whites could "make the free-Negros sensible that a distinction ought to be made between their offspring and the Descendants of an Englishman, with whom they never were to be Accounted Equal."[7]

There was some uncertainty as to whether free blacks were citizens of the republic or whether they constituted a separate legal category of persons. The issue was not resolved until the landmark *Dred Scott* decision was rendered in 1857. Prior to that time, a free black's legal status and rights depended on the state in which he or she resided. The federal government had not addressed the issue as such, although Congress had passed discriminatory legislation against blacks from time to time. The Congress passed legislation in 1792 excluding them from the militia, and in 1810 they were prevented from delivering the mail. In 1820, they were denied the right to hold elective office in Washington, D.C. In addition, Congress turned a blind eye to the treatment of free blacks by the various states, even admitting to the union those whose constitutions contained anti-black measures.

Free blacks found no haven from mistreatment at the hands of the authorities in any state. Northerners who passed acts of emancipation demonstrated what they really thought about blacks by adopting an elaborate body of legislation that created a modified form of slavery. In fact, several states legislated against the entry of free blacks from areas outside their jurisdiction. Their rationalization, in spite of the libertarian rhetoric of the War of Independence, was based on the assertion of white supremacy and black inferiority. One white resident of Indiana who supported the exclusion of blacks from that state felt that "it would be better to kill them off at once, if there is no other way to get rid of them . . . we know how the Puritans did with the Indians, who were infinitely more magnanimous and less impudent than the colored race."[8] While the constitutions of Illinois (1848), Indiana (1851), and Oregon (1857) banned the entry of blacks, other states did not go nearly as far.

Virginia was the first state to adopt measures prohibiting the immigration of free blacks. This law was enacted in 1793. South Carolina passed a similar statute in 1800, Kentucky in 1807, Maryland in 1808, and Delaware in 1810. Ohio did not ban the entry of free blacks, but it required them to post a $500 bond as a guarantee of their good conduct and to provide documentary proof of their free status. North Carolina required the posting of a $200 bond, and Georgia imposed a tax of twenty dollars on all free persons who entered the state.

Although some states declined to prevent or restrict the entry of free blacks, they were not so hesitant to adopt other kinds of discriminatory measures. Whites, demanding that blacks not pose any challenge to their political power, manifested this fear by racist arguments. One Northern legislator believed that it would be injudicious to allow blacks political equality with whites since they were "a peculiar people, . . . incapable of exercising that privilege with any sort of discretion, prudence or independence."[9] The opinion of a delegate to the 1821 New York constitutional convention merits being cited. He feared that the floodgates would be opened once free blacks achieved the right to vote. Not only did they stand a chance of being eligible to participate in future conventions, he complained, but they might serve as jurors or be elected to Congress. The delegate believed that a "southern gentleman" would be offended if he were elected to Congress and found a slave he had freed as a colleague.[10]

Under the circumstances it is hardly surprising that in 1840, 93 percent of the free black population in the North could not vote. In 1860, blacks could vote without restrictions only in the New England states of Maine, Vermont, New Hampshire, Rhode Island, and Massachusetts. These were states where the small black population posed no real threat to white political power. Even so, these black voters faced intimidation at the polls. One Southern senator claimed in 1850 that whites in

Massachusetts "drive them from the polls at an election, and scorn and spit upon them."[11] Black residents of New York could vote if they owned property of a certain value or if they had lived in the state for a specified period of time. In contrast, they could not vote in Pennsylvania, Connecticut, and New Jersey.

The situation was much the same in the Southern and border states. Immediately after the War of Independence, Delaware, Maryland, and Kentucky granted the franchise to blacks but later rescinded it as their number increased. In justifying their behavior, the legislators in Maryland said that free blacks should not "be entitled to the rights of free men." This pattern of disenfranchisement came to prevail in all of the Southern states with the exception of North Carolina and Tennessee.[12] No region of the country could claim completely clean hands on the issue of access to the ballot box from those who had escaped slavery's chains.

The range of restrictive legislation arrayed against free blacks everywhere, coupled with the racist insults leveled against them, led inevitably to questions about their legal status and rights as children of America's soil. Charles Pinckney, who attended the Constitutional Convention as a delegate, noted that in 1787, "There did not then exist such a thing in the Union as a black or colored citizen, nor could I have conceived it possible such a thing could ever have existed in it."[13] Successive U.S. attorneys general maintained that blacks were not citizens. Roger Taney, the attorney general in 1831, was certain that the Constitution had not accorded citizenship to blacks. His opinion was, "The African race in the United States even when free, are everywhere a degraded class, and exercise no political influence. The privileges they are allowed to enjoy, are accorded to them as a matter of kindness and benevolence rather than of right. . . . And where they are nominally admitted by law to the privileges of citizenship, they have no effectual power to defend them, and are permitted to be citizens by the sufferance of the white population and hold whatever rights they enjoy at their mercy."[14]

The issue was not resolved until the controversial *Dred Scott* v. *Sandford* decision of 1857. Born a slave in Virginia, Scott was taken by his owner, Peter Blow, to St. Louis, where he was sold to a physician, John Emerson, in 1832. Dr. Emerson was commissioned to the army at Fort Armstrong, Illinois, in 1835 and Scott accompanied him. Illinois was a state where slavery had been excluded by the Missouri Compromise, but Scott was still held in bondage. In 1836, Emerson took Scott to the Wisconsin Territory where he had moved, a northern area where slavery had been barred by the Missouri Compromise. Emerson was later transferred to Fort Snelling, Minnesota, and Scott again found himself a resident of a state where slavery had been outlawed by the Missouri Compromise. Scott lived in Louisiana with his master after yet

Dred Scott (1795–1858)

another transfer and again in Minnesota. In 1840, Scott returned to St. Louis with Emerson's wife, since she did not accompany him to his new post in Florida. Dr. Emerson eventually returned to St. Louis, where he died in 1843.

Three years later, Scott and his wife, Harriett, whom he had married in Minnesota, brought suit against Mrs. Emerson. They claimed they were entitled to their freedom by virtue of their residence in Illinois, Minnesota, and Wisconsin, areas where slavery had been excluded. Acting against all precedent, the court rejected Scott's petition. Scott filed another petition, and in 1850 the court found in his favor. Mrs. Emerson appealed to the Missouri Supreme Court, and in 1852 it reversed the decision of the lower court. Scott would remain a slave. William Scott, who wrote the decision for the court, held that Missouri was not bound "to respect the laws of other states," meaning that Scott could not claim to be free based on his residence on free soil. The judge ended his opinion with a ringing defense of slavery: "We are almost persuaded," he wrote, "that the introduction of slavery amongst us was, in the providence of God who makes the evil passions of men subservient to His own glory, a means of placing that unhappy race within the pale of civilized nations."[15]

After various legal maneuverings the case was appealed to the U.S. Supreme Court in 1854. The Court heard arguments in 1856 and faced the task of resolving at least two important questions. Was Scott, as a black person, a citizen capable of bringing a suit in a federal court? Was Scott, by virtue of his residence on free soil, a free man? The decision was rendered in 1857.

The Supreme Court, in a 7-to-2 decision, found against Dred Scott. Speaking for the Court, Chief Justice Roger Taney posed the question of black citizenship:

> The question is simply this: Can a negro, whose ancestors who were imported into this country and sold as slaves, become a member of the political community formed and brought into existence by the Constitution of the United States, and as such become entitled to all of the rights, and privileges and immunities, guaranteed by that instrument to the citizen. One of which rights is the privilege of suing in a court of the United States in the cases specified in the Constitution.[16]

The chief justice answered the question in the negative, noting that blacks "are not included, and were not intended to be included under the word 'citizens' in the Constitution and can therefore claim none of the rights and privileges which that instrument provides for and secures to citizens of the United States." Furthermore, states could not confer the right of citizenship on any person "within the meaning of the Constitution."[17] Thus, Scott was a citizen of neither Missouri nor the United States. Taney was certain that this was the intent of the framers of the Constitution because at that time blacks:

> had for more than a century before been regarded as beings of an inferior order, and altogether unfit to associate with the white race, either in social or political relations; and so far inferior, that they had no rights which the white man was bound to respect; and that the negro might justly and lawfully be reduced to slavery for his benefit. He was bought and sold, and treated as an ordinary article of merchandise and traffic, whenever a profit could be made by it. This opinion was at that time fixed and universal in the civilized portion of the white race.[18]

The conclusion that blacks "had no rights which the white man was bound to respect" accurately reflected the place of blacks in society at the time of the War of Independence and later. As was indicated earlier in this volume, the inability of free blacks to testify against whites, serve on juries, or even to vote in most places placed them at the mercy of the dominant group. Free blacks, to reemphasize, had concessions that could be abrogated at any time by white authorities with impunity.

Justice Taney not only underscored the inferior place of blacks but also held that they could never become citizens. As he put it, the federal government lacked the power to "raise to the rank of a citizen anyone born in the United States, who from birth or parentage, by the laws of the country, belongs to an inferior and subordinate class." Dred Scott and all of those who looked like him would not be recognized as citizens of the United States. The black person's legal status had been resolved, or so it seemed.

The Court's decision was quickly denounced by such personages as Frederick Douglass, who angrily described it as the "judicial incarnation of wolfishness."[19] William Still, who was the director of the General Vigilance Committee of Philadelphia, an organization that provided financial and other assistance to escaped slaves, saw the decision as "more discouraging and more prostrating to the hopes of the colored man than any preceding act of tyranny."[20] Few of them could have been surprised, however, given the almost unbroken record of the law and the judiciary in protecting the interests of whites and the slavocracy. Yet the decision had the effect of exacerbating national tensions over the issue of slavery and embarrassed and outraged those whites who supported equal rights for blacks and the emancipation of the slaves. It is doubtful whether the Dred Scott decision made a fundamental difference in the life of any black person, free or slave. Free blacks had experienced many reverses in their struggle for equal rights, so this decision, although bearing the imprimatur of the highest court in the land, was not an aberration.

Not only did free blacks face external pressures, but their community in formation was not immune to inner tensions and conflicts. Scattered evidence suggests, for example, that some free blacks internalized the larger society's pernicious color hierarchy. A white phenotype, because of its association of the aesthetic with the slaveholding class, seemed to have carried weight among some free blacks, particularly those of mixed racial ancestry. Thus, free blacks with a lighter complexion enjoyed greater prestige in their emerging community. But the matter was not always that simple. Free blacks of mixed ancestry tended to be better off economically, since many had received some economic assistance from the white parent. Then, too, mulattoes were more likely to be hired by whites, who accorded them a higher degree of human worth, and they faced fewer limitations on their possibilities. Some of these persons, particularly if they were very light skinned, rejected the black part of their personhood and "passed" for white if circumstances permitted. Whites also aided these differences and made sharp distinctions between those who were black in color and those who were of a lighter hue. One revealing example of this came from the Louisiana Supreme Court in 1856. The court concluded that "in the eyes of Louisiana Law there is . . . all the difference between a free man of color [mulatto] and a slave that there is between a white man and a slave."[21]

During the nineteenth century, if not earlier, Charleston's free mulatto population demonstrated some of the inner tensions of free blacks and the reach of unhealthy white racial attitudes. Absorbing the racial attitudes of the master class, Charleston's mulatto elite founded a benevolent society in 1790 that restricted its membership to peoples of mixed ancestry. Known as the Brown Fellowship Society of Charleston, it admitted to membership only the wealthiest mulattoes, who had to prove their racial heritage.

The Friendly Moralist Society, which was founded in 1838, also restricted its membership to Charleston's free mulatto elite. It was not as prestigious an organization as the Brown Fellowship Society, although its members came largely from skilled artisans. In order to become a member, one had to be "a bona fide free brown man; over the age of eighteen; of moral character, and of good standing in the community."[22] An insecure people in a slave society where whites were free and most blacks were slaves, free mulattoes were aware of their precarious status between the two larger groups. They feared being relegated to the ranks of slaves and sought to distinguish themselves from other blacks on the basis of their partial white ancestry. But the acceptance they sought from whites was never accorded them, at least not as completely as they had desired. In a telling indication of how whites perceived mulattoes, several Southern legislators began in 1860 to consider the issue of the enslavement of free blacks, including mulattoes. The fate of the mixed group would in this and other ways be inextricably linked to that of their darker brethren.

A number of free peoples of African descent, regardless of shade of skin, also owned slaves. Essentially, there were two types of free black slaveowners: those who owned other persons for economic gain and those who had a more humanitarian objective. The first free black slaveowner on record fell into the former category. Anthony Johnson was one of the first Africans brought to Virginia in 1622. He acquired his freedom, and in 1651 he received 250 acres as a "headright" for importing five black persons into the colony. In 1654, Johnson was sued by his black servant John Casor for holding him longer than his "seaven or eight years of Indenture." This extraordinary document deserves to be quoted at length:

> The deposition of Capt. Samll. Goldsmyth taken in open court 8th of March [16]54 sayeth that being att ye house of Anth. Johnson Negro

about ye beginning of November last to receive a Hogsd of tobac, a negro called Jno. Casor came to this depo[nen]t & told him yt hee came into Virginia for seaven or eight years of Indenture; yt hee had demanded his freedome of Antho. Johnson his mayster & further sd yt hee had kept him his serv[ant] seaven years longer than hee should or ought; and desired that this Depont would see yet hee might have noe wronge; whereupon your depont demanded of Anth. Johnson his Indenture. the sd Johnson answered hee never saw any. The negro Jno. Casor replyed when hee came in he had an Indenture. Anth. Johnson sd hee had ye Negro for his life, but Mr. Robert & George Parker sd they knewe that ye sd Negro had an Indenture in one Mr. S[andys?] hand on ye other side of ye Baye. Further sd Mr. Robert Parker & his Brother George sd (if the sd. Anth. Johnson did not let ye negro go free) the said negro Jno Casor would recover most of his Cows from him ye sd Johnson. Then Anth. Johnson (as this dep't. did suppose) was in a great feare. . . . Anth. Johnsons sonne in Law, his wife & his own two sonnes persuaded the old negro Anth. Johnson to sett the sd Jno. Casor free . . . more sth not.

Samll Goldsmyth
Eight March Anno 1654[23]

Although Casor was declared free, Johnson was not satisfied and filed a petition to determine whether Casor was legally a slave or a servant. A summary of the proceedings follows:

Whereas complaint was this daye made to ye court by ye humble peticion of Anth. Johnson Negro ag[ains]t Mr. Robert Parker that hee detayneth one John Casor a Negro the plaintiffs Serv[an]t under pretense yt the sd Jno. Casor is a freeman the court seriously considering & maturely weighing ye premises doe fynd that ye sd Mr. Robert Parker most unrightly keepeth ye sd Negro John Casor from his r[igh]t mayster Anth. Johnson as it appeareth by ye Deposition of Capt. Samll Goldsmith & many probable circumstances. Be it therefore ye Judgement of ye court & ordered that ye sd Jno. Casor negro, shall forthwith bee turned into ye service of his sd master Anthony Johnson and that the sd Mr. Robert Parker make payment of all charges in the suite and execution.[24]

Johnson won his suit, upholding his right as a slaveholder and joining the ranks of those persons who had earlier held him in bondage. Johnson and the other free black slaveowners in this category could hardly have been blind to the profound irony when they became purchasers of human flesh. It showed the enormously corruptive power of slavery, since its victims could also become perpetrators of the infamy.

Most free blacks did not own slaves. This practice, whether stemming from humanitarian imperatives, was simply beyond their financial reach. One estimate for Virginia suggests that only 1.7 percent of free blacks owned slaves in 1830 or 948 persons out of a free population of

55,307. There were only 192 free black slaveowners in North Carolina in 1830, and by 1860 the number had decreased to eight. According to the census of 1830, 2,128 free blacks in the Upper South owned 4,728 slaves and 7,188 slaves were owned by 1,556 blacks in the Lower South.

Most freed persons who owned slaves for economic gain had one or two. A few had more but this was unusual. William Ellison, who was born a slave in South Carolina, eventually acquired seventy slaves, who worked on his cotton plantation in Sumter. Andrew Durnford, who resided in Louisiana, owned twenty-five slaves, and Joseph Hanscome of Charleston had sixteen in 1835. Frankey Miles of Amelia County, Virginia, owned nineteen slaves in 1860, and John Gardner of South Carolina had sixty-two in 1847. These slaveowners, like their white counterparts, approached the slaving business with the detachment they would for any other commercial enterprise. When Andrew Durnford went to Virginia to buy other blacks in 1835, his comments revealed the social distance between himself and those whom he sought to purchase:

> I have two or three bargains on hand, butt so high, that I dare nott come to a conclusion, a woman of 32, her daughter of 12, a boy of 7, a boy of 3 for [$]1,350. I have made an offer of 1,000$.

He was annoyed that some persons thought that he drove a hard bargain. "They all say I wish to have people cheap, I tell them that I must have something for my money."[25]

Black slaveowners were probably no better or worse than whites in the treatment of their slaves. They bought these persons for economic gain and made the usual demands on them. Some exhibited the same blindness to human suffering that had become a characteristic of far too many in the slaveholding class. George Wright, a "coal black free born nigger," reportedly sold his children. According to a former slave, Wright sold them to the "highes' bidder."[26] If the words of some informants are to be believed, slaves did not like being owned by other people of African descent. Given the racial climate and its impact on blacks, these slaves preferred to be owned by whites, if they were to be owned by anyone at all. Perhaps ownership by whites brought a special social status in their own eyes and in those of others. We cannot be certain of this, but the following comment by a slave reveals, through his own lens, what it meant to have a black master:

> You might think, master, dat dey would be good to dar own nation; but dey is not. I will tell you the Truth, massa; I know I'se got to answer, and it's a fact, dey is very bad master's sar, I'd rather be a servant to any man in the world, dan to a brack man. If I was sold to a brack man I'd drown myself. I would dat-I'd drown myself! dought I shouldn't like to do that nudder; but I wouldn't be sold to a colored master for anything.[27]

Slaves may have expected their "colored" masters to treat them better, an expectation based on a presumed tempering effect of a shared heritage. But such persons were slaveowners first; they were persons who had internalized the ethos of a slaveowning class of whom they were junior partners.

Most free blacks owned slaves for benevolent purposes, however. Some purchased spouses, children, and other relatives and emancipated them if the law and circumstances permitted. A number of states, particularly after 1830, made it difficult to manumit slaves, so it was not unusual for individuals to appear in the records as slaves when in practice they were the spouses or children of their free black owners. The following document written in 1806 captures the spirit behind the purchase of many slaves by free persons:

> To all whom these presents may come know ye, that I Peter Hawkins a free black man of the city of Richmond having purchased my wife Rose, a slave about twenty-two years of age and by her have had a child called Mary now about 18 mo. old, for the love I bear toward my wife and child have thought proper to emancipate them and for the further consideration of five shillings to me in hand paid . . . I emancipate and set free the said Rose and Mary and relinquish all my right . . . as master to the said Rose and Mary.
>   Peter Hawkins (seal)[28]

Actions such as this one explain why about one-third of the slaves who were manumitted in the South during the nineteenth century owed their freeedom to the benevolence of other blacks. Unlike those who owned other blacks for business purposes, these individuals challenged the system in the only way in which they could have. They rescued their kin from slavery's tentacles, affirmed their human bonds, and gave a few pinpricks to the institution.

A few states prevented free blacks from owning slaves. Georgia passed such a law in 1818, and in Delaware, Arkansas, and Missouri the courts ruled against it. The courts maintained that given the restrictions under which free blacks lived, they could not be expected to provide protection for their chattel. A Delaware court concluded that the free black person was "almost as helpless and dependant on the white race as the slave himself." But the courts also felt that the practice of free blacks owning slaves undermined the bases of racial slavery. In 1859, an Arkansas court held, "The ownership of slaves by free negroes is directly opposed to the principles upon which slavey exists among us." It noted that slavery's "foundation" rested on *an inferiority of race.* The decision emphasized:

> There is a striking difference between the *black* and *white* man, in intellect, feelings and principles. In the order of providence, the former was

made inferior to the latter; and hence the bondage of one to the other.. . . The bondage of one negro, has not this solid foundation to rest upon. The free negro finds in the slave his brother in blood, in color, feelings, education and principle. He has but few civil rights, nor can have consistent with the good order of society; . . . [He is] civilly and morally disqualified to extend protection, and exercise dominion over the slave.[29]

As the free population increased and some of its members became reasonably well off, class divisions emerged. Free blacks in such Northern cities as Philadelphia reflected this differentiation in marriage choices, residential patterns, and in their friendship networks. In the slave societies of the South, wealth often joined hands with a light complexion to further divide the free population. Light-skinned persons, in the words of a Baltimore observer, tried to "look upwards, not downwards . . . constantly seeking and acquiring too, the privileges of whites."[30]

Some free blacks in the South also tried to distance themselves from the slaves. Endeavoring to gain acceptance from whites, fearing relegation to a slave status, and demonstrating a contempt and rejection of their past, these free blacks once again demonstrated the awesome corruptive power of racial slavery. A few even opposed emancipation. One free black preacher, John Chavis, upheld the rights of the slaveowners by arguing, "The Laws of the Country have had slaves the property of the holder equal to his cow or his horse and that he has a perfect right to dispose of them as he pleases."[31] Other free blacks refused to worship with slaves or to have any social intercourse with them.

Free blacks who engaged in such behavior constituted a minority, however. Examples abound of a strong identity between free blacks and slaves that transcended status, class, and phenotypical differences. Everywhere in the South they attended church together, associated socially, and traded with one another. Slaves, where circumstances allowed, attended schools established by free blacks. Others had passes forged by their literate free brethren and, as has been noted, many were purchased and liberated by them. In short, the bonds that united free blacks and slaves were stronger and more enduring than those that divided them. Similarly, while some internalized negative definitions of themselves and imitated whites, others celebrated a black aesthetic in the expressive arts, placed limits on cultural assimilationism, finding beauty and worth among themselves using their own measures.

CONSTRUCTING IDENTITIES

Discriminated against from the moment they obtained their quasi-freedom, free blacks could hardly protest against their condition until they attained some degree of numerical strength. But this was not always effective, since the white authorities did not readily or easily accept any challenges to the status quo. There was also an important prerequisite for protest and organized programs of self-help. Free blacks had to first develop some consciousness of themselves as a separate people with their own identity, history, interests, and future.

The development of a black identity was not an easy process. Coming from different ethnic groups, black slaves had to forge a common identity in the quarters. This identity defined them as a people who shared a common set of experiences that united them and made them feel a special kinship one with the other. It is difficult to say when this feeling began to emerge, but it was certainly present by the turn of the nineteenth century.

Slaves, of course, were always united by their shared condition of servitude if nothing else. In the case of free blacks, however, we are referring to a public embrace of an identity that included all blacks, slaves and free. It expressed itself in a multitude of ways, including a desire to return to Africa, a changing nomenclature, the formation of self-help organizations, and the struggle for equal rights.

There is no doubt that many African-born persons wished to return to their homelands to escape their life of servitude. Their children must also have harbored a desire to go to their ancestral land, particularly in moments of acute hardship and pain. If Africans could not return while they were alive, at least some hoped that their spirits would be able to do so and find solace with their ancestors. The first surviving public articulation of a desire to return to Africa came from seventy-five black signatories to a petition in Boston in 1787. Strong in the conviction that life in America would remain inhospitable to them, they petitioned the Grand Court "to return to Africa, our native country, which warm climate is much more natural [and] agreeable to us . . . and where we shall live among our equals and be more comfortable and happy, than we can be in our present situation."[32]

Similar sentiments were expressed in Rhode Island in the towns of Newport and Providence. The back to Africa movement was led by the Newport-based African Union Society. The society, founded in 1780, sought to foster moral improvement among blacks and to pioneer self-help programs. Soon it came to embrace emigration to Africa as one of its objectives and in 1787 it explored the establishment of a settlement in Africa, one grounded in Christian principles. The effort was abortive but the idea of a return to Africa survived and gained wider acceptance in time.

This early desire by free persons to emigrate to Africa had two principal thrusts. The primary impetus was their harsh treatment by white America and their desire, in the words of the African Union Society, to escape from the "many disadvantages and evils which are likely to continue on us and our children, while we and they live in this country."[33] A second imperative was to Christianize the Africans and to introduce them to Western civilization. The members of the African Union Society, for example, wanted to help "the natives in Africa from who we sprang, being in heathenish darkness and sunk down in barbarity."[34] As seemingly altruistic as this objective was, it betrayed the degree to which these persons had internalized negative images of Africa and of their heritage. The "civilizing" or "regeneration" or "redemption" of Africa would constitute recurring themes in the thought of black Americans in the nineteenth century. It was, in many respects, indistinguishable from the ethnocentrism and Western chauvinism that undergirded the concept of the "white man's burden" of later vintage or his self-imposed responsibility to transform the rest of the world in accordance with his cultural precepts.

The fledgling idea of black emigration obtained more support and gathered momentum in the nineteenth century. Increasingly disenchanted with their life in America, the prospect of relocating in Africa had a profound appeal among many blacks. Whites who despaired of blacks living on equal terms with them in society and those who disliked the presence of free blacks under any circumstances united to promote African emigration. Others, both black and white, advocated emigration to Haiti or to other parts of the Americas.

The successful free black and property owner Paul Cuffe became the principal architect of African emigration in the early nineteenth century. Born on Cuttyhunk Island in Massachusetts in 1759, Cuffe was the son of a free black man and a Wampanoag Indian. As a young man, he became involved in a coastwide trade in various commodities. By 1806 he had become a successful businessman. In 1808, Cuffe became a member of the Society of Friends, a group that had a long history of antislavery activity. He soon embraced the cause of African emigration and saw a role for himself in transporting those who wished to leave as well as simultaneously developing trade with the various African peoples. Like other emigrationists, Cuffe also wanted to promote the Christianization of Africa.

Although Cuffe was a successful businessman, and probably because of it, he chafed under the restrictions that were a fact of daily life for free blacks. In 1780 along with his brother and others, he petitioned the Massachusetts General Court to be relieved from their tax obligations. The argument that the petitioners used was in conformity with the spirit of the times. They were "aggrieved" because they were not "allowed the Privileges of free men of the State, having No vote or Influence in the Election of those who tax us, yet many of our colour (as is well known) have cheerfully entered the field of battle in the defense of the common cause."[35]

Cuffe made an exploratory visit in 1810 to the British colony at Sierra Leone to determine the feasibility of trade with the Africans as well as to lay the groundwork for American immigrants and the Christianization of the indigenous peoples. Upon his return to America in 1811, he began to recruit volunteers for the African project. In 1815, he set sail with thirty-eight blacks—eighteen adults and twenty children—for Sierra Leone. After a journey lasting fifty-six days, these pioneers disembarked at Freetown, where they were given plots of land by the British. After spending two months in Sierra Leone, Cuffe returned home to a mixed reception by his fellow free blacks.

The African emigration question was hardly without some emotional appeal in free black society. But many blacks were also ambivalent because they were creoles and America, regardless of its terrible imperfections, was their home. Although recognizing the difficulty of their life in America, these persons either refused to emigrate or wanted a part of the United States set aside exclusively for them. In 1817 at a meeting held in the District of Columbia, a number of free blacks requested that Congress create "a territory within the limits of our beloved Union" for them. James Forten, a wealthy and influential free black resident of Philadelphia, noted in January 1817 that blacks "will never become a people until they come out from among the white people."[36]

Complicating the issue was the fact that some whites actively supported the voluntary or forcible removal of free blacks from the country. Thomas Jefferson was an early advocate of the colonization of free blacks elsewhere. In his *Notes on the State of Virginia*, written in 1781–82, he doubted whether free blacks and whites could exist in American society on an equal basis. Jefferson wrote, "Deep rooted prejudices entertained by whites; ten thousand recollections, by the blacks of injuries they have sustained, . . . the real distinctions which nature has made; and many other circumstances, will divide us into two parties and produce convulsions which will probably never end but in the extermination of one or the other race." As late as 1821, Jefferson maintained that "the two races, equally free cannot live in the same government."[37]

Whites sympathetic to this position, as well as those who were energized by more humanitarian impulses, established the American Colonization Society in Washington in December 1816. Henry Clay of Kentucky, who was the sitting Speaker of the House of Representatives, presided at the inaugural meeting. He left no doubt as to his opinion of free blacks and what should be done about them. Clay thought them "useless and pernicious, if not dangerous" and believed that it was best "to drain them off."[38] Not surprisingly, the primary objective of the society was to seek governmental support for the transportation and settlement of free blacks in Africa. Free blacks, even those who quietly supported the colonization idea, were quick to denounce the new organization. Such prominent persons as Richard Allen and James Forten believed that the organization's real intention was to expel free blacks, thereby strengthening slavery. As long as free blacks remained visible, they thought, slaves could see that there was an alternative to servitude.

Given the vigorous opposition of some free blacks to emigration under the aegis of the American Colonization Society or even independently of that organization, Cuffe experienced some difficulty in attracting emigrants. Wracked by failing health, he died in 1817 before he could return to Africa. Yet support for emigration did not disappear, and it would not do so as long as free blacks were unhappy with their treatment in the nation. As Americans, however, many looked askance at being encouraged to abandon their home. In the aftermath of the formation of the American Colonization Society, free blacks in Philadelphia characterized its intentions as "not only . . . cruel, but in direct violation of those principles which have been the boast of this republic." In 1819, they returned to the issue, proclaiming "their most solemn protest against the proposition to send their people to Africa, and against every measure which may have a tendency to convey the idea that they give the project a single particle of countenance or encouragement."[39] The Boston merchant David Walker would later oppose colonization on the grounds that "America is more our country, than it is the whites—we have enriched it with our *blood and tears* . . . and will they drive us from our property and homes, which we have earned with our *blood?*"[40] The free blacks of Pittsburgh emphasized their objection to colonization schemes on the grounds that "Here we were born-here we will live by the help of the Almighty-and here we will die, and let our bones lie with our fathers."[41] Referring to the colonization idea, Frederick Douglass observed in 1859 that "no one idea has given rise to more oppression and persecution toward the colored people of this country than that which makes Africa, not America their home."[42]

Such sentiments notwithstanding, a number of free blacks were willing to abandon America. There was some disagreement as to the appropriate destinations, and many weighed the advantages of Africa, Haiti, Canada, and Central America. In 1820, the American Colonization Society dispatched the *Elizabeth* to Sierra Leone with eighty-six migrants. Their stay at Sierra Leone was only temporary, and the immigrants left almost immediately for the village of Compelar, on Sherbro Island. After much initial difficulty and tension with the local residents, these settlers along with others who arrived subsequently, established a colony in 1822 in what was to become known as Liberia. By 1843, 4,571 colonists had arrived. Not all of these persons were free black volunteers. Some were newly emancipated slaves, and others were rescued from slave ships bound for the Americas.

The Liberian experiment was, in some respects, a disastrous one. The American-born immigrants experienced considerable difficulties adjusting to the African environment. An alarming number fell victim to the ravages of malaria. Of the original 4,571 immigrants, only 1,626 were still alive in 1843. Similar difficulties were confronted by the several thousand free blacks who emigrated to Haiti after 1824, the year of the first departure. Unable to adjust to life on the Caribbean island, many of those who survived returned home.

The urge to emigrate was not a simple exercise in escapism. It was also more than an overt rejection of America. From the standpoint of the emigrants and those who agreed with them, it was the recognition of the painful reality that they were neglected orphans in their own land and things were not likely to improve. For some, emigrationism was also the expression of an emerging black identity, a sense that blacks shared a common past, an unacceptably oppressive present, and a destiny outside the United States. Not all who embraced a common black identity, however, saw their future as being brighter elsewhere. Hence a nascent black identity and emigrationism were not intertwined; the one did not necessarily lead to the other.

Between 1820 and the outbreak of the Civil War, a few prominent free blacks either emigrated of lent their support to the movement. The Reverend Daniel Coker, a distinguished clergyman, was one of the first supporters of emigration. A mulatto, Coker was born in Maryland in 1785. He was educated in New York and became a minister in the newly organized African Methodist Episcopal Church. Elected as first bishop in 1816, he declined the honor in favor of Richard Allen. In 1820, he left for Africa with the first group of persons sponsored by the American Colonization Society.

Coker's example was followed a few years later by John B. Russwurm, who had become editor of *Freedom's Journal,* founded in 1827 in New York as the first black newspaper. Born in Jamaica to a white father and a black mother, Russwurm immigrated to America with his father and obtained a degree at Bowdoin College, becoming only the second black person in the United States to receive a college degree. An early critic of emigration, he nevertheless used the pages of *Freedom's Journal* to air dissenting opinions. In 1829, Russwurm became an acknowledged convert to emigrationism, admonishing fellow blacks to settle in Liberia where "the Man of Colour . . . may walk forth in all the majesty of his creation–a newborn creature–a Free Man!"[43] He left for Liberia later that year never to return.

Perhaps the best known exponent of emigrationism in the nineteenth century was Martin R. Delany. Born a free person in Virginia in 1812, he left with his mother for Charlesburg, Pennsylvania, in 1822. As a young man, he sought his fortunes in Pittsburgh, where he was licensed as a physician. Delany, in time, involved himself in a number of political struggles. He supported the antislavery movement, joined the Temperance Society of the People of Color, and fought for the franchise for free blacks. In 1843, Delany became the publisher and editor of the

Mystery, a black newspaper published in Pittsburgh. Four years later, he and Frederick Douglass became co-editors of the *North Star*, a paper that appeared in Rochester, New York. The two strong-willed men parted company in 1848, and from then on Delany became the most aggressive and articulate exponent of emigration.

Delany's emigrationist position was delineated in a book that he published in Philadelphia in 1852. This work, *The Condition, Elevation, Emigration and Destiny of the Colored People of the United States*, was an eloquent defense of emigration. He despaired of the black person's future in America because "there is no species of degradation to which we are not subject."[44] He did not advocate a particular destination but warned against going to Liberia, which he characterized as "not an independent nation at all; but a *poor miserable mockery–a burlesque* on a government–a pitiful dependency on the American Colonizationists."[45] The Caribbean and Central and South America held greater promise, he argued.

There were other distinguished black supporters of emigration in the 1850s. They included James M. Whitfield, a Buffalo poet and barber, and James Theodore Holly, a shoemaker from Washington, D.C., and a man accomplished in mathematics and the classics. Mary Ann Shadd, who was born in Delaware in 1823 and educated in Pennsylvania, became the best known of the women who supported the movement. Strongly influenced by her father, Abraham Shadd, an ardent abolitionist and advocate for equal rights, Mary Ann Shadd became a schoolteacher and social critic. In 1849, she published a pamphlet, *Hints to the Colored People of the North*, wherein she denounced consumerism by blacks and advocated autonomy and self-respect for the peoples of African descent. By the 1850s, Shadd had become an emigrationist. In 1851 she left for Canada to join the thousands of other blacks who had already relocated in that country. Although she abandoned the United States, Shadd still embraced an integrationist stance, maintaining that blacks in America should eschew separatist tendencies. She espoused these positions in the *Provincial Freeman*, a newspaper she edited. She held the distinction of being the first black woman to edit a newspaper.

By 1858, Delany's efforts were strengthened by the powerful voice of Henry Highland Garnet, a former slave, abolitionist, and missionary. Garnet was born a slave in Maryland in 1815. His family escaped in 1824, eventually taking up residence in New York after a brief sojourn in Maryland. A gifted boy, Garnet attended the African Free School in New York, the Noyes Academy at New Canaan (N.H.), and the Oneida Theological Institute at Whitesboro (N.Y.). A student of theology, Garnet was ordained in the Presbyterian ministry, and in 1842 he became the pastor of the Liberty Street Baptist Church in Troy, New York. An outspoken, fearless man, Garnet quickly established himself as an ardent abolitionist, and in 1849 he declared himself an unrepentant emigrationist, noting, "I would rather see a man free in Liberia, than a slave in the United States."[46]

After a visit to England and a three-year stint in Jamaica as a missionary, Garnet returned to America in 1856. In 1858 he became the president of the African Civilization Society, a proemigration organization boasting black and white membership. As was the case with the earlier African Union Society, this new organization aimed to effect "the civilization and evangelization of Africa and the descendants of African ancestors in any portion of the earth, wherever dispersed."[47] As Americans and as Westerners, members of the society wanted to achieve an African cultural regeneration, betraying like their predecessors a profound cultural chauvinism.

Neither Garnet nor Delany achieved much in the way of practical results. Delany undertook an exploratory mission to West Africa in 1859 in a largely futile attempt to establish a colony. Nor was a mission sponsored by the African Civilization Society any more successful. Yet success cannot be measured solely in terms of the establishment of colonies and the emigration of justifiably disgruntled blacks. These men and others like them were the early Pan-Africanists and the aggressive articulators of a common black identity. Theirs was an expectant search for a space that blacks would control and have their destiny unfold. As Delany expressed it in 1861, "Africa for the African race, and black men to rule them. . . . By black men I mean, men of African descent who claim an identity with the race."[48]

There were several free blacks who spoke passionately in the early decades of the nineteenth century about the need to develop and nurture a black identity. The New York intellectual William Hamilton was one of the first to articulate the dimensions of this emerging identity. As early as 1809, he embraced all those who had an African ancestry since "it makes no difference whether the man is born in Africa, Asia, Europe or America, so long as he is progenized from African parents."[49] Another eloquent call for the creation of a black identity and solidarity came in 1829. Robert Young published his *Ethiopian Manifesto* in New York in that year, urging the "collecting together" of blacks. The more widely known, and arguably the most uncompromising of the early intellectuals, David Walker, also published a book entitled *David Walker's An Appeal in Four Articles; Together with a Preamble to the Colored Citizens of the World, but in Particular, and Very Expressly, to Those of the United States of America*, in 1829. Known historically as *The Appeal*, this work was the earliest detailed formulation of the principles of what has come to be called black nationalism. This ideology asserted the distinctiveness of peoples of African descent, recognized a common heritage and future, and urged blacks everywhere to unite and determine their own destinies and command the future. Accordingly, this ideology was not, in its genesis, merely a reaction to the treatment of blacks by whites, although racial mistreatment certainly gave it immediacy and salience.

David Walker was born a free person in Wilmington, North Carolina, in 1785. His father, who died before his birth, was a slave, and his mother was a free woman. David spent the first four decades of his life in the South before moving to Boston in 1827. He quickly became an "agent" for *Freedom's Journal* and established a small business in used clothing. Walker was a voracious reader and, according to Henry Highland Garnet, "spent all his leisure moments in the cultivation of his mind . . . in order that he might contribute something to humanity."[50]

Walker's wide reading is reflected in the pages of *The Appeal* and in the power of his argument. As someone who had seen slavery all around him and the attendant oppression of free blacks, Walker directed his appeal to "my much afflicted and suffering brethren." He went on:

> I will ask one question here–Can our condition be any worse?–Can it be more mean and abject? If there are any changes will they not be for the better, though they may appear for the worst at first? Can they get us any lower?[51]

Walker stressed that the "wretchedness" of the black condition was a consequence of slavery. He observed that "all the inhabitants of the earth (except however, the sons of Africa) are called *men,* and of course are, and ought to be free. But we (coloured people), and our children are *brutes!!* And of course are, and *ought* to be SLAVES to the American people and their children forever!! to dig their mines and work their farms; and thus go on enriching them, from one generation to another with our *blood* and our *tears!!!!*"

Walker was convinced that "we (coloured people of *these United States of America*), are *the most wretched, degraded and abject* set of beings that *ever lived* since the world began, and that the white Americans having reduced us to the wretched state of slavery, treat us in that condition *more cruel* (they being an enlightened Christian people), than any heathen nation did any people whom it had reduced to our condition." His angry words drew attention to the contradiction between a nation that espoused liberty but held many in bondage. "I have been for years troubling the pages of historians, to find out what our fathers have done to the white *Christians of America,* to merit such condign punishment as they have inflicted on them, and do continue to inflict on us their children," he wrote.

A spirit of angry defiance permeates *The Appeal.* Yet Walker was not merely content to draw attention to America's mistreatment of Africans and their children. His primary objective was to enjoin blacks to unite because disunity had led to their being taken "around the world in chains and handcuffs" as slaves. He denounced blacks who conspired with whites to oppress other blacks:

> Oh Heaven! I am full!!! I can hardly move my pen!!! . . . There have been and are at this day in Boston, New York, Philadelphia, and Baltimore, coloured men, who are in league with tyrants, and who receive a great portion of their daily bread, of the moneys which they acquire from the blood and tears of their more miserable brethren, whom they scandalously delivered into the hands of our *natural enemies.*

Walker wanted to inspire blacks to be the instruments of their own liberation regardless of where they found themselves. Blacks were united by their history, and their destiny rested in collective action:

> I advanced it therefore to you, not as a *problematical,* but as an unshaken and forever immoveable fact, that your full glory and happiness, as well as all other coloured people under Heaven, shall never be fully consummated, but with the *entire emancipation of your enslaved brethren all over the world.* . . . our greatest happiness shall consist in working for the salvation of our whole body.

He knew that eventually the "enslaved children of Africa will have, in spite of all their enemies, to take their stand among the nations of the earth." For all of their suffering, however, Walker was certain that blacks possessed the capacity to be magnanimous towards their oppressors. Blacks, he argued,

> . . . ask them for nothing but the rights of man, viz. for them to set us free, and treat us like men, and . . . we will love and respect them, and protect our country-but cannot conscientiously do these things until they treat us like men. . . . Treat us like men, and there is no danger but we will all live in peace and happiness together. For we are not like you . . . unforgiving. Treat us like men, and we will be your friends.[52]

Lewis Woodson, a Pittsburgh clergyman, was another intellectual who addressed the black condition from a nationalist perspective. Woodson was born a slave in Virginia in 1806 and remained in that condition until his father purchased his freedom at age nineteen. He went to Pittsburgh in the early 1830s and established himself as a prominent clergyman, member of the American Moral Reform Society, and regular contributor to a black newspaper, the *Colored American.* Woodson used the pseudonym "Augustine" when he wrote for the press.

Woodson's letters to the press expressed a strong black identity, a profound sense of difference vis-à-vis whites. He urged the creation of "a national feeling" based on the recognition of a separate identity and experience. "The condition in which we have for generations been living in this land," he wrote, "constitutes us a distinct class. They have been our holders, and we the held. Every power and privilege have been invested with them, while we have been divested of every right."[53] Such views led Woodson to advocate the creation of autonomous communities for blacks that would be beyond white influence. These were to be established in rural areas, and blacks would be able to develop farming and other skills in them. Nothing tangible emerged from his proposals.

Hamilton, Delany, Garnet, Walker, Woodson, and others espoused the ideology of black nationalism. It was an ideology in formation, and these men did not agree on many things, big and small. But they shared a commitment to improving the black condition and spoke in terms of a separate black identity and history, and some even embraced emigration as a solution to the problems that blacks faced. They were, of course, not alone in drawing attention to the injustices inherent in American society. What distinguished them from other prominent leaders such as the abolitionist Frederick Douglass and the clergyman and journalist Samuel Cornish was the aggressive assertion of their blackness, their passionate call for black unity, and their uncompromising rejection of the status quo.

The search for black identity in a land dominated by whites took many forms. Individuals wrote in celebration of their heritage, espoused their racial and cultural distinctiveness, formed organizations, and struggled with their nomenclature. In fact, the contest over the names they would call their organizations and themselves provide ample testimony to the inner turmoil that blacks experienced as they searched for an identity. The changing nature of the names they adopted for their organizations and themselves reflect the difficulty of their quest and the poignancy of their endeavors. The process of naming and renaming was both a search for selfhood and, paradoxically, a recovery of selfhood.

There was, understandably, much tension and ambivalence in the process. Names reflected identity, and a strong black identity did not crystallize overnight. Hence many blacks considered, adopted, and abandoned various names for the peoples of African descent in accordance with their changing sense of identity. Such names included Ethiopian, African, people of color, oppressed Americans, Afro-American, African-American, Colored, Negro, and Afro-Saxon, among others. The choice became rather emotionally charged after about 1820 with the emergence of a creole population, neither totally African nor American, but bridging the two worlds. Mulattoes also faced a special problem, given their mixed racial heritage and their enormous internal struggles over their own identity.

Before 1820, when a significant number of free blacks could still claim African birth, many of their organizations included "African" as a prominent part of their name. Thus, there was the Free African Society,

the New York African Society for Mutual Relief, the New York African
Marine Fund, and the African Methodist Episcopal Church, to name just
a few. There were exceptions, of course. Mulattoes in Charleston, for
example, formed the Brown Fellowship Society. The appellation
"African," in contradistinction to others at this time, had a strong emotional resonance because it invited memories of Africa, affirmed a people's heritage, and paid a proud tribute to their homeland.

As the African-born declined in numbers and their children and
grandchildren took their place, the search for an appropriate name
intensified, and with it grew an inevitable disharmony. The mixed peoples of Louisiana liked "people of color" or "gens de couleur" because of
their French roots. Some persons preferred "African," while others proposed "Colored" or "Black" or "Afro-American." For the advocates of
"Colored," that appellation defined the emergence of a new people; it
was in many respects a word that recognized the range of phenotypes of
which the peoples of African descent were comprised. The name also
appealed to those who wished to reject any identification with Africa. In
1837, a newspaper with the name of the *Colored American* made its
appearance in New York, giving much respectability to "colored" as the
preferred appellation. In justifying the choice, editor Samuel Cornish
maintained:

> We are written about, preached to, and prayed for, as Negroes, Africans,
> and blacks, all of which have been stereotyped, as names of reproach,
> and on that account, if no other, are unacceptable. Let us and our
> friends unite, in baptizing the term "Colored Americans," and hence-
> forth let us be written of, preached of, and prayed for as such. It is the
> true term, and one which is above reproach.[54]

This was not the end of the matter, because it could not be so easily
settled. Nor could a name be mandated by any one person or group of
individuals. There were those who, while celebrating their African
ancestry, had no objections to being called, simply, "American." Frederick Douglass, for one, asserted in 1853:

> We are Americans, and as Americans, we would speak to Americans.
> We address you not as slaves nor as exiles, humbly asking to be per-
> mitted to dwell among you in peace; but we address you as American
> citizens asserting their rights on their own native soil.[55]

The controversy over naming was not spent before emancipation, and
it remained very much alive in later years. It consumed the emotional
energies of many, and it constituted one of the battles that free blacks had
to wage. Unlike some other battles, however, this was a healthy struggle
for self-definition. Nevertheless, it was a double-edged sword. Henry
Highland Garnet recognized this very well when he complained:

How unprofitable it is for us to spend our golden moments in long and solemn debate upon the question whether we shall be called "African," "Colored Americans" or "Africo Americans," or "Blacks." The question should be, my friends, *shall we arise and act like men, and cast off this terrible yoke?* [56]

BUILDING INSTITUTIONS

While free blacks worked to "cast off this terrible yoke," they also directed their energies to a sustained struggle for change and created a diverse set of institutions to serve their needs and the ones of those who would come after. Much of this activity took place in the states of the North where conditions, although considerably less than ideal, facilitated the growth of a black consciousness, the recognition of common needs, the emergence of enlightened and effective leadership, and the capacity to address internal problems.

One of the first efforts by free blacks to act collectively occurred in Philadelphia in 1782. That city boasted a growing and energetic free black population as a result of manumission, migration, and natural increase. Finding strength in numbers and conscious of their mistreatment, six black men sent a relatively mild petition to the state on behalf of "The Black people of the City and Suburbs." The petitioners wanted "liberty to fence in the Negroes Burying ground in the Potters field."[57] As a function of their debasement, blacks could not bury their dead in the cemeteries of the white churches to which they belonged but instead had to use the Potters' Field or Strangers' Burial Ground. The petitioners wanted a special area designated for their own use. It is not clear whether the request was granted, but it portended the aggressiveness that would come to characterize the behavior of free blacks in Philadelphia and in many other places.

It was Philadelphia's good fortune to have produced and attracted a number of persons with unusual leadership abilities. Foremost among them was Richard Allen, who was born a slave in 1760 in Philadelphia. His master, Benjamin Chew, sold the young boy and his family to Stokely Sturgis, a farmer in Dover, Delaware, a few years after Allen was born. Sturgis, who soon fell on hard times, separated the family by selling the boy's parents and some of his siblings. Shortly thereafter, in 1777, Allen and his brother converted to Methodism after listening to a preacher in the woods. As Allen would later recall, "I was awakened and brought to see myself, poor. . . ."[58]

Richard and his brother devoted much of their time to converting their master. Eventually, Sturgis invited Freeborn Garretson, a Methodist preacher, to his farm, and the farmer experienced the conversion that Richard had wanted. The two young men were allowed to purchase their freedom, and Richard spent the succeeding five years working in Delaware, New Jersey, and Pennsylvania. He also became an itinerant preacher, and in 1786 he returned to Philadelphia. Soon he would become one of the foremost leaders of the black population.

Other blacks who played significant roles in the history of blacks in Pennsylvania and the nation included Absalom Jones and James Forten. Jones was born a slave in Delaware in 1747. He learned to read while still a slave, a skill that would later stand him in good stead. At age fifteen, his master sold his mother and his six siblings and took him to Philadelphia. In Philadelphia, Jones got married, furthered his education, and embraced Anglicanism. In 1784 he purchased his freedom and began to assume an active role in his community.

Unlike Allen and Jones, James Forten was born free in Philadelphia in 1766. His father was a successful sailmaker. Young James learned to read and write at the school run by the famous Quaker and humanitarian Anthony Benezet. James served at sea in the War of Independence, where he acquitted himself well. He declined the invitation of the British to go to England once his ship had been captured. He is reputed to have said, "No, No! I am here a prisoner for the liberties of my country; I never, NEVER, shall prove a traitor to her interests."[59] At war's end, he returned home to play a leading role in a variety of causes.

Richard Allen's return to Philadelphia had the kind of consequences that he could hardly have predicted. He was invited to preach at early morning worship at St. George's Methodist Church, and the congregation at those 5:00 A.M. services consisted of free blacks. As his popularity grew, he preached at other places, all the while attracting a growing black audience. We are not certain about the content of his message, but Absalom Jones became one of his adherents. Soon, these free blacks began to discuss the possibility of establishing an independent black organization, an idea that was nothing short of revolutionary. A people had begun to be formed, and they needed their own organizations to give expression to their voices and to affirm their autonomy.

As events unfolded, however, these Philadelphia pathbreakers established an ostensibly secular, mutual aid organization before they formed an independent church. This was the first such organization that was entirely theirs, the first of many that would contain their hopes and dreams. Known as the Free African Society (FAS), the organization boasted such founding members as Richard Allen and Absalom Jones. Its articles of incorporation proclaimed the African ancestry of its members, characterizing themselves as "We, the free Africans and their descendants. . . ."

The FAS was to operate "without regard to religious tenets," although its members had to live "an orderly and sober life." It defined its functions as providing support for the sick and assistance to orphans and widows. It also sought to establish links with free blacks in other cities. A fledgling organization in the best of times, it soon lost Richard Allen, who disagreed with some of the procedural rules that were adopted. Allen and a few others disliked, among other things, the start of each meeting with a fifteen-minute silence. This practice reminded Allen of the Quakers, and he preferred that the organization follow its own course. With Allen gone, having "disunited himself from member- ship with us," Absalom Jones assumed the leadership role.[60]

The Free African Society was only the first of many similar free black mutual aid societies. The first lodge of Freemasons, for example, received its charter in Boston in 1787. Organized by Prince Hall, a for- mer slave, the lodge soon had counterparts in Providence (1797) and Philadelphia (1798). Taken together, these fraternal organizations per- formed social welfare functions for members in economic distress, dis- abled by sickness, widowed, too old for work, or orphaned. Some estab- lished schools advocated better wages and working conditions for their members in the larger society and even supported mission stations in Africa. The African Benevolent Society of Wilmington, North Carolina, made loans to its members, and so did the Brown Fellowship Society of Charleston. On the other hand, the Baltimore Society for Relief in Case of Seizure offered assistance to members who were threatened by kid- nappings or were actually kidnapped to be sold into slavery.

Some of these societies were inspired by the need to foster "moral or mental improvement" among blacks. Such objectives were predicated on the assumption that slavery had had a deleterious effect on its vic- tims. They also reflected a debilitating preoccupation with what whites thought about blacks and a compelling desire to prove their humanity to their detractors. As one writer to the *Colored American* said in 1837:

> I care not how many societies, whose objects are moral or mental improvement, are raised up. They will do good among us. They will tend to clear us from the charge of indolence, or indifference, to our own welfare, which has been heaped upon us; and also, from that foul aspersion as to the inferiority of our intellectual capacities, with which many has [sic] been pleased to brand us.[61]

In accordance with such imperatives, free blacks acting occasion- ally with white friends founded a plethora of literary and "moral improvement" societies, particularly in the North. In 1833, New York City's Phoenix Society appeared. Arthur Tappan, the prominent white abolitionist, was one of the founders. Its membership of "colored young men" pledged themselves to the "improvement of the colored people in morals, literature, and the mechanic arts."[62] To achieve their objectives, the Phoenicians offered a library, a high school, and classes in the evening for adults. Free blacks in Pittsburgh started the Young Men's Literary and Moral Reform Society, and in Boston they founded the Philomothean Society to encourage literary studies. All of these societies and their numerous counterparts elsewhere reflected a people's struggle for self-definition and their efforts to meet their own needs and respond to their own pulls in difficult times. As in the churches, membership in these societies strengthened social relationships even as they performed useful services for their membership and constituency.

The independent black church was the most important and enduring institution that the free persons pioneered. Not surprisingly, it emerged in Philadelphia as an outgrowth of the activities of the Free African Society and its group of energetic and enlightened leaders. Once the FAS had been established, it broadened its activities to include the sponsoring of religious services. Soon, support grew for the establishment of a separate interdenominational place of worship and a school.

Absalom Jones was one of the principal organizers of this effort. Benjamin Rush, the white philanthropist, physician, and abolitionist, lent his support. Planning began seriously in 1791, and it was decided that the church would be named the African Church of Philadelphia. Richard Allen made peace with his brethren, returned to the FAS, and he, Jones, and a few others comprised a committee charged with the difficult task of raising the funds necessary to construct the building. Prominent whites expressed their disapproval of this expression of black independence. The bishop of the Protestant Episcopal Church of Pennsylvania thought the objective of the black people was inappropriate because "it originated in pride."[63] This was precisely the point. White Methodists and Quakers were equally condemnatory of the enterprise.

The thrust toward black religious independence gained considerable momentum in 1792 after an assault on the personhood of the black members occurred in St. George's Methodist Church. The church, finding itself unable to seat all of the congregation comfortably, undertook some renovations. When these were completed, the decision was evidently made to seat the black members in the gallery. Not knowing this, blacks arrived one Sunday morning and assumed their customary seats in the sanctuary when they were told about the changes. The service had already begun and, according to Richard Allen:

We expected to take the seats over the ones we formerly occupied below, not knowing any better. We took those seats; meeting had begun, and they were nearly done singing, and just as we got to the seats, the Elder said, "Let us pray." We had not been long upon our knees before I heard considerable scuffling and loud talking. I raised my head up and saw one of the trustees, H_____ M_____, having hold of the Rev. Absalom Jones, pulling him off his knees, and saying, "You must get up, you must not kneel here." Mr. Jones replied, "Wait until the prayer is over, and I will get up, and trouble you no more." With that he beckoned to one of the trustees, Mr. L_____ S_____, to come to his assistance. He came and went to William White to pull him up. By this time prayer was over, and we all went out of the church in a body, and they were no more plagued by us in the church.[64]

Richard Allen, a pivotal figure in Philadelphia's black community
from 1786 to 1831 and the first proposer of the African Church.

These defiant Christians expedited their plans to build their own house of worship. The stone-laying ceremony occurred in March 1793, and Richard Allen held the place of honor. "As I was the first proposer of the African Church," he later recalled, "I put the first spade into the ground to dig the cellar for the same."[65] Although the disastrous yellow fever epidemic of 1793 interrupted construction, the church was completed in the spring of 1794. Most of the potential members decided to affiliate with the Episcopal Church, a decision that led Richard Allen, a Methodist, to sever his connections with them. Absalom Jones became the *de facto* rector after Allen's departure. He would later become a deacon (1795) and was ordained a priest in 1804. Known as the African Episcopal Church of St. Thomas, the church was formally dedicated on July 14, 1794. Not until 1854, however, was St. Thomas allowed to send a delegate to the state Episcopal convention.

Bethel Church (c. 1794), shown here with the Walnut Street Jail in the background. This church is historically known as Mother Bethel, the first African Methodist Episcopal Church.

Despite the split, Allen continued his efforts to establish a separate Methodist congregation. The opposition of white Methodists notwithstanding, he and his supporters purchased a blacksmith's shop, which was dedicated in July 1794. Known historically as Mother Bethel, this humble church would become the foundation stone of the African Methodist Episcopal Church (AME), the nation's first black denomination.

The road to denominational autonomy was long and difficult. Allen was ordained a deacon in 1799, but ultimate control over the affairs of Mother Bethel resided in the Methodist conference and the white elder at St. George's. As Mother Bethel increased in membership, it sought independence from St. George's. This led to a protracted conflict with St. George's, and in 1816 the Supreme Court of Pennsylvania ruled that Mother Bethel could handle its own affairs. As it turned out, black Methodist congregations that had been formed in other states in the wake of Mother Bethel had similar difficulties with white authorities.

In light of these developments, Richard Allen convened a meeting of African Methodists in Philadelphia in April 1816. This historic gathering, which brought several black congregations together, decided that the faithful "should become one body under the name of the African Methodist Church." Allen was installed as the first bishop of the new denomination. By 1826, the AME boasted 7,937 members and had become an institutional force in black America. Its membership amounted to over 50,000 in 1860 and about 500,000 in 1896.

The struggle to found the AME was replicated in the one to establish the African Methodist Episcopal Zion Church, the second black denomination. Led by James Varick, a free black man, the Zion Methodists abandoned the primarily white John Street Methodist Church in New York City in 1796 after racist treatment. As was the case of their peers at Mother Bethel, they did not start a new denomination immediately but remained a congregation within the Methodist Church. After flirting with the idea of becoming affiliated with the AME, the Zionists acquired full denominational status in 1821. Varick was elected bishop in 1822, a position he held until 1828. The denomination had a membership of 4,600 in 1860.

In addition to giving independent expression to their religious life, free blacks promoted their claims to civil equality by publishing newspapers and periodicals. When *Freedom's Journal,* the first black newspaper, appeared in New York City in 1827, its very name celebrated the "freedom" of those who were no longer property and held out a similar promise to "our brethren who are still in the iron fetters of bondage."[66] The paper was committed to the achievement of civil rights for blacks, the promotion of causes conducive to an improvement in the black condition, and an end to slavery. Although it was under the capable editorship of John Russwurm and Samuel Cornish, the paper was short-lived. Cornish left his job after only six months, and in 1829 Russwurm emigrated to Liberia. Cornish tried to rescue the paper by renaming it the *Rights of All* but it, too, did not survive.

These early ventures into the publishing arena failed, in large measure, because of their small readership and the attendant economic difficulties. This was to be the fate of most black newspapers of the time with a few important exceptions. The *Colored American,* which began publication in New York in 1837, survived until 1841. Under the initial editorship of Cornish, the paper promoted the use of "Colored" as the name for the peoples of African descent and supported independent action by blacks. Cornish hoped that through the agency of the paper "our people may be reached, their minds cultivated, their habits changed and their moral and religious character raised and made uniform."[67]

Several black newspapers began publication in the 1840s. The *National Watchman* appeared in Troy, New York; the *Herald of Justice* in New Haven, Connecticut; and the *People's Press* in New York City, among others. The *North Star*, which was founded by Frederick Douglass in 1847 and renamed the *Frederick Douglass Paper* in 1851, was the only newspaper that would endure for more than a decade. The paper's path was not an easy one; the usual financial problems sapped energies, and white abolitionists opposed it. William Lloyd Garrison, the arrogant and uncompromising opponent of slavery, feared that the *North Star* would compete with his paper, the *Liberator*, and urged Douglass to abandon his plans. Yet the paper survived and enjoyed a substantial white readership.

Black periodicals sought to perform the same functions as the newspapers, and they confronted similar obstacles. The first two black periodicals on record appeared in 1838. The *National Reformer* was published in Philadelphia, and the *Mirror of Liberty* appeared in New York City. They were followed in the 1840s by the *African Methodist Episcopal Church Magazine* (1841) and *L'Album Littéraire* (1843), which appeared in New Orleans and reflected the literary interests of that city's mulatto class. These publications did not survive, but they were succeeded by a host of new ones in the mid- and late 1850s and early 1860s. Some, such as the *Anglo-African Magazine* (1859) and the *Repository of Religion and Literature and of Science and Art* (1858) had a literary emphasis, while the *New Republic and Liberian Missionary Journal* (1856) was unabashedly emigrationist. The appearance of these organs was more important than their uncertain future. They reflected the varied interests of an expanding free black population and addressed the concerns of the black population as a whole.

The inability of most black newspapers and periodicals to survive for an appreciable period of time was in part a function of the low literacy levels among the free people. Many Americans in the nineteenth century were either illiterate or just functionally literate. Yet blacks recognized that one of the avenues to progress, as they defined it, was the acquisition of literacy. As those blacks who attended the Second Annual Convention for the Improvement of the Free People of Color affirmed in 1832, "If we ever expect to see the influence of prejudice decrease and ourselves respected, it must be by the blessings of an enlightened education.[68]

Long before the adoption of this resolution, free blacks had sought access to educational facilities. Several Southern states had made it illegal for slaves to be taught to read and write, but some slaves managed to become literate nevertheless. Whites feared that literate blacks posed a challenge to the racial order. In 1830, for example, a North Carolina law maintained that the "teaching of slaves to read and write, has a tendency to excite dissatisfaction in their minds, and to produce insurrection and rebellion to the manifest injury of the citizens of this state."[69] Some whites, blinded by virulent racism, also opposed the provision of educational facilities for free blacks on the grounds they were incapable of learning or could not progress beyond a certain intellectual level.

Others vehemently opposed their children sharing classrooms with blacks, even threatening and sometimes attacking institutions that were racially integrated. In general, by 1850 none of the Southern states had made provisions for the education of free blacks. By that year, on the other hand, most Northern and Western states had recognized the need to educate their black residents but in separate facilities.

In large measure, the impetus to provide education for blacks in the North came from the free persons themselves. There were, of course, many whites who risked the wrath of their detractors to advocate education for blacks and, in some cases, admitted them to their schools and colleges. When the Noyes Academy in New Canaan, New Hampshire, enrolled blacks in 1835, the townspeople lifted the building off its foundation and, in the words of Senator Isaac Hill, who endorsed the proceedings, they took it "to a place where it could not be used for that purpose."[70] Angry whites destroyed schools that blacks attended in Zanesville and Troy, Ohio; effected the closure of a girls' academy in Canterbury, Connecticut, and a night school in Richmond, Virginia; and forced the abandonment of a proposal to build a college for blacks in New Haven, Connecticut. In 1832, the students at Wesleyan University in Middletown, Connecticut, successfully opposed the admission of a black student, Charles B. Ray. He would later become a prominent abolitionist.

Undeterred by such reverses, blacks and their white allies pursued a number of strategies. In the Northern states they advocated integration of the public schools and improvements in the quality of education that their children received. Secondly, and this appears to have happened in many places, blacks established their own schools with their own resources. Regardless of where the separate schools existed or who established them, they received minimal financial support from the local authorities. Poorly equipped, often staffed with unqualified teachers, and offering a limited curriculum, these schools reflected the second-class status that whites had conferred upon blacks. The *Colored American* denounced such schools in 1837, since they "so shackled the intellect of colored youth, that an education acquired under such circumstances, was, comparatively of little advantage."[71] Black children also confronted the racism of white teachers in these schools, undoubtedly with disastrous consequences for their self-esteem. Before 1860, only in Massachusetts could free blacks attend public schools on equal terms with whites.

In contrast to the public schools, several Northern institutions of higher learning opened their doors to blacks. They included Bowdoin College and Dartmouth in the 1820s, Western Reserve and Oberlin in the 1830s. They were later followed by Oneida Theological Institute, Amherst, Princeton, Harvard Union College, and a few others. Only a handful of blacks were in a position to take advantage of these opportunities, but these institutions had enlarged the possibilities open to them.

By 1860 twenty-eight blacks had graduated from the more prestigious institutions of higher learning.

The need for private schools was greater in the South than in the North given the universal absence of public education in that region. White resistance to any form of educational instruction for blacks, however, never abated in the South. A number of schools operated clandestinely, but they always ran the risk of being closed by whites. Wealthy free blacks, particularly those in Charleston and New Orleans, avoided such harassment by employing private tutors for their children. Their less fortunate brethren had to reconcile themselves to a more uncertain educational future. Even so, they did very well under the circumstances. Baltimore's fifteen African schools, as they were called, had an enrollment of 2,600 in 1860.

The burden of assuming responsibility for their education in many places exacerbated the already precarious economic condition of the vast majority of free blacks. Excluded from a variety of skilled and professional jobs by virtue of their race, most had a marginal existence. Even when some employers were disposed to hiring blacks, whites frequently refused to work with them. White workers, reflecting an acute feeling of insecurity for which not even their sense of racial superiority could compensate, feared the competition of blacks for the available jobs. Whites threatened violence against potential black hirees in New York and Philadelphia in the 1830s. The immigration of almost five million Europeans to the United States between 1830 and 1860 posed additional problems for black workers.

As the Germans, the Irish, and the Scandinavians poured into the country, they competed with blacks for the most menial jobs. In 1838, the *Colored American* published the reaction of one black person to the new foreign presence:

> These impoverished and destitute beings, transported from the transatlantic shores, are crowding themselves into every place of business and of labor, and driving the poor colored American citizen out. Along the wharves, where the colored man once done the whole business of shipping and unshipping—in stores where his services were once rendered, and in families where the chief places were filled by him, in all these situations there are substituted foreigners or white Americans.[72]

The competition for jobs led to violent confrontations between blacks and the Irish, who were their strongest rivals for the least desirable jobs. Such outbursts occurred in Pennsylvania in 1842 and again in 1853. New York also experienced similar violent conflicts between the two groups in 1855 and again in 1863.

Undeterred by the economic discrimination they confronted everywhere, blacks continued to seize the economic opportunities available to them. Most Northern free persons were confined to unskilled service jobs and were, in the case of men, employed as porters, laborers, servants, waiters, and so on. A few were barbers, coachmen, shoemakers, carpenters, or persons employed in shipbuilding, sailmaking, and fishing. Women tended to be located disproportionately in domestic service. On the other hand, in the rural areas of the South most men worked as farmers, laborers, and woodcutters. A smaller proportion performed skilled tasks, working as shoemakers, carpenters, blacksmiths, and coopers. Women worked on the farms as well, but a higher proportion of them were domestics.

There were greater opportunities for blacks in Southern cities as opposed to rural areas. The nature of the jobs varied, of course, depending on the state and its urban economy. Black men in the Lower South found employment as artisans of one sort or another. Such occupations included tailoring, carpentry, barbering, painting, bricklaying, shoemaking, among others. Men in the Upper South found employment in paper mills, iron foundries, restaurants, and in numerous unskilled capacities. Most of the women worked in the households of whites.

A few Southern states or municipal governments excluded blacks from many high-status occupations such as printing, piloting ships, and the making of drugs. In some cases, the law required blacks to pay fees well beyond their financial reach in order to engage in certain occupations. Charleston, for example, imposed high fees on prospective mechanics. In this way, white workers with the requisite skills were shielded from competition. Certain jobs everywhere–usually the most menial–acquired the contemptuous epithet of "nigger work." As one white Southerner expressed it, "No white man would ever do certain kinds of work . . . and if you should ask a white man . . . he would get mad and tell you he wasn't a nigger."[73]

The majority of blacks had no option but to do "nigger work" because that was the basis of their sustenance. A few were able to save what they earned and started their own businesses. Most of these enterprises were small, but they provided a measure of economic independence for their proprietors. New York, Boston, Philadelphia, Charleston, Baltimore, and other cities saw the emergence of barbershops, grocery stores, cookshops, and boarding houses owned and managed by blacks. Fearing the competition, whites often harassed these businesses out of existence. Others would fail without any assistance from whites. But enough free blacks were able to improve their economic situation through shrewd business practices and sometimes as a result of inheritance to join a tiny but growing middle class.

An increasing number of free blacks also became owners of real estate, particularly after 1830. By that time, a sizable number had been free for a generation or two, and a few were able to purchase land. In 1860, however, four out of every five free black households in the South owned no real estate. Among the owners, a few were relatively prosperous according to the standards of the time, but most owned less property than the average white person. Mulattoes in the Lower South who frequently inherited property from their white parents were usually better off than other free peoples. Comprehensive statistics on landownership patterns are not generally available for much of the antebellum years, but one study found that in 1850 urban free blacks as a whole were "roughly one-half as likely as American urbanites in general to own real estate."[74]

As a group, free women in the South controlled 27 percent of the value of the property held by free persons in 1850. This proportion fell to 22 percent in 1860, but the extent of such holdings by women is noteworthy nonetheless. A relatively high proportion of these women, as a study of Petersburg, Virginia, showed, acquired their property later in life, were single, and headed their own households.[75] Some scholars maintain that these women avoided marriage primarily because they lost legal control of their property to their husbands when they married. A woman, if the marriage failed, could lose all that she owned. While this may have been an important factor in a woman's decision to remain single, there were other issues that influenced it. Free black women outnumbered their male counterparts in some places and, on average, were likely to be older. These two factors exacerbated the difficulty of finding a spouse.

Free women, particularly those who were African-born, would scarcely have chosen to remain single, other things being equal. Their creole children undoubtedly shared some of those cultural moorings encouraging marriage that we discussed in Chapter 4. African women, in the main, were products of societies that placed high premiums on reproduction and defined spouseless and childless women as pariahs. Accordingly, the strength of these ancestral kin traditions were powerful factors inducing both men and women to find partners. Free women in America who never married may have found their single status a profoundly unwelcomed and unsought development. Historians who view these women solely through a Western and contemporary lens, concluding that they consciously resisted marriage in order to assert their autonomy, may be in error. In marriage choices and in other aspects of the lives of the peoples of African descent, we must be sensitive to the continuing influence of an Africa that never died.

In spite of their achievements, however, it must be said that the odyssey of the free black person while slavery existed was decidedly bittersweet. Although free from slavery's shackles, these persons were pariahs in the eyes of the larger society. Denied the rights of full citizenship and existing in a racist environment, free blacks embraced various ways of protecting their interests and advancing their cause. Some emigrated to Africa, Canada, and the Caribbean. Others remained to struggle for justice and lay the institutional foundations of black America. And many just lived quiet and unspectacular lives, making the best of their situation. Their struggles were never easy anywhere, and the problems, though varying in regional intensity, were nationwide. Free blacks did not always win their battles, nor did they always agree on which path to pursue. But they created their own passageways, wrestled among themselves for self-definition, and endured.

Notes

1. William Waller Hening, *The Statutes at Large: Being A Collection of All the Laws of Virginia, from the First Session of the Legislature in the Year 1619,* ii (Richmond, 1819–1828), 267.
2. Schweninger, *Black Property Owners,* 66.
3. Ibid.
4. George Fitzhugh, *Sociology of the South; or The Failure of Free Society* (New York, 1854), 264.
5. Donald G. Nieman, *Promises to Keep: African Americans and the Constitutional Order, 1776 to the Present* (New York: Oxford, 1991), 26.
6. Ibid., 22.
7. Ira Berlin, *Slaves Without Masters: The Free Negro in the Antebellum South* (New York: Pantheon Books, 1974), 7.
8. Leon Litwack, *North of Slavery: The Negro in the Free States 1790–1860* (Chicago: University of Chicago Press, 1961), 69.
9. Ibid., 76.
10. Ibid., 77.
11. Ibid., 91.
12. Berlin, *Slaves Without Masters,* 91.
13. Nieman, *Promises to Keep,* 22.
14. Litwack, *North of Slavery,* 52–53.
15. Don E. Fehrenbacher, *The Dred Scott Case: Its Significance in American Law and Politics* (New York: Oxford, 1981), 265.
16. Ibid., 341.
17. Ibid., 346.
18. Ibid., 347.
19. Ibid., 357, 429.
20. C. Peter Ripley, ed., *The Black Abolitionist Papers,* vol. 3 (Chapel Hill: University of North Carolina Press, 1985), 53–54.
21. Ira Berlin, "The Structure of the Free Negro Caste in the Antebellum United States," *Journal of Social History,* 9 (1976), 311–312.
22. Michael P. Johnson and James L. Roark, "'A Middle Ground': Free Mulattoes and the Friendly Moralist Society of Antebellum Charleston," *Southern Studies,* 21 (1982), 248.
23. John H. Russell, "Colored Freemen as Slave Owners in Virginia," *Journal of Negro History,* 1 (1916), 234.
24. Ibid., 235.
25. Schweninger, *Black Property Owners,* 105.
26. Ibid., 106.
27. Ibid., 107.
28. Russell, "Colored Freemen as Slave Owners," 240.
29. Morris, *Southern Slavery and the Law,* 29–31.

30. Berlin, *Slaves Without Masters*, 279.
31. Ibid., 272.
32. Floyd J. Miller, *The Search for a Black Nationality: Black Emigration and Coloniza-tion, 1787–1863* (Urbana: University of Illinois Press, 1975), 5.
33. Ibid., 14.
34. Ibid., 12.
35. Lamont D. Thomas, *Paul Cuffe: Black Entrepreneur and Pan Africanist* (Urbana: University of Illinois Press, 1986), 7; Miller, *The Search for a Black Nationality*, 24.
36. Miller, *The Search for a Black Nationality*, 48–50.
37. Thomas Jefferson, *Notes on the State of Virginia*, William Peden, ed. (Chapel Hill: University of North Carolina Press, 1955), 137–143; William Cohen, "Thomas Jefferson and the Problem of Slavery," *Journal of American History*, LVI (December 1969), 523.
38. Leonard Curry, *The Free Black in Urban America, 1800–1850* (Chicago: University of Chicago Press, 1981), 233.
39. Ibid., 233–234.
40. David Walker, *David Walker's Appeal . . . to the Colored Citizens of the World . . .*, reprint (Baltimore: Black Classic Press, 1993), 84.
41. Curry, *The Free Black in Urban America*, 235.
42. Leonard Sweet, *Black Images of America, 1784–1870* (New York: W. W. Norton, 1976), 43.
43. For a discussion of Russwurm's life, see Bella Gross, "Freedom's Journal and the Rights of All," *Journal of Negro History*, XVII:3 (1932), 241–286.
44. Martin Delany, *The Condition, Elevation, Emigration and Destiny of the Colored People of the United States*, reprint (Baltimore: Black Classic Press, 1993), 14.
45. Ibid., 169–170.
46. Miller, *The Search for a Black Nationality*, 190.
47. Ibid., 193.
48. Ibid., 273.
49. Stuckey, *Slave Culture*, 201.
50. Ibid., 188.
51. Walker, *David Walker's Appeal*, 22.
52. The preceding quotations are taken from Walker, *David Walker's Appeal*, 27, 34, 42–43, 50, 85–90.
53. Miller, *Search for a Black Nationality*, 96.
54. Stuckey, *Slave Culture*, 209.
55. Ibid., 224.
56. Ibid., 225.
57. Gary B. Nash, *Forging Freedom: The Formation of Philadelphia's Black Community, 1720–1840* (Cambridge: Harvard University Press, 1988), 94.
58. Carol V. R. George, *Segregated Sabbaths: Richard Allen and the Emergence of Independent Black Churches, 1760–1840* (New York: Oxford, 1973), 26.
59. Nash, *Forging Freedom*, 52.
60. Ibid., 111.
61. Pease and Pease, *They Who Would Be Free*, 134.
62. Ibid., 135.
63. Nash, *Forging Freedom*, 116.
64. Richard Allen, *The Life Experience and Gospel Labors of Rt. Rev. Richard Allen* (Nashville, 1960), 25.
65. Ibid., 28.
66. Pease and Pease, *They Who Would Be Free*, 24.
67. Ibid., 114.
68. Litwack, *North of Slavery*, 113.
69. Morris, *Southern Slavery and the Law*, 347–348.
70. Litwack, *North of Slavery*, 120.

71. Ibid., 137.
72. Ibid., 163.
73. Berlin, *Slaves Without Masters*, 234.
74. Curry, *The Free Black in Urban America*, 40.
75. Suzanne Lebsock, "Free Black Women and the Question of Matriarchy: Petersburg, Virginia 1784–1820," *Feminist Studies*, 8 (1982), 271–292.

The Opposition to Slavery

The nature of the enslaved persons' reactions to their condition over time remains a controversial issue. The institution of slavery lasted in America for more than two centuries; this was a long period of time by any measure. From the early seventeenth century to 1865, millions of people of African descent labored in America as slaves, but not always under the same circumstances. Some worked in households, others served on plantations, a few were industrial workers, and still others performed a range of other jobs, skilled and unskilled. Black slaves came from many ethnic backgrounds in Africa, but by far the majority were American-born. There were gender differences as well, and undoubtedly generational ones. Never a static institution, slavery also changed over time, and with it the responses of its victims.

The question of resistance cannot be satisfactorily addressed before we briefly consider the emotional issue of how slavery affected those who lived under the institution. After all, the history of black America up to 1865 is largely the history of an enslaved group, the nature of their oppression, and their efforts to order their lives and create a new people. When freedom came, black slaves, as persons, could not walk away as if nothing had happened. To grant the possibility that slavery must have had an impact on its victims is, fundamentally, to affirm the humanity of the black person. Africans and their children were people, too, with all of the vulnerabilities and strengths manifested by humans everywhere. Their burdens under American slavery were great and unremitting, and their struggles to maintain their selfhood were extraordinary. In the end, these struggles must have exacted a psychic toll on everyone. Henry Bibb, an escaped slave, was certain that "No tongue, nor pen ever has or can express the horrors of American Slavery." Similarly, Harriet Jacobs assured the readers of her autobiography, "You never know what it is to be a slave; to be entirely unprotected by law or custom; to have the laws reduce you to the condition of a chattel entirely subject to the will of another." Frances Kemble captured the pain of slavery when she reported on her visit to the hut of an ailing woman on a Georgia plantation in the 1830s:

> As I bent over today trying to prop her into some posture where she might find some ease, she took hold of my hand, and with the tears streaming over her face, said: I have worked every day through dew and damp, and sand and heat, and done good work; but oh, missis, me old and broken now; no tongue can tell how much I suffer.[1]

A particularly poignant comment on what it must have meant to be human property came from an enslaved man who labored as a woodcutter on the banks of the Ohio River during the nineteenth century. A white abolitionist reported having the following conversation with him:

"Halloo, there! Where are you going?" I called to him.
"Gwine chopping in de woods!"
"Choppin for yourself?"
"Han't got no self."
"Slave, are you?"
"Dat's what I is."[2]

No contemporary historian can recapture the above sentiments. Nor can anyone completely understand the range of emotions and responses that these persons betrayed as a consequence of their condition. The enslaved experienced the quiet joys of family life, intimacy with friends, the pain of loss, the anger and frustration of hopes dashed, possibilities contained, and life chances restricted. Accordingly, the enslaved, as is the case with other human beings, harbored a complex package of emotions, as a close reading of their recorded memories clearly reveals.

It is beyond question as we have suggested, that the culture of the slaves helped provide them with one of the bases of their psychological sustenance. Their culture defined, nourished, and shaped them. The issue of slave culture, however, must be separated from the question of the impact of slavery on its victims. Some contemporary historians have tended to focus primarily on the slaves' culture and have confused or conflated the two questions. That slaves did not exist in a world of cultural chaos is abundantly established, at least for the nineteenth century. But, as we have argued, this culture lacked the absolute power, the independent agency ascribed to it, to neutralize racial slavery's canons. The slaves' culture and their networks of relationships tempered the effects of the psychic wounds that were inflicted, but they could not prevent the targets from being hit in a multitude of ways from a multitude of directions. Nor could their culture and support systems always kill the pain, heal all the wounds, and remove all the scars.

Although the ways in which slavery affected the personhood of its victims remains imperfectly understood, it can be maintained that there was a wide range of psychological responses to the institution. These responses were shaped by a number of variables, such as whether the person was African-born or American-born; the age at which an African was enslaved; the size of the black population at any one time; the presence or absence of cultural institutions; and the degree, frequency, and nature of the interaction with whites. Africans who arrived in the seventeenth century undoubtedly experienced a profound feeling of alienation. Usually young adults, they were scattered throughout the colonies, and their numbers were never adequate to establish meaningful and sustaining relationships. Bereft of support systems in an alien land and culture, exposed to debasement by whites, these persons must have experienced something akin to a social death. As their numbers increased, fostering the growth of social institutions and the possibility of relationships, their feelings of marginality must have diminished. Africans retained as much of their cultural heritages as their situation allowed, but how they processed their condition psychologically during that long first century and later cannot be easily determined.

The majority of the slaves in the nineteenth century were born in America. By 1820 blacks had been under white domination for two hundred years and slavery had become a way of life, even if it was becoming increasingly confined to the South. Most black children were born as slaves; most black people were human property, subject to the controlling mechanisms of the larger society and the unceasing assaults on their personhood. Children were socialized into their subordinate role, acquiring along the way the lessons they would need to help them navigate their way through the institutional passageways to their advantage. The psychic price that these persons paid as the victims of oppression for more than two centuries must have been great. Yet although no one could escape from slavery's pernicious reach and unholy influence, not everyone was affected in the same way. Some must have become the childlike, carefree, master-loving, and psychologically maimed Sambo that white Southerners described during the nineteenth century. Others, at the other extreme, by sheer mental fortitude and luck avoided most of the traumatic effects of the institution that held them in thrall. In between—and constituting the vast majority—were a range of personality types. These were the persons who, in varying degrees, bore psychic wounds and scars as a consequence of their condition. But they were not so damaged as to become the stereotypical Sambo. Like most persons today, these slaves functioned normally in spite of their travail, absorbed their blows, and proceeded to confront the next challenge. Most slaves maintained a psychic balance, but no one remained untouched by slavery's blows. Observing slavery's corrosive effect, Frances Kemble was impressed by "the miserable results of the system on everything connected with it–the souls, minds, bodies, and estates of both races of men."[3]

It is precisely because there were so many personality types among the slave population, as one would expect among all peoples, that generalizations on this issue must be cautiously advanced. Never predominantly psychological lepers nor composed primarily of persons always on the barricades, slaves displayed a complex of emotional reactions to their condition depending on the circumstances, the stage in their life course, and the mood of the moment. Slaveowners were constantly surprised at the way even a most trusted Sambo-like person could engage in acts of violence, sabotage, and resistance. No one could predict how enslaved persons would behave when the opportunities for freedom beckoned, when their political consciousness became aroused, or when they had been pushed to the breaking point. Consequently, those masters who had some understanding of their human property realized that they could not rest easily and that the seeming fidelity of their chattel could be readily transformed into defiance and rebellion. The overseer who observed that a person who "put his confidence in a Negro . . . was simply a Damned Fool" was undoubtedly correct. Edwin C. Holland, a South Carolina planter, observed in 1822 that the slaves were "The Jacobins of the country against whom we should always be on guard." He saw them as "the *anarchists* and the *domestic enemy;* the common enemy of civilized society, and the barbarians who would IF THEY COULD become the destroyers of our race."[4] As is the case with any other group of people, slaves recognized the boundaries beyond which they could not be pushed without provoking their resistance. Masters and overseers knew that too, and few believed that their human property were uniformly tractable individuals who collaborated in their oppression.

The rules that governed master-slave relationships were constantly being negotiated. Slavery was an institution based on coercion, but there was often much give and take in practice. Contented slaves made better workers, and masters were not reluctant to accommodate the wishes of their chattel if that did not mean any diminution in their authority. The work routine could be modified, rations increased, and minor concessions granted if it were in the master's best interest to do so. In 1767, for example, a number of slaves took their complaints against a slave driver to the owner who lived in Charleston. The slaves were upset about the amount of work that they were expected to accomplish daily under the task system. Evidently, they had a case, since the owner confessed that "there is sometimes a great difference in Tasks, . . . I was sorry to see Poor Caesar amongst them for I knew him to be an honest, inoffensive fellow and that if any will do without severity, he will."

That slaves exercised some degree of control over the workplace seems to be generally accepted. One nineteenth-century white South Carolinian observed that the "daily task does not vary according to the arbitrary will and caprice of their owners, and although [it] is not fixed by law, it is so well settled by long usage, that upon every plantation it is the same. Should the owner increase the work beyond what is customary, he subjects himself to the reproach of his neighbors, and to such discontent amongst his slaves as to make them of but little use to him."[5]

The negotiated nature of the work routine can be seen in the experiences of the slaves who worked on James Henry Hammond's farm in Silver Bluff, Georgia, between 1831 and the 1850s. Hammond, a South Carolinian, inherited the farm in 1831 and reported on the frequent negotiations with his slaves over a number of issues, including their opposition to the gang system. When forced to do gang labor, Hammond noted, they were "doing badly." In 1847 when Hammond wanted to deny the slaves a number of their customary days off at Christmas because of his unhappiness with their work, he was "persuaded out of my decision by the Negroes." As Drew Faust has noted, "Hammond and his slaves arrived at a sort of accommodation on the issue of work. But in this process, Hammond had to adjust his desires and expectations as significantly as did his bondsmen."[6]

Slaves who extracted concessions from their owners worked more willingly and ironically strengthened the institution of slavery. From their vantage point however, the slaves were testing the limits of the system, effecting an improvement in their work situation and reducing their physical burdens. Slaves, unlike modern unionized workers, could not withdraw their services without serious repercussions. Usually, they had to express their unhappiness by peacefully insisting on the honoring of customary rights and ensuring that the work routine was not pushed beyond the limits of their endurance. None of this posed any serious threat to the survival of slavery, but their vigilance and protests earned them some limited control over the labor arrangements.

Slaves also developed a number of techniques to show their unhappiness with their condition. Some of these acts of protest were inspired by their dislike of a particular job assignment, negative reactions to a master or an overseer, resentment at being physically abused, or the normal and pervasive desire to be free. These persons feigned illness, malingered, treated their tools carelessly, went on go-slows, neglected their duty, pretended not to understand an assignment, or engaged in acts of sabotage. Such behavior enraged masters and overseers, but there was hardly any corrective action that brought satisfactory results. Characterized as day-to-day resistance, these actions by the slaves punctured the efficiency of the institution, but they did little to derail it. The slaves, however, must have reaped psychological rewards in striking back in the only way they knew how, by withdrawing their labor or by not working diligently or at their maximum level.

Evidence also suggests that nineteenth-century slaves converted some of their master's property to their own use. Slaves evidently stole ground provisions, tobacco, liquor, animals to be slaughtered, and whatever else they fancied. The extent of such pilfering cannot be determined, but most slaves probably did not engage in it. If they had, there would have been chaos on the farms, plantations, and in the households, and white society would have responded with all of its might to curb it, if it could not be eliminated.

Was the incidence of theft by slaves an act of resistance or was it a symptom of their condition, the absence of an appropriate code of ethical conduct? The answer may not be readily apparent, because we do not fully understand the ethos or the values that informed the behavior of the slaves. Slaves stole from their masters as well as from other whites, and a distinction should be made between the two categories. Slaves who stole from persons other than their masters took various forms of property but most frequently money, horses, and clothes. If caught and convicted, they suffered whippings, execution, or banishment from the state.

The majority of the slaves stole from their own masters, and most of the thefts involved food. We are more concerned with this category of thefts, because of their wider incidence and because they seem to tell us more about slave behavior than the other form of thievery. Slaves justified their stealing food on the grounds that it supplemented their diet. A former slave admitted, "I used to steal some chickens 'cause we didn't have enough to eat, and I didn't think I done wrong, 'cause the place was full of 'em."[7] Other slaves expressed no moral qualms for such thefts on the grounds that they constituted an exchange for their labor, an unsanctioned quid pro quo. Frederick Douglass maintained that such appropriation of the master's property should not be considered thefts. Rather, "such taking is not stealing in any just sense of the word." Since the slave was himself the master's property, how could he possibly be guilty of stealing, since everyone and everything belonged to the master? In Douglass's expressive phraseology, the slave was merely "taking his meat out of one tub and putting it in another."[8]

At one level, thefts by slaves had profound political implications. In some cases they represented a challenge to the authority of the slave-owners, reflected the slaves' attempt to share in the fruits of their labor, and enriched their table or pockets in the process. Slaves "took" that which they saw as partially theirs and undoubtedly congratulated themselves if they got away with it. These acts were not consciously designed to destroy the institution, although some historians have mistakenly argued otherwise. Slaves were not so naive as to believe that that would occur. Theft was one of the weapons that the enslaved used to contest the power of the masters and create small victories for themselves.

The secular ethos of slave society appears to have condoned such behavior. Slaves who engaged in thefts did not suffer any ostracism, and their peers were not likely to inform on them. On the contrary, such persons enjoyed the vicarious admiration of the community for the successful assault on the master, and to report them would have been an act of disloyalty. As one slaveowner noted with some exaggeration, a slave who stole "will never be informed upon by his fellow laborers, for an informer, in [the slaves'] eyes, is held in greater detestation than the most notorious thief."[9] In the contest between the oppressor and the oppressed, the usual moral constraints and judgments did not apply. The situation would be different if a slave stole from another slave; the community's wrath and disapprobation would descend upon the villain.

Yet the matter of theft from the master must have posed some moral problems for those who had embraced Christianity. The Baptist Association of Virginia, for example, denounced thefts in 1816 and called for the expulsion of members when they "cannot be convinced of his or her error." The association was alarmed "that many Coloured persons, who are Members of our Church, hold the abominable opinion that it is no crime, in the sight of God, to steal their master's property, arguing that it is taking their own labor; . . . many of them, acting upon this principle, have thereby brought great reproach upon the cause of Religion."[10] In addition, white preachers and some black ones, too, denounced stealing and enjoined their congregations to avoid the temptation. We may assume that some Christianized slaves understood the religious strictures against theft, although, as will be shown, they may have neutralized any guilt that resulted from their contravention. Christianized slaves, furthermore, represented only a portion of slave society; many more evidently remained untouched by this religion.

A former slave who recalled his peers' stealing hogs on Saturday for their barbecue on Sunday morning confessed, "As none o' our gang didn't have no 'ligion, us never felt no scruples bout not getting the 'cue ready fo' Sunday."[11] This person, and those like him, obviously placed no moral significance on their "theft"; it was not an issue for them. Other persons did have 'ligion, however, and they could not treat the matter so lightly. Yet by viewing the appropriation of the master's property as "taking" rather than stealing, Christianized slaves neutralized the ethical question that their behavior would, under different circumstances, have raised.

The incidence of theft cannot be seen solely in economic terms or merely as a contest for power between masters and slaves. Nor was it, in its principal thrust, a rejection of the moral code of white society. Theft was, inevitably, a product of the condition of servitude, and to assess it in moral terms misses the point. Taking from the master was a clandestine way for slaves to share in the fruits of their labor and partake of the crops they had tended and the animals for which they had cared. From the masters' position, such behavior was theft; from the standpoint of the slaves it bore no such negative connotation. Taking from the master was legitimized culturally and was characterized as neither "right" nor "wrong." It was almost as normal as a day's work. The escaped slave Charles Ball admitted, "I never was acquainted with a slave who believed that he violated any rule of morality by appropriating to himself anything that belonged to his master if it was necessary to his comfort."[12] One master who observed that "the colored preachers were the greatest and most active thieves" said more than he recognized. For some, there was no incompatibility between the embrace of Christian strictures against theft and taking from the masters; different yardsticks applied. A former slave said it well: "Where you labor there shall ye reap."[13]

Slave society was never idyllic and had the same internal tensions as others, perhaps more so. Faced with pressures from both outside and inside their community, these persons reacted in a variety of ways. Some of these reactions took the form of aggressive or violent behavior directed at whites and other blacks. Between 1740 and 1794, for example, slaves killed at least twenty-four whites in Virginia.[14] Other whites were assaulted and women raped, although the incidence of the latter does not appear to have been as great as the general populace believed. Some whites were poisoned by slaves, a practice that seems to have peaked in the eighteenth century, the high-water mark of the African-born population. Slaves also committed arson against their master's property with some regularity.

Slaves who assaulted whites and destroyed their property faced severe penalties if caught, tried, and convicted. Not all of these cases ended up in the courts, to be sure, since the masters exercised enormous private powers of discipline over their human property and were not hesitant about using them. Attacks on whites violated the slave codes and challenged white authority and white supremacy, regardless of the motivation for the offense. In many cases, slaves struck out at whites as a consequence of their rejection of their condition, an expression of pent-up anger and frustration. Such outbursts, usually independent acts, terrified the white populace, and the assailants paid the price. Not all forms of violence by slaves were clearly politically inspired and designed to overthrow the system, although historians disagree on this point. Some slaves, it can be conjectured, rejected the legitimacy of the legal system that held them in bondage. By so doing, they called into question the hegemonic power of whites. Yet we should grant that not every act by a slave was dictated by whites or constituted a conscious reaction to their power.

ABANDONING SLAVERY

Many slaves claimed their freedom by running away. This practice, usually characterized as *marronage*, began sometime after the arrival of the Africans during that long first century. It will be recalled that John Punch fled with two white servants in 1640. Punch was the first to appear in the records, but we can never be certain that he was the first to flee. The incidence of flight increased as the black population expanded, and whites adopted horrendous measures to curb the practice. In 1643 the Virginia legislators required runaway servants to serve an additional period of time equivalent to two times the period for which they fled. In addition, they had to be branded with the letter "R" so that all would know. Between 1661 and 1670 Virginia passed ten laws pertaining to the control of runaways.[15]

The laws relating to the treatment of runaway slaves tell us a great deal about white perception of blacks, the place whites assigned them in society, and what constituted acceptable punishment for blacks who challenged their status, condition, and role. The laws also reveal much about the psychology of the people who prescribed the mutilation of other humans. A South Carolina law passed in 1712 allowed the death penalty for slaves who escaped "in order to deprive [their] master or mistress of [their] service."[16] Slaves who ran away temporarily received punishments ranging from whipping to branding and mutilation. The law ordered that a woman who had escaped four times be "severely whipped . . . branded on the left cheek with the letter R, and her left ear cut off."[17] Those who fled for a fifth time faced death or had the "cord" of their legs above the heel cut.[18] Some of these measures were modified in later years, but the South Carolina law continued to sanction the use of violence against runaways.

The Georgia slave code of 1755 also permitted violence used in the capture of runaways. Such slaves could be killed with impunity, although the law encouraged their return alive. Those who brought a runaway back alive received a higher reward than those who brought back a scalp and ears. New York also adopted a measure in 1755 permitting whites to "shoot or otherwise destroy" slaves older than fourteen who were found without a pass more than a mile away from home. Those who murdered these slaves were not to be "impeached, censured or prosecuted for the same."[19] This law was passed during the heat of the French and Indian War, and its stringency may have been a function of that crisis.

Runaway slaves everywhere confronted laws that meted out the severest forms of punishment to them. These persons posed a serious threat to the survival of the slave system; hence white society had to respond with all of the terror at its command. The Georgia legislature defended its law of 1755 on the grounds that it deterred slaves "who will be tempted to desert from their masters."[20] Years later, James H. Hammond, a Georgia slaveowner, supported the use of chains and irons in disciplining runaways: "If we pretend to own slaves, they must not be permitted to abscond whenever they see fit; and if nothing else will prevent it these means must be resorted to."[21]

The slaveowners, to be sure, exercised enormous disciplinary powers over their recaptured runaways. More often than not, the legal authorities were never involved, and masters drew upon their own arsenal of cruelty to punish those who came back or were recaptured. Slaves were fettered, whipped, branded, had limbs chopped off, castrated, and humiliated in numerous ways. These measures sometimes worked as a deterrent. They gave the owners, the overseers, and others ample opportunity to wield almost untrammeled power over their chattel without fear of legal retribution or societal ostracism. At the other end, the runaways bore the physical scars and undoubtedly the psychological wounds of their quest for freedom. The lesson was not lost upon those slaves who had remained behind. But for many, the desire to be free dwarfed considerations such as the probability of capture and barbaric forms of punishment.

We are now beginning to acquire some understanding of those persons who braved all risks and escaped. We can assume that during the long formative period most of the escapees were African-born, since they enjoyed numerical superiority for many years. In fact, for a good portion of the seventeenth century, almost all the slaves were African-born. The circumstances of their birth and enslavement had a significant bearing on the nature of their resistance to slavery.

Slaves who ran off in the formative years appear to have done so in groups of three or more. This pattern seems to have lasted into the early years of the nineteenth century. Significantly African-born and probably unfamiliar with the terrain, slaves must have found comfort in numbers. But perhaps there was a more important imperative at work. These African-born slaves came from cultural backgrounds where collective behavior was emphasized and the needs of the group predominated. Thus, in order to understand the style and expression of their challenge to slavery, we must situate those protests culturally. Of course, the realities of life in America would modify these cultural predispositions, but in resistance and other matters, behavior had to be culturally sanctioned.

Effects of the Fugitive Slave Law. Brutally tracking down fugitive slaves on their way to the north.

Escape in the formative period, as opposed to the creolized patterns of the nineteenth century, was seen essentially as an enterprise that involved the group. Some strong group ties had been forged on the ships that transported slaves to the Americas, but a cooperative ethos had existed in their societies long before the misfortune of their enslavement. Throughout the eighteenth century, newspaper advertisements for the recovery of African runaways stressed that they had escaped as a group. Slaveowners hoped for the return of four "new Gambia men," four men from the "Fullah Country," and various other ethnic combinations.[22] Robert Carter, a Virginia planter, reported in 1727 the escape of seven Africans he had recently purchased. Evidently, recent arrivals from Africa were more likely to escape in their first year than in succeeding years, and the white authorities made allowances for that possibility. The Maryland Assembly, for example, in 1725 authorized the mutilation of escaped slaves but excluded Africans during their first year of residence in the colony.[23]

A disproportionate number of the early escapees were men, but it must be remembered that men also formed the greater proportion of the African-born slaves. Most barely knew English, having spent only a few months or a year or two in the colonies. When recaptured, some were unable to identify themselves or to indicate who had purchased them. For many, their destination was uncertain and they sought refuge wherever they could find it. A few may have hoped that they would be able to return to Africa. One Virginia slaveowner reported that a male slave and his daughter "went off with several others, being persuaded that they could find the Way back to their own Country."[24]

Slaves within reach of rivers or the ocean often fled to them, vainly searching for boats that would facilitate their journey to freedom. Charleston became one of the principal destinations for slaves who harbored the desire to return to Africa. Others hoped to travel by river to final destinations in the North or the South. Northern runaways sometimes headed for Canada. So serious had the exodus become that New York passed a law in 1705 and again in 1715 and 1745 imposing the death penalty on slaves escaping to Canada.[25] A few slaves departed from South Carolina for the Spanish settlement of St. Augustine, Florida, with the expectation that they would be welcomed and their freedom recognized. Long the foes of the English, the Spaniards actively encouraged their slaves to flee. In 1733 the king of Spain went as far as granting freedom to all slaves who escaped from the English colonies. Although the edict was not immediately implemented, word spread and a steady stream of slaves deserted their English masters and fled to St. Augustine. In 1738, the runaways had their right to a settlement confirmed, and the town and fort of Gracia Real de Santa Teresa de Mose came into existence. The settlement was abandoned in 1763 when the English assumed control of Florida and the residents fled to Cuba.

Runaway slaves sometimes found sanctuaries among the Indians, but this could not always be depended upon. Among the Northern Indian nations, the Senecas and Onondagas of New York and the Minisinks of Long Island welcomed black escapees. Some found refuge among the Mohawks as well. In Florida, the Seminoles provided sanctuary for runaways, but reduced many of them to a form of servitude, similar to the slavery they thought they had abandoned. The Chickasaws, Choctaws, Creeks, and Cherokees also enslaved blacks. In fact, the Cherokees became notorious in the eighteenth century for catching runaways and returning them.

In 1730, seven Cherokees went to England where they signed a treaty with the king agreeing that "if any Negro slaves shall run away into the woods from their English masters the Cherokee Indians shall endeavour to apprehend them and either bring them back to the plantation from whence they run away or to the Governor, and for every Negro so apprehended and brought back the Indian who brings him shall receive a gun and a match coat."[26] Identifying with some Indian nations, as opposed to the whites, some runaways supported the indigenous peoples, particularly the Seminoles, in their struggles with the U.S. government. Blacks, for example, participated on the side of the Indians in the Second Seminole War, which began in 1835.

White authorities tried, with some success, to discourage any collaboration between Indians and blacks. Clearly, it was in their interest to prevent these two groups from making common cause against those who exercised an oppressive power in society. Indians were repeatedly asked not to welcome runaways. In 1732, Pennsylvania whites pleaded with the Indians not to provide a home for runaways since slaves were "the support and livelihood of their masters, and get them their bread."[27] Other Indians were threatened with reprisals if they harbored slaves. In 1721 the governor of South Carolina signed an agreement with the Upper and Lower Creeks requiring them "to apprehend and secure any Negro or other Slave which shall run away from any English Settlements to our Nation." When it was believed in 1735 that the Tuscaroras were sheltering black runaways, South Carolina legislators declared that if such behavior and other depredations continued, "the next step on the like Provocation we shall endeavour to extirpate them."[28]

Many escapees did not flee to Indian nations but tried to establish their own settlements. The establishment of free enclaves was a feature of many slave societies in the Americas. Runaway blacks created communities in Brazil, Jamaica, Mexico, Cuba, Venezuela, and in other places. The Africans desired to recreate a way of life similar to the one they had known in their homelands. These settlements were to be run by blacks for blacks and were to be free from white control and influence. Free communities probably appeared in the American colonies in the second half of the seventeenth century, but there is firm evidence that they existed in the early years of the eighteenth century. In 1725, the Maryland legislature took note of the "sundry" slaves who "have of late Years runaway into the Back-Woods, some of which have there perished," a suggestion that they must have lived in a community of some sort. In 1729, the governor of Virginia reported the news of "some runaway Negroes beginning a settlement in the Mountains." This community was destroyed by the whites.[29] Most of the settlements were established in topographically inhospitable parts of the colonies and states. Mountainous sections and swamps proved to be particularly attractive, even if they afforded a harsh existence. The Great Dismal Swamp in North Carolina and southern Virginia became one of the principal settlement areas. So too were equally unpleasant parts of South Carolina, Georgia, Louisiana, Florida, Mississippi, and Alabama.

African-born slaves had a greater tendency to establish runaway communities than did their creole counterparts. These persons, many of them unacculturated to the ways of the society that held them in bondage, simply withdrew from it. For some it was only a partial withdrawal because they continued a clandestine trade with agreeable whites. Others carried on hit-and-run attacks on whites, stealing provisions and intimidating them. Most of the communities were rather small, except for that in the Great Dismal Swamp, which may have had 2,000 residents at its peak. Theirs was a harsh life, but slaves were no strangers to a difficult existence, and many managed to preserve their freedom for varying lengths of time.

During the nineteenth century, the runaways, particularly creoles, were more likely to seek refuge in the free states of the Union. This was not a viable option available to their peers before the end of the War of Independence and the demise of slavery in the North. More aware of their possibilities than the African-born by virtue of their birth in America, creoles saw a better future for themselves in New York City, Philadelphia, and Boston, and not in maroon (runaway) communities. Such persons had no former lives to recreate; theirs was a journey to freedom and to new opportunities, or so they hoped. They were likely to be skilled persons, fluent in English, familiar with the ways of whites, and predominantly male, young, and unmarried.

The decision to escape, particularly for persons with families, was never an easy one. Fleeing with a family, especially with young children, heightened the chances of recapture, to say nothing of all the other hazards—the weather, hunger, pursuing dogs—that could be encountered. Accordingly, most men with spouses and children fled alone. Henry Bibb, who escaped, recalled that leaving his family was "one of the most self-denying acts of my whole life, to take leave of an affectionate wife, who stood before me on my departure, with dear little Frances in her arms, and with tears of sorrow in her eyes, as she bid me a long farewell. It required all the moral courage that I was master of to suppress my feelings while taking leave of my little family."[30] By all indications, women were less likely to escape, probably electing to stay behind with their children.

Yet there is some evidence that families escaped together, despite the inherent difficulty of the enterprise. One of the most famous of such escapes was that involving the abolitionist Henry Highland Garnet. In 1824, then only a boy of nine, his entire family escaped from Maryland to freedom in Wilmington, Delaware. Henry had to be carried on the backs of the adults when he tired. There were probably eight persons among the family group, including Henry's sister, his parents and other relatives.

Those persons who ran away demonstrated enormous courage. Many took off with the expectation that they would be gone permanently. Some had a change of heart as they confronted hunger, inclement weather, inhospitable terrain, and the awful fear of the unknown. These persons returned after a few days to face their punishment and perhaps to try again at a more propitious time. Others who did not harbor thoughts of permanent absence but merely deserted temporarily in order to escape punishment returned after they thought their masters' passions had cooled. Those who visited relatives and friends without permission came back in their own time to pay the penalty for trying to cement personal bonds and to celebrate their humanity.

All of these acts of defiance could not be engaged in lightly, and collectively they must have taken their toll on those who would be free, if even temporarily. But for those who headed for free territories, the rigors of the journey would test their internal fiber; the promise of freedom would be their sustenance. And they needed a good deal of luck to navigate their way smoothly, and guile to elude and deceive their pursuers or the army of suspicious whites they encountered.

The extraordinary odyssey of William and Ellen Craft dramatizes the courage and ingenuity of the runaways, as well as a desire for freedom that only persons who never experienced that state could fully understand. Ellen was a light-skinned mulatto slave who was born in 1826 in Clinton, Georgia, and later moved with her owner to Macon. William was also a slave born in Georgia. He had a black phenotype and worked as a carpenter. Although they belonged to different owners, they met in the 1840s, fell in love, and decided to marry. The wedding took place in 1846, but the young couple remained uneasy, fearing that they might be separated through sale, as had been the fate of so many other families.

By 1848, the couple had developed a novel plan for escape to the North. Ellen, who could be mistaken for a white person because of her light skin, was to be dressed as a male plantation owner and would pretend to be William's master. William would play the role of the trusted valet accompanying his master, who needed help for his rheumatic condition. As part of the scheme, a poultice was placed on Ellen's face to dissuade questions from the curious, since she was obviously in no physical shape to respond. Furthermore, since Ellen could not write, her right arm was placed in a sling, reducing the possibility of her being asked to sign any documents. The couple passed through Charleston, Wilmington, Richmond, Washington, and Baltimore before arriving at Philadelphia, their destination. They traveled by boat, coaches, and trains for four days, fearful at one moment and hopeful at the next.

Ellen and William recounted their experiences in the narrative *Running a Thousand Miles for Freedom*, which appeared in 1860. They told of their often narrow avoidance of discovery and of the fears they harbored. The last night was particularly difficult, since freedom was so near at hand. They recalled that while they waited in Baltimore: "We felt more anxious than ever, because we knew not what that last dark night would bring forth. It is true we were near the goal, but our poor hearts were still as if tossed at sea; and, as there was another great and dangerous bar to pass, we were afraid our liberties would be wrecked, and, like the ill fated Royal Charter, go down forever just off the place we longed to reach." But their worst fears never materialized, and their spectacular escape was celebrated by the abolitionists. Wendell Phillips,

*Ellen Craft (1826–1897) in the disguise used in her 1848 escape from
slavery.*

a white abolitionist, predicted that "future historians and poets would
tell this story as one of the most thrilling in the nation's annals."[31]

Other slaves, desperate for freedom, employed similar creative,
albeit dangerous, methods. A number had themselves crated and
shipped to their intended destination, frequently with fatal consequences. One individual who survived such an ordeal was Henry "Box"
Brown of Virginia. According to Brown, a voice urged him to "Go get a
box, and put yourself in it," as a means of facilitating his escape to
Philadelphia. Accordingly, he had one of the appropriate size constructed and he arranged to have himself shipped by a friend. He took

supplies of biscuits and water with him, but his ordeal was made almost unbearable when the crate was placed wrong side up and he endured a twenty-six-hour ride in that position. He went on to play an active role in the antislavery movement.

Escaping slaves quite frequently received assistance along the way from friendly blacks and sympathetic whites, chiefly abolitionists and Quakers. It is difficult to reconstruct the extent and pervasiveness of this support, which is shrouded in myth. This network of assistance has been characterized as constituting an underground railroad, whereby persons supportive of the runaways provided them with food, lodging, advice, and funds. Prominent "conductors" have been said to include Levi Coffin and Thomas Garrett, prominent white Quakers, as well as William Still, a black Philadelphian, and Harriet Tubman, an escaped slave.

Harriet Tubman has been variously characterized as "Moses" and "the greatest heroine of the age." She was born a slave in Dorchester County, Maryland, in 1821. In her early years she worked as a domestic but later became a field hand, becoming quite famous for her physical strength. While still a young woman she was seriously injured, a condition that made her fall asleep at unpredictable moments. Harriet escaped to Pennsylvania in 1849 and dedicated her life to freeing those who remained in bondage. She soon returned to Baltimore and "conducted" her sister and her two children to freedom. Thereafter, she reputedly assisted in the escape of as many as 200 slaves.

Possessed of extraordinary organizational skills and daring, Tubman developed quite a reputation among many slaves. One runaway slave, Thomas Cole, noted that he would have welcomed her assistance since he "was hopin and prayin all de time dat I could meets up wid dat Harriet Tubman woman."[32] William Still, who aided many escaping slaves in his position as secretary and executive director of the General Vigilance Committee, was effusive in his assessment of Tubman's contribution to the cause of freedom: ". . . in point of courage, shrewdness and disinterested exertions to rescue her fellow-men," he noted, "she was without equal. . . . Her like it is probable was never known before or since."[33]

The majority of the slaves did not run off, nor did they engage in acts of violence or rebellion. Their failure to do either should not be taken as a measure of their contentment with their condition. In fact, we should not expect to find a people always poised for overt rebellious behavior for 250 years, always conspiring and occupying the trenches. Ebbs and flows in such behavior depended on the circumstances, the possibilities, and the changing levels of political consciousness. Certain developments internal to the slaves—the presence of a network of relationships, the growth of religious and other institutions, the emergence of a settled family and community life—tempered the harshness of their

Harriet Tubman was known as "the greatest heroine of the age".

daily experiences as chattel. Freedom as a desired state was never absent for the vast majority; the will to embrace it when it came was never crushed. But not all of the slaves' daily energies were consumed by activities designed to effect the institution's violent end; they had to confront numerous immediate and seemingly more mundane daily needs and concerns. Such preoccupations did not negate their involvement in or their embrace of acts of resistance; these demands simply rendered involvement more difficult.

The form that resistance took, as has been noted earlier, also had to receive cultural sanction. Those African-born slaves who interpreted their misfortune in religious terms and as a result of the white man's sorcery would not have embraced violence as a means of effecting their liberation. Such sorcery had to be confronted in other ways. This meant resorting to more rituals in a quest for stronger sorcery to defeat that of the enemy. We must, therefore, not ignore the cultural dimensions in our understanding of slave behavior in this and other ways.

Creole slaves, at least those born in the nineteenth century, would have had other ideas about the reasons for their condition. But we cannot ignore the possible tempering effect of Christianity on the use of violence against one's enemies. Not all slaves were Christians, and not all would have absorbed Christian dogma uncritically, so we can only speculate on how they processed what they heard and how it informed their behavior.

USING VIOLENCE

Many African-born slaves and creoles rejected whatever cultural restraints existed against acts of violence against their oppressors. Such behavior was the ultimate act of defiance against slavery, a conscious attempt to destroy it and to liberate its victims. For some, the decision to shed blood to effect their freedom probably came quickly and easily; for others it came only after a careful assessment of their condition and an evaluation of the chances of success and the consequences of failure. Always aware of the armed might of white society, conscious of the organizational difficulties that stood in their way, and faced with the absence of appropriate weapons, most slaves must have despaired of any chance of success. Once they had decided to resort to violence, however, a crucial bridge had been crossed. Like the decision to escape permanently, the rejection of bondage was now complete and the person had laid claim to himself, the consequences not withstanding.

Slaves conspired to rebel with some degree of frequency, and an insecure white society was constantly alert to rumors of revolt. But the actual resort to organized violence was not a continual feature of slave life in America. One recent scholar has identified "at least nine slave revolts in America between 1691 and 1865."[34] Conspiracies, of course, far exceeded that number. None of these revolts ended slavery, but this is only one measure of their importance. They gave expression to the need of the participants—and those who supported them—to chart their own destinies and live according to their own rules. Slavery had not destroyed their spirits; it had blighted their possibilities, but it had not rendered them impotent. Such challenges reminded whites that they could not take their chattel for granted and it made them painfully aware that their control of the slaves would never be unchallenged.

The first significant organized challenge to slavery occurred in New York City in 1712. Most of the slaves in the city at the time were African-born, and they numbered slightly less than a thousand. The organizational details of the revolt are scant. It is known, however, that they drew upon their traditional customs to enjoin the conspirators to secrecy and doubtlessly to emphasize the seriousness and sanctity of the enterprise. According to the evidence, they swore "themselves to secrecy by Sucking ye blood of each others hand."[35] They then collected guns, daggers, knives, swords, and other weapons with which to assault the whites "for some hard usage they apprehended to have received from their masters."[36] Twenty-four slaves began the uprising by burning a building and shooting the whites who rushed to the scene. Nine whites lost their lives, and seven were wounded. The outnumbered rebels were soon defeated by the local militia with the assistance of the townspeople. A number of them escaped into the woods, where they committed suicide rather than return to slavery. Others surrendered when they found it impossible to find food and their hunger became unbearable. The authorities arrested seventy blacks, of whom twenty-five were convicted and nineteen executed.[37]

The courts imposed, in the words of New York Governor Robert Hunter, "the most exemplary punishments that could be possibly thought of." One convicted man was "to be broke upon a wheel and so to continue languishing until he be dead"; another was ordered "hung up in chains alive and so to continue without any sustenance until he be dead." This person, according to one observer, the Reverend John Sharpe, survived for five days, "though often delirious by long continuance in that posture, through hunger, thirst and pain." A third slave "was to be burned with a slow fire that he may continue in torment for eight or ten hours."[38]

The rebellion unleashed a panic among the white citizenry in New York and other states in the North. The New York Assembly rushed through a statute "for preventing, suppressing, and punishing the conspiracy and insurrection of Negroes," creating special courts for slaves accused of conspiracy against the established order. Massachusetts, Rhode Island, and Pennsylvania introduced legislation designed to control the entry of new slaves into their territory.

Several years after the New York uprising, a number of slaves resorted to organized violence against whites in Stono, South Carolina. Known as the Stono Rebellion, the incident occurred in September 1739 with large consequences for the black and white populations alike. The conspirators, who numbered about twenty at the outset, were primarily African-born and seemed to have wanted to fight their way to St. Augustine and a life of freedom among the Spaniards. After taking guns from a local store, they killed a number of whites, setting fire to their houses and destroying other forms of property as well. Their numbers increased as they went on, their confidence grew with each successful assault, and their journey was flavored with ecstatic shouts of "Liberty."

Twenty-five whites were killed before the exhausted slaves, having traveled about ten miles, decided to rest. According to one account, their number had "increased every minute by new Negroes coming to them, so that they were above Sixty, some say a hundred, on which they halted in a field and set to dancing, Singing and beating Drums to draw more Negroes to them."[39]

The festivities soon came to an end, however, for the whites surprised them with devastating consequences. Quickly responding, the slaves "gave 2 Fires, but without any damage. We return'd the Fire and bra't down 14 on the spot; and pursuing after them, within 2 Days kill'd twenty odd more, and took about 40; who were immediately some shot, some hang'd, and some Gibbeted alive. A Number came in and were seized and discharged; and some are out yet, but we hope will soon be taken." Eventually, most of the rebels were rounded up and, in the words of a contemporary, "many of them having been put to the most cruel Death."[40]

Predictably, the authorities responded with stiffer controls on the slave population. The resulting slave code of 1740 was comprehensive in its scope. On the one hand, it included provisions that sought to prevent masters and "other persons having the care and government of slaves" from "exercising too great rigor and cruelty over them."[41] Whites could be punished for maiming their slaves, and they had to make adequate provisions for their daily needs. On the other hand, the law tightened the arsenal of control imposed on the slaves. Now defined as personal chattels, they were denied the right to congregate, to become literate, or even to earn money. In further circumscribing the liberty of the slaves, the code restricted the masters as well. They faced severe penalties if they failed to enforce the measures that had been enacted. In denying the slaves certain rights, slave society also imposed chains on itself. This was a stark irony, one of the many prices that whites paid for enslaving blacks.

The largest uprising in terms of the number of slaves who participated began in Louisiana on January 8, 1811. This revolt has not yet been satisfactorily studied, but we know that 400 or 500 slaves were involved. It began in German Cost County, located to the northwest of New Orleans. Poorly armed with knives, clubs, and some guns and under the leadership of Charles Deslondes, a mulatto, the slaves headed for the capital city. They burned plantations along the way, and their number gradually increased. The information is scant, but it appears that only two white persons were killed by the insurgents.

When news of the insurrection spread, many whites panicked and fled from their houses. Acting quickly, members of the militia along with about sixty U.S. soldiers and vigilantes, attacked the slaves and routed them. By January 11, sixty-six slaves had been killed and another seventeen had fled and "are supposed generally to be dead in the woods, as many bodies have been seen by the patrols." A number of the rebels were arrested and held for trial. Many of the accused refused to provide details of the conspiracy when asked to do so, although some pleaded no contest. Twenty-one of them received the death penalty and were shot. White society responded with improved security measures, and the governor noted that the rebellion had made whites more vigilant and cognizant of the threats to their safety.[42]

Of all the overt and violent assaults on slavery, the Nat Turner rebellion was the most dramatic and far reaching. This rebellion occurred in Southampton, Virginia, in August 1831. Southampton County had about 6,500 whites and 9,500 blacks. Approximately one-fifth of the black population were free persons. Two-thirds of the white population owned slaves, with an average ownership of ten or eleven. Most of the slaves were probably creoles and had been born in Virginia or in adjacent states. The vast majority were field hands.

Nat Turner, the best-known leader of the American slave revolts, was born in Southampton in 1800. As a boy and a slave of Benjamin Turner, he demonstrated an impressive intellect and learned to read. When he was nine he was sent to live on the property of Benjamin Turner's son, Samuel. A year later, upon Benjamin's death, he formally became Samuel's property. Young Nat was strongly influenced by Christianity and spent much of his time praying and fasting. Believing that he was "ordained for great purpose in the hands of the Almighty," Turner became a preacher and waited for the revelation of his mission.

In the wake of Samuel Turner's death, Nat was sold to Thomas Moore, a Southampton farmer in 1822. In 1828, he would recall, he had a vision "and the Spirit instantly appeared to me and said the Serpent was loosened, and Christ had laid down the yoke he had borne for the sins of men, and that I should take it on and fight against the Serpent, for the time was fast approaching when the first should be last and the last should be first." When Thomas Moore died in 1829, Nat became the property of his son Putnam, then a nine-year-old boy. In 1829, Moore's widow married Joseph Travis, and he assumed control of the estate and the slaves on it.

Turner's vision in 1828 convinced him that he had been chosen to undertake the destruction of slavery. Consequently, when an eclipse of the sun occurred in 1831, he felt certain that this was a sign from God that he should execute his mission. He confided his plans to four other slaves–Sam, Hark, Nelson, Henry–and the planning began in earnest. The rebellion was set for July 4, a day when the whites would be involved in their holiday celebrations. But General Nat, as he came to be known, fell ill on July 4 and the revolt had to be postponed.

Turner resumed his plans in August after he received another sign on August 13; the sun reportedly dimmed and assumed an array of colors. Shortly after midnight on August 21, Nat and his small army struck. Joined by a few additional recruits, they began their assault on the sleeping whites. Joseph Travis and his wife were the first to be killed, and many others would experience a similar fate. The number of the insurgents gradually increased, although many slaves declined the invitation to join, some saving their masters from the violence that was being unleashed all around them.

Within twenty-four hours, as many as sixty or eighty blacks had joined the revolt. By August 23, fifty-seven whites had been killed, but the revolt was then sputtering to an end as the white authorities prepared a massive military response. Although Turner and a few others eluded capture, most were put in jail to await their trial. Nineteen or twenty of these persons were sentenced to death and executed. Many more, in the words of the *Richmond Whig*, were slaughtered "without trial and under circumstances of great barbarity."[43] Turner was arrested on October 30, tried rather quickly and sentenced to death. While he awaited his execution, he dictated an account of his life to a white attorney, Thomas R. Gray. Known as the *Confessions of Nat Turner*, this document is the most reliable account of his life and the circumstances of the revolt. Turner was executed on November 11, 1831, remaining unrepentant to the end. "I'm ready," he said as he faced execution.

In the aftermath of the revolt, Southern whites and their Northern sympathizers searched for scapegoats. Many blamed abolitionist meddling. Others accused free blacks of stirring up the slave population. Few whites came to the conclusion that the desire for liberty gave motive force to the insurgents. As white Virginians contemplated the presence of an unpredictable black population, some supported emancipation if it were accompanied by colonization elsewhere. But, slavery was too important to the economy for it to be legislated out of existence. Consequently Virginians passed measures designed to further control their slaves and the free blacks. The militia was strengthened, and black preachers were forbidden to conduct religious services. Free blacks could no longer possess weapons, and assaults on whites carried the death penalty. Maryland, North Carolina, Mississippi, Alabama, and other states also adopted measures to minimize the risk of slave insurrections.[44]

Regardless of legislative efforts to control the slave population, conspiracies to overthrow slavery were a fact of life for whites. Reports of

Nat Turner and his companions waged a revolt on white slave owners in Virginia on August 23, 1831.

conspiracies scared the master class, and the often exaggerated details of such plots brought forth terrible reprisals. Rumors abounded, too, and they tell us much more about white fears than what they reveal about black behavior. Most conspiracies never ended as fullscale revolts; an ever-vigilant security system often nipped them in the bud, or slaves terminated them on their own volition. No Southern state seemed to have been immune to slave conspiracies, and a few Northern states had their share as well.

The "Great Negro Plot," which occurred in 1741 in New York City, is perhaps the best known of the eighteenth-century conspiracies. Historians have long dismissed it as the figment of white imagination, but a more recent study has questioned that interpretation.[45] By 1741 New York City's slaves constituted about one-fifth of the population. Certainly, they were in a demographically superior position to that of their brethren who revolted in 1712. When the authorities heard that blacks were planning to burn down the city and kill the whites, panic ensued. The tension was exacerbated by a series of inexplicable fires. A witch-hunt extracted "confessions" from some of the accused. In this crazed atmosphere, the authorities arrested 154 blacks and 24 whites, accusing them of conspiracy. No black person was safe from the terror. The lieutenant governor was certain that "if the truth were ever known, there are not many innocent Negro men."[46]

The authorities and the white citizenry alike cared not for the truth, such was the hysteria that prevailed. Whites were predisposed to believe everything they heard, and the trials were exercises in bedlam and injustice. In the end, thirteen black men were burned at the stake and seventeen were hanged. Four whites were also hanged for their alleged roles in the conspiracy. Slaves may have talked in general about liberating themselves, but it is not certain that a fully developed conspiracy existed. Suffice it to say, white fears ran amok, and not for the last time.

In contrast to the events in New York, there is incontrovertible evidence that the slaves in Richmond conspired to liberate themselves in 1800. According to the accounts of the conspiracy, a number of slaves and free blacks used religious and social gatherings to recruit participants for a planned rebellion. The leader, Gabriel Prosser, was a twenty-four-year-old artisan, described as "a fellow of courage and intellect above his rank in life." His principal assistants included his two brothers, Solomon and Martin, and his friends Jack and Ben.

Throughout the spring of 1800, the leaders encouraged others to enlist, often asking the potential recruit: whether he was "willing to fight the white people for his freedom." It is not clear how many responded to the call. Gabriel spoke of 10,000 men, but this was an artful exaggeration. Potentially, thousands stood ready to support the revolt at some stage, but first it had to get off the ground. Unfortunately for the slaves, it rained torrentially on August 30, the day of the attack. Morale was seriously undermined, and security collapsed. The authorities got word of the affair, responded swiftly, and arrested a number of persons. About forty individuals were tried and sentenced to death, Gabriel Prosser among them. One observer noted that the condemned persons "exhibited a spirit, which, if it becomes general, must deluge the Southern country in blood. They manifested a sense of their rights, and contempt of danger, and a thirst for revenge which portend the most unhappy consequences."[47] One unrepentant conspirator told his captors that he did no more than what General George Washington, the founding father, had done for his people. "I have nothing more to offer than what General Washington would have had to offer, had he been taken by the British officers and put on trial by them," he explained. "I have ventured my life in endeavoring to obtain the liberty of my countrymen, and am a willing sacrifice to their cause."[48]

The prediction that the revolt portended "unhappy consequences" was accurate because the incidence of conspiracies never abated in succeeding years and the Turner revolt confirmed white society's fears. In 1822, whites uncovered a major conspiracy in Charleston, and its scope intensified their insecurity. This conspiracy was characterized by a nineteenth-century abolitionist as "the most elaborate insurrectionary project ever formed by American slaves."[49] The leader was Denmark Vesey, a man who had purchased his freedom years earlier.

The city of Charleston had a majority black population at the time of the projected revolt. The 1820 census reported a population of 14,127 blacks to 10,653 whites. Whites, of course, exercised power in all of its dimensions, and most blacks were slaves. Many of Charleston's free blacks, however, were skilled persons, literate, aggressively independent, and assertive. Endeavoring to keep free blacks in their places and betraying their lack of confidence in themselves, whites responded by restricting their access to certain jobs, imposed a poll tax on them, closed one of their churches, and engaged in other acts of harassment. Under the circumstances, it is not surprising that some free blacks would have embraced violence to transform their situation and found common cause with the slaves.

Denmark Vesey, "who stood at the head of this conspiracy," according to court records, chafed under these restrictions. He was familiar with the great slave revolt in St. Domingue and drew inspiration from it. He seems to have been well known among blacks, and during his trial the court observed that "he appears to have been constantly and assiduously engaged in endeavoring to embitter the minds of the coloured population against the white."[50] Conveniently, the court ignored the grievances of the blacks and the stark injustice of their condition. Vesey was not alone. He was assisted by trusted associates such as Monday Gell, Gullah Jack, and Peter Poyas, who were all slaves.

The revolt, however, was stillborn. When the authorities were alerted to the plan, they arrested and tried 131 persons and executed 35 of them. Thirty-one were banished from the state, and the others were acquitted. As usual, whites panicked and used the courts to terrorize blacks. Individuals were convicted on the flimsiest charge as whites showed who was actually in charge. As the judges admitted in the aftermath of the trial, "the terror of example we thought would be sufficiently operative by the number of criminals sentenced to death." Many of the condemned remained defiant to the end. Most admitted no wrongdoing, and Bacchus Hammett epitomized their refusal to be psychologically vanquished even as death approached. He "went to the gallows *laughing and bidding his acquaintances in the streets* 'good bye.'"[51]

In the final analysis, Hammett's behavior captured the nature of slave resistance in all of its forms. Those who challenged the institution overtly demonstrated enormous courage and an unremitting defiance of the system of slavery and those who operated it. Some escaped to more hospitable environments, and others lost their lives in their quest for freedom. Far more endured their travail, employing less spectacular forms of opposition, but pricking the system nonetheless while struggling to keep their balance.

In spite of their efforts, the slaves never posed a successful revolutionary challenge to the institution of slavery. This should not be entirely surprising. During the long first century, the Africans and their children constituted a small minority of the overall population of the colonies and were distributed over a vast geographic area. With lives disrupted and lacking a critical mass of their peers, it is understandable that only one violent and notable challenge to slavery occurred before 1720. The New York rebellion of 1712 took place in an urban area that had a slave population slightly less than one thousand, a seemingly inadequate number to take on the armed might of the whites even if there had been full participation in it.

But, as we have suggested earlier, there may have been cultural imperatives at work among the African-born that militated against the use of violence. For some, slavery was perceived as a misfortune and the result of sorcery. Consequently, as Monica Schuler has suggested, "if slaves defined slaveowners as sorcerors, there surely could be no acceptance of bondage."[52] Such sorcery, however, could be defeated not by a resort to violence but only by the victims' application of a stronger form of sorcery. Thus, some members of a deeply religious enslaved population contested the power of their enslavers by drawing upon their arsenal of religious beliefs and practices. That this was largely ineffective in a Western environment is beside the point. In time, the larger and more creolized slave population would show a greater tendency to conspire and embrace violence to end their oppression.

Yet there was never a rebellion anywhere that involved the participation of more than a few hundred slaves. In addition, a resort to organized violence was not a particularly frequent occurrence even in the nineteenth century. Several factors may help us to understand why this was the case. We cannot ignore the fact that white society had a monopoly of armed power, watched the servile population very closely, and punished threats to the social order swiftly and brutally. The controlling mechanisms of white society—the army, militia, local patrols, and the judiciary—bolstered the enormous private disciplinary power that the slaveowners or their surrogates wielded. White society's assertion of a self-proclaimed racial superiority over the peoples of African descent—slave or free—sanctioned its exercise of power. Ironically, however, it also led an insecure white society to remain frenetically vigilant to any threats to the societal order from which many of its members profited and to devote much of its energies to its protection. Slaves, in retrospect, stood little chance of success if they assaulted such a system frontally; the forces arrayed against them were too deeply entrenched and powerful.

But there were other limiting factors as well. In terms of its size, the slave population of the nineteenth century posed the greatest potential challenge to the institution. But it was a population constantly beset by externally induced problems that consumed much of its psychic energies just to survive. The appalling forcible break-up of an estimated two million marriages between 1820 and 1860 and the removal of probably as many as one million persons from the border states and the Upper South to the Lower South and Texas after 1790 created untold misery in black lives. Starkly reminiscent of the disruptions caused by the international slave trade, such atrocities contradict the uniform picture of a sedentary slave population in the nineteenth century.

Such unremitting pressures, under different circumstances, probably would have produced more frequently organized violent responses. But slaves, it seems, were acutely aware of the impossibility of defeating the whites given the absence of military wherewithal. They were, however, able to take advantage of divisions in white society to claim their freedom. This occurred, to some extent, in the War of Independence. When white America went to war with itself in 1861, many thousands of the enslaved also seized the opportunity to liberate themselves.

The insecurity of their lives and the disruptions notwithstanding, slaves had to function as persons. The spectacular population growth after 1820–in spite of a high infant mortality rate–tells us much about the world of the slaves and its inner drives. Fully 73 percent of blacks were under age thirty in 1860; a high proportion of them consisted of children. Family ties, concern for the safety of kith and kin, and the presence of a disproportionate number of children not likely to have yet experienced slavery in all of its harshness were all factors that must have blunted any tendency toward violence. If slavery's end had not been hastened by the Civil War, a large, mature, and numerically confident slave population would, in all likelihood, have fulfilled white society's nightmares.

White society's arsenal of control was not limited to the exercise of physical power. We have maintained throughout this study that the society attempted at every turn to debase blacks and to inflict a thousand psychological wounds on them. Although the majority of the black population maintained a psychic balance, we cannot fully capture the nature of the internal price they paid. The struggle to maintain a degree of selfhood and to reject, or at least limit, the hegemonic power of whites remains the most poignant and compelling aspect of the black odyssey. Slaves had to create a psychic enclave, hidden from a hostile outside world. The most sustained struggle against slavery took place in the heads of its victims, in their battle against becoming psychological lepers and the compliant, unthinking workers that their masters would have loved.

As a group, the enslaved peoples struggled to meet their own needs as individuals, lovers, parents, children, and friends. These quiet battles were not spectacular. But these human challenges were infinitely more difficult for the enslaved to confront than they were for those who owned them, and more debilitating in their demands. Overt acts of resistance such as flight and rebellion required a kind of courage that many did not have. Yet those who worked to meet their own needs as well as those of kith and kin, carving passageways in slavery's complex edifice, also demonstrated a compelling resilience, courage, and inner strength.

Such life struggles, along with the cultural spaces they created, affirmed the slaves' humanity. As human beings, they were compelled to contest the forces that oppressed them, using the weapons at their disposal. Violence constituted one form of resistance and time-tested religious practices another. Most, if not all, tried to maintain their sanity and their humanity refusing to define themselves as property. As human beings, they created and recreated the institutions and culture that reflected their circumstances and met their needs. But we should not view their creative energies as being inspired fundamentally by the need to resist their oppressors. Nor should we see these cultural motions as reflecting a resigned accommodation to slavery. The reasons for the slaves' cultural vitality resides elsewhere. There is no question that the culture that they created soothed their souls and made their lives more tolerable. But the unconscious imperative behind this cultural production was both human and universal, namely the timeless and irrepressible need by all peoples to claim, define, and mark their own ground. Resistance was more than an act of violence or escape; for the slaves it also constituted a relentless and painful struggle to maintain their personhood, to remain human, and to be themselves.

Notes

1. Henry Bibb, *Narrative of the Life*, 65; Harriet Jacobs, *Incidents in the Life of a Slave Girl*, 56; Frances Kemble, *Journal*, 268.
2. Cited in Charles T. Davis and Henry Louis Gates, eds., *The Slave's Narratives* (New York: Oxford University Press, 1985).
3. Kemble, *Journal*, 276.
4. Stampp, *The Peculiar Institution*, 88; Fredrickson, "Masters and Mudsills," 39.
5. Morgan, "Work and Culture," 598.
6. Drew Gilpin Faust, "Culture, Conflict, and Community: The Meaning of Power on the Antebellum Plantation," *Journal of Social History*, 14 (1980), 86.
7. Rawick, *The American Slave*, vol. 4, 1181.
8. Douglass, *My Bondage and My Freedom*, 189–191.
9. Alex Lichtenstein, "'That Disposition to Theft, With Which They have Been Branded': Moral Economy, Slave Management and the Law," *Journal of Social History*, 21 (1988), 422.
10. Sylvia R. Frey, *Water From the Rock: Black Resistance in a Revolutionary Age* (Princeton: Princeton University Press, 1991), 308.
11. Rawick, *The American Slave*, vol. 2, 2–3.
12. Charles Ball, *Slavery in the United States: A Narrative of the Life and Adventures of Charles Ball, a Black Man*, reprint (New York: Negro Universities Press, 1969), 231.
13. Eric Foner, *Nothing But Freedom: Emancipation and its Legacy* (Baton Rouge: Louisiana State University Press, 1983), 58; Lichtenstein, "That Disposition to Theft," 422.
14. Philip J. Schwarz, *Twice Condemned: Slaves and the Criminal Laws of Virginia, 1705–1865* (Baton Rouge: Louisiana State University Press, 1988), 142.
15. Jordan, *White Over Black*, 107.
16. Higginbotham, *In the Matter of Color*, 178.
17. Jordan, *White Over Black*, 112.

18. Higginbotham, *In the Matter of Color,* 177.
19. Edgar McManus, *Black Bondage in the North* (Syracuse: Syracuse University Press, 1973), 121.
20. Higginbotham, *In the Matter of Color,* 234.
21. Stampp, *The Peculiar Institution,* 174.
22. Gerald W. Mullin, *Flight and Rebellion: Slave Resistance in Eighteenth Century Virginia* (New York: Oxford, 1972), 43.
23. Kulikoff, *Tobacco and Slaves,* 332.
24. Mullin, *Flight and Rebellion,* 43.
25. McManus, *Black Bondage,* 110.
26. Michael Donald Roethler O.S.B., "Negro Slavery Among the Cherokee Indians, 1540–1866," PhD Dissertation (Fordham University, 1964), 27; Wood, *Black Majority,* 262.
27. McManus, *Black Bondage,* 109.
28. Wood, *Black Majority,* 261, 260.
29. Herbert Aptheker, "Maroons within the Present Limits of the United States," *Journal of Negro History,* 24 (1939), 169; Kulikoff, *Tobacco and Slaves,* 238–239.
30. Bibb, *Narrative of the Life and Adventures of Henry Bibb,* 46.
31. R. J. M. Blackett, *Beating Against the Barriers: Biographical Essays in Nineteenth-Century Afro-American History* (Baton Rouge: Louisiana State University Press, 1986), 106, 90.
32. Benjamin Quarles, "Harriet Tubman's Unlikely Leadership," in Leon Litwack and August Meier, eds., *Black Leaders of the Nineteenth Century* (Urbana: University of Illinois Press, 1988), 48.
33. Ibid., 49.
34. Blassingame, *The Slave Community,* 216.
35. Herbert Aptheker, *American Negro Slave Revolts* (New York: Columbia University Press, 1943), 33.
36. Kenneth Scott, "The Slave Insurrection in New York in 1712," *New York Historical Society Quarterly,* 45 (1961), 46.
37. Ibid., 62.
38. McManus, *Black Bondage,* 129–130.
39. Peter Wood, *Black Majority,* 316.
40. Aptheker, *American Negro Slave Revolts,* 35; Wood, *Black Majority,* 319.
41. Sirmens, "The Legal Status of the Slave," 471.
42. Aptheker, *American Negro Slave Revolts,* 523.
43. Ibid., 301.
44. For a full discussion of the Turner revolt and its aftermath, see Stephen Oates, *The Fires of Jubilee: Nat Turner's Fierce Rebellion* (New York: Harper and Row, 1975); Herbert Aptheker, *American Negro Slave Revolts;* Eric Foner, ed., *Nat Turner* (Englewood Cliffs, NJ: Prentice-Hall, 1971).
45. T. J. Davis, *The "Great Negro Plot" in Colonial New York* (New York: The Free Press, 1985).
46. McManus, *A History of Negro Slavery in New York,* 136.
47. For accounts of the conspiracy see Mullin, *Flight and Resistance; Aptheker, Negro Slave Revolts;* Douglas R. Egerton, *Gabriel's Rebellion: The Virginia Slave Conspiracies of 1800 and 1802* (Chapel Hill: University of North Carolina Press, 1993).
48. Robinson, *Slavery in the Structure of American Politics,* 9.
49. John Lofton, *Insurrection in South Carolina: The Turbulent World of Denmark Vesey* (Yellow Springs, OH: Antioch Press, 1964), vi.
50. Richard C. Wade, "The Vesey Plot: A Reconsideration," *Journal of Southern History* (1964), 158.
51. Ibid., 147.
52. Monica Schuler, "Afro-American Slave Culture," *Historical Reflections,* 6:1 (1979), 132.

Black Abolitionists

The struggle against slavery was not undertaken by the slaves alone. Nor did it involve only flight, acts of sabotage, or violence. Beginning with the Quakers in the seventeenth century, many persons waged an ideological assault on the institution. At first, most white antislavery persons tended to condemn the institution, advocating its containment but not its immediate destruction. Nor were they supportive of equal rights for blacks. In contrast, the abolitionists, who emerged prominently in the nineteenth century, organized themselves into groups that promoted the emancipation of the slaves and appealed to the nation to cleanse itself of slavery's infamy. Free blacks and white abolitionists found a common ground in this struggle, but the alliance was not always an easy one. Most white abolitionists were ambivalent on the question of civil equality for blacks. In fact, the emancipation of the slaves and the achievement of equality had an immediacy for blacks that their white friends did not always understand. As the black abolitionist Theodore Wright said as he admonished the New England Anti-Slavery Convention: "You have never felt the oppression of the slave. You have never known what it is to have a master, or to see your parents and children in slavery."[1]

Many whites came to embrace antislavery and abolitionism, usually after much soul searching. Some were influenced during the eighteenth century and later by ideas associated with Enlightenment Rationalism. In essence, this body of thought maintained that slavery was illegal, unjust, and a violation of natural law. Several intellectuals advocated emancipation as a natural consequence of this injustice. The English abolitionist Granville Sharp, who was certain that slavery violated the law of God and the law of reason, pleaded for "immediate redress, because, to be in power, and to neglect . . . even a day in endeavoring to put a stop to such monstrous injustice and abandoned wickedness must necessarily endanger a man's *eternal* welfare." The Philadelphia schoolteacher and humanitarian Anthony Benezet and men such as the pamphleteer and lawyer James Otis and Nathaniel Appleton, a merchant, shared similar positions. Otis for example, believed that "the colonists are by the law of nature free born, as indeed all men are, white and black . . ."[2] These abolitionists in varying degrees, also drew their inspiration from the republican tenets of liberty and equality.

Individuals who fell under the influence of the Protestant revivalism of the eighteenth and early nineteenth centuries were also receptive to reform, if not to a full-fledged assault on slavery. The view that slaveholding was sinful was accepted by some, but most knew that abolition would not come anytime soon. The American Methodists were evidently an early exception although they would later retreat from their 1784 stance that "it is our bounden duty to take immediately some effectual method to extirpate this abomination from among us."[3] To many who became a part of the evangelical tradition, blacks enjoyed spiritual equality with whites. Not yet ready to endorse immediate emancipation before the 1830s, these Christians at least envisioned the eventual demise of slavery. The libertarian and egalitarian ideologies of the War of Independence also played crucial roles in raising the question of property in persons and advancing the cause of abolition, at least in the North, where slavery was at its weakest.

There was, of course, no single abolitionist movement. Nor did the white advocates of emancipation share the same motivations, objectives, and perspectives. Some became abolitionists because it was an act of moral expiation, a conscious attempt to disassociate themselves from the institution of slavery because they were convinced that it was a sinful practice. Not necessarily sympathetic to blacks and their ultimate fate, these persons' sole objective was to seek Christian redemption for themselves. Others favored gradual emancipation because slavery was not only immoral but it also contradicted the ideals upon which the nation was founded. Believing, however, that blacks were not yet ready for the responsibilities of freedom, they wanted to move slowly while preparing the prospective freed persons for their eventual incorporation into the larger society.

A third category of white abolitionists consisted of those who supported emancipation but doubted that blacks and whites could live together on the basis of equality. For them, emancipation was tied to colonization. A virulent racism undergirded much of their thinking, since they feared that free blacks could not function well when released from slavery's chains but would be a burden on society and the source of all manner of social ills. At the other extreme were those abolitionists who advocated immediate emancipation and the creation of a just society for all peoples.

Most of the early abolitionist societies denied membership to free blacks. The first one was established in Philadelphia in 1775, eventually acquiring the imposing name of The Pennsylvania Society for Promoting the Abolition of Slavery, the Relief of Free Negroes Unlawfully Held in Bondage and for Improving the Condition of the African Race. Others quickly followed in New York (1785), Delaware (1788), Maryland (1789), and elsewhere. Most of these organizations attracted few members, and they tended to be Quakers, Methodists, and Presbyterians. One estimate of the overall size of the membership of the various organizations was made in 1827. Benjamin Lundy who edited the *Genius of Universal Emancipation,* an abolitionist newspaper, reported that the slave states had 106 antislavery societies with a combined membership of 5,150. In contrast, the Northern states had 1,475 members in 24 organizations. By far, the majority of the organizations in the slave states were located in the Upper South.

Although these organizations existed to promote the welfare of those in bondage, they were prisoners of the racism of the times. The exclusion of blacks from their membership rolls was one thing, but it was quite another to urge free blacks to "impress" upon slaves "the necessity of contentment with their situations."[4] These organizations saw slavery ending gradually. Society at large would eventually come to share their opposition to the institution. Slaveowners should rest assured, however, that emancipation would not be accompanied by economic disaster, since they would be compensated for the loss of their human property. Undoubtedly, the antislavery organizations in the North drew encouragement from the passage of laws gradually ending slavery in the aftermath of the War of Independence. Their Southern counterparts fell on hard times, however, as slavery gained in strength and the abolition movement declined, becoming the recipient of much resentment from the white public at large.

The abolition movement experienced a dramatic change in its style, composition, and objectives after 1830. This was the consequence of changes within black society, the nature and structure of slavery in the South, and the success of the movement for emancipation in England. These transformations produced new leaders with different agendas and a greater sense of urgency.

By 1830, the free black population, particularly in the North, had swelled its ranks as a consequence of the war, natural increase, the legislative process of gradual emancipation, and flight from the South. With increasing numbers came confidence and a spirit of assertiveness. Black organizations emerged, newspapers appeared, institutions were established, and vigorous debates took place on such matters as emigration, strategies for the achievement of equal rights, and emancipation. The appearance of David Walker's *Appeal* reflected this new aggressive spirit and an uncompromising stance on the slavery question. Blessed with leaders of enormous competence, eloquence, energy, and political sophistication, free blacks began to campaign for the liberation of their enslaved brethren, giving a dimension and an immediacy to the struggle that it had hitherto lacked.

To blacks and their white friends alike, it was clear by 1830 that slavery in the South was not on the verge of extinction. Not only was the Southern slave population increasing, but a confident slaveowning class brooked no interference with the institution and welcomed opportunities for its expansion. Those who had entertained notions that slavery would disappear in the fullness of time had to reassess their strategy and launch a more aggressive assault on it. New leaders were emerging with an impatience that the movement had not yet seen. Far from excluding blacks from their organizations, white abolitionists now actively sought their cooperative involvement, although few welcomed them as equals.

Abolitionists, black and white, drew encouragement from the successes their counterparts were experiencing in England. In 1823, the British parliament adopted a pathbreaking measure for the amelioration of the condition of the slaves in the Caribbean. Despite the resistance of the slaveowners, the law freed all children once they reached the age of six, admitted slave testimony in the courts, and provided for their religious instruction. Restrictions were imposed on the master's power to separate families and mistreat slaves with impunity. In essence, Parliament adopted the principle of the gradual emancipation of the approximately three million slaves in the islands. The Act of Emancipation was not formally passed until 1833, but by 1830 the handwriting was on the wall.

The publication of the overtly abolitionist newspaper the *Liberator* by a white man named William Lloyd Garrison in 1831 was one of the first significant salvos in the new struggle against slavery. A passionate opponent of slavery, Garrison grew up in Newburyport, Massachusetts. Deeply religious, he fell under the influence of the abolitionist Benjamin Lundy and by the late 1820s he had enthusiastically embraced the cause of emancipation. In 1829 he advocated "the right of the free states to demand a gradual abolition of slavery, because, by its continuance, they participate in the guilt thereof."[5] His language became increasingly vituperative in later years, the tone strident, the anger unrestrained, and the passion unmistakable.

The *Liberator* received strong support from blacks, and it was their patronage that largely sustained it in its early years. The paper became an effective organ for the cause it represented, but a broadly based organization was needed to harness abolitionist energies and give them practical expression. Accordingly, on December 4, 1833, three blacks and sixty whites met in Philadelphia to found the American Anti-Slavery Society. Their primary objectives were "the entire abolition of slavery in the United States" and the improvement of "the character and condition of the people of color." This organization, revolutionary in intent and biracial in its composition, broke new ground and spawned a number of affiliates in Massachusetts, Maine, New York, Ohio, and other Midwest and Northeastern states.

Some of these auxiliary organizations were integrated, but others were completely black or white, depending on the racial temper of the environs and their location. Blacks, of course, had been accustomed to being excluded from white organizations and founded their own. In 1826, for example, blacks in Massachusetts established the Massachusetts General Colored Association to promote the cause of emancipation. Four years later, a number of prominent black leaders met in Philadelphia to found what would become known as the Negro Convention Movement. There were only twenty-six persons present at the first meeting, but they represented Pennsylvania, Maryland, New York, Rhode Island, Virginia, and Connecticut. Bishop Richard Allen of the AME was one of the principal organizers, and so was Hezekiah Grice, a butcher and ice dealer from Maryland. The Convention Movement did not limit its concerns to abolition; it discussed a wide range of issues including emigration, temperance, economic and self-help opportunities, and the struggle for equality.

The Convention Movement which met annually for a number of years, attracted the national black elite. But there were numerous local organizations that enjoyed grass roots support and worked quietly to advance the cause. Such groups existed in places like Troy, Michigan; Rochester, New York; Philadelphia; Newark, New Jersey; and Nantucket, Massachusetts. These branches operated on a shoestring but nevertheless were able to scrape up enough funds to support the work of the parent organizations as well as their own.

Although men have generally received more attention in the recounting of the story of the black abolitionists, women also played a significant role in it. Black and white women were originally excluded from membership in the American Anti-Slavery Society. They protested against this discrimination and won the support of several men. When women were finally admitted in 1839, the policy change helped to cause a split in abolitionist ranks. In opposing the role of women in the organization, the white New York abolitionist Lewis Tappan maintained

When the Constitution of the A. Anti S. Soc. was formed in 1833, and the word "person" introduced, *all concerned* considered that it was to be understood as it is usually understood in our benevolent Societies.

All have a right to be *members,* but the *business* to be conducted by *men.* . . . Women have equal rights with men, and therefore have a right to form societies of women only. Men have the same right. *Men* formed the Amer. Anti S. Society.[6]

White men and black men alike shared the same perceptions of women, their place in society, and their capacities. Ideally, women were to occupy a separate domestic sphere and were thought to possess the virtues of piety and purity. They were to devote their lives to their family and defer to the needs and desires of their men. Middle-class white women epitomized these virtuous qualities, but black women and their poor white peers were deemed to be impure and lacking in respectability because of the contaminating influences of their class and their allegedly promiscuous sexuality. Black men absorbed the larger society's definition of what constituted women's proper sphere as well as what made a woman "respectable" in the eyes of others.

A few examples of the views of free black men on the roles of women may be cited. Richard Allen, for example, joined in the denunciation of a woman who declined "to submit to her husband as a dutiful wife." Frederick Douglass, a supporter of women's rights, was nonetheless certain that young women needed "A knowledge of domestic affairs," since "a well regulated household, in every station of society is one of woman's brightest ornaments." Similarly, the abolitionist, Charles B. Ray maintained that "Daughters are destined to be wives and mothers–they should, therefore, be taught to know how to manage a house, and govern and instruct children." The noted clergyman and abolitionist the Reverend J. W. C. Pennington believed that women were unsuited for ordination or for other professional jobs "where mighty thought and laborious investigation are needed." Women possessed a certain sensitivity that enabled them to function as activists, but not in leadership positions where they would be the rivals of men. Samuel Cornish said it well:

Woman was created to be the "help-meet," and not the idol or slave of man; and in everything truly virtuous and noble, she is furnished by our bountiful Creator, with all the intellectual, moral and physical requisites for her important place.[7]

Thus, although women were not quite the equals of men, they could perform subordinate roles in the abolitionist movement and bring moral legitimacy to it as well. "In any enterprise for the improvement of our people–either moral or mental, our hands would be palsied without women's influence . . . ," wrote one observer in 1837. As was the case with other issues, some black men dissented from these positions. John C. Bowers, who belonged to a men's literary society in Boston, championed education for women. Writing in 1834, he argued that "a female soul, without education, is like marble in a quarry previous to being polished by the hands of the artist." James Forten, Jr., the son of the sailmaker and wealthy entrepreneur, believed that men "startle at the idea of women rising equal to them in . . . intellectual strength." Recognizing the incongruity in black men oppressing black women, since both were victims of an unjust societal order, Forten admonished: "It is not for us to . . . cry aloud against persecution, and . . . play the part of persecutors."[8]

Women, realizing that the abolition struggle was also theirs, refused to be excluded from it. In 1832, "females of color" in Salem, Massachusetts, formed the Female Anti-Slavery Society of Salem. The society was renamed the Salem Female Anti-Slavery Society in 1834 and opened its membership to white women. Similar societies were formed in New York City, Philadelphia, Rochester, and Nantucket. As their numbers grew, black female abolitionists attended women's antislavery conventions in New York in 1837 and in Philadelphia the following year. Sarah Forten, the gifted sister of James Forten Jr., and a pioneer female abolitionist, condemned slavery in her many literary contributions to the *Liberator*. In 1831, for example, she reminded whites that they had once been oppressed by British colonialism. Forten was concerned that they

> . . . quite forgot
> That bondage once had been their lot;
> The sweets of freedom now they know,
> They care not for the captive's wo[e].[9]

Female abolitionists included members of the black elite as well as those who lived at survival levels. The more privileged included Charlotte Forten, the wife of the sailmaker and a member of the Philadelphia Female Anti-Slavery Society. So too were Grace and Sarah Douglass, a mother and daughter who went on to hold leadership positions in the organization. Mary Ann Shadd was active as a teacher and abolitionist and then as a newspaper editor in Canada. Others included Sarah Parker Remond, a Philadelphian who traveled as an abolitionist speaker in the 1850s, and Frances Ellen Watkins Harper, a poet, lecturer, and feminist. Harper was noted for the poems she read at her lectures, including the following one, which was published by the *Anti-Slavery Bugle* in Salem, Ohio, in 1858:

BURY ME IN A FREE LAND
You may make my grave wherever you will,
In a lowly vale or a lofty hill;

You may make it among earth's humblest graves
But not in a land where men are slaves.

I could not sleep if around my grave
I heard the steps of a trembling slave;
His shadow above my silent Tomb
Would make it a place of fearful gloom. . . .

I ask no monument proud and high
To arrest the gaze of passers by;
All that my spirit yearning craves,
Is—bury me not in the land of the slaves.[10]

In what is probably the earliest written assault by a black person in the American colonies on slavery, the poet Phillis Wheatley denounced the institution in a letter she wrote to Sansom Occom, an Indian preacher in New England. Wheatley was responding to a letter she had received from Occom, and excerpts were published in two Boston newspapers in March 1774:

I have this Day received your obliging kind Epistle, and am greatly satisfied with your Reasons respecting the Negroes, and think highly reasonable what you offer in Vindication of their natural Rights: Those that invade them cannot be insensible that the divine Light is chasing away the thick Darkness which broods over the Land of Africa; and the Chaos which has reigned so long, is converting into beautiful Order, and reveals more and more clearly, the glorious Dispensation of civil and religious Liberty, which are so inseparably united, and there is little or no Enjoyment of one without the other: Otherwise, perhaps, the Israelites had been less solicitous for their Freedom from Egyptian Slavery; I do not say they would have been contented without it, by no Means, for in every human Breast, God has implanted a Principle, which we call Love of Freedom; it is impatient of Oppression, and pants for Deliverance; and by the leave of our Modern Egyptians I will assert, that the same Principle Lives in us. God grant Deliverance in his own way and Time, and get him honor upon all those whose Avarice impels them to countenance and help forward the Calamities of their Fellow Creatures. This I desire not for their Hurt, but to convince them of the strange Absurdity of their Conduct whose Words and Actions are so diametrically opposite. How well the Cry for Liberty, and the reverse Disposition for the Exercise of oppressive Power over others agree,—I humbly think it does not require the Penetration of a Philosopher to determine.[11]

Harriett Tubman and Sojourner Truth were two of the best-known women associated with the cause of emancipation during the nine-

Sojourner Truth (c.1797–1883), evangelist and reformer.

teenth century. While Tubman developed a reputation as a "conductor" on the Underground Railroad, Truth became famous speaking against the institution of slavery. Truth, who does not appear to have belonged to any of the antislavery organizations, preferred to carry on her struggle independently. She was born a slave in Ulster County, New York, and obtained her freedom in 1827 when she had reached the age of thirty. An eloquent speaker, Truth never learned to read or write, showing thereby how slavery had blunted her life chances. Fearless and outspoken, she linked the struggle for emancipation with the fight for women's rights. Few in attendance could forget her speech to a women's-rights convention in Akron, Ohio, in 1851. Her eloquence was stunning as she laid bare the nation's unequal treatment of black women. There are several versions of Truth's speech to the convention. The most widely known, highly controversial, and probably apocryphal account was published in 1863. Written by the abolitionist and feminist Frances Dana Gage, it quoted Truth as declaring:

> Nobody eber helps me into carriages, or ober mud-puddles, or gibs me any best place! And arn't I a woman? Look at me! Look at my arm! I have ploughed, and planted, and gathered into barns, and no man could head me!–And ar'n't I a woman? I could work as much and eat as much as a man–when I could get it–, and bear de lash as well–and ar'n't I a woman?[12]

Sojourner Truth's attempt to fuse the two struggles was not unusual for black female abolitionists. Theirs was not just a struggle confined narrowly to achieving the end of slavery. Black women embraced a number of causes designed to improve the condition of their people at the local levels as well. Hence they engaged in efforts aimed at racial uplift, encouraging self-help programs, fostering temperance and moral improvement as well as the provision of greater educational opportunities for the young and old alike. Black men embraced these causes as well, often in the abstract. But the women, particularly those with enough time, volunteered their services at the local levels in order to see their ideas through to fruition.

For black and white abolitionists, the 1830s represented a decade when emancipation seemed within reach. Their ranks increased as many Northern whites fell under the influence of an evangelical Christianity that condemned slavery as sinful. The liberation of the slaves constituted a path to one's own redemption. As the Reverend Beriah Green noted, "There is no way for us to escape from guilt and corruption of heart, but by cordially and joyfully yielding to our colored brethren the sympathies of our common humanity." Wendell Phillips, arguably the most intellectually gifted of the white abolitionists, agreed. "If we never free a slave, we have at least freed ourselves in the effort to emancipate our brother man," he confessed.[13]

The religious revivals of the 1820s led by Charles Grandison Finney and others helped create in the converts a favorable disposition to reforms, particularly if they cleansed society and advanced the cause of God's kingdom on earth. By depicting slavery as a sin, the true believers had no option but to fight for its destruction. William Jay, a white abolitionist, confessed, "I do not depend on any man as an abolitionist who does not act from a sense of religious obligation."[14] Similar sentiments were echoed in 1852 by the Reverend William Goodell, who wrote: "Whatever our missionary and evangelizing orators intended, whatever *they* were thinking of, they were God's instruments for putting into the minds of others 'thoughts that burned,' for the emancipation of the enslaved."[15] Not surprisingly, clergymen comprised a disproportionate share of the leadership of the abolition societies.

Yet not all who came to view slavery as sinful enlisted with the abolitionists. Most had no connection at all with the institution and were concerned only with their personal redemption, leaving the abolitionist struggle to others. For them, slavery was a societal evil, not a personal sin. Others eschewed any participation in organized causes and distanced themselves from the movement. But a sufficient number of persons acted on their convictions, primarily in the Northeast and the Midwest, to form a vocal and significant minority. The American Anti-Slavery Society claimed a membership of 250,000 in 1838 for itself and allied organizations. This was probably the high-water mark of the movement's membership. The succeeding years saw a shift in strategy as well as various internal schisms that must have weakened its strength and appeal.

During the 1830s, the abolitionists adopted the strategy of appealing to the nation's conscience to eliminate slavery's sin. Characterized as moral suasion, the objective was to use peaceful means to convince white society to honor the ideals upon which the republic was founded. Abolitionists used their newspapers to express their views, sent petitions to Congress, flooded the mailboxes of the Northern states with antislavery literature, and gave speeches wherever they could. Among the whites, William Lloyd Garrison, evangelist Theodore Wright Weld, New York merchant Lewis Tappan, attorney Wendell Phillips, and Alabama lawyer and planter James Birney played distinguished roles in the cause for freedom. White women such as Lucretia Mott of Philadelphia, feminist Susan Anthony, Quakers Sarah and Angelina Grimké, and women's rights advocate Elizabeth Cady Stanton lent their talents and energy to the movement.

No matter how well meaning and committed the whites were, they could not fully share the pain of the black abolitionists who had been slaves themselves and who still had relatives and brethren in bondage. Black abolitionists knew that as long as slavery remained, all blacks were diminished as persons. While they welcomed white support for emancipation, recognizing that it was whites who had the power to legislate an end to slavery, the black abolitionists understood the uniqueness of their role. "We occupy a position, and sustain relations which [white abolitionists] cannot possibly assume. They are our allies—ours is the battle," wrote one black observer in 1841. Frederick Douglass agreed. "The man who *suffered the wrong* is the man to *demand redress*," the former slave maintained.[16]

White abolitionists knew that black abolitionists could speak with an authority about the institution that they lacked. John A. Collins, an agent of the American Anti-Slavery Society, told Garrison in 1842, "The public have itching ears to hear a colored man speak, and particularly a *slave*. Multitudes will flock to hear one of this class speak. . . . It would be a good policy to employ a number of colored agents, if suitable ones can be found."[17] This view was quite common, and whites made a point of encouraging escaped slaves to address antislavery gatherings. Several blacks attained much prominence as a consequence of their graphic descriptions of their lives as slaves and their often heroic escape from its tentacles. Frederick Douglass was a particularly impressive speaker, and so too were Henry Bibb, William Wells Brown, and Ellen and William Craft.

Douglass, who became the best-known black leader of his day, had a gripping story. He was born a slave on Maryland's Eastern Shore in 1818. His mother, Harriet Bailey, was a slave, and his father was a white man. "Of my father, I know nothing," Douglass would later write. His grandmother cared for him in his infancy, and his mother remained but a shadow in his life. "The slavemother can be spared long enough from the field to endure all the bitterness of a mother's anguish, when it adds another name to a master's ledger, but *not* long enough to receive the joyous reward afforded by the intelligent smiles of her child," he wrote. At age six he was separated from his grandmother when he was moved to his master's residence, some twelve miles away from the plantation on which he was born.

Douglass was a precocious child, curious, observant, and sensitive. He experienced slavery's torments early, and he would never forget them. He recalled seeing his Aunt Hester being brutalized by his master, Aaron Anthony. He described her "wrists . . . firmly tied, and the twisted rope . . . fastened to a strong staple in a heavy wooden joist above, near the fireplace. Here she stood, on a bench, her arms tightly drawn over her breast. Her back and shoulders were bare to the waist. Behind her stood old master, with cowskin in hand, preparing his barbarous work with all manner of harsh, coarse, and tantalizing epithets. The screams of his victim were most piercing. He was cruelly deliberate, and protracted the torture, as one who was delighted with the scene. Again and again he drew the hateful whip. . . ."

At age seven the young boy was sent to Baltimore to live with Hugh and Sophia Auld, relatives of Aaron Anthony. Upon Anthony's death, Frederick was sent back to the country while the estate was being probated. When the settlement was completed, Frederick formally became the property of Hugh Auld, and he returned to Baltimore for the remainder of his childhood. Sophia Auld taught Frederick to read, but when her husband learned of it he exploded and forbade the instruction. Hugh Auld ranted that "learning would spoil the best nigger in the world." He was certain that "if you learn him how to read, he'll want to know how to write; and, this accomplished, he'll be running away with himself." This prophecy was fulfilled.

Former slave, Frederick Douglass (1817–1895) was one of the best known and influential black abolitionists.

As he grew into adolescence, Frederick read about the antislavery movement and began to develop a political consciousness. At age sixteen he was moved, yet again, to the Eastern Shore to live with Thomas Auld, Aaron Anthony's son-in-law. He was hired out to farmer Edward Covey, a man who had the reputation of "a nigger breaker." Covey and Frederick engaged in a battle of wills for the next several months. On one occasion, Covey punished the adolescent boy in a manner that vividly demonstrates the absolute power that the slaveowners or their surrogates exercised over their chattel. As Douglass described the scene, Covey "went to a large gum-tree, and with his axe cut three large switches, and, after trimming them up neatly with his pocket-knife, he ordered me to take off my clothes. I made him no answer, but stood with my clothes on. He repeated his order. I still made no answer, nor did I move to strip myself. Upon this he rushed at me with the fierceness of a tiger, tore off my clothes, and lashed me till he had worn out his switches." Eventually, Covey and the young man came to blows and Frederick asserted his physical supremacy, reclaiming his personhood in the process. As he exulted later: "He only can understand the deep satisfaction I experienced, who has himself repelled by force the bloody arm of slavery. . . . It was a glorious resurrection." For Douglass, "this battle was the turning point in my life 'as a slave.' . . . I was *nothing* before; I WAS A MAN NOW." And he made the fateful, self-affirming decision to reject slavery.

A plan to escape in early 1836 was betrayed and Douglass was jailed briefly. Upon his return to Hugh Auld's household in Baltimore, Douglass's desire to escape increased. Over the next two years he developed detailed plans for himself and his fiancée, Anna, a free woman who worked as a housekeeper in Baltimore. On September 3, 1838, Douglass fled and after some anxious moments, traveling by ferry and train, he arrived in New York two days later. Anna soon joined him, and their marriage was solemnized, on September 15, merely twelve days after Douglass had claimed his freedom. James W. C. Pennington, himself a runaway slave, was the officiating clergyman. Douglass and his bride then headed for New Bedford, Massachusetts, and a life that would alter the course of his people's history. In 1841 after he spoke at an abolitionist meeting at Nantucket, he made such a great impression that he was invited to become a lecturer for the Massachusetts Anti-Slavery Society, a role he would play for a few years.[18]

Henry Bibb's personal trajectory was also filled with drama and courage. In 1837, Bibb, a Kentucky slave, escaped to Ohio. Upon his return to the South to help free his wife, he was recaptured but escaped a second time. His story contained all the ingredients that thrilled abolitionist audiences, and he became a lecturer who was much in demand in the 1840s. At one such lecture, the audience reportedly "cheered, clapped, stamped, laughed, and wept by turns."[19] William Wells Brown, another escaped slave from Kentucky, also lectured widely in the 1840s. Similarly, William and Ellen Craft excited audiences with their recounting of the circumstances of their remarkable escape from Georgia in 1848.

The saga of the slaves who rebelled on the schooner *Amistad* and accidentally sailed it to Long Island also quickened the pulse of abolitionists in 1839 and 1840. Fifty-three slaves had risen aboard the schooner off the coast of Cuba in 1839, seizing control of the vessel and the Spanish crew. Led by Joseph Cinqué, a strong, imposing man, they planned to sail to Africa, but they lacked the requisite navigational expertise. By the time the vessel arrived in New York after a circuitous two-month journey, only thirty-nine slaves were alive. American authorities detained the vessel and took the occupants into custody to await the resolution of their fate by the courts. Were these people still slaves, and if so should they be returned to their Spanish masters? Or had they reclaimed their freedom?

When the abolitionists got word of the *Amistad's* odyssey, they used the affair to generate public sympathy for the cause of freedom. They focused on the transcendental issue of human rights and dramatized the evils of property in persons. The Supreme Court heard the case in 1841 after a lower court had ruled that the captives should be freed. The verdict was appealed with the strong support of President Martin Van Buren. After hearing lengthy arguments, the Court's majority upheld the decision of the lower court. Speaking for the majority, Justice William Story affirmed the "ultimate right of all human beings in extreme cases to resist oppression, and to apply force against ruinous injustice."[20] With the case decided, black and white abolitionists raised funds to send the surviving thirty-nine Africans to Sierra Leone.

Abolitionists knew that they were likely to win support for their cause if the white public read firsthand accounts of slavery and identified with the victims. Persons who escaped were encouraged to tell their stories in graphic detail, emphasizing the nature of slavery and, if they were runaways, the circumstances surrounding their escape. Some of these narratives were penned by former slaves, but many were ghost-written. While a few accounts stretched the boundaries of credibility, in the main they were truthful. The writers were aware that some of the events they described could be dismissed as fabrications, so they took pains to establish their veracity. Harriet Jacobs, who published her gripping *Incidents in the Life of a Slave Girl* in 1861, assured her readers that "this narrative is no fiction. I am aware that some of my adventures may seem incredible; but they are nevertheless strictly true." Jacobs noted that she had "not exaggerated the wrongs inflicted by Slavery; on the contrary, my descriptions fall short of the facts."[21]

The *Narrative of the Life of Frederick Douglass, an American Slave*, published in 1845, was the most popular of the antebellum narratives. Greeted enthusiastically by abolitionists and Northern whites, it sold 30,000 copies by 1850, an extraordinary achievement for the time. Other successful autobiographies included *Narrative of William W. Brown, a Fugitive Slave* (1847), *The Life of Josiah Henson, Formerly a Slave, Now an Inhabitant of Canada* (1849), *The Narrative of the Life and Adventures of Henry Bibb* (1849), and *The Fugitive Blacksmith; or Events in the History of James W. C. Pennington* (1849).

Josiah Henson's narrative became the basis of Harriet Beecher Stowe's fictional character, Uncle Tom. When *Uncle Tom's Cabin* was published in 1851, the novel achieved instant success as it provided a portrait of slavery at its unimaginable worst. It had a profound impact on white sensibilities and helped win sympathy for the abolitionist cause. Yet the novel was no real substitute for the lived experiences of those who had been slaves. Their accounts needed no fictional embroidery; theirs were the poignant tales of suffering, endurance and a painfully achieved triumph. As one reviewer concluded in 1849: "narratives of slaves go right to the hearts of men."[22]

In addition to popularizing their experiences at home, black abolitionists sought an international stage as well. Most were attracted to England, a country that boasted a vigorous antislavery movement prior to the passage of the Act of Emancipation in 1833. According to a recent scholar, these black visitors to England "were interested not in raising arms and men to combat oppression, but in erecting a moral cordon around America that would isolate her from the international community." The boundaries of this cordon, according to Frederick Douglass, were "Canada on the North, Mexico in the West, and England, Scotland and Ireland on the East, so that whereever a slaveholder went, he might hear nothing but denunciation of slavery, that he might be looked down upon as a man-stealing, cradle-robbing, and woman-stripping monster, and that he might see reproof and detestation on every hand."[23]

The first free black American to cross the Atlantic to London was probably James McCune Smith, who did so in 1831. Failing to gain admission to a medical school in the United States, Smith attended the University of Glasgow, graduated as a physician in 1837, and later became a noted abolitionist. Others went in succeeding years to study and to promote the cause of antislavery. Between 1840 and 1860 several black abolitionist leaders sailed for England, often visiting Scotland and Ireland as well to promote the cause of antislavery in America. The list included Frederick Douglass, J. W. C. Pennington, Henry Highland Garnet, Martin Delany, Alexander Crummell, William and Ellen Craft, and Josiah Henson.

These visitors addressed enthusiastic audiences, frequently describing their experiences as slaves. They visited cities and villages, speaking to the privileged as well as to workers. Some linked their struggle for freedom with that of oppressed peoples everywhere. The English public responded with financial support for their cause. Some tried to get their sister churches in America to denounce slavery, and others gave much needed moral support. Black abolitionists felt at home in England. In 1846 Douglass wrote to Garrison from Dublin that "one of the most pleasing features of my visit thus far has been a total absence of all manifestations of prejudice against me, on account of my color. The change of circumstances in this, is particularly striking. I go on stage coaches, omnibuses, steamboats, into the first cabins, and in the first public houses, without seeing the slightest manifestation of that hated and vulgar feeling against me. I find myself not treated as a *color*, but as a *man*—not as a thing, but as a child of the common Father of us all."[24] Douglass, of course, exaggerated. Other black abolitionists confronted the ugly face of English racism and reported on their unhappy experiences.

Although the black abolitionists were united on the urgency of emancipation, they did not all agree on the means. They came to the issue from different philosophical perspectives and debated among themselves and with whites the question of the strategy appropriate for the struggle. Perceptions and ideas changed over time as abolitionists developed a deeper understanding of the battle they were waging, the forces arrayed against them, and the tenacity of slavery. As in all reform movements, tactics and strategies changed as circumstances warranted and new people entered the fray. The abolitionist movement muddled along, but it never lost its focus.

Abolitionist leaders were divided on the feasibility of "direct action" as a strategy. Direct action normally connoted the use of violence, but by the 1850s it came to include rescuing runaway slaves who were being returned to their owners, the boycotting of slave-grown products, and tax resistance. In 1829, David Walker's *Appeal* had openly endorsed the use of violence to end slavery. "Remember Americans, that we must and shall be free and enlightened as you are," he wrote. "Will you wait until we shall, under God, obtain our liberty by the crushing arm of power? Will it not be dreadful for you? . . . We must and shall be free I say, in spite of you. . . . And wo, wo, will be, to you if we have to obtain our freedom by fighting."[25] Walker may have paid with his life for such incendiary language, since he died under mysterious circumstances in 1830, after several Southern newspapers and citizens had denounced him.

Such an eloquent call to direct action could not be lightly dismissed by either blacks or whites. Some white abolitionists distanced themselves from it, and blacks appear to have maintained a discreet public silence. The outbreak of Nat Turner's rebellion in 1831 confirmed the slaveowners' worst fears about the security of their system and exacerbated tensions. The abolitionists, including Walker, were blamed for inciting the slaves.

Placing their faith in the transforming power of moral suasion in the 1830s, almost all black abolitionists shied away from any endorsement of direct action. Meeting in 1834, the National Negro Convention declared its support for a peaceful opposition to slavery. The Declaration of Sentiments that the convention endorsed said that the struggle in which blacks were engaged "is not for blood, but for right." To that end, blacks should use "spiritual" and not "carnal" weapons.[26] William Whipper, a businessman from Pennsylvania, was reportedly the author of the declaration. Some of those who rejected violence may have been convinced that slave rebellions stood no realistic chance of success. Others were disinclined to alienate their white allies, many of whom would have been frightened away by appeals for direct action. But here and there was an occasional voice raised in support of a more aggressive stance in the fight for freedom.

In 1838, for example, the otherwise moderate Samuel Cornish admitted the need for direct action. Cornish, who was born free in Delaware, served as a Presbyterian minister and successively as editor of *Freedom's Journal, the Rights of All,* and the *Colored American.* A strong advocate of self-help programs and "moral improvement," Cornish was also a tireless proponent of equal rights for blacks.

But Cornish grew weary at the lack of improvement in the black condition. In 1837 he admitted, with some sorrow, "that we have yet to learn what virtue there would be in using moral weapons . . . against a kidnapper or a midnight incendiary with a lighted torch in his hand." Two years later he asserted that "offensive aggression" was "indispensable to personal liberty and rights."[27] If this was not an endorsement of violence, it came very close. Cornish was probably right to be cautious. It was not an easy matter for a small free black population to publicly advocate direct action in the 1830s. But it may be guessed that privately many saw some justification for it.

Not until 1843 was there another dramatic call for violence, reminiscent of the one made by David Walker. The silence was broken by the redoubtable Henry Highland Garnet in his address to the National Colored Convention, held in Buffalo. The former slave argued that the slaves should liberate themselves through their own efforts. The time had come for them to abandon their patience and use other options:

> TO SUCH DEGRADATION IT IS SINFUL IN THE EXTREME FOR YOU TO MAKE VOLUNTARY SUBMISSION . . . NEITHER GOD, NOR ANGELS, OR JUST MEN, COMMAND YOU TO SUFFER FOR A SINGLE MOMENT. THEREFORE IT IS YOUR SOLEMN AND IMPERATIVE DUTY TO USE EVERY MEANS, BOTH MORAL, INTELLECTUAL, AND PHYSICAL THAT PROMISE SUCCESS. . . . Brethren, arise, arise! Strike for your lives and liberties. Now is the day and the hour. Let every slave throughout the land do this and the days of slavery are numbered. You cannot be more oppressed than you have been— you cannot suffer greater cruelties than you have already. Rather die freemen than live to be slaves.

Concluding his courageous speech, the clergyman once more enjoined the slaves to reject their condition:

> Let your motto be RESISTANCE! RESISTANCE! RESISTANCE!–No oppressed people have ever secured their liberty without resistance. . . . Labor for the peace of the human race, and remember that you are three million.[28]

Garnet's unequivocal call for violence represented the coming of age of black abolitionism. Regardless of whether the speech gained popular approval, a crucial debate was joined. A bright young abolitionist had

Henry Highland Garnett urged his fellow brethren to strike for their lives and liberties.

raised an issue that had to be confronted, and sides had to be taken. Garnet articulated the quiet feelings of many, even as he challenged his colleagues to declare where they stood. The speech was a bold assertion of independence from the proponents of moral suasion and a rejection of those who counseled moderation. By a vote of eighteen in favor and nineteen against, the convention did not endorse the publication of the address, but the fact that eighteen persons in attendance supported the dissemination of such an incendiary speech was victory enough for Garnet.

Garnet's speech spawned much controversy. Frederick Douglass, still developing as an abolitionist, opposed its content and tenor. So did William Wells Brown and Charles Lenox Remond, the New York abolitionist. A few white abolitionists were outraged, including Maria W. Chapman from Boston. Chapman doubted that Garnet was responsible for the ideas that he espoused: "We say emphatically to the man of color, trust not the counsels that lead you to the shedding of blood. That man knows nothing of nature, human or Divine,–of character–good or evil, who imagines that a civil and servile war would ultimately promote freedom." Garnet reacted angrily to this assault on his independence of thought, noting, "If it has come to this, that I must think and act as you do, because you are an abolitionist or be exterminated by your thunder, that I do not hesitate to say your abolitionism is abject slavery." Rejecting Chapman's charge that he received counsel from others, he added: "I have expected no more from ignorant slave-holders and their apologists, but I really expected better things from Mrs. Maria W. Chapman, an antislavery poetess, and editor *pro tem* of the *Boston Liberator.*" He ended in a note of angry defiance, "In the meantime, be assured that there is one black American who dares speak boldly on the subject of universal liberty."[29]

The issue of violence as a means of ending slavery was again addressed four years later at the 1847 National Colored Convention held at Troy, New York. The delegates received a report from a committee headed by Frederick Douglass charged to study the "best means to Abolish Slavery and Caste in the United States." After much discussion and compromise, the delegates approved the report's denunciation of violence: "All argument put forth in favor of insurrection and bloodshed, however well intended, is either the result of unpardonable impatience or an atheistic want of faith in the power of truth as a means of regenerating and reforming the world."[30]

This was not the end of the matter, however. Upon reflection, Douglass announced in 1849 that he would be pleased to hear "that the subtle armies which have been engaged in beautifying and adorning the South were engaged in spreading death and devastation there."[31] This embrace of violence by the important and influential leader did not mean that he rejected moral suasion altogether. As he wrote in the *North Star,* also in 1849, the "only well grounded hope of the slave for emancipation is the operation of moral force."[32] When he addressed an audience composed primarily of whites on July 5, 1852, in Rochester, New York, the former slave asked:

> What to the American Slave is your Fourth of July? I answer: a day that reveals to him . . . the gross injustice and constant cruelty to which he is the constant victim . . . your celebration is a sham; your boasted liberty, an unholy license; your national greatness, swelling vanity. . . . There is not a nation on earth guilty of practices, more shocking and bloody, than are the people of these United States.[33]

Divisions in the ranks of abolitionists were, of course, nothing new. The American Anti-Slavery Society had experienced a major rupture in 1840 when those who were disenchanted with Garrison's leadership withdrew and founded the American and Foreign Anti-Slavery Society. There were several reasons for the split into two wings—one more radical in approach and associated with Garrison and New England, the other more moderate in its orientation and enjoying the support of men like Lewis Tappan, Joseph Leavitt, and James G. Birney.

Some abolitionists had become uncomfortable with Garrison's denunciation of the churches for their failure to embrace antislavery. His support of the exercise of leadership roles in the movement by women alienated many men who argued that women's rights issues should be divorced from antislavery. Garrison's detractors also shrank from his refusal to endorse any participation in the institutional life of the nation and his rejection of electoral activity. While these internecine quarrels were more vigorously conducted by whites, blacks were not unaffected by them and chose sides in accordance with their own philosophical positions. Although most blacks remained with the Garrisonian wing, men such as the clergymen Theodore S. Wright and Amos G. Beman allied with the rival group.

The energies of the black abolitionists were not dissipated by these disputes. Although they were also divided over means, the common ground was their own personal involvement in the struggle. They could ill afford to be distracted from the struggle when their own liberty was at stake. In fact, although blacks remained members of the two integrated national organizations, they increasingly went in their own directions after 1840. They had become confident, mature, and skilled as leaders and many chafed under white direction and leadership. The Convention Movement became their primary forum, and it was at these irregularly held gatherings that many battles over means and direction were fought.

The alliance between white and black abolitionists was never an easy one. Blacks were only too well aware that a good number of their white colleagues were racist. Some whites opposed social interaction with blacks; others doubted their intellectual capacity and opposed any form of black independence. Even Garrison was not above demonstrating an unacceptable arrogance in his attitude toward blacks. In 1853, for example, in one of his feuds with Frederick Douglass, he announced that the antislavery struggle had reached a point that it "transcended the ability of the sufferers from American Slavery and prejudice, *as a class*, to keep pace with it, or to perceive what [are] its demands, or to understand the philosophy of its operations."[34]

While most white abolitionists were committed narrowly to the destruction of slavery, blacks wanted the elimination of all forms of racial oppression and the creation of a just society as well. Some whites publicly disassociated themselves from the struggle for equal rights or gave it only lukewarm support. In 1842, a black newspaper took white abolitionists to task for not "destroying every barrier in their power, which is closed against us and retards our progression."[35] This was a serious charge, and one that had much validity. In their struggle for equal rights, blacks felt compelled to point out the hypocrisy of their white friends even as they welcomed their support and cooperated with them on various levels. But as black abolitionist Theodore S. Wright told the integrated audience at the New York State Anti-Slavery Convention in 1837, "Prejudice must be killed or slavery will never be abolished. . . . Abolitionists must annihilate in their own bosoms the cord of caste."[36]

The struggle against slavery on the one hand and for equal rights on the other must have exacted an awful psychological price from black abolitionists. By 1850, the end of slavery was nowhere in sight, although there were a few successes in the equal rights campaign in the North. The white and black abolitionists who had shifted to political activity in the 1840s could also not claim any advances in their fight. The New York-based Liberty party, which was organized in 1840, committed itself to emancipation but was singularly unsuccessful at the polls. The Free Soil Party, which was founded in 1848, was essentially antislavery in its orientation, but basically it sought to prevent the expansion of slavery into the new territories. It elected five persons to Congress in the 1848 elections, but overall its impact on the course of the freedom struggle was negligible.

There were significant changes in the temper of the black abolitionists—as well as that of their white colleagues—in the 1850s. It was a decade of enormous setbacks for the movement, and strategies had to be reevaluated and changed. Wearied by years of struggle and disappointment, abolitionists increasingly came to accept the stark truth that they had not accomplished much. In fact, the possibility of a further expansion of slavery loomed. In 1845 Texas was admitted into the Union as a slave state, and there was reason to believe that this would not be the last such occurrence.

The passage of the Fugitive Slave Act in 1850 represented a major blow to the abolitionists and their cause. Southern slaveowners and their defenders had long complained about the support given to runaways by the opponents of slavery. It will be recalled that the Constitution had sanctioned the return of "persons held to service and labor" to their owners, an unmistakable reference to escaped slaves. In 1793 Congress gave practical expression to this clause by passing a law allowing slaveowners to enter other states to capture and reclaim their property. The legal deck was stacked against the escapees, since they were denied the right to testify in court on their own behalf, to *habeas corpus,* or even to a jury trial. Since such a law placed all blacks at the mercy of slave catchers, some Northern states passed measures that gave these black victims the rights that the federal laws had denied them. Known as liberty laws, they afforded some measure of protection to black victims and permitted the prosecution of the kidnappers.

Not surprisingly, the constitutionality of the liberty laws was tested in the courts. The state of Pennsylvania had passed a liberty law in 1826 that imposed penalties on kidnappers. In 1837, Edward Prigg, a slave catcher, was indicted for kidnapping a woman and her two children and returning them to their owner in Maryland. Upon his conviction, Prigg appealed to the U.S. Supreme Court. In a controversial decision, the Court ruled that the Pennsylvania liberty law was unconstitutional and upheld the federal Fugitive Slave Law of 1793. The decision, by implication, struck down similar liberty laws in other states and granted slaveowners the right to reclaim their property anywhere. The Court, however, held that states need not cooperate with the federal authorities in their pursuit of runaways.

This proslavery decision did not stanch the flow of escapees, nor did it prevent sympathetic persons from providing them with assistance. A few Northern states even passed new liberty laws, and there were enough judges who ruled in favor of escapees and against the kidnappers to provide Southerners with causes for complaint. In an attempt to placate the Southerners, Congress adopted a new fugitive slave law in 1850. This draconian statute required all citizens to aid law enforcement authorities in the capture and return of runaways. Abducted persons were denied the right to a legal hearing or a trial by jury. Those persons who opposed the authorities in their efforts to seize runaways or aided and harbored them were subject to harsh punishments. The commissioners who were to be appointed to oversee the operation of the law received a higher fee if they approved the return of an accused runaway than if they declined to do so.

Clearly, the act upheld the interest of Southern slaveowners and posed a severe threat to the security of free blacks everywhere. Those who lacked free papers could be seized and reenslaved, and even those who possessed them were at risk as well. Free blacks knew only too well that the law was never on their side; it never operated as a guardian and protector of their rights. Consequently, in the aftermath of the law, an estimated 20,000 free blacks fled to Canada in search of a sanctuary. Their flight was a telling commentary on the black person's plight in America, on the unfriendliness of the system in which they lived and the unpalatable choices it forced them to make.

Most free blacks did not flee, however. Many joined sympathetic whites in denouncing the law and they vowed resistance to it. William Still believed that blacks had a "duty to stay here and fight it out." Others concluded that flight would only "embolden our oppressors to renew efforts to pass those *hellish black laws.*" Blacks in Syracuse pledged to defend themselves with "daggers in our pockets."[37] Groups of persons armed themselves for collective defense. Taking note of the fear that the law generated and the dislocation in black lives that it created, *Frederick Douglass' Paper* lamented in 1851, "The night is a dark and stormy one.

We have lost some of our strong men.–Ward has been driven into exile; Loguen has been hunted from our shores; Brown, Garnet and Crummell, men who were our pride and hope, we have heard signified their unwillingness to return again to their National field of labors in this country. Bibb has *chosen* Canada as his field of labor–and the eloquent Remond is comparatively silent."[38]

In an effort to sabotage the enforcement of the law, blacks as well as whites rescued some of those who were taken up. An increasingly angry Frederick Douglass was certain that "The only way to make the Fugitive Slave Law a dead letter [is] to make half a dozen or more dead kidnappers."[39] William Garrison expressed the view that if the "Revolutionary fathers were justified in wading through blood to freedom and independence, then every fugitive slave is justified in arming himself for protection and defence,–in taking the life of every marshal, commissioner, or other person who attempts to reduce him to bondage. . . ."[40]

Under the circumstances, the slave catchers met with a good deal of opposition in the discharge of their duties. Ordinary citizens were particularly outraged when runaways who had lived in freedom for many years were seized. One woman in Philadelphia who was arrested had escaped from Maryland twenty-two years earlier and an Indiana man was recaptured after nineteen years. Others such as William and Ellen Craft eluded the authorities and fled to England. President Fillmore denounced the Bostonians who helped the Crafts in their escape and offered federal help to their owners in their efforts to reclaim their property. Bostonians were particularly aggressive in rescuing runaways who were apprehended. When in 1851 a number of black men rescued Shadrach Minkins, an escaped Virginia slave, Fillmore demanded the prosecution of all "aiders and abettors of this flagitious offense." Henry Clay, the prominent Southern politician and would-be president was so outraged by the incident that he wanted to know "whether we shall have a government of white men or black men in the cities of this country."[41]

Perhaps the most celebrated case of direct resistance to the law occurred in September 1851 at Christiana, a town in Pennsylvania. Two escaped slaves from Maryland had been provided sanctuary by a black resident of Christiana. When the slaveowner, accompanied by the authorities and his friends, attempted to seize the escapees, they encountered strong resistance from some well-armed black men. By the time the meleé ended, the slaveowner had lost his life and the blacks had fled. An angry Fillmore dispatched the marines to assist the local authorities in restoring order and rounding up the participants in the affair. Enraged whites pursued blacks indiscriminately and they were "hunted like partridges upon the mountains," according to one contemporary observer.[42] Another person who was on the scene reported:

I was in the Red Lion Hotel; there were a number of United States Marines; I asked one what they were doing here; he said, "We are going to arrest every nigger and d—-d abolitionist. . . ." I walked away. Sure enough they scoured the country for miles around, arresting every colored man, boy and girl they could find.[43]

Ultimately, thirty-six blacks and five whites stood accused for their alleged involvement in the affair. The three most prominent leaders of the blacks–William Parker, Alexander Pinckney, Abraham Johnson–had escaped to Canada.

The Christiana "riot," as it came to be called, produced an angry reaction from Southern whites and Northerners as well. In North Carolina, the *Raleigh Standard* threatened that "if the accused were not punished . . . WE LEAVE YOU! Before God and man . . . if you fail in this simple act of justice, THE BONDS WILL BE DISSOLVED." A Rochester, New York, newspaper was particularly strident:

Let the negroes buy as many revolvers as they please; but they may rest assured that the first one that is used by them against our citizens will be the signal for the extermination of the whole negro race from our midst. If they wish to provoke *a war of the races*, by re-enacting the bloody scenes of Christiana, they will find our civil and military authorities, and our citizens at large, prepared to defend themselves, and to put down their murderous assaults, with an avenging arm that will carry retribution justice home to such vile traitors and assassins. If the issue is to be forced upon us, to decide whether the white races are to maintain their rights and their position, or whether *negro mob law* is to govern and ride rampant over our laws, constitution and liberties–let it be known at once, that our people may be prepared for the emergency.[44]

Many Northern whites did not embrace such rhetoric, however. White abolitionists used the event to denounce slavery, and some newspapers urged a sympathetic understanding of the circumstances that provoked the riot. Although black abolitionists were fearful of reprisals against blacks everywhere, some defended the behavior of their brethren at Christiana. Frederick Douglass, James McCune Smith, and Charles W. Ray, among others, publicly expressed their support. Douglass contended:

. . . the only way to meet the man-hunter successfully, is with cold steel and the nerve to use it. The wretch who engages in such a business is impervious to every consideration of truth, love and mercy, and nothing short of putting him in bodily danger can deter him. The colored people must defend their rights, if they would have their rights respected. To shape their muscles for the fetters, and to adjust their wrists for the handcuffs at the bidding of the slaveholder, is an example of non-resistance, quite as radical as any class of men in the country could wish, and while it might excite the sympathy of a few, it could not fail to bring down upon the whole race to which they belong, the scorn and contempt of every brave man. I have but one lesson for my people in the present trying hour; it is this: *Count your lives utterly worthless, unless coupled with the inestimable blessing of liberty*[45]

Endeavoring to underscore the seriousness of the riot, the government charged those who were arrested with treason. The grand jury that heard the charges indicted thirty-six blacks and five whites. Eventually, the government abandoned the case after the first defendant–a white man–was found not guilty. This unexpected development was the direct consequence of the popular ridicule that the trial had generated in the North. Abolitionists and their friends poked fun at a frightened government that had overreacted and brought palpably unjust charges against the defendants. Deeply embarrassed and unwilling to further the abolitionists' interests by this obvious blunder, the federal authorities relented.

Incidents such as the one at Christiana continued to inflame tensions between the North and the South. White Southerners reacted angrily to the widespread resistance to the fugitive slave law, and many of their leaders doubted whether they should continue to remain in the Union. Only a small number of escapees were ever returned to their owners, a fact that added to the resentment in the South. By 1860 only 332 persons had been reenslaved. Yet, it should be added, almost all of the suspects who were taken up lost their freedom. Only eleven avoided the fate of reenslavement during the 1850s.

With the passage of the fugitive slave act and the insecurity it generated, emigration, as we have seen, became increasingly attractive as an option to many blacks. When the Supreme Court rendered the Dred Scott decision in 1857, the tension heightened, and many more were further disposed to abandon their native land. Two years later, the white abolitionist John Brown led a small military assault on the federal armory at Harpers Ferry, Virginia, and brought the nation closer to the breaking point.

An uncompromising opponent of slavery, Brown had fought against the adoption of slavery in Kansas in the mid-1850s. Eventually, he conceived of a plan to invade the South, overrun the armory at Harpers Ferry and distribute the weapons to the slaves. The ensuing conflagration would end in the liberation of the slaves through their own efforts. Brown failed to obtain the support of many sympathizers; most doubted that the plan stood any realistic chance of success. Undaunted, Brown

proceeded with his plans, and he and his twenty-one committed supporters, including five blacks, began their ill-fated assault on the armory
on October 16, 1859.

The response by the militia was swift and effective. Brown lost ten
men in the conflict, and he and the others were arrested and charged
with treason. During the trial, the intrepid abolitionist delivered a passionate speech in his own defense. In this extraordinary address, Brown
maintained:

> Had I interfered in behalf of the rich, the powerful, the intelligent, the
> so-called great . . . or any of that class . . . it would have been all right;
> and every man in this court would have deemed it an act worthy of
> reward rather than punishment![46]

The court remained unmoved, and Brown was sentenced to death.
A number of black women in Brooklyn praised Brown as "a Saviour
commissioned to redeem us, the American people, from the great
National Sin of Slavery."[47] While many prominent Northerners extolled
Brown for the nobility of his actions, white Southerners and Northern
conservatives denounced him with unrestrained ferocity. Most Southerners blamed Northerners, particularly the abolitionists, for what had
happened. Several newspapers wondered if the Union could survive the
assault. Others launched a more aggressive defense of their peculiar
institution. "We regard every man who does not boldly declare that he
believes African slavery to be a social, moral, and political blessing an
enemy to the institutions of the South," proclaimed a newspaper published in Atlanta.[48]

As the 1850s drew to a close, the nation stumbled awkwardly from
crisis to crisis. Blacks were marginalized in many of the quarrels that
divided whites, but it was their fate that constituted the core of the disputes. The abolitionists as a group had helped keep the issue of slavery
at the forefront of the nation's debates, but they had not achieved their
objective. They, and the Northern politicians who shared an antipathy to
slavery, kept the South on the defensive. Yet the abolitionists did not
cause the war that would eventually bring them success. They pricked
the nation's conscience relentlessly and vigorously, but the roots of the
war resided in the institution itself and the increasingly irreconcilable
differences between the sections over its expansion and place in the
land of the free. Black abolitionists, in particular, appealed to the nation
to cleanse itself of the horror of slavery and to create an egalitarian society. Comparatively few in number, they conducted a courageous campaign, but one that suffered internal stresses and strains. In the process,
free blacks created many institutions to aid in their struggle. These
institutions would survive long after slavery disappeared and met a

wide range of needs. In the course of the long and wearying struggle, blacks proved unyielding against overwhelming odds. That was success enough, although it was not the one they sought.

Notes

1. Jane H. Pease and William H. Pease, "Ends, Means, and Attitudes: Black White Conflict in the Antislavery Movement," *Civil War History*, xviii (June 1972), 121.
2. David Brion Davis, "The Emergence of Immediatism in British and American Anti-slavery Thought," *Mississippi Valley Historical Review*, XLIX (1962), 211; Roger Burns, ed., *Am I Not a Man and a Brother: The Anti Slavery Crusade of Revolutionary America 1688–1788* (New York: Chelsea House Publishers, 1977), 103.
3. Ibid., 218.
4. Benjamin Quarles, *Black Abolitionists* (New York: Oxford, 1969), 11.
5. Louis Filler, *The Crusade Against Slavery, 1830–1860* (New York: Harper & Row, 1960), 57.
6. Shirley Yee, *Black Women Abolitionists: A Study in Activism, 1828–1860* (Knoxville: University of Tennessee Press, 1992), 8.
7. Ibid., 55–59.
8. Julie Winch, "'You Have Talents—Only Cultivate Them': Female Literary Societies and the Abolitionist Crusade," in Jean Fagan Yellin and John C. Van Horne, eds., *The Abolitionist Sisterhood: Women's Political Culture in Antebellum America* (Ithaca: Cornell University Press, 1994), 110.
9. Ibid., 104.
10. C. Peter Ripley, ed., *Witness for Freedom: African-American Voices on Race, Slavery, and Emancipation* (Chapel Hill: University of North Carolina Press, 1993), 103.
11. Charles W. Akers, "'Our Modern Egyptians': Phillis Wheatley and the Whig Campaign against Slavery in Revolutionary Boston," *Journal of Negro History*, LX:3 (1975), 406–407.
12. See Nell Irvin Painter, "Difference, Slavery, and Memory: Sojourner Truth in Feminist Abolitionism," in Yellin and Van Horne, *The Abolitionist Sisterhood*, 141. See also Painter's fine biography, *Sojourner Truth: A Life, a Symbol* (New York: Norton, 1996).
13. Jane H. Pease and William H. Pease, *They Who Would Be Free: Blacks Search for Freedom, 1830–1861* (Urbana: University of Illinois Press, 1990), 11.
14. Filler, *The Crusade Against Slavery,* 23.
15. C. Loveland, "Evangelicalism and 'Immediate Emancipation' in American Antislavery Thought," *Journal of Southern History*, 23 (1966), 172.
16. For a discussion of this issue, see Pease and Pease, *They Who Would Be Free*, 3–16; 68–93.
17. Larry Gara, "The Professional Fugitive in the Abolition Movement," *Wisconsin Magazine of History*, xlviii (1965), 196.
18. The preceding account of Douglass' life draws on Douglass, *My Life and My Bondage*, and on William S. McFeeley, *Frederick Douglass* (New York: Norton, 1991).
19. Logan and Winston, *Dictionary of American Negro Biography*, 44.
20. Howard Jones, *Mutiny on the Amistad: The Sign of a Slave Revolt and its Impact on American Abolition, Law, and Diplomacy* (New York: Oxford, 1987), 190.
21. Jacobs, *Incidents in the Life of a Slave Girl*, xiii.
22. R. J. M. Blackett, *Building an Antislavery Wall: Black Americans in the Atlantic Abolitionist Movement, 1830–1860* (Baton Rouge: Louisiana State University Press, 1983), 26.
23. Ibid., 6.

24. Ibid., 107.
25. Walker, *David Walker's Appeal*, 89.
26. Carleton Mabee, *Black Freedom: The Nonviolent Abolitionists from 1830 Through the Civil War* (New York: Macmillan, 1970), 57.
27. Ibid., 277.
28. Joel Schor, *Henry Highland Garnet: A Voice of Black Radicalism in the Nineteenth Century* (Westport, CT: Greenwood Press, 1977), 55.
29. Ibid., 59–60.
30. Ibid., 81.
31. Quarles, *Black Abolitionists*, 225.
32. Mabee, *Black Freedom*, 65.
33. Edward Countryman, *Americans: A Collision of Histories* (New York: Hill and Wang, 1996), 184.
34. Pease and Pease, "Ends, Means, and Attitudes", 123.
35. Ibid., 124.
36. Gerald Sorin, *Abolitionism: A New Perspective* (New York: Praeger, 1972), 108.
37. Ripley, *Black Abolitionist Papers*, iii, 56.
38. Litwack, *North of Slavery*, 249.
39. McPherson, *Battle Cry of Freedom*, 84.
40. Jane H. Pease and William H. Pease, "Confrontation and Abolition in the 1850s," *Journal of American History*, 58 (1972), 929.
41. McPherson, *Battle Cry of Freedom*, 82–83.
42. Jonathan Katz, *Resistance at Christiana* (New York: Thomas Y. Crowell Co., 1974), 123.
43. Ibid., 125.
44. ibid., 138–139.
45. Ibid., 153.
46. Elbert Smith, *The Death of Slavery: The United States, 1837–1865* (Chicago: University of Chicago Press, 1967), 158.
47. Sweet, *Black Images of America*, 154.
48. McPherson, *Battle Cry of Freedom*, 212.

Emancipation

Slavery ended officially in 1865 with the adoption of the Thirteenth Amendment to the Constitution. Its legal demise came 246 years after the first blacks landed at Jamestown and almost eight decades after the new nation adopted its Constitution. This is a short time for the historical imagination but a long time for the successive generations of black people who lived as chattel. If there were any slaves alive in 1865 who had been born in 1787, they had lived through momentous changes in the life of black America and witnessed many disputes among whites concerning their peculiar institution and the place of blacks in the land where most of them had been born.

Paradoxically, the years after 1787 had seen the slow death of slavery in the North as well as its expansion and entrenchment in the South. The assault by some Northerners on the institution elicited a very strong defense of it as Southerners asserted a pugnacious and unwavering doctrine of white supremacy and maintained that slavery was "a positive good" for blacks. Slavery had powerful friends in high places, and many of the nation's leaders were slaveowners. Of the first seven men elected to the presidency, five owned slaves. Slaveholders had included speakers of the House of Representatives, members of the cabinet, and justices of the Supreme Court, including Judge Taney of the Dred Scott decision fame. Time and time again these white men who determined the nation's political fate worked out flawed and controversial compromises on the slavery question, postponing the resolution of an issue that had to be faced in an increasingly modern world. By 1860 slavery in the Americas existed only in Brazil, Cuba, Puerto Rico, and the United States.

In retrospect, it can be seen that the sectional antagonists on the slavery question were captives of their distinctive brands of racism. Northern whites who attacked slavery did not articulate, in the main, a virulent ideology of white supremacy. Yet they could not claim a moral highground on the matter, since their discriminatory treatment of the free blacks in their midst spoke volumes about their racial beliefs and attitudes. Northerners had banned slavery, but they had not exorcised racism from their consciousness. Writing in 1833, the white feminist and abolitionist Lydia Maria Child observed that "the form of slavery" was absent in the North but its "very spirit . . . is here in all its strength."[1] Southerners delighted in drawing attention to Northern hypocrisy, much to Northerners' discomfiture. On the other hand, Southerners promoted a belligerent brand of racism with no apologies. In the end, the broad differences between the antagonists rested on the place of human property in the nation, its feasibility and morality. The immorality of the racism that legitimized slavery and the treatment of free blacks was not the central issue or even one that invited much division among whites. Until whites came to see racism and slavery as inextricably related, the nation's soul would never be at peace. For some, the recognition that racism defiled the nation and its institutions proved as elusive in the nineteenth century as it has been in the twentieth.

Speaking for the white majority and ignoring the presence of native American peoples and blacks, the *New York Tribune* concluded in 1855: "We are not one people. We are two peoples. We are a people for Freedom and a people for Slavery. Between the two, conflict is inevitable."[2] The "we" in the *Tribune's* comment obviously included only Caucasians. But even within the *Tribune's* definition of who could claim to be an American, it overstated the case. Not all white Northerners, perhaps not even a bare majority, opposed slavery as long as it remained in the South and did not invade their soil. Conversely, not all white Southerners supported the peculiar institution and rose to its defense. In addition, as the plight of free blacks in the North demonstrated and events after 1865 would continue to underscore, freedom for them was limited and came with a number of strings attached. Legally, it meant, and would mean, what whites wanted it to mean. The dichotomy between slavery and freedom that the *Tribune* posed was a false one; Northern whites were more opposed to slavery than they were committed to freedom and its full meaning for blacks. Yet the *Tribune's* thoughtless equation of being American with being white (a characteristic of some of the writing of our own times) is important, nonetheless. Blacks remained the "Other"; their two centuries of residence in America had not changed the perception of them as alien held by the dominant group.

Although blacks were never formally involved in the political process, it was their condition as slaves and to a lesser extent as free persons, that shaped much of the national debates among whites during the antebellum years. The invisible presence of blacks in the halls of political power was a stark reminder to sensitive whites of the nation's moral deficiencies and its failure to abide by its stated principles. Even the South's defense of its social system and its raucous bellicosity on the slavery issue may have betrayed an uneasy conscience, as if it needed to convince itself of the morality of its actions and sought to substitute angry posturing for its conscience.

Yet there was no cordon sanitaire that separated the North from the South, no impenetrable wall divided the sections. Slavery accounted for the perverse distinctiveness of the South because it was the foundation of that region's peculiar social order. But slavery's existence belied the pervasiveness of a racism that knew no sectional boundaries. On the racial question, the essential difference between the sections was the unabashed virulence of Southern racism, and not its absence in the North. Antislavery Northerners wanted to cleanse the nation of slavery's evil, enhance the moral superiority of wage labor, and reduce the political power of the slavocracy. Underneath, the differences between the North and the South portended a struggle over the nation's soul, a battle for the guardianship of its ideals. As the *New York Times* noted in 1857:

> The great States of the North, are not peopled exclusively by quidnuncs and agitators. . . . Nevertheless, we do give ourselves great and increasing concern over the existence of Slavery in States over whose internal economy we have no right and no wish to exercise any control whatever. Nevertheless, we do feel, and the feeling is growing deeper in the northern heart with every passing year, that our character, our prosperity, and our destiny are most seriously involved in the question of the perpetuation or extinction of slavery in those States.[3]

Southerners were the wayward kin who tarnished the family name with their unholy indulgence, but they were kin nonetheless. This familial quarrel—at times bitter, at times conciliatory—reflected the conflicting pulls and emotions inherent in such domestic estrangements.

Members of the family were divided over its character and image, and they competed for control of its power and resources. They debated questions surrounding the right to private property of whatever stripe and the degree of autonomy that each state, or each unit in the family, should have. Blacks were not members of this national family. Stephen Douglas, a senatorial candidate in Illinois in 1858, for example, denounced his rival Abraham Lincoln for thinking "the Negro is his brother. I do not think the Negro is any kin of mine at all. . . . This government was made by white men, for the benefit of white men and their posterity, to be executed and managed by white men."[4] No wonder that the disputes were noted for the absence of a passionate concern for the lives and fate of those who were not acknowledged members of the family, those who passed their lives in the service of others.

By 1860 the accumulated passions aroused by the disputes of the preceding decades seemingly could no longer be contained. During the 1850s, whites had struggled over slavery's expansion and worked out a flawed compromise. Between 1854 and 1856, proslavery and antislavery forces clashed violently in Kansas, each faction trying to influence the residents of that territory to either endorse or reject slavery. Kansas eventually threw its lot with the antislavery forces in 1857, but not before much blood had been shed. "Bleeding Kansas" revealed the depth of the national passions and presaged a more costly internecine conflict.

The Supreme Court's Dred Scott decision created additional tensions in 1857, even if the decision was not particularly surprising to many. A year later, the debates touching on slavery in the Illinois senatorial election provided a remarkable airing of conflicting opinions on the nation's foremost unresolved dispute. At center stage was Abraham Lincoln, a relatively unknown lawyer and the candidate of the Republican party, which had been founded four years earlier. Sharing the limelight was Stephen Douglas, the candidate of the Democratic party. Each man spoke on behalf of many others; each at times reflected white society's feelings, beliefs, fears, and contradictions on the slavery question.

Lincoln's position was the more principled of the two, but it was never an overtly abolitionist position, nor did it endorse the creation of an egalitarian society. Lincoln expressed strong support for the containment of slavery, saying that the institution would disappear ultimately. But its "ultimate extinction," according to Lincoln, would not occur soon: "I do not mean . . . it will be in a day, nor in a year, nor in two years. I do not suppose that in the most peaceful way ultimate extinction would occur in less than a hundred years at the least; but it will occur in the best way for both races in God's good time, I have no doubt."[5] Slaves, in this rendering, could look forward to their liberation in the mid- to late twentieth century.

Lincoln did not promote social interaction between the races. A black person, however, "in the right to eat the bread, without leave of anybody else, which his own hand earns is my *equal and the equal of* Judge Douglas, and the equal of every living man." This, did not mean intellectual equality, the candidate stressed. Although he personally condemned slavery, Lincoln assured his white countrymen, "I am not, nor ever have been in favor of bringing about in any way the social and political equality of the white and the black races. . . . I am not nor ever have been in favor of making voters or jurors of negroes, nor of qualifying them to hold office, nor to intermarry with white people; and I will say in addition to this that there is a physical difference between the races which I believe will forever forbid the two races living together on terms of social and political equality."[6]

Stephen Douglas took exception to Lincoln's desire to limit the expansion of slavery. He was convinced that Southerners did not seek its expansion, but it was their constitutional right to take their property with them as they desired. Douglas did not believe that blacks were the equal of whites. "The signers of the Declaration," he argued, "had no reference to the negro . . . or any inferior and degraded race."[7] The Democratic candidate openly pandered to the racism of his audiences, characterizing his opponents as "Black Republicans." When the Illinois voters spoke, they sent Douglas to the Senate.

The Lincoln-Douglas debates showed a predominantly white nation at war with itself over the human worth it ascribed to blacks who occupied the same space. Can any one doubt that blacks—slave and free—who were aware of the tenor of the debates were assaulted psychologically by assertions that they were an inferior species of humans? Free blacks, in particular, were not silent observers to the disputes and followed them with interest and concern. In 1859, many of them had celebrated John Brown's assault on Harper's Ferry and accorded him a revered status. A year later, they watched the course of the presidential campaign with more than usual interest.

In many respects, the election campaign of 1860 was a replay of the Illinois senatorial race two years earlier. Abraham Lincoln was the surprise nominee of the Republican party, and Stephen Douglas was the candidate of the Democratic party, which had split into Northern and Southern factions over the slavery question. Douglas represented the Northern Democrats, who were less strident than their Southern counterparts on the issue of slavery's expansion but nevertheless embraced federal protection for slavery wherever it existed. Southern Democrats, along with Northern Whigs and others, formed the Constitutional Union party and nominated John Bell of Tennessee to be their standard bearer.

White Southerners were alarmed by Lincoln's nomination. In their eyes—despite much evidence to the contrary—he represented the antislavery forces that would destroy Southern society and institutions. John J. Crittenden of Kentucky, a Democratic congressman, denounced the Republicans for thinking it was "their duty to destroy . . . the white man, in order that the black might be free. . . . [The South] has come to the conclusion that in case Lincoln should be elected . . . she could not submit to the consequences, and therefore, to avoid her fate, will secede from the Union."[8] Others agreed.

The Republican party took great pains to distance itself from the antislavery movement and to destroy any perception that Lincoln's election posed a threat to slavery. Lincoln assured the country, "Wrong as we think slavery is, we can yet afford to let it alone where it is, because that much is due to the necessity arising from its actual presence in the nation."[9] Nevertheless, Democrats linked the Republicans to the cause of antislavery and charged them with the promotion of racial equality for blacks. Others raised the specter that a Lincoln victory would provide the impetus for slaves to escape to the North and compete with whites for jobs. In response, the Republicans proudly proclaimed themselves the "White Man's Party."

Many free blacks who had the right to vote supported Lincoln's candidacy. Frederick Douglass and a few others, however, refused to do so because the Republican party "promises to be about as good a Southern party as either wing of the old Democratic Party."[10] They threw their support to Gerrit Smith, who had been nominated by the Radical Abolitionist party. While it stood no realistic chance of winning the presidency, the Radical Abolitionists supported the emancipation of all slaves. In advocating support for Smith, Douglass wrote, "Ten thousand votes for GERRIT SMITH at this juncture would do more, in our judgment for the ultimate abolition of slavery in this country, than two million for ABRAHAM LINCOLN, or any other man who stands pledged before the world against all interference with slavery in the slave states, who is not pledged to the abolition of slavery in the District of Columbia, or anywhere else the system exists, and who is not opposed to making the free states a hunting ground for men under the Fugitive Slave Law. . . ."[11]

The election of Lincoln to the presidency galvanized the South into secession from the Union. Unwilling to remain in a Union that seemed to threaten their interests, slaveowners and others wanted to preserve a world that had been built on the coerced labor of blacks and legitimized by racist ideology. The governor of Georgia, Joseph E. Brown, assured his constituents that black slavery "is the poor man's best Government. Among us the poor white laborer . . . does not belong to the menial class. The negro is in no sense his equal. . . . He belongs to the only true aristocracy, the race of *white men*."[12] Seven states severed ties with the Union, and their representatives met in Montgomery, Alabama, in February 1861 to found the Confederate States of America and to write a provisional constitution. Jefferson Davis of Mississippi was elected the provisional president.

The Confederacy justified its perverted existence on the doctrine of racial supremacy. The new nation, unlike the Union, saw no need to embrace the concepts of equality and justice. In fact, its *raisón d'etre* was a repudiation of those ideas and a celebration of white oppression of blacks. Confederate Vice President Alexander Stephens articulated the essential difference between the ideals upon which the Confederacy rested and those of the Declaration of Independence. To him, the Confederate government was founded upon ideas "exactly the opposite" of the Declaration: "Its foundations are laid, its cornerstone rests, upon the great truth that the negro is not equal to the white man; that slavery . . . is his natural and normal condition. This, our new government, is the first in the history of the world based upon this great physical, philosophical, and moral truth."[13]

The impending war between the states would not, however, be fought over the slavery question. President Lincoln was committed to the preservation of the Union and not to the destruction of slavery. In his inaugural address, he pledged to respect Southern institutions and was generally conciliatory to his erring kin. "We are not enemies, but friends," Lincoln declared. "Though passion may have strained, it must not break our bonds of affection."[14]

But passion had already taken over. Confederate guns assaulted the Union troops at Fort Sumter, South Carolina, in April 1861 and the die was cast. Frederick Douglass and other abolitionists applauded Lincoln's decision to save the Union: "He who faithfully works to put down a rebellion undertaken and carried on for the extension and perpetuity of slavery, performs an antislavery work," he wrote. Almost alone among the early observers of events as they unfolded, Douglass was confident that the emancipation of the slaves was a prerequisite for the preservation of the Union. He was certain that

> Any attempt now to separate the freedom of the slave from the victory of the Government, . . . any attempt to secure peace to the whites while leaving the blacks in chains . . . will be labor lost. The American people and the Government at Washington may refuse to recognize it for a time; but the "inexorable logic of events" will force it upon them in the end; that the war now being waged in this land is a war for and against slavery; and that it can never be effectually put down till one or the other of these vital forces is completely destroyed.[15]

Blacks, whether slaves or free, had an emotional involvement in the war that was different in texture from that which engulfed whites on both sides of the dispute. Blacks in the North were not immune to expressions of patriotic fervor, but for them the war had a meaning deeper than just the preservation of the Union. Affronted by the South's brazen action in defense of slavery, free blacks must have felt personally wounded, and slaves who were aware of the war's ramifications must have quietly bided their time. A few free blacks in the South, particularly in New Orleans and Charleston, supported the Confederacy. Some acted out of fear of reprisals from whites; others had fallen victim to sectional pride and confused the interests of whites with their own. A few were slaveowners who sought to protect their own interests. Writing to the governor of South Carolina, a number of Charleston's free blacks expressed their support for the war:

> In our veins flows the blood of the white race, in some half, in others much more than half white blood, . . . our attachments are with you,

our hopes and safety and protection from you, . . . our allegiance is due to South Carolina and in her defense, we will offer up our lives, and all that is dear to us.[16]

Many Northern whites who knew that the war was not an emancipation crusade reminded their free black neighbors that it was "a white man's war." But this hardly deterred blacks from expressing their loyalty to the Union and volunteering their support for it. Any struggle against proslavery forces was their own. And many, like Frederick Douglass, believed that the war would bring about slavery's end.

There were obstacles, however, that stood in the path of free blacks serving in the Union's army. They had been forbidden by a federal statute to serve in state militias and had also been excluded from the nation's army. Consequently, some petitioned the government to allow them to serve in the war. The secretary of war, Simon Cameron, however, rejected such early requests, noting in 1861 that his department "has no intention at present to call into the service of the Government any colored soldiers."[17]

This slap in the face did not seem to lower the degree of enthusiasm shared by free blacks for the war. It was hardly the first time that white society had treated them like pariahs. But their early recognition that the conflict could be transformed into a war for emancipation gave them the resolve to keep trying for induction into military service. Not all free blacks in the North approved of such endeavors, however. Some maintained that the war was a proslavery exercise in the sense that its impetus was to preserve the Union and keep slavery where it existed. A black person who wrote to the *Anglo-African*, a New York newspaper, emphatically opposed blacks' serving in the war: "No regiments of black troops should leave their bodies to rot upon the battlefield beneath a Southern sun, to conquer a peace based upon the perpetuity of human bondage," he wrote.[18]

Other blacks could not conceive of fighting for a Union that denied them the basic rights of citizenship and debased them as persons. "If the colored people," wrote an Ohio man, "under all the social and legal disabilities by which they are environed, are ever ready to defend the government that despoils them of their rights, it may be concluded that it is quite safe to oppress them . . . it is absurd to suppose that the fact of tendering our services to settle a domestic war when we know that our services will be contemptuously rejected, will procure a practical acknowledgement of our rights."[19]

The writer spoke the views of many, but such voices constituted a minority among free blacks outside of the slave states. Yet, as the war began, small cracks appeared in the wall of opposition to the participation of blacks. General Benjamin F. Butler, who commanded the federal forces in Virginia, for example, provided sanctuary to escaped slaves and used them in the service of the union. Why should the Confederacy "be allowed the use of this property against the United States and we not be allowed its use in aid of the United States?" Butler enquired. The general's actions were followed by his peers. Butler wanted his government, however, to determine the legal status of the confiscated human property. "Are these men, women and children slaves? Are they free?" he asked the War Department.[20] A partial answer came with the passage of the Act of Confiscation on August 6, 1861. The act was silent on the legal status of these persons, but it permitted the confiscation of the property of those engaged in treasonous conduct, such as secession. In essence, this meant that slaves who were directly involved in the Confederate War effort could be seized. A few weeks later, on August 30, General John C. Frémont issued a proclamation emancipating all the slaves of the Confederates in Missouri. Lincoln rejected the order, maintaining that it went beyond the act of August 6, which allowed only the confiscation of slaves directly involved in the war effort. While this pleased the proslavery forces and those who still maintained that the war was not being fought to liberate the slaves, abolitionists like Frederick Douglass were outraged. "To fight against slaveholders, without fighting against slavery," Douglass observed, "is a half-hearted business, and paralyzes the hands engaged in it. . . . Fire must be met with water. . . . War for the destruction of liberty must be met with war for the destruction of slavery."[21]

The Lincoln administration was not yet prepared to admit blacks to the army formally, liberate all the slaves in occupied rebel states, or even declare emancipation as one of the objectives of the war. Although the North had suffered spectacular defeats at Bull Run in Virginia and victory over the Confederacy was nowhere in sight, two centuries of deepseated racism prevented the Union from enlisting black troops. On the other hand, the Confederacy benefitted from the labor of its slaves in a variety of ways. They produced and cooked the food for the army, transported war supplies, built fortifications, and freed the white soldiers from a range of menial and backbreaking chores. Frederick Douglass, in his usual expressive phraseology, claimed, "the very stomach of this rebellion is the negro in the form of a slave. Arrest that hoe in the hands of the negro, and you smite the rebellion in the very seat of its life."[22]

The Union took its first tentative steps against slavery in 1862, but not in the Confederacy, where it was strongest. Acting under pressure from Radical Republicans and abolitionists, Congress struck at slavery in the District of Columbia where it was most vulnerable. The measure abolished slavery in the national capital and granted slaveowners $300 for the loss of each one of their chattel. After some deliberation, Lincoln signed the measure into law, prompting Douglass to declare: "It is the first step, toward a redeemed and regenerated nation."[23]

The emancipation of the 3,000 slaves in the district was the occasion for celebration by free blacks. Churches held services of thanks, and many persons commemorated the occasion with speeches and passed resolutions of gratitude. J. Madison Bell, a black poet who lived in San Francisco, expressed the sentiments of many in the following way:

> Thank God! from our old ensign
> Is erased one mark of shame
> Which leaves one less to rapine
> One less to blight our fame[24]

The jubilation in the nation's capital was tempered by the knowledge that many whites, including Lincoln, wanted to transport free blacks outside of the country. The president was not a newcomer to the idea of colonization. As early as 1854 he confessed, "My first impulse would be to free all the slaves, and send them back to Liberia, to their own native land."[25] When Congress abolished slavery in the District of Columbia, it also appropriated $100,000 to help resettle those newly freed as well as others who "may desire to emigrate." In July 1862, Congress approved the spending of an additional $500,000 for colonizing confiscated slaves elsewhere.

President Lincoln lobbied among free blacks for support of his colonization scheme. But he found little support for a proposal that rested on the premise that blacks could live in the United States only as slaves. "There is an unwillingness on the part of our people," Lincoln told a visiting delegation of black men in 1862, "harsh as it may be, for you free colored people to remain among us."[26] Lincoln expressed the sentiments of many whites, and few of them could contemplate a situation where all blacks were free. Senator Henry Clay, a dogged defender of the white South and its institutions, expressed the view in 1830 that it "would be unwise" to liberate the slaves "without their removal or colonization." A farmer in Mississippi guessed that "the majority would be right glad [to abolish slavery] if we could get rid of the niggers. But it wouldn't never do to free 'em and leave 'em here. I don't know anybody hardly, in favor of that. Make 'em free and leave 'em here and they'd steal everything we made. Nobody couldn't live here then." A Northern editor was alarmed at "the danger of encouraging a distinct and inferior race to abide in the same community with us. They are aliens and enemies and some mode should be adopted to rid the country of their presence."[27]

Many free blacks took issue with such racist assessments of them. They reiterated the position that America was their native land and that they would not abandon it voluntarily. Others denounced the injustice of such colonization schemes. A number of Philadelphians informed the president, "We can find nothing in the religion of our Lord and Master teaching us that color is the standard by which He judges his creatures, either in this life or in the life to come." A. P. Smith, who resided in New

Jersey, went to the heart of the matter in a letter that he sent to Lincoln. "Pray tell us," he enquired, "is our right to a home in this country less than your own?"[28]

The spectacle of the president actively working to remove from the nation persons who were born there must have wounded the esteem of all black persons. Frederick Douglass was so outraged by such behavior that he accused Lincoln of harboring "contempt for negroes."[29] Yet a few hundred blacks continued to leave, as in previous years, for Canada, Haiti, and Liberia. An adamant and angry majority refused to budge. The black abolitionist Robert Purvis gave a ready explanation for the rebuff to the president: "The children of the black men have enriched the soil by their tears, and sweat, and blood. Sir we were born here, and here we choose to remain."[30]

The question of the future of free blacks did not disappear but it lost its immediacy for the white Union authorities as the war continued and the Confederacy proved to be more tenacious than had been anticipated. By mid-1862 Congress was ready to strengthen the Confiscation Act passed a year earlier. This development was a pragmatic response to the behavior of slaves held by the Confederate states and the growing realization that blacks and their labor constituted one of the principal foundations of the war effort in the rebel states.

From the inception of the war, thousands of blacks deserted the slaveowners and fled to the Union troops for sanctuary. In addition, the Union forces controlled sizable chunks of Confederate territory and the slaves that worked thereon. In May 1862, David O Hunter, the commander of the Union forces in the Southeast, ordered the emancipation of the slaves in South Carolina, Georgia, and Florida. He did this without consulting the president, who promptly rescinded the order. Hunter's actions, even if they exceeded his authority, reflected the fact that he recognized that the Union stood a much better chance of winning the war if Southern secessionists were divested of their property in slaves.

It was this thinking, along with the growing number of contraband slaves, that led to the enactment of the new confiscation law. It provided for the confiscation of the slaves owned by Southern "traitors" and declared them "forever free." The implications of this measure were far-reaching. The war was being transformed from a war to save the Union into a war to save the Union and liberate the slaves. Faced with the prospect of a war of attrition and uncertain of ultimate victory, the Union began to adjust its policy on the slavery question and its attitude to the use of black soldiers. The impending change of heart was a pragmatic response to the requirements of a war that was not progressing well; it was not the product of a conviction that it was the morally correct thing to do. As the governor of Iowa, Samuel Kirkwood, wrote: "When this war is over & we have summed up the entire loss of life it has imposed on the country I shall not have any regrets if it is found that a part of the dead are *niggers* and that *all* are not white men."[31]

The Militia Act of July 1862 showed strong congressional support for the use of black soldiers. Among other measures, the bill authorized the use of blacks in "any war service for which they may be found competent." The act was not implemented immediately, since there were still significant voices of opposition to it. President Lincoln, never one for rash action, had also begun to give serious consideration to a general emancipation of the slaves. He conveyed his intention to his cabinet, which persuaded him to wait until the military fortunes of the Union had changed and emancipation would not be perceived as the desperate act of a power that was on the verge of being vanquished.

The issue of emancipation and the fate of the slaves was clearly not the principal concern of the Lincoln administration. The preservation of the Union was paramount, and the president never ceased to make that known. In a letter written in mid-1862 to Horace Greeley, the New York newspaper editor, Lincoln wrote:

> My paramount object in this struggle *is* to save the Union, and is *not* either to save or to destroy slavery. If I could save the Union without freeing *any* slave I would do it, and if I could save it by freeing *all* the slaves I would do it; and if I could save it by freeing some and leaving others alone I would also do that. What I do about slavery, and the colored race, I do because I believe it helps to save the Union; and what I forbear, I forbear because I do *not* believe it would help save the Union. . . . I shall try to correct errors when shown to be errors; and I shall adopt new views so fast as they shall appear to be true views.
>
> I have here stated my purpose according to my view of *official* duty; and I intend no modification of my oft-expressed *personal* wish that all men every where could be free.[32]

The president's primary anguish was that for a Union threatened with collapse. From his perspective, and that of those committed to its survival, this was a defensible position. But there were others whose interests compelled attention as well. Free blacks and slaves could hardly have put the survival of the Union above freedom and justice for themselves. Even those who wished to enlist in the Union's army knew that they would be fighting for a side that scorned them as persons. Their hope was that the war contained the seeds of slavery's destruction and the promise of a just society.

The course of a war is seldom predictable, however. A war, particularly a prolonged one, also has the capacity to transform the antagonists in significant ways. Lincoln, for one, certainly had no idea in early 1861 when the war began that he would issue a preliminary Emancipation Proclamation a year and a half later. But such was the extraordinary announcement that he made on September 22, 1862. The Union's forces had just held their own at the battle of Antietam, Maryland, and the president believed the time had come to change the course of the war. In his historic announcement, he warned the secessionists to return to the national fold by January 1, 1863, or their slaves "shall be then, thence forward, and forever free." The rebel states thus were given the option to return to the Union, and in so doing, preserve slavery.[33]

The reaction to this announcement was, understandably, mixed. Blacks who had much to gain from its potential implementation expressed a guarded approval. Some, including many white abolitionists, criticized the proclamation because it did not free the slaves immediately and it would not abolish the institution in those states that laid down their arms by January 1. Slavery remained untouched in the border states. In Lincoln's defense, it may be suggested that he lacked the constitutional authority to divest citizens of their property unless they were engaged in an act of war against the state. Under the circumstances, the president had no power to free the slaves in the loyal states.

The preliminary Emancipation Proclamation gave the rebel states time to reconsider their past and future actions. For them, however, there was not much incentive to abandon their struggle; the war had gone quite well for them and this was hardly the time to settle. There was also much more at stake. The rebel states wanted to have their institutions free from assault by others, and they wanted the unconditional respect of the North. It was not clear that either would be forthcoming; a return to the Union would not heal their wounds nor shield them from abuse. Under the circumstances, the proclamation stood little chance of achieving its objective.

As January 1, 1863, approached, many wondered whether the president would abide by his pledge. Subjected to much pressure from supporters and opponents, Lincoln seemed to remain committed to the notion that the destruction of slavery was a prerequisite for the success of the Union. He still believed, however, that free blacks and whites could not live together in freedom; he tied emancipation to colonization elsewhere as late as December 1862. Lincoln also indicated that he did not anticipate a complete end to slavery until 1900, thirty-eight years later.

Lincoln kept his word. Characterizing emancipation an "act of justice," he signed the document that would effect a fundamental transformation in the relationship between blacks and whites in the United States. Because it is of such crucial importance in the history of black America, it needs to be quoted at length:

Whereas, on the twentysecond day of September, in the year of our Lord one thousand eight hundred and sixty two, a proclamation was issued by the President of the United States, containing, among other things, the following, to wit:

"That on the first day of January, in the year of our Lord one thousand eight hundred and sixty-three, all persons held as slaves within any State or designated part of a State, the people whereof shall then be in rebellion against the United States, shall be then, thenceforewards, and forever free; and the Executive Government of the United States, including the military and naval authority thereof, will recognize and maintain the freedom of such persons, and will do no act or acts to repress such persons, or any of them, in any efforts they make for their actual freedom. . . . "

And by virtue of the power and for the purpose aforesaid I do order and declare that all persons held as slaves within said designated States, and parts of States, are, and henceforward shall be free; and that the Executive government of the United States, including the military and naval authorities thereof, will recognize and maintain the freedom of said persons.

And I hereby enjoin upon the people so declared to be free to abstain from all violence, unless in necessary self-defence; and I recommend to them that, in all cases when allowed, they labor faithfully for reasonable wages.

· And I further declare and make known that such persons of suitable condition, will be received into the armed service of the United States to garrison forts, positions, stations, and other places, and to man vessels of all sorts in said service.

And upon this act, sincerely believed to be an act of justice, warranted by the Constitution, upon military necessity, I invoke the considerate judgment of mankind, and the gracious favor of Almighty God.

As important as the proclamation was for the course of the war and the history of black America, it is necessary to underscore the point that it did not apply to the border states, which remained loyal to the Union. Thus, the 450,000 slaves in Missouri, Maryland, Kentucky, and Delaware saw their legal condition unchanged. In addition, slaves in Union-occupied territory in Virginia, Louisiana, and Tennessee were not covered by the proclamation. Taken together, as many as 700,000 slaves, almost one-fifth of the slave population, were excluded. Clearly, the proclamation was as much an expression of military expediency as it was an attempt to punish the secessionists. Its inapplicability to those slaves who, by happenstance, resided in the loyal areas exposed its overriding objectives and robbed it of much moral legitimacy.

Apart from liberating the slaves in the rebel states, the proclamation paved the way for enlisting blacks in the service of the Union. All "persons of suitable condition" would now be welcomed. Its signing was greeted by an unprecedented outpouring of joy among blacks. Contemporaries described the jubilant church services, the concerts, the singing, dancing, ecstatic shouts, and tears that expressed a people's triumph after the long years of adversity. An anthem sung on the occasion captured the spirit of the celebrations:

> Sound the loud timbrel o'er Egypt's dark sea,
> Jehovah hath triumphed, his people are free.

One woman led a congregation in Washington in singing:

> Go down, Abraham, away down in Dixie's land,
> Tell Jeff Davis to let my people go.

And few supporters of emancipation could have remained unmoved by the actions of former slaves in South Carolina who claimed their place as Americans and raised their voices in song:

> My country, 'tis of thee,
> Sweet land of liberty
> of thee I sing . . .

The poet John Greenleaf Whittier welcomed the proclamation and expressed the thoughts of the liberated:

> O dark, sad millions, patiently and dumb
> Waiting for God, your hour, at last, has come
>   And Freedom's Song
> Breaks the long silence of your night of wrong!
>
> Arise and flee! Shake off the vile restraint
> of ages! but, like Ballymena's saint,
>   The oppressor spare,
> Heap only on his head the coals of prayer!
>
> Go forth, like him! like him, return again,
> To bless the land whereon in bitter pain
>   Ye toiled at first,
> And heal with freedom what your slavery cursed![34]

The Emancipation Proclamation, at one level, merely ratified a process that had been underway since the war started. Throughout the rebel states, as we have indicated, thousands of slaves had claimed their freedom by joining the invading Union troops or had escaped to the free states, effectively undermining the institution. Others refused to work for their masters unless they were paid. The institution was hemorrhaging, but no one could have predicted when it would finally suc-

Emancipation Proclamation. A celebration of newly freed slaves in Winchester, Massachusetts.

cumb. The Confiscation Acts of 1861 and 1862, as well as the Emancipation Proclamation, accelerated and legitimized the quest for freedom, but they did not create it.

The proclamation enlarged the possibilities for those blacks who were already free or who remained slaves in the Confederacy, but it could not transform white attitudes toward them. Some of the troops in the Union army opposed the intent of the Proclamation and disliked the notion that the nature of the war was being changed. As one of them declared: "I am as much in favor for the Union as any one but I am not in favor of shedding my blood for the sake of the black tribe although I think Slavery is a ruination to our government."[55] President Lincoln received a note from an officer stationed in Virginia claiming, "a decided majority of our Officers of all grades have no sympathy with your policy; nor with anything human. They hate the Negro more than they love the Union."[56]

FIGHTING FOR FREEDOM

Although the Emancipation Proclamation had transformed the war into a struggle for emancipation, blacks who had much to gain or lose from its outcome were not to be afforded a central place in the military effort.

The door for the enlistment of blacks was opened, but they were excluded from service on the front line and confined "to garrison forts, stations, and other places." But, as with other aspects of the war, matters changed. The military reverses suffered by the Union and the increasingly difficult task of finding an adequate number of white men to fight by 1863 led to dramatic policy changes. As many as 100,000 had deserted by the end of 1862, probably constituting at times as high a proportion as one tenth to one eighth of the enlistees. With widespread concern over the number of casualties, some whites were willing to accept the enlistment of blacks, since it meant that white lives would probably be saved. One soldier observed that the dead white men could not be replaced, "but if a nigger dies, all you have to do is send out and get another one."[37] A song that became popular among whites in the North in 1863 reflects the mood that helped make black enlistment feasible:

> Some tell us 'tis a burnin shame
> To make the naygers fight;
> An' that the thrade of bein' kilt
> Belongs but to the white;
> But as for me, upon my soul!
> So liberal are we here,
> I'll let Sambo be murthered instead of myself
> On every day in the year.

In fact, blacks had been unofficially admitted into the army in Louisiana, Kansas, and the South Carolina sea islands, by the summer of 1862. In early 1863 the War Department was willing to approve the creation of black regiments in Massachusetts, Connecticut, and Rhode Island. These regiments experienced no difficulty in attracting recruits, as the men responded with alacrity and enthusiasm. The *Christian Recorder*, a black newspaper published in Philadelphia, urged the men: "Go with the view that you will return freemen. And if you should never return, you will die with the satisfaction of knowing that you have struck a blow for freedom and assisted in giving liberty to our race in the land of our birth."[38] Blacks who enlisted derived enormous pride from being able to serve the cause of freedom "I felt freedom in my bones," said one man, remembering his reaction as he stood for his first roll call. Having once been officially excluded from serving in their nation's army, many now felt a special vindication. To these soldiers, it was a sign of better things to come; it was the first step toward equality and full citizenship. Becoming a soldier "was the biggest thing that ever happened in my life, I felt like a man with a uniform on and a gun in my hand," a former slave reminisced. Such confidence in their possibilities was plain enough for everyone to see. "Put a United States uniform on his back and the *chattel* is a man," a white soldier maintained.[39]

Blacks were actively recruited into the army by such prominent persons as Frederick Douglass, Martin Delany, and Henry Highland Garnet. The government established the Bureau of Colored Troops in May 1863 to coordinate the recruitment efforts and to name the white officers who commanded the segregated black regiments. By war's end, about 180,000 black men had served in the Union's army, constituting about one-tenth of all the troops who fought on that side. Table 10.1 breaks down the number who served in each state. A number of black women, including Harriet Tubman, also assisted in the war effort, serving the troops in a variety of domestic capacities. Many black men were recruited into the navy as well, beginning as early as September 1861.

As Table 10.1 demonstrates, the enlistees represented a high proportion of the available black men in the Northern free states and the border states. This was an important measure of their commitment to the cause of emancipation. Fewer blacks were able to enlist in the Confederate slave states. These soldiers, despite their obvious enthusiasm for service, found life in the army as difficult as it had been for them as civilians. They served in segregated regiments, received less pay (until 1864) than their white counterparts, the worst medical care, and were often assigned the most menial and backbreaking tasks. Many white officers did not expect much from them at first and treated them with obvious condescension. Accustomed to expressions of white arrogance in civilian life, the black recruits were sensitive to such treatment in the army. Some challenged the authority of the white officers when it was clear to them that they were being demeaned because of their race. "I am as good as any white man, and I'll be damned if I'll be bossed over by any of them," insisted one recruit.[40] They objected to certain forms of punishment such as bondage that reminded them of slavery, and they chafed under a system of military justice that often reflected the biases of civilian society. Black troops comprised 21 percent of all the soldiers executed for crimes although they constituted less than 10 percent of the men in uniform.[41]

In addition to racist slights and treatment, blacks were angered that none of them served as commissioned officers at first. Major General N. P. Banks believed that black officers would be "detrimental to the service" and be a source of demoralization for "the white troops and the negroes." Unwilling to be so disparaged, the soldiers demanded a change of policy. Toward the end of the war, the War Department relented and named some black commissioned officers. They included the emigrationist Martin Delany. The soldiers also launched a vigorous campaign to obtain equal pay. "Now your Excellency," some wrote to President Lincoln, "we have done a Soldier's duty. Why can't we have a Soldier's pay?"[42] Congress acquiesced in June 1864.

TABLE 10.1

Black Soldiers in the Union Army and Black Male Population of Military Age in 1860, by State

| | BLACK MALE POPULATION AGES 18 TO 45 | | | BLACK SOLDIERS | |
STATE	FREE	SLAVE	TOTAL	NUMBER CREDITED TO THE STATE	PERCENTAGE OF BLACK MEN AGES 18 TO 45
Northern free states					
Maine	272	–	272	104	
New Hampshire	103	–	103	125	
Vermont	140	–	140	120	
Massachusetts	1,973	–	1,973	3,966	
Connecticut	1,760	–	1,760	1,764	
Rhode Island	809	–	809	1,837	
New York	10,208	–	10,208	4,125	
New Jersey	4,866	–	4,866	1,185	
Pennsylvania	10,844	–	10,844	8,612	
District of Columbia[a]	1,823	–	1,823	3,269	
Ohio	7,161	–	7,161	5,092	
Indiana	2,219	–	2,219	1,537	
Illinois	1,622	–	1,622	1,811	
Michigan	1,622	–	1,622	1,387	
Wisconsin	292	–	292	165	
Minnesota	61	–	61	104	
Iowa	249	–	249	440	
Kansas	126	–	126	2,080	
Subtotal	46,150	–	46,150	37,723	
Black soldiers recruited in Confederate states but credited to Northern free states[b]				(5,052)	
Total				32,671	71

NOTE: The percentage of each state's black military–age population that entered the army is merely an approximation, because fugitive slaves frequently enlisted in regiments outside their home states (the number of black soldiers credited in Kansas and the District of Columbia, for example, was notably swelled by such enlistments), and other population movements make the 1860 census figure somewhat inadequate for comparison with enlistment statistics. Because early Massachusetts, Connecticut, and Rhode Island black regiments recruited throughout the North, state-by-state computation of population percentages for the free states would be misleading: hence, only a regional percentage is given.

[a]Congress had already ended slavery in the District of Columbia at the time these population figures were compiled.

TABLE 10.1 CONTINUED

| STATE | BLACK MALE POPULATION AGES 18 TO 45 | | | BLACK SOLDIERS | |
	FREE	SLAVE	TOTAL	NUMBER CREDITED TO THE STATE	PERCENTAGE OF BLACK MEN AGES 18 TO 45
Union slave states					
Delaware	3,597	289	3,886	954	25
Maryland	15,149	16,108	31,257	8,718	28
Missouri	701	20,466	21,167	8,344	39
Kentucky	1,650	40,285	41,935	23,703	57
Total	21,097	77,148	98,245	41,719	42
Confederate states					
Virginia	9,309	92,119	101,428	5,919[c]	6
North Carolina	5,150	55,020	60,170	5,035	8
South Carolina	1,522	70,798	72,320	5,462	8
Florida	131	12,028	12,159	1,044	9
Georgia	583	83,819	84,402	3,486	4
Alabama	391	83,945	84,336	4,969	6
Mississippi	130	85,777	85,907	17,869	21
Louisiana	3,205	75,548	78,753	24,052	31
Texas	62	36,140	36,202	47	(less than 1)
Arkansas	22	23,088	23,110	5,526	24
Tennessee	1,162	50,047	51,209	20,133	39
Subtotal	21,667	668,329	689,996	93,542	
Black soldiers recruited in Confederate states but credited to Northern free states[b]				5,052	
Total				98,594	14
Other areas	2,041[d]	2,041	5,991[e]		
Total for all areas	90,955	745,477	836,432	178,975	21

[b]Enlisted under the act of July 4, 1864, that permitted Northern state agents to recruit blacks in the Confederate states.

[c]See *Official Records*, ser. 3, vol. 5, p. 662. Virginia, 5.723; West Virginia, 196.

[d]California 1,918, Oregon 38, Colorado 5, Nebraska 15, Nevada 27, New Mexico 16, Utah 5, Washington 17.

[e]Colorado Territory 95, and state or territory unknown 5,896.

SOURCES: Population figures come from a report by the superintendent of the Census, based upon the 1860 census (see pp. 87–88); the number of black soldiers credited to each state is given in the 1865 report of the Bureau of Colored Troops (*Official Records*, ser. 3, vol. 5, p. 138).

SOURCE: Ira Berlin, ed., *Freedom: A Documentary History of Emancipation, 1861–1867,* Series ii, The Black Military Experience, (Cambridge University Press, Cambridge and New York, 1982), p. 12.

Black soldiers were singled out by Confederate armies for the most brutal treatment. Black men in uniform reminded Southern whites that they had been divested of their human property. Resentful of this development, alarmed at the potential collapse of their social order, and mortified by the spectacle of former slaves confronting them in battle, Southern white soldiers reacted with particular ferocity in any combat with blacks. Confederate troops summarily executed captured black soldiers. Their officers suffered similar fates. One white soldier in North Carolina reported that members of a black regiment were "taken prisoner [and] afterwards either bayoneted or burnt. The men were perfectly exasperated at the idea of negroes opposed to them [and] rushed at them like so many devils."[43] Describing the treatment of blacks who were captured by Confederate troops in North Carolina in 1864, a Union sergeant said:

> All the negroes found in blue uniform or with any outward marks of a Union soldier upon him was killed–I saw some taken into the woods and hung–Others I saw stripped of all their clothing, and they stood upon the bank of the river with their faces riverwards and then they were shot–Still others were killed by having their brains beaten out by the butt end of the muskets in the hands of the Rebels–
>
> All were not killed the day of the capture–Those that were not, were placed in a room with their officers, they [the officers] having previously been dragged through the town with ropes around their necks, where they were kept confined until the following morning when the remainder of the black soldiers were killed.[44]

The Confederacy steadfastly refused to acknowledge captured black soldiers as prisoners of war and accorded them no rights. The Confederate secretary of war, James Seddon, directed his troops, "never to be inconvenienced with such prisoners . . . summary execution must therefore be inflicted on those taken." The men took such orders seriously. In 1864 at Fort Pillow, Tennessee, they murdered scores of black soldiers and some whites after they had surrendered. "Kill the damned Niggers," the Confederate soldiers shouted as the butchery continued. General Nathan Forrest who commanded the Confederate troops, boasted, "It is hoped that these facts will demonstrate to the Northern people that negro soldiers cannot cope with Southerners." He would later emphasize that he regarded "captured negroes as I do other captured property and not as captured soldiers."[45] The treatment of black soldiers by the Confederate troops was a horrible expression of hatred and racism gone amok.

Black soldiers, however, must have especially enjoyed their confrontations with former owners. Some undoubtedly had scores to settle with members of the slavocracy and must have reclaimed parts of their personhood in so doing. Time and time again Confederate troops fearing reprisals avoided surrendering to black troops or fled at their approach. One white soldier reported that in 1865 at Fort Blakely, Alabama, the Confederate soldiers were "panic-struck. Numbers of them jumped into the river and were drowned attempting to cross, or were shot while swimming. Still others threw down their arms and run for their lives over to the white troops on our left, to give themselves up, to save being butchered by our niggers [;] the niggers did not take a prisoner, they killed all they took to a man."[46] Perhaps it was this need to dominate former oppressors that contributed to the extraordinary bravery of some of these soldiers. In May 1863, for example, as the First Louisiana Regiment prepared to assault Port Hudson, Louisiana, a Confederate bastion, the troops were fortified by the recognition that the war had become theirs and the outcome would be fraught with personal, racial, and professional meaning. George H. Baker, a poet, commemorated the battle in the following way:

"Now," the flag-sergeant cried,
"Though death and hell betide,
Let the whole nation see
If we are fit to be
Free in this land; or bound
Down, like the whining hound-
Bound with red stripes of pain
In our old chains again!"
Oh! What a shout there went
From the black regiment![47]

By the time the battle ended, almost two hundred black soldiers had died. In spite of their defeat, General N. P. Banks, who was in command, observed, "The position occupied by these troops was one of importance, and called for their utmost steadiness and bravery. . . . It gives me pleasure to report that they answered every expectation. No troops could be more determined or more daring."[48] The *New York Times,* which had entertained doubts about the ability of black troops, agreed:

Those black soldiers had never before been in any severe engagement. They were comparatively raw troops, and were yet subjected to the most awful ordeal than even veterans ever have to experience–the charging upon fortifications through the crash of belching batteries. The men, white or black, who will not flinch from that will flinch from nothing. It is no longer possible to doubt the bravery and steadiness of the colored race, when rightly led.[49]

The Fifty-Fourth Massachusetts Infantry Regiment captured the popular imagination in the battle of Fort Wagner, South Carolina, in July

1863. Fighting alongside white soldiers, the Fifty-Fourth led the attack on the Confederate stronghold. Essentially a suicide mission, the men confronted heavy fire from the enemy soldiers at the fort. The regiment lost 34 men, and 146 were wounded and 92 were reported captured or missing. The *Atlantic Monthly* magazine celebrated the bravery and sacrifice of the men by noting, "Through the cannon smoke of that dark night, the manhood of the colored race shines before many eyes that would not see."[50]

Brigadier General George C. Strong was equally impressed by the valor of the black troops. "Under cover of darkness," he reported, "they had stormed the fort, faced a stream of fire, faltered not till the ranks were broken by shot and shell; and in all these severe tests, which would have tried even veteran troops, they fully met my expectations, for many were killed, wounded, or captured on the walls of the fort." An eyewitness agreed: "I saw them fight at Wagner as none but splendid soldiers, splendidly officered, could fight, dashing through shot and shell, grape, canister, and shrapnel, and showers of bullets, . . ."[51]

The record is replete with similar expressions of praise for the battlefield performance of black soldiers. They accepted dangerous assignments or volunteered for them. Wishing to prove their mettle to the nation at large and fighting for the cause of black freedom, they displayed the requisite enthusiasm, and courage. President Lincoln recognized their contributions to the changing fortunes of the Union's forces when he wrote in mid-1863:

> I know . . . that some of the commanders . . . in the field . . . now believe that the emancipation policy and the use of colored troops constitute the heaviest blow yet dealt to the rebellion and that at least one of the important successes could not have been achieved but for the aid of black soldiers.[52]

Lincoln, whose capacity as a leader grew as the war continued, chided his white countrymen for their opposition to the use of black soldiers. He predicted that at war's end, "There will be some black men who can remember that, with silent tongue, and clenched teeth, and steady eye, and well-poised bayonet, they have helped mankind on to this great consummation; while, I fear, there will be some white ones, unable to forget that, with malignant heart, and deceitful speech, they have strove to hinder it."[53]

Black casualties in the war were often disproportionately higher than those for whites. But that was the price they were willing to pay for the defeat of the Confederacy and the emancipation of their people. In spite of their military hardships–high casualties, lower pay, racial discrimination–contemporary accounts suggest that they never lost sight of their principal mission and that they conducted themselves with confidence and even good humor.

The story is told of an elderly black man who visited Robert E. Lee, the Confederate general during the war:

"General Lee," said the visitor, "I been wanting to see you a long time. I'm a soldier."

"Ah? To what army do you belong–to the Union army or to the Southern army?"

"Oh, General, I belong to your army."

"Well, have you been shot?"

"No, sir, I ain't been shot yet."

"How is that? Nearly all of our men get shot."

"Why, General, I ain't been shot 'cause I stay back whar de generals stay."[54]

The role of the black enlistees increased as the war dragged on. By 1864, there were about 100,000 black men in uniform, in more than 60 regiments. In all, blacks participated in 449 battles and lost 37,300 men. Although they were deployed in almost all of the principal battles, the lot of providing support services for the army fell disproportionately on their shoulders. Still, enough of them served on the front lines to continue to receive favorable notice for their valor. Although the Union lost the Battle of Olustee in Florida in early 1864, General Truman Seymour could still report:

> The colored troops behaved creditably,–the Fifty-Fourth Massachusetts and First North Carolina like veterans. It was not in their conduct that could be found the chief cause of failure, but in the unanticipated yielding of a white regiment.[55]

Black soldiers, in spite of their proven abilities, constantly had to prove to their white peers that they could discharge all of their military responsibilities. White soldiers, like the majority of white society, found it difficult to exorcise a racism that had become systemic. Their deeply held belief that blacks were inferior accounts for the surprise that white soldiers expressed at the frequently outstanding performance of the black troops. Consider the observation of Colonel S. G. Hicks, who commanded the troops at Union City, Tennessee, in 1864: "And here permit me to remark that I have been one of those men who never had much confidence in colored troops fighting, but those doubts are now all removed, for they fought as bravely as any troops in the fort."[56]

As the Confederate forces retreated in 1864, their beleaguered Congress considered the question of arming the slaves. This was a discussion born of desperation, a clear indication that the Confederate cause was in deep trouble. This contemplation of the use of slaves, however, was similar to the North's belated recognition that its success depended on black military support. In endorsing the arming of slaves, the *Jackson Mississippian* maintained, "Yankee success is death to the institution . . .

. . . so that it is a question of necessity–a question of choice of evils. . . .
We must . . . save ourselves from the rapacious North, WHATEVER
THE COST."[57]

Supporters of this position recognized that even if the Confederate
cause prevailed, the arming of the slaves and their service in war might
enhance the cause of their emancipation. But this was a risk some were
prepared to take. The *Mississippian* gave voice to such concerns: "Let
not slavery prove a barrier to our independence. Although slavery is one
of the principles that we started to fight for . . . if it proves an unsur-
mountable obstacle to the achievement of our liberty and separate
nationality, away with it!"[58] As their military fortunes worsened, the
Confederate House of Representatives endorsed the arming of slaves in
February 1865. General Robert E. Lee supported the measure, but there
were important voices of dissent. Howell Cobb, of Georgia, a former
speaker of the U. S. House of Representatives who became a Confederate general, could hardly conceal his displeasure at the prospect of
blacks in the service of the Confederacy: ". . . the moment you resort to
negro soldiers your white soldiers will be lost to you," he complained.
". . . The day you make soldiers of them is the beginning of the end of
the revolution. If slaves will make good soldiers our whole theory of
slavery is wrong."[59] Cobb had a point. But his fears were never realized,
since the Confederate Senate refused to go along with the House and the
measure was stillborn.

By refusing to arm their slaves even to aid their cause, Confederate
politicians emphasized that there was no place in "Southern Civilization" for blacks except as slaves. The debate over the use of slaves in the
Confederate army aroused racist passions, and opponents of the measure–and supporters–reaffirmed their commitment to white supremacy.
The use of such soldiers, observed one newspaper, would mean that
poor whites would be "reduced to the level of a nigger."[60] It may be suggested that in this instance the principles of the Southerners, albeit pernicious ones, triumphed over self-interest and expediency.

In the end, the debate had little political or military significance.
President Lincoln was reelected in the election of 1864 in spite of scur-
rilous attacks from racist Democrats who accused him and the Republicans of all manner of evils, including the promotion of miscegenation.
The Emancipation Proclamation was renamed the "Miscegenation
Proclamation." The specter of huge numbers of blacks who were no
longer slaves continued to frighten many Northern whites, to say nothing of their Southern counterparts. A New York Catholic newspaper,
which should have been guided by higher principles, denounced Lincoln as "brutal in all his habits. . . . He is obscene. . . . He is an animal. . . . Filthy black niggers, greasy, sweaty, and disgusting, now jos-
tle white people and even ladies everywhere, even at the President's
levees."[61]

Undeterred, Lincoln renewed his support for the adoption of a constitutional amendment–the Thirteenth Amendment–to end slavery. Such a measure had been passed in the Senate in mid-1864, but Democrats marshalled enough opposition to defeat it in the House. But much had changed between June 1864 and January 1865, when the two legislatures gave the measure the required two-thirds majority. The amendment was ratified by the states by the end of the year, although Delaware, New Jersey, and Kentucky–all loyal states–declined to do so.

With the adoption of the Thirteenth Amendment, the rest was an anticlimax. After its resounding defeat at Richmond, the Confederacy gave up the struggle in April 1865, and the nation now had to tend its self-inflicted wounds. Joyful beyond belief, the newly-freed blacks proclaimed Lincoln a Messiah as they contemplated the start of a new life, or so it seemed in those halycon days. Frances Ellen Watkins Harper was moved to write this simple patriotic poem of praise and hope:

> God bless our native land,
>   Land of the newly free,
> Oh may she ever stand
>   For truth and liberty.
>
> God bless our native land,
>   Where sleep our kindred dead,
> Let peace at thy command
>   Above their graves be shed.
>
> God bless our native land,
>   Bring surcease to her strife,
> And shower from thy hand
>   A more abundant life.
>
> God bless our native land,
>   Her homes and children bless,
> Oh may she ever stand
>   For truth and righteousness.[62]

Fannie Berry, a domestic slave in Richmond, recalled the day when the Confederacy surrendered:

Never was no time like 'em befo' or since. Niggers shoutin' an' clappin' hands an' singin'! Chillun runnin' all over de place beatin' tins an' yellin'. Ev'ybody happy. Sho' did some celebratin! Run to de kitchen an' shout in de winder:

> *Mammy, don't you cook no mo'*
> *You's free! You's free!*

Run to the henhouse an' shout:
Rooster, don't you crow no mo'
You's free! You's free!
Ol' hen, don't you lay no mo' eggs,
You's free! You's free!

Go to de pigpen an' tell de pig.
O'l pig, don't you grunt no mo'
You's free! You's free!

Tell de cows:
O'l cow, don't you give no mo' milk,
You's free! You's free![63]

But there was angry retribution as well. Caddy, a slave woman in Mississippi, "threw down" her hoe when she heard of the surrender. According to the account rendered by her descendants, ". . . she marched herself up to the big house, then, she looked around and found the mistress. She went over to the mistress, she flipped up her dress and told the white woman to do something. She said it mean and ugly. This is what she said: *KISS MY ASS!*"[64]

Emancipation came two and a half centuries after the English began using coerced black labor on America's soil. Ironically, by seceding, Southerners hastened the destruction of the institution that they wanted to preserve and the cherished social order that they created. President Lincoln had no plans to interfere with slavery in 1861, and were it not for the war, it would most certainly have survived for some time longer. No one could have predicted its life expectancy with certainty or the manner of its passing. But slavery was in no danger of succumbing from the abolitionists' onslaught in 1861, and there had been no slave rebellions of consequence since 1831. This, of course, was hardly a prescription for complacency or inertia insofar as white society was concerned. Slavery was also still highly profitable at the outbreak of the war, and no one claimed that its material strength had been spent.

Under the circumstances, it took a bloody and prolonged war to end an institution that had become deeply embedded in the nation's fabric and in its psychology. The war to save the Union eventually became a war to liberate the slaves. The North faced the prospect of defeat if the slaves had not been freed. But emancipation was never predicted in early 1861, and many whites came to embrace that possibility only when the war appeared to be increasingly protracted and even unwinnable and the destruction of the Union loomed. Essentially a pragmatic decision born of military necessity, emancipation lacked moral legitimacy. Had whites in the North and the South abandoned slavery because it was morally wrong, the nation would have been spared much of the racially sanctioned atrocities that followed in the wake of 1865 and that contradicted the timeless principles upon which the nation was founded.

Emancipation had personal significance for every black person. The four million slaves were no longer chattel, and the profound meaning that freedom held for them can only be imagined. Many of them had claimed their freedom before war's end by escaping, negotiating for wages, and refusing to work for their masters or to be relocated to safer ground. Thousands of blacks served in the Union's forces, thereby contributing to their liberation. Many acquired leadership skills in battle, forged alliances and friendships with white soldiers, and demonstrated a boundless confidence in themselves and their possibilities. In 1863, Frederick Douglass wrote: "Once let the black man get upon his person the brass letters, U.S.; let him get the eagle on his button, and a musket on his shoulder and bullets in his pocket, and there is no power on earth which can deny that he has earned the right to citizenship."[65] Many would try to cash in on these claims after 1865. Emancipation had closed an unhappy chapter in black life, but its promise would not be easily achieved.

Still, the disappointments that freedom brought were not present in the days that immediately followed the war. The moment had to be savored, emotions expressed, and unbounded praise rendered. The following ballad celebrated the release from slavery's chains and the affirmation of a people's spirit:

Slavery chain done broke at last!
Broke at last! Broke at last!
Slavery chain done broke at last!
Gonna praise God till I die!

Way up in that valley,
Pray-in' on my knees,
Tell-in' God a-bout my troubles,
And to help me if He please.

I did tell him how I suffer,
In the dungeon and the chain;
And the days I went with head bowed down,
An' my broken flesh and pain.

I did know my Jesus heard me
'Cause the spirit spoke to me,
An' said, "Rise, my chile, your children
An' you too shall be free."

I done 'p'int one mighty captain
For to marshal all my hosts;
An' to bring my bleeding ones to me,
An' not one shall be lost.

Now no more weary trav'lin',
'Cause my Jesus set me free,
An' there's no more auction block for me
Since He give me liberty.

Notes

1. Ruth Bogin and Jean Fagan Yellin, Introduction in their *Abolitionist Sisterhood*, 7.
2. Foner, *Politics and Ideology*, 53.
3. Eric Foner, *Free Soil, Free Labor, Free Men: The Ideology of the Republican Party Before the Civil War* (New York: Oxford, 1970), 311.
4. McPherson, *Battle Cry of Freedom*, 182.
5. Ibid., 187.
6. Ibid., 186.
7. Ibid., 184.
8. Ibid., 230.
9. Smith, *The Death of Slavery*, 164.
10. James McPherson, *The Negro's Civil War: How American Negroes Felt and Acted during the War for the Union* (Urbana: University of Illinois Press, 1982), 8.
11. Ibid., 9.
12. McPherson, *Battle Cry of Freedom*, 243.
13. Ibid., 244.
14. Ibid., 263.
15. McPherson, *The Negro's Civil War*, 17–18.
16. Leon Litwack, *Been in the Storm So Long*, 17.
17. McPherson, *The Negro's Civil War*, 21.
18. Ibid., 31.
19. Ibid., 29–30.
20. McPherson, *Battle Cry of Freedom*, 355.
21. Ibid., 354.
22. Ibid.
23. Benjamin Quarles, *The Negro in the Civil War* (Boston: Little Brown, 1953), 140.
24. Ibid., 141.
25. Ibid., 145.
26. McPherson, *Battle Cry of Freedom*, 508.
27. Allan Nevins, *Ordeal of the Union*, 4 vols. (New York: Charles Scribner's Sons, 1947–1951), i, 422–423.
28. Quarles, *The Negro in the Civil War*, 149–150.
29. McPherson, *Battle Cry of Freedom*, 509.
30. Quarles, *The Negro in the Civil War*, 157.
31. Ira Berlin, Barbara Fields et al., *Slaves No More: Three Essays on Emancipation and the Civil War* (New York: Cambridge University Press, 1992), 46.
32. John Hope Franklin, *The Emancipation Proclamation* (Garden City, NY: Doubleday, 1963), 28.
33. Ibid., 40.

34. Ibid., 143.
35. Glatthaar, *Forged in Battle*, 28.
36. Ibid., 10.
37. Litwack, *Been in the Storm So Long*, 67.
38. Ibid., 77.
39. Glatthaar, *Forged in Battle*, 79.
40. Ibid., 113.
41. Ibid., 118.
42. Ibid., 176, 171.
43. McPherson, *Battle Cry of Freedom*, 566.
44. Ibid., 793.
45. *Ibid.*, 793; Hondon B. Hargrove, *Black Union Soldiers in the Civil War* (Jefferson, NC: McFarland, 1988), 172, 176.
46. Glatthaar, *Forged in Battle*, 158.
47. Quarles, *The Negro in the Civil War*, 216.
48. Hargrove, *Black Union Soldiers*, 136.
49. Glatthaar, *Forged in Battle*, 130.
50. McPherson, *Battle Cry of Freedom*, 686.
51. Hargrove, *Black Union Soldiers*, 158.
52. Ibid., 160.
53. McPherson, *Battle Cry of Freedom*, 687.
54. Quarles, *The Negro in the Civil War*, 266–267.
55. Hargrove, *Black Union Soldiers*, 167.
56. Ibid., 169.
57. McPherson, *Battle Cry of Freedom*, 832.
58. Ibid., 833.
59. Ibid., 835.
60. Ibid., 836.
61. Ibid., 790.
62. Quarles, *The Negro in the Civil War*, 346.
63. Litwack, *Been in the Storm So Long*, 172–173.
64. Ibid., 187.
65. McPherson, *Battle Cry of Freedom*, 564.

Further Reading

The literature on black life between 1619 and 1863 is now so enormous that I shall confine my suggestions to recently published works and those that are easily accessible. The periodical literature is particularly vast, and it is impossible to mention those titles here. I refer readers to Paul Finkelman's eighteen-volume compilation of 400 articles on slavery. I shall identify the relevant volumes in the essay that follows. In keeping with the philosophical tone of this book, I shall recommend only those works that deal significantly with the history of black Americans, as opposed to the history of the nation.

GENERAL WORKS

There are numerous general studies of the evolution of black life and culture. John Hope Franklin and Alfred A. Moss Jr., *From Slavery to Freedom: A History of Negro Americans,* 7th edition (New York, 1994) is a classic work. John M. Boles *Black Southerners: 1619–1869* is also useful. Other noteworthy surveys include Vincent Harding, *There Is a River: The Black Struggle for Freedom in America* (New York, 1981); and August Meier and Elliott M. Rudwick, *From Plantation to Ghetto,* 3rd edition (New York, 1976). For significant studies that focus on the instiution of slavery over the long haul, see John Blassingame, *The Slave Community: Plantation Life in the Antebellum South* (New York, 1979); Peter Kolchin, *American Slavery, 1619–1877* (New York, 1993); and

Ulrich B. Phillips, *American Negro Slavery*, reprint (Baton Rouge, 1966), which is an older work that has endured in spite of its racially inspired claims. Stanley Elkins, *Slavery: A Problem in American Institutional and Intellectual Life* (Chicago, 1959) triggered a substantial debate on the impact of slavery on its victims and remains a valuable resource. It should be read along with Ann Lane, ed., *The Debate Over Slavery: Stanley Elkins and his Critics* (Urbana, 1971).

Recent debates on the historiography of slavery are addressed by a fine set of articles republished in Paul Finkelman, ed., *Slavery and Historiography* (New York, 1989). Readers interested in questions relating to the historiography of slavery in the Americas as a whole should also consult Paul Finkelman, ed., *Comparative Issues in Slavery* (New York, 1989). See also Frank Tannenbaum, *Slave and Citizen*, reprint (Boston, 1992). For an excellent discussion of methodological approaches to the study of the peoples of African descent, see Sidney Mintz and Richard Price, *The Birth of African American Culture: An Anthropological Perspective* (Boston, 1992).

AFRICA AND THE PEOPLING OF BLACK AMERICA

The study of blacks in the Americas should be preceded by a wide reading in the history and culture of the African societies from which they descended. A fine general history of Africa is Philip Curtin et al., *African History* (New York, 1978). For studies of specific regions see Anne Hilton, *The Kingdom of Kongo* (Oxford, 1985); John K. Thornton, *Kingdom of Kongo: Civil War and Transition, 1641–1718* (Madison, 1983); Wyatt MacGaffey, *Religion and Society in Central Africa: The BaKongo of Lower Zaire* (Chicago, 1986); Jan Vansina, *Paths in the Rainforests: Toward a History of Political Tradition in Equitorial Africa* (London, 1990); Joseph C. Miller, *Kings and Kinsmen: Early States Among the Mbundu of Angola* (Oxford, 1976); Robin Law, *The Oyo Empire, c. 1600–c. 1836* (Oxford, 1977); Alan F. C. Ryder, *Benin and the Europeans, 1485–1897* (London, 1969); I. A. Akinjogbin, *Dahomey and its Neighbours, 1708–1818* (London, 1967); J. K. Fynn, *Asante and its Neighbors, 1700–1807* (Evanston, 1971); Anthony G. Hopkins, *An Economic History of West Africa* (New York, 1973); Philip D. Curtin, *Economic Change in Precolonial Africa: Senegambia in the Era of the Slave Trade* (Madison, 1975); and Walter Rodney, *A History of the Upper Guinea Coast 1545–1800* (Oxford, 1970). For studies of African slave systems, see Suzanne Miers and Igor Kopytoff, eds., *Slavery in Africa: Historical and Anthropological Perspectives* (Madison, 1977); Paul Lovejoy, *Transformations in Slavery: A History of Slavery in Africa* (Cambridge, 1983); and Patrick Manning, *Slavery and African Life: Occidental, Oriental, and African Slave Trades* (Cambridge, 1990). John Thornton provides a provocative discussion of the Africans' impact on the Americas in *Africa and Africans in the Making of the Atlantic World, 1400–1680* (Cambridge, 1992).

The slave trade to the Americas is well studied. For an outstanding discussion of the numerical distribution of the slaves, see Philip D. Curtin, *The Atlantic Slave Trade: A Census* (Madison, 1969). The best general study of the organization of the trade is James A. Rawley, *The Transatlantic Slave Trade: A History* (New York, 1981). Other significant works are Jay Coughtry, *The Notorious Triangle: Rhode Island and the African Slave Trade, 1700–1807* (Philadelphia, 1981); Herbert S. Klein, *The Middle Passage: Comparative Studies in the Atlantic Slave Trade* (Princeton, 1978); Joseph E. Inikori and Stanley L. Engerman, eds., *The Atlantic Slave Trade: Effects on the Economics, Societies, and Peoples in Africa, the Americas, and Europe* (Durham, 1992); Henry A. Gemery and Jan S. Hogendorn, eds., *The Uncommon Market: Essays in the Economic History of the Atlantic Slave Trade* (New York, 1979); and David Galenson, *Traders, Planters, and Slaves: Market Behavior in Early America* (New York, 1986). Two popular and readable accounts are Daniel P. Mannix and Malcolm Cowley, *Black Cargoes: A History of the Atlantic Slave Trade, 1518–1865* (New York, 1962); and Basil Davidson, *The African Slave Trade* (Boston, 1961). The domestic slave trade in the United States is described by Michael Tadman, *Speculators and Slaves: Masters, Traders, and Slaves in the Old South* (Madison, 1989). A still useful discussion of the abolition of the trade is W. E. B. Du Bois, *The Suppression of the African Slave Trade to the United States of America, 1638–1870*, reprint (New York, 1969). See also the articles republished in Paul Finkelman, ed., *Slave Trade and Migration: Domestic and Foreign* (New York, 1989).

THE FOUNDATIONS OF BLACK AMERICA

The controversy over the European antecedents of racism and slavery is addressed in a series of essays in the *William and Mary Quarterly*, 3rd Series, vol. LIV: 1 (January 1997). Slavery in medieval England is discussed in David A. E. Pelteret, *Slavery in Mediaeval England* (Woodbridge, Suffolk, 1995). Four significant studies of slavery and the law are Alan Watson, *Slave Law in the Americas* (Athens, 1989); A. Leon Higginbotham Jr., *In the Matter of Color: Race and the American Legal Process: The Colonial Period* (New York, 1978); Thomas D. Morris, *Southern Slavery and the Law, 1619–1860* (Chapel Hill, 1996); and Mark Tushnet, *The American Law of Slavery, 1810–1860: Considerations of Humanity and Interest* (Princeton, 1981). For the evolution of slavery in Virginia, see T. H. Breen and Stephen Innes, *"Myne Owne Ground": Race and Freedom on Virginia's Eastern Shore, 1640–1676* (New York, 1980). Slavery in early South Carolina is examined by Peter H. Wood, *Black*

Majority, Negroes in Colonial South Carolina from 1670 Through the Stono Rebellion (New York, 1974); and Daniel Littlefield, *Rice and Slaves: Ethnicity and the Slave Trade in Colonial South Carolina* (Baton Rouge, 1981). For Georgia, see Betty Wood, *Slavery in Colonial Georgia, 1730–1775* (Athens, 1984); and Julia Floyd Smith, *Slavery and Rice Culture in Low Country Georgia, 1750–1860* (Knoxville, 1985). The story of slavery in early North Carolina is recounted in an admirable work by Marvin L. Michael and Loren Lee Cary, *Slavery in North Carolina, 1748–1775* (Chapel Hill, 1995). Allan Kulikoff ranges more widely in *Tobacco and Slaves: The Development of Southern Cultures in the Chesapeake, 1680–1800* (Chapel Hill, 1986). For New York, see Edgar J. McManus, *A History of Negro Slavery in New York* (Syracuse, 1966); and for New England, see William Piersen, *Black Yankees: The Development of an Afro-American Subculture in Eighteenth Century New England* (Amherst, 1988). Gwendolyn Midlo Hall, *Africans in Colonial Louisiana: The Development of Afro-Creole Culture in the Eighteenth Century* (Baton Rouge, 1992) is particularly important. For a collection of significant articles on the early history of slavery and the enslaved, see Paul Finkelman, ed., *Colonial Southern Slavery* (New York, 1989). An important comparative analysis is presented in Peter Kolchin, *Unfree Labor: American Slavery and Russian Serfdom* (Cambridge, 1987).

THE CHANGING STRUCTURE OF BLACK SOCIETY

The ideological bases of racism is the subject of much controversy among scholars. Excellent treatments of this issue can be found in Winthrop D. Jordan, *White Over Black: American Attitudes Toward the Negro, 1550–1812* (Chapel Hill, 1968); Audrey Smedley, *Race in North America: Origin and Evolution of a World View* (Boulder, 1993); and Alden T. Vaughan, *Roots of American Racism, Essays on the Colonial Experience* (New York, 1995). A collection of proslavery thought is Eric McKitrick, ed., *Slavery Defended: The Views of the Old South* (Englewood Cliffs, 1963). See also William Stanton, *The Leopard's Spots: Scientific Attitudes Toward Race in America, 1815–59* (Chicago, 1960). Aspects of black-white interaction are addressed by Mechal Sobel, *The World They Made Together: Black and White Values in Eighteenth Century Virginia* (Princeton, 1987). An excellent study of the slaveowning class is James Oakes, *The Ruling Race: A History of American Slaveholders* (New York, 1982).

An early but still valuable discussion of the nature of slavery is Kenneth Stampp, *The Peculiar Institution: Slavery in the Antebellum South* (New York, 1956). A more recent and outstanding analysis of the physical aspects of the slave's condition is William M. Dusinberre, *Them Dark Days: Slavery in the American Rice Swamps* (New York, 1996). The labor regimen and the internal economies of the slave population are covered in Ira Berlin and Philip D. Morgan, eds., *Cultivation and Culture: Labor and the Shaping of Slave Life in the Americas* (Charlottesville, 1993); and by the same editors, *The Slaves' Economy: Independent Production by Slaves in the Americas* (London, 1991); Larry E. Hudson Jr., ed., *Working Towards Freedom: Slave Society and Domestic Economy in the American South* (Rochester, 1994); Mary Turner, ed., *From Chattel Slaves to Wage Slaves: The Dynamics of Labour Bargaining in the Americas* (Bloomington, 1995); and Roderick McDonald, *The Economy and Material Culture of Slaves: Goods and Chattels on the Sugar Planations of Jamaica and Louisiana* (Baton Rouge, 1993). See also the collection of articles reprinted in Paul Finkelman, ed., *Economics, Industrialization, Urbanization and Slavery* (New York, 1989); and Robert Fogel and Stanley Engerman, *The Economics of American Negro Slavery*, 2 vols. (New York, 1989). Industrial slavery is examined by Robert Starobin, *Industrial Slavery in the Old South* (New York, 1970); Ronald L. Lewis, *Coal, Iron, and Slaves: Industrial Slavery in Maryland and Virginia, 1715–1865* (Westport, 1979); and Charles B. Dew, *Bond of Iron: Master and Slave at Buffalo Forge* (New York, 1994).

For studies that provide broad treatments of slavery primarily for the nineteenth century, see Leslie Owens, *This Species of Property: Slave Life and Culture in the Old South* (New York, 1976); Charles Joyner, *Down by the Riverside: A South Carolina Slave Community* (Urbana, 1984); Richard Wade, *Slavery in the Cities: The South, 1820–1860* (New York, 1964); Claudia Goldin, *Urban Slavery in the American South, 1820–1860: A Quantitative History* (Chicago, 1976); and George Rawick, *From Sundown to Sunup* (Westport, 1972).

The end of slavery in the North is well treated by Arthur Zilversmit, *The First Emancipation: The Abolition of Slavery in the North* (Chicago, 1967). See also Donald L. Robinson, *Slavery in the Structure of American Politics, 1765–1820* (New York, 1971); and David Brion Davis, *The Problem of Slavery in the Age of Revolution, 1770–1823* (Ithaca, 1975). The articles republished in Paul Finkelman, ed., *Slavery, Revolutionary America, and the New Nation* (New York, 1989) are highly recommended. The role of blacks in the War of Independence is discussed by Benjamin Quarles, *The Negro in the American Revolution* (New York, 1973), and Duncan J. McLeod, *Slavery, Race and the American Revolution* (Cambridge, 1975). For the impact of the Haitian Revolution on black Americans, see Alfred N. Hunt, *Haiti's Influence on Antebellum America: Slumbering Volcano in the Caribbean* (Baton Rouge, 1988).

THE DEVELOPMENT OF FAMILY LIFE

The two most important studies of the black family under slavery are Herbert Gutman, *The Black Family in Slavery and Freedom, 1750–1825* (New York, 1976); and Ann Patton Malone, *Sweet Chariot: Slave Family and Household Structure in Nineteenth Century Louisiana* (Chapel Hill, 1992). Wilma King examines the lives of slave children in *Stolen Childhood: Slave Youth in Nineteenth-Century America* (Bloomington, 1995). Outstanding articles on women and the family are republished in Paul Finkelman, ed., *Women and the Family in a Slave Society* (New York, 1989). The expanding literature on enslaved women includes Deborah Gray White, *Ar'n't I A Woman?: Female Slaves in the Plantation South* (New York, 1985); Jacqueline Jones, *Labor of Love, Labor of Sorrow: Black Women, Work, and the Family from Slavery to the Present* (New York, 1985); Elizabeth Fox Genovese, *Within the Plantation Household: Black and White Women of the Old South* (Chapel Hill, 1988); and Darlene Clark Hine and David Barry Gaspar, eds., *More Than Chattel: Black Women and Slavery in the Americas* (Bloomington, 1996). See also Brenda E. Stephenson, *Life in Black and White: Family and Community in the Slave South* (New York, 1996).

THE BLACK RELIGIOUS EXPERIENCE

Readers should develop some understanding of African religions before they begin their study of the beliefs and practices of the enslaved. Some indispensable works are John S. Mbiti, *African Religions and Philosophy* (New York, 1969); Geoffrey Parrinder, *West African Religion* (New York, 1970); and M. Fortes and G. Dieterlen, eds., *African Systems of Thought* (London, 1966). There are several outstanding studies of the religious experiences of slaves, although most of them focus primarily on the beliefs of the Christianized minority. They include Eugene Genovese, *Roll Jordan Roll, The Worlds the Slaves Made* (New York, 1974); Albert J. Raboteau, *Slave Religion: The "Invisible Institution" in the Antebellum South* (New York, 1978); Mechal Sobel, *Trabelin' On: The Slave Journey to an Afro-Baptist Faith* (Westport, 1979); John B. Boles, ed., *Masters and Slaves in the House of the Lord: Race and Religion in the American South, 1740–1870* (Lexington, 1988); Albert J. Raboteau, *A Fire in the Bones: Reflections on African-American Religious History* (Boston, 1995); and Margaret Washington Creel, *"A Peculiar People": Slave Religion and Community–Culture Among the Gullahs* (New York, 1988). See also the outstanding set of articles reprinted in Paul Finkelman, ed., *Religion and Slavery* (New York, 1989). An excellent article on Muslims is Michael A. Gomez, "Muslims in Early America," *Journal of Southern History*, LX:4 (1994): 671–710.

Related works on the religious beliefs and practices of the enslaved include James Melvin Washington, ed., *Conversations with God: Two Centuries of Prayers by African Americans* (New York, 1994); Gayraud S. Wilmore, *Black Religion and Black Radicalism: An Interpretation of the Religious History of Afro-American People*, 2nd edition (Maryknoll, 1983); Milton C. Sennett, *Black Religion and American Evangelicalism:*

White Protestants, Plantation Missions and the Flowering of Negro Christianity, 1787–1865 (Metuchen, 1975); and Donald J. Mathews, *Religion in the Old South* (Chicago, 1977).

SOCIAL AND CULTURAL LIFE

The best general treatment of the nature and evolution of black culture is Lawrence Levine, *Black Culture and Black Consciousness: Afro-American Folk Thought from Slavery to Freedom* (New York, 1977). Paul Finkelman has republished seminal articles on various aspects of black culture in his edited works, *Medicine, Nutrition, Demography, and Slavery* (New York, 1989) and *The Culture and Community of Slavery* (New York, 1989). For an important study of the music of the enslaved, see Dena J. Epstein, *Sinful Tunes and Spirituals: Black Folk Music to the Civil War* (Urbana, 1977). Black humor is the subject of Mel Watkins, *On the Real Side: Laughing, Lying, and Signifying–The Underground Tradition of African American Humor* (New York, 1994). On architecture, see John Vlach, *Back of the Big House: The Architecture of Plantation Slavery* (Chapel Hill, 1993). The decorative arts are addressed in John Vlach, *The Afro-American Tradition in Decorative Arts* (Athens, 1990). For issues relating to medical practices, consult Todd L. Savitt, *Medicine and Slavery: The Diseases and Health Care of Slaves in Antebellum Virginia* (Urbana, 1978); and Kenneth F. Kiple and Virginia Himmelsteib Kiple, *Another Dimension to the Black Diaspora: Diet, Disease, and Racism* (Cambridge, 1981). See the following for various aspects of black life and culture, Thomas L. Webber, *Deep Like the Rivers: Education in the Slave Quarter Community, 1831–1865* (New York, 1985); Paul D. Escott, *Slavery Remembered: A Record of Twentieth Century Slave Narratives* (Chapel Hill, 1979); William D. Piersen, *Black Legacy: America's Hidden Heritage* (Amherst, 1993); Ted Ownby, ed., *Black and White: Cultural Interaction in the Antebellum South* (Jackson, 1993); Roger D. Abrahams, *Singing the Master: The Emergence of African-American Culture in the Plantation South* (New York, 1993); Robert Farris Thompson, *Flash of the Spirit: African and Afro-American Art and Philosophy* (New York, 1984); and Joseph E. Holloway, ed., *Africanisms in American Culture* (Bloomington, 1990).

TOWARD FREEDOM

There are three fine general works on blacks who were free before 1863, namely Leon Litwack, *North of Slavery, The Negro in the Free States, 1790–1860* (Chicago, 1961); Ira Berlin, *Slaves Without Masters: The Free Negro in the Antebellum South* (New York, 1975); and James

Oliver Horton and Lois E. Horton, *In Hope of Liberty: Culture, Community and Protest Among Northern Free Blacks, 1700–1860* (New York, 1997). Narrower studies include Leonard P. Curry, *The Free Black in Urban America, 1800–1850* (Chicago, 1981); and James Oliver Horton, *Free People of Color: Inside the African American Community* (Washington, 1993). Several outstanding articles on free blacks have been republished by Paul Finkelman, ed., *Free Blacks in a Slave Society* (New York, 1989).

Free blacks are the subjects of several useful local studies, including John Hope Franklin, *The Free Negro in North Carolina, 1790–1860* (Chapel Hill, 1943); Letitia Woods Brown, *Free Negroes in the District of Columbia, 1740–1846* (New York, 1972); James Oliver Horton and Lois Horton, *Black Bostonians: Family Life and Community Struggle in the Antebellum North* (New York, 1979); Gary B. Nash, *Forging Freedom: The Formation of Philadelphia's Black Community, 1720–1840* (Cambridge, 1988); Julie Winch, *Philadelphia's Black Elite: Activism, Accommodation and the Struggle for Autonomy, 1787–1848* (Philadelphia, 1988); Suzanne Lebsock, *The Free Women of Petersburg: Status and Culture in a Southern Town* (New York, 1984); Herbert E. Sterkt, *The Free Negro in Antebellum Louisiana* (Rutherford, 1972); Michael P. Johnson and James L. Roark, *No Chariot Let Down: Charleston's Free People of Color on the Eve of the Civil War* (Chapel Hill, 1984); and Bernard E. Powers Jr., *Black Charlestonians: A Social History, 1822–1885* (Fayetteville, 1994). The legal status of free blacks is addressed in Don H. Fehrenbacher, *The Dred Scott Case: Its Significance in American Law and Politics* (New York, 1981). For studies that discuss the War of Independence, its ideology, and blacks, see Benjamin Quarles, *The Negro in the American Revolution* (Chapel Hill, 1961); Sylvia R. Frey, *Water From the Rock: Black Resistance in a Revolutionary Age* (Princeton, 1991); and Ira Berlin and Ronald Hoffman, eds., *Slavery and Freedom in the Age of the American Revolution* (Charlottesville, 1983).

Free blacks, as slaveowners, have been studied by Michael P. Johnson and James L. Roark, *Black Masters: A Free Family of Color in the Old South* (New York, 1984); and Larry Koger, *Black Slaveowners: Free Black Slave Masters in South Carolina* (Jefferson, 1985). Loren Schweninger presents an important analysis of the economic status of blacks in *Black Property Owners in the South, 1790–1915* (Urbana, 1990).

The struggle to create an identity is the concern of Sterling Stuckey, ed., *The Ideological Origins of Black Nationalism* (Boston, 1972), and his *Slave Culture: Nationalist Theory and the Foundations of Black America* (New York, 1987). See also Jennifer Fleischner, *Mastering Slavery: Memory, Family and Identity in Women's Slave Narratives* (New York, 1996); and Victor Ullman, *Martin Delany, The Beginnings of Black Nationalism* (Boston, 1971). Three books by Wilson Jeremiah Moses are particularly significant. They are *The Golden Age of Black Nationalism, 1850–1925* (New York, 1988); *Alexander Crummell: A Study of Civilization and Discontent* (New York, 1989); and *Classical Black Nationalism: From the American Revolution to Marcus Garvey* (New York, 1996). The significance of David Walker is addressed in Peter P. Hinks, *To Awaken My Afflicted Brethren: David Walker and the Problem of Antebellum Slave Resistance* (University Park, 1997). On emigrationism, see J. W. St. G. Walker, *The Black Loyalists: The Search for a Promised Land in Nova Scotia and Sierra Leone, 1783–1870* (London, 1976); and Floyd J. Miller, *The Search for a Black Nationality: Black Emigration and Colonization, 1787–1863* (Urbana, 1975). Two studies of the experiences of blacks in Liberia are Tom W. Shick, *Behold the Promised Land! A History of Afro-American Settler Society in Nineteenth Century Liberia* (Baltimore, 1980); and Antonio McDaniel, *Swing Low, Sweet Chariot: The Mortality Cost of Colonizing Liberia in the Nineteenth Century* (Chicago, 1995). An important biography of Paul Cuffe is Lamont D. Thomas, *Paul Cuffe: Black Entrepreneur and Pan Africanist* (Urbana, 1986).

The literature on the organizations created by free blacks is growing. In particular, see Carol V. R. George, *Segregated Sabbaths: Richard Allen and the Emergence of Independent Black Churches, 1760–1840* (New York, 1973); Jane H. Pease and William H. Pease, *They Who Would Be Free: Blacks Search for Freedom, 1830–1861* (Urbana, 1990); James T. Campbell, *Songs of Zion: The African Methodist Episcopal Church in the United States and South Africa* (New York, 1995); David E. Swift, *Black Prophets of Justice, Activist Clergy Before the Civil War* (Baton Rouge, 1989); and Penelope L. Bullock, *The Afro-American Periodical Press, 1838–1909* (Baton Rouge, 1981).

THE OPPOSITION TO SLAVERY

Studies of the resistance to slavery are numerous. The best general works are Herbert Aptheker, *American Negro Slave Revolts* (New York, 1943); and Eugene Genovese, *From Rebellion to Revolution: Afro-American Slave Revolts in the Making of the New World* (New York, 1968). Some of the best articles on resistance are reprinted in Paul Finkelman, ed., *Rebellion, Resistance, and Runaways Within the Slave South* (New York, 1989). For studies of specific revolts or conspiracies, see T. J. Davis, *Rumor of Revolt: The "Great Negro Plot" in Colonial New York* (New York, 1985); Joseph C. Carroll, *Slave Insurrections in the United States, 1800–1865*, reprint (New York, 1973); Douglas R. Egerton, *Gabriel's Rebellion: The Virginia Slave Conspiracies of 1800 and 1802* (Chapel Hill, 1993); John Lofton, *Insurrection in South Carolina: The Turbulent World of Denmark Vesey* (Yellow Springs, 1964); Robert S. Starobin, ed., *Denmark Vesey: The Slave Conspiracy of 1822* (Englewood

Cliffs, 1970); Herbert Aptheker, *Nat Turner's Slave Rebellion: Including the Full Text of the So-called "Confessions" of Nat Turner Made in Prison in 1831* (New York, 1966); Eric Foner, ed., *Nat Turner* (Englewood Cliffs, 1971); John B. Duff and Peter M. Mitchel, eds., *The Nat Turner Rebellion: The Historical Event and the Modern Controversy* (New York, 1971); Stephen B. Oates, *The Fires of Jubilee: Nat Turner's Fierce Rebellion* (New York, 1975); and Henry Irving Tragle, ed., *The Southampton Slave Revolt of 1831* (Amherst, 1971).

Flight from slavery is not particularly well studied. Three of the best studies are Gerald W. Mullin, *Flight and Rebellion: Slave Resistance in Eighteenth Century Virginia* (New York, 1972); Freddie L. Parker, *Running for Freedom: Slave Runaways in North Carolina 1775–1840* (New York, 1993), and Gary Collison, *Shadrach Minkins: From Fugitive Slave to Citizen* (Cambridge, Mass., 1997). The Underground Railroad is the subject of Larry Gara, *The Liberty Line: The Legend of the Underground Railroad* (Lexington, 1961). For a collection of important articles on escaped slaves, consult Paul Finkelman, ed., *Fugitive Slaves* (New York, 1989). Analyses of resistance in the Americas, seen comparatively, are Richard Price, ed., *Maroon Societies: Rebel Slave Communities in the Americas* (Garden City, 1973); and Michael Mullin, *Africa in America: Slave Acculturation and Resistance in the American South and the British Caribbean, 1736–1831* (Urbana, 1992).

BLACK ABOLITIONISTS

Many of the best articles on the antislavery movement are reprinted in Paul Finkelman, ed., *Antislavery* (New York, 1989). The outstanding general account of the black abolitionists is Benjamin Quarles, *The Black Abolitionists* (New York, 1969). See also C. Peter Ripley, ed., *Witness for Freedom: African American Voices on Race, Slavery, and Emancipation* (Chapel Hill, 1993); Carlton Mabee, *Black Freedom: The Nonviolent Abolitionists from 1830 through the Civil War* (New York, 1970); R. J. M. Blackett, *Building an Antislavery Wall: Black Americans in the Atlantic Abolitionist Movement, 1830–1860* (Baton Rouge, 1983); C. Peter Ripley, ed., *The Black Abolitionist Papers*, vol. iii (Chapel Hill, 1985); and Jane H. Pease and William H. Pease, *They Who Would Be Free: Blacks Search for Freedom, 1830–1861* (Urbana, 1990). The roles of women in the movement are described by Shirley Yee in *Black Women Abolitionists: A Study in Activism, 1828–1860* (Knoxville, 1992); and in several articles in Jean Fagan Yellin and John C. Van Horne, eds., *The Abolitionist Sisterhood: Women's Political Culture in Antebellum America* (Ithaca, 1994). Black abolitionists also receive some attention in Martin L. Duberman, ed., *The Antislavery Vanguard* (Princeton, 1965); Gerald Sorin, *Abolitionism: A New Perspective* (New York, 1972). There are a number of biographical studies of major abolitionists. Frederick Douglass is studied by Benjamin Quarles, *Frederick Douglass* (New York, 1970); Philip S. Foner, *Frederick Douglass: A Biography* (New York, 1964); Waldo E. Martin Jr., *The Mind of Frederick Douglass* (Chapel Hill, 1984); David W. Blight, *Frederick Douglass' Civil War: Keeping Faith in Jubilee* (Baton Rouge, 1989); and William McFeely, *Frederick Douglass* (New York, 1991). For biographies of Henry Highland Garnet, see Joel Schor, *Henry Highland Garnet, A Voice of Black Radicalism in the Nineteenth Century* (Westport, 1977); and Earl Ofari, *Let Your Motto Be Resistance: The Life and Thought of Henry Highland Garnet* (Boston, 1972). Sojourner Truth is the subject of Carlton Mabee with Susan Mabee Newhouse, *Sojourner Truth: Slave, Prophet, Legend* (New York, 1993); and Nell Irvin Painter, *Sojourner Truth: A Life, a Symbol* (New York, 1996). See also Earl Conrad, *Harriet Tubman* (Washington, 1943); William E. Farrison, *William Wells Brown: Author and Reformer* (Chicago, 1969); William Cheek and Aimee Lee Cheek, *John Mercer Langston and the Fight for Black Freedom* (Urbana, 1989); and R. J. M. Blackett, *Beating Against the Barriers: Biographical Essays in Nineteenth Century American History* (Baton Rouge, 1986).

EMANCIPATION

A good general discussion of events leading up to the Civil War and the war itself is James McPherson, *The Battle Cry of Freedom: The Civil War Era* (New York, 1988). For important analyses of blacks and the war, see Benjamin Quarles, *The Negro and the Civil War* (Boston, 1953); James M. McPherson, *The Negro's Civil War: How American Negroes Felt and Acted During the War for the Union* (New York, 1965); Dudley Taylor Cornish, *The Sable Arm: Negro Troops in the Union Army, 1861–1865* (New York, 1956); Hondon B. Hargrove, *Black Union Soldiers in the Civil War* (Jefferson, 1988); and Ervin L. Jordan Jr., *Black Confederates and Afro-Yankees in Civil War Virginia* (Charlottesville, 1995). The role of blacks in the war is nicely illuminated in the volumes of documents with informed introductions prepared under the auspices of the Freedmen and Southern Society Project at the University of Maryland. See Series 1, Volume 1, *The Destruction of Slavery*, eds., Ira Berlin, Barbara J. Fields, Thavolia Glymph, Joseph P. Reidy, and Leslie S. Rowland (New York, 1985); Series 1, Volume 2, *The Wartime Genesis of Free Labor: The Upper South*, eds., Ira Berlin, Steven F. Miller, Joseph P. Reidy, and Leslie S. Rowland (New York, 1993); Series 1, Volume 3, *The Wartime Genesis of Free Labor: The Lower South*, eds., Ira Berlin, Thavolia Glymph, Steven F. Miller, Joseph P. Reidy, Leslie S. Rowland, and Julie Saville (New York, 1990); and Series 2, *The Black Military Experience*, eds., Ira Berlin, Joseph P. Reidy, and Leslie S. Rowland (New York,

1982). The introductions to three of these volumes are conveniently available in Ira Berlin, Barbara J. Fields, Steven F. Miller, Joseph P. Reidy, and Leslie S. Rowland, eds., *Slaves No More: Three Essays on Emancipation and the Civil War* (New York, 1992). For related issues, see James McPherson, *The Struggle for Equality: Abolitionists and the Negro in the Civil War and Reconstruction* (Princeton, 1964); Joseph T. Glatthaar, *Forged in Battle: The Civil War Alliance of Black Soldiers and White Officers* (New York, 1990); and John Hope Franklin, *The Emancipation Proclamation* (New York, 1963). For two fine books on the aftermath of slavery, see Leon F. Litwack, *Been in the Storm So Long: The Aftermath of Slavery* (New York, 1979); and Eric Foner, *Reconstruction: America's Unfinished Revolution, 1863–1877* (New York, 1988).

Photo Credits

Index